CHILE:

The State and Revolution

CHILE:

The State and Revolution

IAN ROXBOROUGH

PHILIP O'BRIEN

JACKIE RODDICK

Assisted by
MICHAEL GONZALEZ

HM HOLMES & MEIER PUBLISHERS, INC.
New York

First published in the United States in 1977

by Holmes & Meier Publishers, Inc.

101 Fifth Avenue

New York, New York 10003

Library of Congress Cataloging in Publication Data

Roxborough, Ian.
   Chile: the state and revolution.

   Bibliography: p.
   1. Chile – Politics and government – 1970–
2. Unidad Popular.   3. Chile – History – Coup d'état,
1973. I. O'Brien, Philip, joint author. II. Roddick, Jackie, joint author.
III. Title.
F3100.R68   320.9'83'064   75–35896
ISBN 0–8419–0234–8

Printed in Great Britain

To all those who fought for Socialism in Chile

Contents

Preface

The overthrow of President Salvador Allende and the Popular Unity Government on 11 September 1973, and the massive repression of the Chilean working class and its organizations that followed were a major defeat for both the Chilean working class and for the international working class movement as a whole. The pogrom against the thousands of Latin American exiles living in Chile has been a great blow against all those fighting the oppressive dictatorships of Latin America.

It may seem churlish to analyse critically the events and policies leading up to the coup, when thousands of workers and left-wing militants are being exiled, imprisoned, tortured and executed. Many of those engaged in resistance and dying for it are members of political parties which we criticize. President Allende himself died fighting for his beliefs in a situation when a lesser man could have slipped quietly across the border to a life of comfortable and respectable ease. Nevertheless, although we pay tribute to the courage and sincerity of Allende and many members of his government, we feel it is necessary to criticize, and to criticize sharply, many of the policies followed by Popular Unity.

We believe an analysis of the three years to be of use not only for our Latin American comrades but also for comrades here in Europe. We hope that this analysis has not been carried out in a sectarian way or in a complacent 'I told you so' spirit, nor on the basis of an *a priori* judgement. We intend our analysis of the Chilean experience to be a contribution to an understanding of events which we regard as crucial for future debates on the tactics and strategies for achieving socialism. For we believe that the essential lessons of Chile are not peculiar to Chile (although of course many aspects were peculiarly Chilean), but that they yield general truths about the class struggle in capitalist countries. As such these lessons should be considered and debated as widely and as openly as possible.

Finally, let there be not the slightest doubt that we support all those fighting the military junta. We feel that all militants, regardless of their differences, should unite in solidarity with the Chilean people. This solidarity should be effective, and should carry on for the duration of the struggle of the Chilean people against capitalism and imperialism, and against bloody and barbaric repression. It is important that all those fighting and resisting the coup receive help in their struggle, help which should take the form, not only of material and moral assistance, but of an on-going political campaign that ensures that those now in power in Chile receive neither aid, trade, credits, investments nor acceptance in any sphere of activity. Let it be not said that the military junta were able to consolidate their power thanks to the indifference of comrades in our countries. The struggle will be long and difficult. We must do all we can to help it succeed.

Each part of the book has been the result of collective discussions and mutual criticism. Mike Gonzalez wrote the chronology and edited, rewrote and reorganized the whole book to such an extent that his name should by rights appear on the title cover.

We would like to record our thanks to the Director of the Institute of Latin American Studies at the University of Glasgow, Peter Flynn, for his support. Many other people have given us assistance. We would like to thank especially members of the Chile Solidarity Campaign, Chris Kay for his help particularly with Chapter six, and all those Chileans who helped us to understand and appreciate Chile. In addition we wish to thank Paul Stiff and Paul Walton for their help in enabling this book to see the light of day.

Glasgow, May 1974

1 Imperialism and Class Structure in Chile

This book is essentially concerned with the story of Chilean politics between 1970 and 1973, under the government of President Salvador Allende: with the tragic history of the 'Chilean road to socialism'. But it would be wrong to begin such a story in 1970 or 1969, in an undefined landscape and with a set of protagonists which might belong to any country in the world. If challenged in 1970 about their faith in the 'Chilean road', most supporters of President Allende would have defended themselves by claiming that Chile was a unique country, with a unique set of social and political conditions which had to determine the choice of a 'road to socialism'. One can take issue with their belief that the Chilean road to socialism was unique – one can point to its close parallels in the 'British . . .' and 'Italian road to socialism', as advocated by their respective Communist parties. But like every other country, Chile really is unique in many ways. It has a peculiar economy and social structure, and its different classes and political parties have been through a unique, not-to-be underestimated historical experience. Every road to socialism must adapt itself to national conditions. And so we begin this book with two chapters on the national conditions prevailing in Chile when Allende came to power.

In the case of Chile, three important specific 'national conditions' spring to mind. First, Chile has one of the strongest working classes in Latin America. It is an industrial country, with more than 70% of the population living in urban areas; a revolution in Chile would not have to be primarily a peasant revolution. Chilean workers have a history of economic militancy and political struggle which goes back to the 1880's when the nitrate mines were opened up in the north, and the Chilean Communist Party has enjoyed mass support on a nation-wide basis since it was founded in the 1920's. By any measure, the Chilean working class is one of the two or three key working classes in the continent. Bolivia also has a strong revolutionary working class tradition, particularly in the mines, but the country is still predominantly a country of peasants: Argentina has a larger working class and a stronger industrial base, but the history of the Argentinian working class is closely tied with that strange and confusing political movement, Peronism. If socialist revolutions are to be made by a working class using Marxist principles, then Chile would be a logical place to expect the Latin American revolution to begin.

Secondly, in 1970, in stark contrast to such important countries in Latin America as Argentina and Brazil, Chile seemed to have a firmly founded bourgeois democracy and what conventional political scientists would no doubt describe as a 'democratic culture'. While military regimes, torture and the violation of elementary human rights prevailed elsewhere, Chile thought of itself proudly as 'the England of Latin America'. A period of outright military dictatorship between 1924 and 1931 was virtually forgotten, and the occasional revival of more direct means of repression of the working class by bourgeois governments (the banning of the Communist Party in 1948, the periodic use of troops to break up strikes) was easily ignored. Since the 1930's, the working class movement in Chile had numbered its martyrs in ones and twos, until the September 1973 coup. Compared with the brutality of bourgeois rule in Brazil, Chile's record was something to be proud of. And even during the dictatorship of the 1920's, military men had generally used imprisonment and exile rather than torture and murder to control their opponents. One could say that violence was not the automatic first weapon of the Chilean bourgeoisie.

Thirdly, in 1970 (and since its emergence as a nation state) Chile was a dependent economy, an economy wholly organized in terms of the workings of the international capitalist market dominated by Europe and America. For the whole of its national history, Chile has been a country to which economic change happened because of conditions beyond its control. Even Chilean capitalists have had very little say in the occasional drastic shifts in the country's system of production, and very little control over the profound social upheaval which such shifts bring in their wake. The economic levers have always been controlled from outside the country, initially by colonial Spain, then by imperialist Britain, and since the 1920's by the imperialist USA.

Economic dependency has had far-reaching effects on Chilean society, and in many ways it is the most important 'national condition' for foreigners to grasp, for it is the one which differentiates Chile's historical experience from the experience of European countries with political institutions which are very much the same. There would never have been a military dictatorship in the 1920's for instance, if the European market for Chile's principal exports, nitrates, had not collapsed after Germany invented an artificial nitrate during the First World War. That single shift in world markets threatened the country's entire social structure, and forced a realignment of Chilean politics to take account of the increased pressure from urban middle sectors and the organized working class.

One can even trace the initial growth in political consciousness of the Chilean working class to dependency, for the fact that from the late nineteenth century, foreigners with a different language and culture so obviously controlled the mines, and could call on a supposedly 'national' government to suppress the strikes of Chilean workers on behalf of British interests, did a great deal to encourage the growth of Chile's first working class party. In 1970, this constant experience of national frustration at the hands of foreign interests seemed to be one of the 'Chilean road's' principal strengths. The palpable fact of imperialism, the visible resentment of American power, the alliance of local Chilean monopolists with all-powerful American companies, made it seem relatively easy to put forward a programme for an electoral transition to socialism, based on the interests and desires of the majority of the population. It was thought that workers, peasants and most of the 'middle classes' – petty bourgeoisie, white collar workers and small or medium-sized capitalists without foreign connections – could be mobilized to defend their own interests against the tiny minority of wealthy Chileans and foreign businessmen who controlled the economic fortunes of everyone else. Under the guise of an alliance of democratic and anti-imperialist forces, the Communist Party of Chile has been putting forward such a programme since the 1930's. In 1970, the Popular Unity coalition allowed itself to believe that with such a programme revolutionaries would be able to use the language and instruments of bourgeois patriotism against the bourgeoisie itself.

The experience of Chile between 1970 and 1973 has shown that it is not so easy. The Chilean middle classes, in spite of their own conflicts of interest with monopoly capital, were not willing to accept socialism with a patriotic face. Given the threat of revolution, they turned back towards a nationalist ideology of the old kind, a nationalism whose primary function was to limit and suppress the advances of the 'subversive' working class.

But if the national condition of dependency did not do very much to strengthen the Chilean road to socialism, in practice, it was nonetheless one of the most important influences on the struggle of Popular Unity. For not only Allende himself was constrained by the limits which a dependent economy set on his economic policies, the degree to which Chilean socialism was made vulnerable by a fall in the world price of copper or the disappearance of American credits and American supplies of spare parts. At the same time, the very strengths of Popular Unity – for instance, its ability to make use of a State apparatus which has played a crucial role in the economy since 1891 – were also the result of a long history of attempts to balance a singularly ill-balanced economy and society.

Economic Dependence and the National Bourgeoisie

For a country with abundant natural resources (iron, copper, coal and good agricultural land, as well as natural fertilizer) Chile's industrial development came very late. Chile had a history of spurts of industrial growth whenever for some reason the sources of imported manufactured goods from Europe and the USA went dry – during perods of depression or war. But these spurts tended to come to an end once the first crisis was over, and the means of importing foreign goods was available again. Chile's national bourgeoisie showed very little interest in industrialization. The first conscious attempt to foster Chilean industrialization did not come until the election of a Popular Front government in 1938, which put forward a systematic programme of State investment and State protection for native industry, under the joint banner of the Radical, Communist and Socialist parties.

Until 1938, Chile was primarily a country which exported minerals and agricultural products to the industrial countries of the west, and for the previous eighty years the country's ruling élite had been committed to the practice of a *laissez-faire* economics which tended to favour British and American manufactured imports. Even today, after thirty years of industrial development, the whole Chilean economy balances precariously on the international price of one export: copper. For industrialization through the substitution of local manufactures for those which were previously imported, within the framework of a dependent capitalist economy, has proved to be an elusive road to economic development. Machinery, spare parts and technical skills still have to be imported from the imperialist countries at a high price. Furthermore, in spite of the fact that in the nineteenth century it was one of Chile's principal sources of exports, Chilean agriculture in the twentieth century has plumbed the depths of inefficiency. In spite of the potential of the land itself, Chilean farmers have not produced enough to meet the demands of the population. Much of the revenue from copper has to be spent abroad to secure food imports, if the population is to be fed.

The history of economic dependence in Chile goes back a long way: through the era of American imperialism (from 1920 to the present) and the previous era of British imperialism (from Independence to 1920), right back to the period when Chile was dominated, economically and politically, by colonial Spain.

Colonial Chile

With its conquest by Spain, Chile became integrated into the expanding capitalism of the sixteenth century. From that point onwards, the development of the colonial economy was restricted to the production of exports whose ultimate destination was the markets of western and central Europe. As was typical in the bulk of Spanish colonial possessions, the first export was gold. However, Chilean gold mines were poor, and from the seventeenth century onwards produced very little.

Yet Chile could and did play another role which was equally in keeping with the essential elements of a colonial economy tied to Spain. The three elements in the colonial economic system were (1) a series of mining cores in Mexico and Peru, (2) agricultural and ranching areas peripheral to the mining cores developed for the supply of foodstuffs and raw materials and (3) a commercial system designed to funnel silver and gold as specie and bullion to Spain to pay for goods produced by western Europe and funnelled through one Spanish port for distribution to the colonies.[1] Within this system, Chile's role was to furnish agricultural products and raw materials to Lima, capital of the Viceroyalty of Peru. In the early period, Chile exported tallow and a certain amount of wheat, and remained a predominently pastoral economy.

In 1687 an earthquake destroyed Lima and Peru's wheat-producing areas, leaving Chilean wheat, which had already begun to make inroads on the

Peruvian market, as the market's only supplier. Wheat prices rose, and Chilean livestock producers turned their land over to the production of cereals in order to take advantage of the new market. This shift in the nature of Chilean agricultural production brought with it changes in the rural social structure, and in particular, the expansion and consolidation of the *hacienda* system. The *haciendas* quickly came to occupy the bulk of the best land in Chile's fertile central valley, incorporating a dependent peasantry which remained tied to the *hacienda* through various forms of tenancy, share-cropping, and more or less permanent indebtedness. This system, which ensured the continuing presence of a relatively stable and dependent labour force, socially isolated by the authoritarian paternalism of the great *haciendas*, was to provide a solid social base for the power of the great rural landowners throughout the eighteenth and nineteenth centuries, and well into the twentieth.

There were some rudimentary attempts during the eighteenth century to develop a domestic industry, particularly in textiles, rigging and hides. But as Spanish colonial power yielded, from 1778 onwards, to the direct imperialist penetration of Britain and France, all such attempts at independent development were arrested. At the same time, as trade between the Spanish colonies and the new imperialist powers increased, a growing antagonism appeared between the needs and interests of the colonists and the Spanish effort to maintain control over them. It was the wealth of the colonies which supported the declining metropolitan economy of Spain, but from the colonists' point of view, greater freedom of trade with the ultimate sources of western European manufactured goods was desirable. It was this fundamental conflict of interest which finally gave rise to the Wars of Independence.

Independence, British Imperialism, and the Local Bourgeoisie

The Chilean ruling class was formed in the period of colonial rule: a relatively cohesive ruling class dominated by Central Valley landowners from the region around Santiago, the oligarchy who made their living from the proceeds of agriculture and the exploitation of rural labour on the international market, meanwhile increasing the prosperity of the Central Valley itself by exploiting their control over State revenues from mineral exports.

From Independence until 1920, this small élite retained all the essentials of power within the new nation-state, using its control over the armed forces to suppress occasional challenges to its rule from landowners further south and mine-owners in the northern desert and the area around Concepción. It was a distinctly capitalist élite, dependent for its prosperity on the vagaries of the international market, with a marked preference for international standards of consumption, French furnishings and frequent visits to the 'civilized' atmosphere of Paris and London. Nevertheless, not all its economic and political importance was the result of the capitalist spirit: a good part of its importance as a ruling class must be put down to the benefits of a central geographical position and control over the army, for from a strictly economic point of view, mining often contributed at least as much to the total national wealth. Even at this early date, too, British capital and British families controlled the export-import business.

Unlike many Latin American republics, Chile did not emerge from the struggle for Independence with a weakened central authority. Elsewhere the war against centralized Spanish authority led to an upsurge of *caudillismo*, rule by chiefs, the rule of more or less autonomous landowners who retained exclusive authority in their own private fiefdoms. Political alliances between chiefs were subject to rapid and sudden change, and the system was highly unstable. Chile, however, escaped the phase of *caudillismo* thanks in part to the strength of its armed forces, who remained obedient to Santiago. A strong and powerful State emerged, controlled by a succession of dynamic presidents and ministers (the key figure being Diego Portales) who represented at once the personal interests of the Central Valley landowners, and the interests of the bourgeoisie as a whole in maintaining order. The central authority established by the Spaniards remained intact, and so did the class structure. The responsibility for framing a Constitution which would serve the interests of the dominant classes fell to Portales, who created an authoritarian political system with a strong presidency, safeguarding the nation's political cohesion, and arrogating to the government the task of providing the economic policies and physical infrastructure which were necessary if the export sector of the economy was to continue its expansion. It was a mercantilist policy, rather than a policy of strict *laissez-faire*, and the landowners of the Central Valley were able to follow it with pleasure largely because the tax revenue for investments in infrastructure came from elsewhere: from taxes on mineral exports. Thus from the earliest post-Independence days, the Chilean ruling élite had a powerful State apparatus at its disposal, without having to shoulder any great share of the cost.

Under President Portales and his successors, post-Independence governments took some steps to further Chile's economic independence, though they did relatively little to disturb British control over trade. The transport of goods between Chilean ports was reserved exclusively to Chilean shipping, to encourage the development of a national merchant marine. Revenues from export and import duties were used to improve amenities in Santiago and provide railways and other infrastructural works throughout the Central Valley. Valparaíso was carefully promoted as the chief port on the west coast of South America. With government encouragement, a number of local industries were established, the most important being food processing, beer, footwear, soap and candles. Yet the export sector continued to be the key sector of the economy.

Between 1845 and 1860, foreign trade trebled. The first export boom was in wheat destined for the gold-mining areas of California and later Australia. Silver, copper and coal exports also increased rapidly: between 1850 and 1875, Chile was the world's main copper exporter. This export boom helped finance a growing urbanization, and gave the commercial bourgeoisie established in

Santiago and Valparaíso, increased power. Anglo-Chilean families such as the Edwards, later famous for their ownership of *El Mercurio*, ceased to think of themselves primarily as Britons abroad and began to take an active part in Chilean politics.

In the 1850's, mining capitalists, the new commercial bourgeoisie and the growing urban classes joined forces and began to agitate politically around a programme of liberal reforms – constitutional reform of the authoritarian State, administrative decentralization, a more democratic suffrage, and State supervision of education. This was the time of the foundation of the Radical Party. It signified the beginning of a successful rebellion by the rest of the bourgeoisie against the exclusive domination of the State apparatus by Central Valley landowners. The result was a compromise: existing ties between the oligarchy and mining and commerce, whether economic ties or the ties of kinship, were already becoming too close to make a civil war profitable, and no section of the bourgeoisie was happy at the growing radicalism which their own dispute seemed to be provoking among the miners and urban artisans. The result was a careful extension of the old élite's political control to new sectors of the bourgeoisie, and the imposition of a policy of *laissez-faire*.

Fundamentally, even the exporters in the Central Valley had very little to gain from a policy of heavy taxation on mineral exports in which they were beginning to invest themselves, or on imports which they consumed – less than they had to gain from reinforcing their own ties with the profitable mines and import-export businesses. In other circumstances, the proceeds of taxes on exports might have been used to accumulate funds for increased domestic investment and a State-sponsored development of national industry, as the proceeds of taxes on mineral exports had been used to build railways in the Central Valley. But there was increasing pressure from Britain to reinforce the demand for an introduction of free trade, as well as the pressure from mine-owners and importers for a reduction in their tax burden. From the 1860's, *laissez-faire* economic theories dominated the political scene. A banking system free from any State control was established (later to be an important source of perpetual problems with inflation) and from 1864, Chile adopted reciprocal free trade agreements with most of the leading industrial countries of the world. In the 1870's and 1880's, the authoritarian State was gradually weakened, other sectors of the bourgeoisie were allowed greater access to political power, State intervention in the economy was dismantled and the first effort to establish manhood suffrage was introduced.

Free trade weakened Chile's incipient industries decisively, for without State protection and encouragement they could hardly compete against competition from Europe and the USA. So the Chilean economy remained absolutely dependent on its capacity to pay for imported manufactures and luxury goods. One result of this dependence was periodic economic and social crises, whenever world demand for Chilean products declined, as happened for example with the closing of the Californian and Australian markets for Chilean wheat from 1858 onwards, or later when Chile's technically unsophisticated mining industry was unable to compete on the world market. There was a particularly severe economic crisis between 1873 and 1878, when a decline in mining exports coincided with a rapid spurt in world competition in wheat, thanks to the opening up of virgin agricultural land in Canada, the USA and Australia.

Chile of the Nitrates

In an economy as totally dependent on a small number of exports as Chile's the whole fabric of politics and society depends on the fate of those exports. When a key export is threatened, society as a whole is also threatened, and new economic and political forms of organization have to be invented to take the place of the old. As a result, periods of collapse in the export market have also been, in Chile, periods of fundamental political and social change.

In theory, the Chilean bourgeoisie could have tried to overcome the crisis of the 1870's by improving their competitive position through the introduction of new techniques in mining and new methods of production in agriculture, by increasing their own economic efficiency. Instead, it found another solution. With British aid, the Chileans declared war on Bolivia and Peru in 1879 and annexed the Atacama desert, the world's source of nitrates. The war gave Chile a world monopoly over nitrates. It also revived the pattern of the authoritarian State in at least one respect: income from export revenues on nitrates became the fundamental source of income for the State itself, and through State channels, enriched the southern economy as a whole. The era of nitrates in Chile was an era of liberalism run rampant. By a curious irony, it also established the pattern of an economy in which the State was of supreme importance, a pattern which has endured to the present day.

Laissez-faire policies resulted in a number of lost opportunities when the war was over. Chilean industry had expanded rapidly during the war with Bolivia and Peru, and was able to produce all that was necessary for the war effort: but when the war ended, and the country was once again able to make use of export earnings to import manufactured and luxury goods, industrial growth slowed down once again. After the war, the Chilean government was left in possession of a number of mines which had been nationalized by the Peruvians, and whose owners had long since lost or sold their shares. Instead of keeping the mines and running them for its own profit, the government decided to hand them back to their 'original' owners. The result was that John North, an English adventurer, was able to buy up cheaply large numbers of shares using loans from a bank in Valparaíso, and thus using Chilean finance acquired a large part of the nitrate industry for himself. Over the next twenty years, most of the nitrate mines passed into the hands of foreigners, and Chile's economic prosperity came to depend on a mining enclave which was almost entirely in foreign hands.

There was one brief attempt to reverse this process, which collapsed because of the opposition of the national bourgeoisie to any State intervention in the economy, and their sympathy with the foreign investors. In 1889, President Balmaceda made a strong appeal for the formation of a national bourgeoisie not tied to imperialist interests, to break up the growing British monopoly on economic activity in the nitrate areas, guided and helped by the State. In a speech in Iquique, centre of the nitrate industry, he declared: 'We must invest the surplus in productive works so that when the nitrate deposits are exhausted or lose their importance because of discoveries of new deposits or scientific progress, we shall have established a national industry and created with it and the state railways, the basis for new investments.'[3] The bulk of the ruling class thought differently, and resented what seemed to them to be an attempt to increase presidential power once again, and return Chile to the days of Portales. Balmaceda was defeated in a brief civil war (1891) in which his opponents were financially assisted by the British nitrate owners. The mass of the population remained uninvolved and indifferent.

With Balmaceda died the last attempt for thirty years to impose a strong government capable of pursuing policies in the national interest, which ran counter to the interests of specific fractions of the bourgeoisie. After the civil war, came what is loosely known in Chile as 'the parliamentary regime': loosely, because the executive power remained in the hands of the president (there was no Prime Minister, and no system of party politics designed to give the executive an automatic parliamentary majority). Congress ruled supreme. No cabinet was able to pursue policies which offended in any way the shifting and largely unprincipled political alliances between members of Congress. Meanwhile, the business of politics became a matter of the equitable distribution of patronage from the State's enormous revenues, among different regional interests and the various competing political parties with their urban clientele, and politics itself became a prosperous business.

With the rapid development of the nitrate industry, under foreign ownership, came a boom in State expenditure of unprecedented proportions. State revenues doubled in every decade from 1880 onwards, with 97% deriving from taxes on foreign commerce. Before Balmaceda's death, a State railway system was established; the armed forces were modernized, with the help of imported German and British experts and a great deal of subsequent expenditure on European armaments; a national system of public education was founded, also with the help of German experts. The numbers directly employed by the State grew to about 50,000 by 1925, expenditure on public works and infrastructure boomed and the population of the urban areas grew very quickly.

The nitrate boom gave Chile, for the first time, a substantial middle class of professionals, white-collar workers employed in finance and commerce, and State employees. Political parties with a secure mass base in the urban areas emerged for the first time. The oligarchy was able to counterbalance their strength for a time by relying on its own control over the rural electorate, but the days in which family connections and tradition could ensure its hegemony were clearly numbered. The new urban classes, however, were not a particularly violent strain on the existing system of politics. Political parties like the Radical Party won much of their support among the middle classes through the dispensation of State patronage, and the edge of politics everywhere was blunted by massive corruption. The urban clientele of the politicians provided a useful counterweight to the growing militancy of the working class, especially in the mining areas (there were 53,000 nitrate miners in 1915, more than the contemporary number of State employees). The politics of the parliamentary regime was straight-forward, when it came to any compromise with the lower classes: the 'social question' – the question posed by an aroused and politicized working class – was a question for the police and the troops. In 1907, 3,000 striking miners and their families were massacred by troops after a demonstration in the nitrate port of Iquique.

The era of the collapse of nitrates

Balmaceda's prophecy came true. With the invention of synthetic nitrates during the First World War, the bottom fell out of the market for natural nitrates and the Chilean economy entered a profound crisis. It had not yet managed to recover when the collapse of the world market in 1929 and the ensuing world crisis dealt it another heavy blow.

The parliamentary regime collapsed with this new and profound social upheaval. Suddenly, its middle class base in the urban areas became unreliable: large sectors of the middle class began demanding fundamental social reforms, better wages as a protection against inflation, social security, and the legalization of trade unions – which State employees and white collar workers were quick to form. The threat of a combination of these sectors and a working class with strong left-wing traditions was very grave. In spite of President Alessandri's attempts to capitalize on the sentiment for social change in 1920, and effect a subsequent programme of reform legislation, the politicians of the old regime could not adjust to the new situation and were unwilling to make any sacrifices in their old privileged position. The result was military intervention in 1924. The stability of the system required an end to the politics of simple repression and the beginning of a new political system, which would combine some repression with a number of important concessions to the lower orders. When the political representatives of the bourgeoisie proved that they were unwilling to take the necessary steps, the military moved in to do it for them. Between 1924 and 1931, Chile was governed by a classic 'Bonapartist' regime.

The collapse of nitrates was followed by the fortunate rediscovery of copper as the main base of the Chilean economy. Partly because of the failure of Chile to develop technical skills adequate for its exploitation, partly because of a new alliance between the Chilean government and the USA (based on large American loans), control over the rich copper deposits went to American companies using a new mining technology. Once again, Chile's main production sector became a foreign enclave, and the 'reformist' military government took no steps to bring it under national control. The fundamental alliance between the ruling sectors of the Chilean bourgeoisie and foreign capital, which had been characteristic of the nitrate era and very largely characteristic for the period before as well, was continued in the twentieth century with a new ally – the USA.

Between 1924 and 1940, however, Chilean governments rediscovered an interest in the encouragement of national industry. The first signs of a return to old mercantilist policies came with the military dictatorship of Ibáñez in 1928, when an Institute of Industrial Credit was established using revenues from the newly set up social security banks. Supposed concessions to the middle class served the dual purpose of providing national industry with a source of savings.

Chilean exports were recovering from the nitrate collapse when the Great Depression arrived. Between 1929 and 1932 the value of Chile's exports fell by 88% – the steepest decline in the world. The expansion of industry stopped, and the military dictatorship fell.

It was only with the Popular Front governments of the late thirties and early forties that economic growth began again. This time it was based on import substitution industrialization, and a concentrated government effort to speed up the industrialization process, both indirectly, by creating inducements which made domestic industry more profitable (e.g., tariff and exchange controls) and directly via the State Development Corporation (CORFO) which created or contributed to the expansion of a number of important industries. Yet much of the import substitution industrialization took the form of creating final consumer goods industries based on existing demand patterns, i.e., on the demands of the wealthier classes for high quality luxury goods. Production continued to be geared to a grossly unequal distribution of wealth and income. This method of industrialization could not solve the fundamental problems of the Chilean economy. Rather, it created a high cost, inefficient industry dependent for its survival on the import of intermediate goods (machinery and spare parts) and State subsidies. Taxes and foreign exchange from the unstable export base, copper, were essential. When revenue from copper was insufficient, the Chilean government relied on the inflow of foreign capital, in the form of private investment or public loans, to cover its foreign exchange deficit; and on inflationary deficit financing, printing money to cover a gap in resources, to cover the State's commitments at home. In the new economic order, the government could not afford a drastic cut in State expenditure to match State income, without risking a dangerous industrial and social crisis. As a result, inflation became a perpetual problem, one which grew worse whenever there was a sharp fall in the international price of copper. One of the greatest misfortunes of Popular Unity was that the price of copper fell between 1970 and 1972.

By the end of the nitrate era and the beginning of the copper era, Chile's economic pattern was firmly fixed. A great deal of the country's prosperity depended in one way or another on the revenue from foreign companies who controlled the export of Chile's mineral wealth. Much of this revenue, if not all, was funnelled through the State apparatus into the rest of the urban economy. The State was of vital economic importance, first as a source of employment, then after the Popular Front as a source of funds for investment in industry. It was also the State which guaranteed the economic environment in which private industry could operate – tax concessions for manufacturers, tariff protection against foreign competition, a legal machinery for dealing with the problem of working class militancy in the face of inflation. In 1971, an economist in the Communist Party was to estimate that 50% of supposedly private investment in 1969 was subsidized by the State, and total State expenditure in the same year amounted to 46% of Gross National Product.[4]

Growth of Working Class Organization

The predominance of agriculture in the Chilean economy of the eighteenth and nineteenth centuries meant that the working class remained very small until the latter half of the nineteenth century. Its beginnings lie in the various mining industries of Chile: copper, coal, silver, and at the turn of the century, nitrates. This mining proletariat was poorly organized at first, but it was not lacking in combativity. The first workers' uprising is recorded in Chanarcillo in 1834 and from then on, the history of the working class is studded with demonstrations and uprisings followed as a matter of course by repression.

Protest by the working class at their conditions of work and pay during the period from 1850 to 1880 was sporadic, since it lacked a coherent form of organization. The first forms of class organization developed by the Chilean working class were the mutualist associations, a primitive form of trade unionism dominated by utopian socialist and liberal ideas. Despite their inadequacies, the mutualist associations grew rapidly, and by 1879 there were more than seventy throughout Chile.

The real qualitative jump in the development of the Chilean working class came after 1880, with the development of the nitrate mining industry. In 1880 there were 2,848 workers engaged in nitrate production, according to one estimate; by 1890, this figure had jumped to 13,060. The development of the nitrate industry was accompanied by a corresponding boom in railways, public works, and coal mining. A conservative estimate of the number of industrial workers in Chile in 1890 would be 150,000, and according to the same source, by 1900 there were between 200,000 and 250,000, many of them recent immigrants from the countryside.[5] This rapid growth of the working class brought with it a dramatic increase in the number of strikes and demonstrations from 1890 onwards. Nevertheless, the working class continued to be dominated by an essentially bourgeois ideology and was consequently unable to develop a viable trade union organization.

The key role in the development of independent working class organizations was played by the Democratic Party. Founded as a splinter group of the Radical

Party, it was essentially a liberal, parliamentary party with a substantial following among the petty bourgeoisie; but it organized centres for workers, artisans and members of the liberal professions where current problems could be discussed, and thus contributed a great deal to the development of working class political consciousness. Nevertheless, in time, its petty bourgeois orientations became a constraint, as the working class developed more solid forms of economic organization.

The period after 1890 saw a confused struggle between different forms of trade union and different political tendencies: liberalism, anarchism and socialism. Socialist trade unionism really began with the founding of the Chilean Workers' Federation (FOCH) in 1911, though the nitrate miners had evolved a militant form of mutualist society which was keenly conscious of the fundamental role played in society by manual labour. Then in mid-1912, a breakaway faction of the Democratic Party led by a printer turned journalist, Luis Emilio Recabarren, established the Socialist Workers' Party (POS). Recabarren became the father figure of the Chilean working class, its most important political leader in this century. Immediately, he turned his attention to encouraging trade unionism and politics among the nitrate miners of the north.

The Chilean working class, then, was formed in the first place in the nitrate fields, an imperialist enclave in the far north of the country. Conditions of work were harsh, and the miners could scarcely fail to see themselves as exploited. They worked under conditions where mortality was high; they suffered from the companies' attempts to introduce forms of super-exploitation, such as the infamous 'truck' system – where miners were paid in tokens which could only be exchanged at the company store. Union organization was difficult and often illegal; organizers were persecuted, and the army was regularly brought in to suppress strikers. There were, in fact, a number of massacres, the most notorious the slaughter of three thousand men, women and children in the schoolhouse of Santa Maria de Iquique.

It took decades of ideological and organizational struggle to develop autonomous organizations of the working class. Once they were established, revolutionaries in the Chilean working class waged a ceaseless struggle throughout the subsequent years to maintain the independence of the class and protect it from attempts by the bourgeoisie to reassert its ideological and political control over the workers' organizations. That this struggle for the political independence of the working class has not always met with unlimited success is eloquently demonstrated by the fact that the bourgeoisie did establish control over sections of the labour movement in the nineteen-thirties and forties, during the Popular Front and the Radical governments which followed.

The Essentials of a Stable Political System

Pick up almost any book on Chile written before 1973, and you will find a reference to Chile's long history of constitutionalism and democracy, to its impressive record of political stability and democratic change.[6] Chile used to be held up as a model to other Latin American countries. The logical culmination of this tradition of constitutional development, in many eyes, was Popular Unity's attempt to initiate a peaceful, constitutional road to socialism.

The road to socialism proved less peaceful than planned. Because of the limitations of the bourgeois State, even a State like Chile's, the peaceful road to socialism had necessarily to stop short of the goal of socialist transformation, or become an armed road. Sooner or later the historical choice, Revolution or Restoration, Socialism or Barbarism, had to be posed. It was posed in 1973, and the outcome decided by a military coup with a violence and degree of bloodshed for which there has been little precedence in Chilean history. Yet the tradition of discussing Chilean politics in terms of liberal democracy and constitutionalism dies hard, as may be seen in the British Communist Party's call to defend Chilean 'democrats' against the military junta. It dies hard because it has a certain foundation in fact.

One should not understate the violence which has occasionally accompanied the class struggle in Chile, or the degree of repression employed by the ruling classes in defence of their interests. The Chilean Left had a kind of litany of working class massacres in the first three decades of the twentieth century, used to illustrate the scale of working class struggle on Popular Unity's various ceremonial and political occasions – Santa Maria de Iquique, San Gregorio, La Coruña, all of them strikes by nitrate miners in which the troops were brought out, with the consequent loss of hundreds and at least once, thousands of lives. One could construct a modern litany to match: the massacre of the Plaza Bulnes in 1948, when troops shot two demonstrators, the massacre of El Salvador in 1965, when troops were brought out to repress a strike of copper miners and killed six miners and miners' wives, the massacre of Puerto Montt (the subject of one of Victor Jara's songs) when police dislodged a camp of squatters at the cost of twelve dead and more wounded, in 1969. But still, it is noticeable that from 1930 – and until 1973 – the Chilean bourgeoisie was able to rely on more skilful political solutions to its social problems than the straightforward and costly application of brute force. Christian Democracy and the so-called 'Revolution in Liberty' was not based on the notion that the 'social question' was a question for the police, however much in practice President Frei may have been willing to rely on the troops when he had no better or more beguiling tricks up his sleeve.

What were the essential elements in this stable political system? A key factor, perhaps, was the relative unity of the ruling class itself. There has never been a revolutionary war in Chile between those whose wealth was originally based on the land and those whose wealth was based on industry – for a variety of reasons, perhaps, for the Central Valley oligarchy of the 1850's was as much in favour of capitalism as any mining or commercial interests of the day, and in any case a real industrial bourgeoisie did not develop until very late, perhaps

not until the 1920's. But whatever their potential divisions, the various industrial, commercial, landed or mining fractions of the bourgeoisie have always
been able to maintain an essential unity in the face of a potential threat to the
bourgeois order as a whole. They did it in 1850, when for a brief moment it
looked as though the liberal ideology of the mining families might spark more
rebellious notions among the miners and urban artisans. They were quite
capable of doing it again in 1970, whatever their momentary quarrels when
Allende came to power. Unity, too, has a solid economic foundation. Since
1850, the Chilean oligarchy has shown a noticeable ability to diversify its
economic interests and make connections with other wealthy families through
marriage, just as other fractions of the bourgeoisie have shown a noticeable
tendency to try to buy their way into the ranks of the élite by acquiring landed
estates. In 1964, in spite of the decline in the importance of agriculture as a
profitable economic investment, a survey of big businessmen showed that
almost half of them owned farms or had relatives who owned farms.

More important still, when it has been in its own class interest, the Chilean
bourgeoisie has always been able to combine concessions to workers or the
middle class with a certain degree of repression of the most militant elements,
when some concession had to be made in order to preserve the domination of
the bourgeoisie as a whole. The most painful period of transition of the
bourgeoisie was perhaps the period of military dictatorship between 1924 and
1931, when the end of the parliamentary regime itself and all sorts of bitterly
feared social concessions were forced on an unwilling congress – legal limitations
of the rights of property, legalization of the right of workers to form trade
unions and under certain circumstances, the right to strike. But when in 1927
it became clear that the alternative to military rule (with all the feared changes)
was a growing Communist Party and a dangerously broad united movement
of the urban working class and the middle sectors, prominent political opponents of military rule publicly invited Colonel Ibáñez to establish himself as
president.

Between 1920 and 1973, one could say, the bourgeoisie returned again and
again to a single basic political strategy: the strategy of a reformist alternative
to Communism, the promise of fundamental change without a real revolution,
coupled with periodic suppression of political parties or workers who would not
submit. This was Ibáñez's strategy in 1927, when he coupled a vicious attack on
Communists and anarchists with appeals to the urban middle class trade unions
and the implementation of 1924 legislation which made trade unions legal.
Divide, and rule. In spite of the Communist Party's resolute opposition to the
legal unions (which involved State control over finances, and the registering of
names of officials with the government bureaucracy) there were more than 300
legal unions by 1930.

Given the class structure of Chile, this kind of political strategy could count
on several potential sources of strength, besides its chances of dividing the
organized working class. One was the fact that Chile had a relatively large

middle class, for an underdeveloped country. The middle classes are always more ready to believe a reformist bourgeois politician than to trust a revolutionary or working class one, and the Chilean State could offer the powerful extra inducement that reformist parties were an excellent source of State jobs. The persistence of clientelism has been characteristic of Chilean politics because of the economic importance of the State itself. Another strength of reformist politics was the fact that import-substitution left the Chilean proletariat relatively weak in numerical terms, and the urban lumpenproletariat relatively strong.

Still, one would conclude that Chilean politics from 1930 to 1970 was in a precarious state of balance. The control of the bourgeoisie over large sectors of the salaried middle class could not be guaranteed, because the nature of Chile's economic system encouraged persistent inflation – and inflation led very quickly to the emergence of white collar trade unions with close ties with the labour movement and a persistent tendency to confront bourgeois governments whenever there was an attempt to impose a freeze on wages in the hopes of reducing inflation. Inflation, too, made it very difficult to envisage a stable compromise with the working class: the pressure on bourgeois governments to try to hold back price increases by imposing a cut in workers' real incomes was too strong.

Reformist political projects in Chile have had a relatively brief life span, in spite of the natural advantages which bourgeois politicians have had in controlling access to jobs in the State apparatus. The Radical Party was a successful reformist party in the first two decades of the twentieth century, with a perfect combination of clientelist politics and crusading ideology, but the nitrate crisis almost ruined its relationship with white collar workers and State employees who provided its mass base. The Party was revived because the intervention of a military dictatorship threw all political forces into disarray, and even more important, because of the Communist Party's own decision to press for the formation of a Popular Front. Even so, from its second chance at power in 1938 to its second defeat as a party capable of ruling Chile in 1950 (when the party's white collar base rebelled at an attempt to impose a wages freeze), the Radicals' political hegemony only lasted twelve years. The heyday of any particular Chilean reformism has always been short.

2   Class and Party from Popular Front to Popular Unity

Dependency and bourgeois institutions

The central theme of this chapter will again be the dependent nature of the Chilean economy, the consequences of which largely explain the economic and social developments of the period 1920 to 1970. The growth and changing consciousness of working class organization during this period, and particularly during the crises of the nineteen-twenties and thirties, will be set against the background of a situation of dependency which not only determined the tempo of the class struggle in Chile, but which also contained the source of the long term economic crisis which politicians tried without success to solve between 1952 and 1970, when Salvador Allende assumed the Presidency.

As we have shown, one of the historical peculiarities of 'Latin America's most stable democracy' was the development of a strong State apparatus and a democratic political system which was, paradoxically, to provide Popular Unity with some initial advantages in putting its programme into operation when Allende came to power. The political system inherited by Popular Unity provided the president, for example, with a certain margin of political independence from a parliament still controlled by the Right, as well as the power to initiate executive action without first submitting it for parliamentary approval. Further, Chile's Constitution allowed the State to limit the rights of private property in the interests of social need and to provide every inhabitant with a minimum standard of living. In fact the State had done very little since 1925 to guarantee that minimum living standard for all; yet this populist and on occasions anti-imperialist and anti-capitalist ideology was ingrained in the rhetoric of both the principal multi-class parties of the period – the Radicals and the Christian Democrats – and was clearly influential within the ranks of the salaried white-collar middle class.

These initial advantages, a strong presidency and widespread support among significant sectors of the middle class for a radical-sounding ideology, were to foster UP's most characteristic illusions. They led to the belief that there was a natural political alliance between working class and middle class, and to the conviction that the working class could capture the existing State institutions through elections. Yet these institutions had been constructed by the bourgeoisie in order to fulfil one prime function; to provide the ruling classes with the kind of institutional flexibility which would enable them to contain and neutralise the rising militancy of the Chilean working class. The relative independence of the president *vis-à-vis* parliament, for example, was used throughout the 1926–1970 period to allow different presidents to take a stand whenever the immediate threat from the working class passed certain limits, and to introduce extremely repressive measures even when these ran contrary to the supposedly democratic traditions of the Chilean polity.

The rhetoric of populism was first adopted by the military in 1925, then briefly taken up by the ruling Radical Party, and finally emerged in a more virulent and sophisticated form under the guise of the 'Revolution in Liberty' advocated by the Christian Democrats in 1964. It was employed throughout this period with the clear object of muting the appeal of an already strong Marxist ideology within the working class or among its potential allies and, where possible, to divide the working class against itself. The military had played the game very successfully between 1925 and 1931; the Christian Democrats' attempt to repeat the experiment, however, met with less success, as by 1964 the parties and trade union organizations of the Chilean working class were considerably stronger than they had been forty years before.

Any attempt to explain the peculiarities of Chile's bourgeois institutions or to understand the emergence of Popular Unity itself, therefore, must begin with what nineteenth century Chilean aristocrats used to call 'the social question' – the development of independent working class parties and organizations of various kinds, the emergence of an independent working class consciousness. The bulk of the present chapter, therefore, is devoted to a history of Chile's working class parties and a study of their politics, from their emergence in the nineteen-twenties and thirties to the elections of 1970. Two events in this long history are of key importance, moments at which the future politics of the working class was determined; the formation of the Popular Front of Socialists, Communists and Radicals in 1936, and the banning of the Communist Party in 1948, which brought any further attempts at alliance to an abrupt end.

The politics of the Chilean working class

The single most important point is that the Chilean working class is represented by not one, but two Marxist parties with a mass base: the Communist Party founded officially in 1922 but not recognized by the Comintern until later, and the Socialist Party which was founded as a rival in 1933. The history of the working class in Chile largely revolves around their divisions and their united fronts. Unity of the two parties was the key to working class support for Radical presidential candidate Aguirre Cerda and the Popular Front platform of 1936. Bitter rivalry between Socialists and Communists was later to have a critical effect in aiding the bourgeoisie to contain the working class during the period of Chile's subsequent industrialization. The final defeat of the working class during this period, economically and politically, was marked by the *Ley Maldita* or 'Evil Law' which outlawed the Communist Party in 1948, a defeat which inaugurated a period of collaboration between the working-class parties and led in turn to the formation of a series of united fronts culminating in the UP coalition, formed in 1969.

The existence of a second Marxist party which was neither Communist nor Social Democratic has also been profoundly important in the history of the Chilean working class, though perhaps never as critically important as it was to become in 1970–73. From the time of the *Ley Maldita*, when they split into two legally separate parties which subsequently came together again, the Socialists have clearly been divided into a revolutionary current (usually with a bare majority of the party's supporters behind it) and a reformist current closely associated with the PC. One can see the potential for such a division in the period when the party was formed, and particularly in the splitting of the Socialist Party over the question of whether or not to take part in an alliance with a bourgeois party, the Radicals, in the Popular Front itself. From 1953 onwards, the revolutionary wing of the Socialists, besides arguing against the formation of popular front-style alliances, has also argued that it is impossible for Chile's national capitalist class to develop the country, and has clearly rejected the Communists' theory that a socialist revolution would require a prior bourgeois democratic revolution, which could develop local industry; a revolution in 'stages'. In effect, the revolutionary wing of the Socialist Party has accepted since 1953 Trotsky's theory of the 'permanent revolution': that the tasks of the bourgeois democratic revolution in a colonial or neo-colonial country can only be fulfilled by the working class, in the course of making its own, clearly socialist revolution.

The importance of this tendency within the Socialists stems from its role in attempting to push Popular Unity as a whole towards the left. One cannot approach the history of Popular Unity, therefore, without first analysing the history of the Socialist and Communist parties.

The Emergence of the Working Class Parties

Both parties emerged as a result of Chile's crisis of dependency in the nineteen-twenties. The bulk of the Chilean economy, then as now, depended on revenues from the foreign enclave which exported Chile's minerals: any threat to the world market for the country's single foreign export was a threat to the whole Chilean economy, especially since much of the national economy was dependent on the redistribution of nitrate revenues through the State apparatus.

The strongest political group within the working class in the nineteen-twenties was the Socialist Workers' Party, which had its own trade union confederation, the Chilean Workers' Federation, and dominated the important nitrate miners as well as organized workers in the rest of the country; its influence reached as far as the province of Magallanes in the extreme south. In the first wave of economic problems and social unrest caused by the collapse of nitrates, the Socialist Workers' Party decided to join the Third International.

The sharp cut in State revenues and the rising rate of inflation had created a profound political crisis, resulting in the paralysis of the existing parliament and the rapid radicalization of large sections of the salaried middle class, particularly those whose employment depended directly on the State. The existing political order seemed even to these social layers to be breaking up, and to be scarcely worth preserving. In Russia, as the working class was well aware, workers and peasants had shown that it was possible to overthrow the old regime and had begun to build a new social order. Could the new Chilean Communist Party do the same?

For many reasons, the answer was no. In fact, the nitrate crisis tended to weaken the position of those leaders, notably Luis Emilio Recabarren, who had taken it into the Third International. The nitrate miners formed the strongest and by far the most class conscious section of the Socialist Workers' Party and of the working class as a whole. The collapse of the nitrate industry caused the breakdown of their trade union organizations and the scattering of individual militants throughout the whole of Chile – resulting in a brief upsurge of peasant militancy, as the miners returned to their homes in the central valley, but in an overall loss of party cohesion. With its strongest base shattered, the Party was not in any positon to carry out the reorganization – the imposition of a democratic centralist model of party discipline, for example, and the preparation of cadres prepared to lead an insurrection – which would have been necessary in order to establish a party built on the Leninist model.

Outside the mining areas, the base of the new Communist Party lay in areas where the workers were less sure of their class position, among tramworkers, seamen, and workers in the metallurgical and other small industries (for all the contemporary industries in Chile were quite small). Here the party was exposed to strong libertarian pressures from local anarcho–syndicalists and the I.W.W. When Recabarren returned from a visit to Russia in 1923 and attempted to put through a programme of 'Bolshevization', he met with strong opposition. Local party units had been accustomed to complete independence, and refused to implement the new order of discipline. Their rebellion briefly threatened to overturn Recabarren's control of the Party. Furthermore the party's existing practices strongly inclined it towards taking political action through the trade unions and the ballot box, and Recabarren does not seem to have been a forceful enough figure to impose single-handed the idea that the party should now look to the violent overthrow of the State. The new Communist Party was therefore incapable of providing revolutionary leadership, even in the potentially revolutionary conditions of 1923. Ultimately, this failure was to cost it the chance to consolidate any kind of permanent dominance within the working class.

Since the working class could not provide a solution, the necessary violent action was taken by the armed forces, who intervened in 1924 to put an end to the paralysis of the existing political system by imposing a solution of their own, over the heads of the elected representatives of the bourgeoisie. Their solution involved an attempt to reconcile the working class to the existing order by granting it some concessions, and to accord yet more concessions to the salaried white collar middle class; in this way they hoped to build a stronger base of support. On the other hand, the remaining threat represented by those sectors of the working class who refused to be reconciled was solved by overt and systematic repression. It was this combination of responses which was to characterize Chilean politics for the next forty years.

The intervention of the armed forces was triggered by two current problems: the point-blank refusal of all the political parties to put into effect the pro- gramme of reforms on which the incumbent president, Arturo Alessandri, had been elected in 1920, and the decision of parliament to vote itself a salary increase when the officers, like many State employees, had not received any pay at all for many weeks. A new constitution was drawn up and its imple- mentation guaranteed by the military; new legislation made trade unions legal again and created a certain measure of social security for manual workers and salaried white collar employees. The parliamentary system was replaced by a strong presidential regime capable of balancing the immediate costs and benefits of such concessions against the larger interests of preserving the dom- ination of the bourgeoisie as a whole; on the other hand, the virtual right under the parliamentary system of any section of the bourgeoisie to veto any law not in its own most immediate interest, was removed.

The military remained in power until 1932, although the movement of progressive junior officers who had instigated the coup and then taken control of it, and who at least pretended to be sympathetic to the claims and organiza- tions of the working class, was gradually whittled away until in 1926 a leader emerged who was conservative enough to be acceptable to the bourgeoisie. From 1926 to 1931, Chile was ruled by a military dictator, Colonel Carlos Ibáñez del Campo, who began his period of rule by outlawing the Communist Party and imprisoning or exiling many of its leading militants. Ibáñez also took steps to solve the existing crisis of dependency which had led to a fall in State revenues; he sought out a new imperialist patron willing to lend Chile substantial amounts of money, and found such a patron in the USA. The USA was already quite willing to establish itself in any country in Latin America where British influence seemed to be faltering. Where the British had con- trolled the nitrate mines, the USA had now begun to control copper.

The constitution which was passed on military insistence in 1925 was to last till 1973. It required the State to guarantee every inhabitant and his family a reasonable standard of living, and provided that the State should also guaran- tee the inviolable right of private property, although it could limit any such right in the interests of social needs. Trade unions had been legalized (a major concession) and simultaneously hobbled with restrictions which limited them to the level of a factory organization, and to those factories which employed more than 26 men. In the current industrial structure of the country, which was heavily dominated by artisan industries, this legal restriction was an effective form of repression. At the same time, on paper at least, the unions and the workers they represented were offered substantial economic concessions in exchange for joining the new legal trade union.

The anarcho-syndicalists refused to register their union under the new legal system. The Communist Party split. Recabarren committed suicide in 1924, just after the military coup. His party was confused over what attitude to take towards the officers, first supporting them, then quickly withdrawing support once again. Divisions appeared within the party which were to carry over into the 1930s, and heavily influence the formation of the new Socialist Party in 1933.

Some Communists, like the anarcho-syndicalists, were in principle opposed to both the military and the legal unions; this faction retained control of the party and formed the basis of the Communist Party which re-emerged from the dictatorship in 1931, after suffering several years of bitter repression. In 1927, this rump of the old party did manage to achieve a 'Bolshevik' style organization, based on cells. It followed the 'ultra-left' politics of the International's third period, and was later accepted into the Comintern as a full-fledged member.

But others argued for support of the progressive wing of the armed forces (the officers behind the coup of 1924 included one of the later founders of the Socialist Party, Marmaduke Grove, and some at least obviously held an ideology substantially to the left of Ibáñez, which led them to join with the deposed President Alessandri in attempts to overthrow the dictator in 1928 and 1929). This faction also argued that what was needed was an alliance of the working class and the salaried middle class, to pressure the military into granting real reforms. And it supported or at least was willing to make use of the new legislation for officially recognized trade unions.

The dictatorship was toppled in 1931, not by any political organization of its opponents but by the Great Depression, which revived Chile's crisis of dependency in an even more severe form. Ibáñez had succeeded in solving the old nitrate crisis by mortgaging the Republic to the hilt in order to maintain his programme of social reforms and assure the position of State employees, thus stabilizing the political order. When the Depression followed the nitrate crisis, Chile was forced to renege on its external debts, and the bourgeoisie withdrew political support from the Ibáñez regime. The collapse of Ibáñez unleashed old and new political resentments in a great flood. There was a succession of military coups, as the armed forces proved to themselves that no one in their ranks could solve the new crisis. Out of one such coup, mounted in co-operation with a small independent Socialist group led by one of the old progressive officers of the 1924 period, Marmaduke Grove, the twelve-day wonder of the Socialist Republic emerged. Besides providing president Allende with most of the legislation which he would later use to take over industries in 1970 and 1971, the Socialist Republic led directly to the formation of the Socialist Party.

The Socialist Republic plays a double role in Chilean history. On the one hand, it was the dying flare of that generation of officers who had been radicalized by the crisis of dependency in the nineteen-twenties. The number of officers involved in this radicalization was quite small (perhaps four or five besides Grove himself) but their weight in the original military intervention in 1924 had seemed substantial at the time and they continued to be a rallying point for sectors of white-collar workers who had also turned towards an anti-imperialist and anti-oligarchic ideology to explain their discomforts of the 1920s and of the Great Depression. In its concrete actions, the Socialist Republic was not really 'socialist': its basic idea was to create employment through public works financed by the printing of money. However, it denounced economic liberalism and held fast to the constitutional theme that Chile's economy should provide for the people's needs. Its proclamation did mention the possibility of a rational socialist economic order, and was certainly both virulently anti-imperialist, and bitterly opposed to the existing class of local capitalists who had sold Chile to the forces of imperialism and left it completely vulnerable to the chaos of the world market.

The officers and the independent leftists who made the coup could count on that section of the old Communist Party which had always supported an alliance between progressive officers, working class, and salaried middle class, the section which had its base in the urban areas rather than in the mines, and in the legal unions or among artisans and workers in industries too small to be unionized. The new Socialist Party would inherit much of the opportunist politics of the 1924 period, and many of the libertarian sectors with which Recabarren had had such problems in 1923 – the libertarian tradition may go some way to explaining why the Socialists have so rarely been able to operate as a unified political force. The principled rump of the PC which was still strong in the coal mines, the remaining nitrate mines, and among metallurgical workers, rejected the politics of the Socialist Republic as social demagogy, and although this political line owed much to the current position of the Comintern during the ultra-left period, it also contained an element of truth.

At the same time, the Socialist Republic appealed to all those sectors of the working class and the salaried middle classes who had been anarcho-syndicalist or independent in the 1920s and who were now looking for new answers and a new focus for political action. The anarcho-syndicalists were clearly declining in influence within the working class, partly because of their own opposition to legal unions, but partly also because their ideology could offer very few answers in a period of overt political repression by the State machine. The Communist Party had similarly kept its principles and its independence during the 1920s period, yet it too had failed to provide a political answer to the crisis. Now that its relations with the Third International were much closer, and its politics had become much more sectarian, many workers had other reasons for refusing to join it. For all the sectors who were dissatisfied with the old politics, and all the new socialist groups which had sprung up as soon as the dictatorship was over, offering new answers for Chile's political problems, the Socialist Republic offered a great ray of hope: the possibility that for the first time ever, the working class and its political representatives might take State power. This hope was quickly reflected in the results of the new elections for president, held in the same year, in order to restore the country to civilian rule. The key figure in the Socialist Republic, Marmaduke Grove, and the secretary-general of the Communist Party, Elías Lafferte, both stood as candidates. Grove won 60,856 votes, a third of the number of votes taken by the victorious returning president Arturo Alessandri, while Lafferte as the Communist Party candidate won 4,128. Clearly, the Communist Party had lost a substantial part of the 70,000-odd trade unionists who had been part of its Federation of Chilean Workers in 1924. Later the newly formed Socialist Party would be able to consolidate its own trade union support in the *Confederación Nacional Sindical*, formed in 1934 from the amalgamation of two existing federations, one of them representing industrial and professional trade unions in Santiago, the other representing legal and unregistered unions throughout the country.

The Socialist Party was founded officially after the elections in April 1933, on the basis of a merger of several small socialist groups. It had more than 400 founding members. Some of the groups involved were revolutionary Marxists, some of them much more vaguely left-wing, and clearly about half the founding members were of petty-bourgeois origin (though as petty-bourgeois elements were involved immediately in creating a 'principled' faction within the party to oppose entry into the Popular Front, any assertion that the party's first political problems were caused by the weight of the petty-bourgeoisie within it should be treated with care). Internally, the party was quickly faced with problems created by its tendency to be dominated by the cliques formed around 'great chiefs'. By no very strange coincidence, the chiefs tended to be prominent political figures from the earlier period, and representing the more opportunist wing of the party. Grove was obviously important, but so was a man identified with the old politics of the alliance between progressive officers, working class, and salaried middle class – Oscar Schnake.

The experience of dictatorship had forced the working class parties to reconsider their policies; the new political platform of the Socialist Party, therefore, was the fruit of such a reconsideration. It accepted Marxism as the foundation of its interpretation of reality, basing its analysis on the class struggle, the class character of the bourgeois State, the need for a new socialist order, the need for a forceful revolution to overthrow the existing State and the subsequent necessity of a dictatorship of the working class. Verbally, the party also accepted the principle of internationalism, while interpreting internationalism as something which could be limited to the South American continent: concretely, the Socialists proposed the formation of a Federation of Socialist Republics of Latin America. An official declaration made a year later (when Trotskyists expelled from the Communist Party joined the Socialist Party) had this to say on the problem: 'Chilean and Latin American workers are not generally interested in the existing Internationals, nor the reformist Second, nor the extremist Third, nor the Fourth in formation. On the contrary, to bring conflicts of this kind into our country would divide the working class to the benefit of the oligarchy and imperialism, causing the working class to lose touch with its own specific problems.'

The Popular Front and its Aftermath

In 1935, the Communist Party's 'ultra-left' phase came to an abrupt end, when the Third International adopted a policy of broad-based popular fronts with all supporters of democracy including the progressive and democratic bourgeoisie. The Chilean Communist Party promptly suggested the formation of such a popular front between itself, the Socialists, and the Radical Party, to contest the presidential elections of 1938 on an anti-Fascist programme not dissimilar to those being put forward in Europe. At the time there was a lively Fascist movement in Chile, drawing its inspiration from the Spain of Primo de Rivera and Mussolini's Italy: it too was a result of the effect of the crisis of dependency on the petty-bourgeoisie.

For almost a year, the Socialists refused to consider the idea of a 'hybrid' alliance of this kind (as they called it), counterposing their own idea of a Workers' Front which would not include the bourgeois Radicals. But in March, 1937, in spite of internal opposition, the Socialists agreed to join the Popular Front. In December, a unity conference of the existing Socialist and Communist trade union federations was called, in which the one large Radical union, the Union of Chilean White-Collar Workers, also participated. There the parties of the Popular Front formed a new Confederation of Chilean Workers which was meant to embrace workers of all political tendencies. The anarcho–syndicalists, however, refused to join.

In 1938, Radical presidential candidate Aguirre Cerda was elected and the Popular Front came to power.

Industrialization

The themes of anti-Fascism and the need for basic reforms to improve the living conditions of the poor ('Bread, Clothing and a Roof') dominated the electoral platform of the Popular Front. But the point in its platform which was to have the most lasting effect on Chilean society was an anti-imperialist gesture, which promised that the new government would put a substantial tax on copper exports and use it to fund a new agency to foster Chile's industrialization. In 1938, the State Development Agency, CORFO, was established.

The Popular Front's programme of industrialization was not in any sense intended to replace private capital. At first CORFO's role was limited to supplying credit, incentives and advice to private investors. At the time (during and immediately after the Second World War) this kind of measure

was sufficient to create a brief industrial boom. Since imports from the manufacturing countries had largely been cut off as a result of the war, Chilean
industrialists could count on the demand for products which had previously
been imported to provide them with a market of their own. Very little was
needed initially in the way of skilled labour or even capital outlay. Aided and
abetted by a whole range of government policies – low taxes on manufacturing
establishments and tariff policies which provided a great deal of protection
against imported consumer goods, while letting in goods used in the manufacturing process with very little duty attached – manufacturing grew spectac-
ularly. The manufacturing growth rate reached a high 2.98: that is for a
growth of 1% in the economy as a whole, manufacturing grew 2.98% between 1940 and 1945.

After a rapid downturn in the growth of industry between 1945 and 1950,
when the manufacturing countries resumed their exports, CORFO was
forced to intervene more directly in the manufacturing process and itself
created a number of important industries, including a steel industry. When
these industries began to make a profit, however, they were quickly turned
back to private enterprise. The pattern of a 'national' industry heavily financed
and protected by the State but run by private capitalists on their own behalf,
had been established, and was to remain a key feature of Chile's industrial
structure until the election of Popular Unity. As a bourgeois party, with many
private capitalists within its own ranks, the Radical Party was not interested in
encouraging State-ownership of industry, and it continued to hold the presidency long after the original Popular Front was dissolved in 1941.

The Popular Front usually received much of the credit for the rapid growth
of Chilean industry during and after the Second World War. It could be said
that encouraging capitalist development through State intervention was its
historical mission from the outset, whether or not this played a prominent role
in the Front's electoral campaign. Many of those who had been radicalized by
the nitrate crisis and the Great Depression felt that these disasters were proof
that a country which only produced primary products would always be
powerless in the face of imperialism. Those who were turning to Marxism saw
that the classic Socialist revolution was supposed to be made by an industrial
proletariat of a kind which barely existed in Chile, and some of them argued
that the only political solution open to Chilean revolutionaries (apart from
waiting for a proletarian revolution in the industrial countries) was to join in the
struggle to force industrialization on the national bourgeoisie. In July, 1933,
the Chilean Communist Party had set out a very similar idea in the theory of
stages: 'In Chile it was necessary to make a bourgeois democratic revolution,
whose central objective should be, in our case, to put an end to the domination
of international monopolies and large landowners, by nationalizing the
imperialist firms, establishing relationships with the socialist world, giving land
to the peasants, and thus *creating the material bases for an independent industry*, the
democratization of the Republic, and the final struggle for socialism'.[1]

The Socialist Party of the day was in a poor position to take any stand on this conception of the tasks of the Chilean revolution. Its first official statements had argued that the only solution to Chile's problems was a Socialist revolution and the complete transformation of the existing free enterprise economy. But in spite of its bitter criticisms of the national bourgeoisie for their historical sell-out to imperialism, the party could offer no specific reasons as to why local capitalists should be incapable of making Chile into a powerful industrial country if the profits which had always been exported were brought under national control and invested productively. Sections of the leadership moved quickly towards complete acceptance of the PC programme, justifying their change of position on the basis of the need in any revolution to conciliate the middle class. Those who were critical saw the question as one which revolved around the inevitable betrayal of the working class in any political alliance with sectors of the bourgeoisie (in other words, what was at issue was not the possibility or otherwise of capitalist development, but the correctness or incorrectness of the Popular Front and the impossibility of making a revolution by peaceful and electoral means). The question of whether the Socialists were committed to a socialist revolution or not was not discussed, though in fact this was what the debate was about. In 1939, Schnake, who had been the most prominent defender of the Popular Front within the Socialist Party, became the Minister in charge of CORFO, and the debate was at an end (though in 1941, a section of the party left to form a new Socialist Workers' Party, which broke away over the issue of the Popular Front).

Import-substitution industrialization did not solve the fundamental contradictions of Chile's dependent economy, however. It only resulted in the re-emergence of old problems in new forms.

The new policy of conscious industrialization did have some effect in strengthening the position of the Chilean proletariat, but scarcely a dramatic one. In the years between 1940 and 1952, the number of workers employed in manufacturing jumped from 298,000 to 408,000, from 15% of the working population to 19%. But after 1952, the percentage remained the same and even slightly declined (in 1970, it was 18.9%). The workers employed in very small industries and the independent craftsmen also became somewhat less important as a result of industrialization, although their numbers remained very high by comparison with the industrial countries of Europe. In 1925, workers employed by firms with less than 5 employees accounted for 70% of the manufacturing labour force, while in 1950 only 50% of manufacturing workers were employed in industries that small. But 50% is still an incredibly high figure, and though it continued to decline, the vast number of small firms of this kind would pose a problem for Popular Unity in 1970.

There were other problems with the post-Popular Front pattern of economic development. Industrialization was carried out behind high tariff walls; protection of national industry was often indiscriminate, and led to the proliferation of many inefficient industries catering for the demands of high income groups. By the standards of the industrial West, even the factories in Chile's industrial sector continued to be small. Furthermore, those industries which had been created produced the kind of goods demanded by those who had money, in a country with a very unequal distribution of income. Chile did not produce the goods necessary to satisfy the needs of the majority of its people for 'Bread, Clothing and a Roof' as they had been promised by the Popular Front.

The end result was a mixed economy, with a large State-owned sector, whose responses to the series of crises which beset it were short-sighted and *ad hoc*. The country was still highly dependent on imported goods from the industrial countries, this time in the form of imported machines for production and their replacement parts. The foreign exchange necessary to import machines still came from the export of minerals (copper now, rather than nitrates). Whenever there was a drop in world demand for Chile's chief export, copper, the Chilean economy as a whole fell into recession.

The old contradiction between the need of Chile's governments to cut their State budget when faced with a decline in the revenues from taxes on minerals, and the fact that any such action immediately created an economic and political crisis because of the large number of workers and salaried middle class dependent on the State, was to govern the political history of Chile after the Popular Front just as it had during the nitrate crisis. One might even say that the contradiction had become more acute. After the Popular Front, the economy as a whole was much more dependent on State intervention and State aid to industry, and the expenditure which could be cut back was increasingly limited. The salaried middle classes, even those in the State sector, had organized into unions and professional associations (thanks in part to the effects of the nitrate crisis itself). Furthermore, from the years of the Popular Front onwards, they constituted the mass base of the Radical Party itself (as they were later to account for much of the mass base of the Christian Democrats) – a dangerous sector to alienate.

Inflation had been a problem in Chile since 1879, but it only became the cornerstone of political conflicts after 1938. Between 1879 and 1940 the rate of inflation averaged 8.7% per year; between 1940 and 1950, it jumped to 18% and in the years to come it was to rise even higher. Part of the problem was the government's inability to reduce expenditures when faced with a drop in revenues, and was compounded by its unwillingness to confront the need to change archaic production relations in agriculture, still dominated by the old estates, in spite of the fact that food production in Chile consistently failed to keep up with the growing urban demand. The Radical governments and those which followed them from 1952 to 1964, were unwilling to challenge the interests of the propertied classes even in the hope of gaining increased productivity from the land. The need to import food and pay for it with precious foreign exchange added another burden to Chile's balance of payments, and made the economic crisis which resulted from any drop in the country's sales of copper more acute.

An inflationary process usually leads to industrial conflict, as workers and the salaried middle class struggle to keep their wages equal to the rising cost of living. But during the 1940s and 1950s, the conflict over wages in Chile began to take the form of head-on collisions between the government and the trade unions, as governments tried to 'solve' the problem of inflation by forcing workers to accept a decline in their standard of living. This most dangerous of contradictions was eventually to make the political balance achieved at such cost as a result of the crises of the nineteen-twenties and thirties, and embodied in the popular Front itself, completely unworkable.

The Popular Front and Working Class Politics

The immediate effect of the Popular Front was to usher in a period of social peace, paid for by the spurt in industrialization. There were relatively few strikes during the period from 1938 to 1945, because although real income fluctuated with inflation, the real incomes of both workers and salaried employees were increasing. Workers' salaries rose 20% in real terms between 1940 and 1945, while those of white-collar workers rose 25%.

The political effects of the Popular Front, however, were disastrous for both working class parties. In effect, both had put themselves at the service of the bourgeoisie: 'The shamelessness reached such extremes that an agreement was reached with respect to the peasantry, promising not to organize unions of agricultural workers in order to avoid "creating difficulties for the government".'[2] And this in spite of the fact that between 1939 and 1940 the Socialists themselves had spent considerable effort on organizing a movement of peasants to demand agrarian reform.

The party to pay the highest price for its compromises during this period was the Socialist Party. In 1940, it claimed 50,000 registered members and dominated the Confederation of Chilean Workers. By 1950, the party's influence had declined precipitously while that of the Communists had risen. Worse still, the party cadre was badly demoralized and split. From 1941, when the dissolution of the Popular Front agreement and the death of President Aguirre Cerda opened up new possibilities, the bases of the Socialist Party argued forcefully for a change of programme, the withdrawal of the party from the incumbent Radical administration (which was moving ever more clearly to the Right) and a presidential candidate and electoral platform of its own based on the real interests of the working class. Technically, at every party congress the demand for this turn to the left was won, but in practice the votes of party militants had only a limited effect. Between congresses the leading personalities within the party were possessed of extraordinary talents for manoeuvring to keep their own places in the administration. Twice during this period Grove 'left' the party to continue with his preferred policy of collaboration. Meanwhile, there were Socialists in most of the Cabinets from 1941 to 1948, whether it was party policy or not. The Socialists were paying a heavy price for their original organization around a few 'chiefs'.

The working class was shortly to pay an even heavier price for this Socialist entanglement in the politics of class collaboration. In January 1945, there was a strike in the nitrate zone, and the government declared a number of miners' trade unions illegal. On the 28th the Confederation of Chilean Workers called a vast protest meeting in the Plaza Bulnes facing the Presidential Palace: troops guarding the Palace opened fire on the demonstrators and two of them, a Socialist and a Communist, were killed. (This is the event commemorated in Pablo Neruda's poem *The dead in the square*.) The government immediately moved to patch up the new crisis, by inviting the Socialists (who were currently out of office) into the Cabinet, including in its invitation the leading Socialist militant in the Confederation itself, Bernardo Ibáñez Arroyo. The Socialists accepted: when other workers proposed a general strike to protest against the murders, they refused to participate and chose instead to divide the Confederation. From 1946 onwards, there were two Confederations of Chilean Workers, one Socialist, led by Ibáñez Arroyo (comprising workers in flour-milling and baking, chemicals, the hospital service and some textile workers) and one Communist (covering the miners, metallurgical workers, construction workers and other textile workers).

In September 1946, the Radical presidential candidate, Gabriel González Videla, was elected with the support of the Communist Party, which in spite of the blood on the hands of the previous Radical incumbent, was still following its policy of a 'Democratic Alliance' with the progressive bourgeoisie. The Socialist Party, following the demand of its party congress, put up a presidential candidate of its own, and did not participate in the new administration. Communist cabinet ministers subsequently began firing the most notable Socialist militants within their departments, in what the Socialist Party charged was a campaign of persecution. The Socialists also claim that there were a number of violent clashes between the two parties, in which five of their militants died. Relations between Socialists and Communists could hardly have been worse.

The bourgeoisie was soon able to put this division of the working class to good use. In 1947, President González Videla was looking for an excuse to break with the Communist Party in order to satisfy the demands of American businessmen, and the pressures of the Cold War. In October, the Communist-dominated coal miners went on strike. The coal zone was an important Communist base. González Videla offered the miners some concessions and declared the strike illegal when they refused to accept them. He had the open support of the Socialist Party, and for a time there was even the suggestion that the administration would make the Socialist section of the Confederation of Chilean Workers 'official'. The strike was broken.

A similar attempt to break the railmen's strike later the same year was less successful, since the Socialist Party now officially condemned those of its members who supported the government. But the damage was done. In 1948, on the basis of a successful offensive against the working class, González Videla was able to pass the Evil Law or *Ley Maldita*, called officially the 'Law for the Defence of Democracy', which outlawed the Communist Party and deprived its members of any right to vote in elections, as well as providing heavy penalties for 'Communists' involved in encouraging strikes. A concentration camp for Communist Party members and other trade union militants was established in Pisagua, an abandoned mining camp in the northern desert. The Socialists now moved to expel those of their members who had supported the President consistently in his anti-Communist drive and voted for the *Ley Maldita*. Nevertheless, a few Socialists, including Grove, continued to support González Videla. The government itself granted these people the official title of 'Socialist Party of Chile'.

From 1947, the Socialist Party was officially divided, with one section (the Socialists of Chile) co-operating openly if only briefly with an extremely repressive government. The majority of the Socialists had lost much of their mass support, and had even been forced to take another name: the Popular Socialist Party. Between 1947 and 1958, they set about trying to rebuild the party on the ashes of its experience of the Popular Front.

The Watershed 1947-1958

The result of Popular Front politics and the rivalry between Socialists and Communists within such a framework, was a decisive and lasting defeat for the working class as a whole. The *Ley Maldita* remained in force from 1947 to 1958. Throughout this period, the Communist Party was illegal and could make no political moves in its own name; the same law which had banned the party provided the government with a means of imprisoning any trade unionist who encouraged 'illegal' strikes.

The *Ley Maldita* marks a watershed in the politics of the Chilean working class. One of its ultimate effects was to create great pressure on Communists and Socialists alike (both factions of Socialists) to submerge the extremes of sectarian rivalry in the interests of unity within the working class as a whole. Rightly or wrongly, the history of the working-class during the next twenty-odd years would be a history of the Socialist-Communist alliance, an alliance in which each party would try to maintain its own political line, without bringing its relations with the other party to the point of open rupture. By a stroke of bitter irony, this alliance was inaugurated by the class collaborationist 'Socialist Party of Chile', now repenting of the worst of its follies, which in 1952 joined with the still illegal Communist Party to form a People's Front and present its own candidate for presidency and its own platform. The candidate chosen was Salvador Allende. In 1958, when the Socialist Party had succeeded in reuniting its two factions, Socialists and Communists formed the

Popular Action Front (FRAP), and once again presented Salvador Allende as a candidate. The same alliance had Allende as its candidate again in the Presidential elections of 1964. The Popular Action Front was thus the direct forerunner of Popular Unity, though in 1969 the alliance was widened to include other minority parties.

Still more important in the short-term, however, was the revival of a single trade union confederation, which this time did genuinely embrace all political currents within the working class. The CUT (*Central Unica de Trabajadores*), the new trade union federation, was founded on the initiative of all those sectors who had been least compromised by the Popular Front period and taken less of a beating from the *Ley Maldita*, sectors that on the whole were on the margins of the organized working class: the students, the anarcho–syndicalists, and the white-collar workers.

The Radical government of González Videla was finally defeated when his attempts to cut wages began to affect the salaried middle class, who provided the government's own mass base. In 1950 the bank employees went on strike, causing a cabinet crisis and the collapse of the government's counter-inflation policy, and in fact, the end of the government itself as an effective political force. After this victory, the leaders of the bank employees' trade union took a sudden sharp turn towards the ultra-left (to the considerable embarrassment of the whole trade union movement) going so far as to fake their own kidnapping in order to try and force the president to resign. Other white collar workers were moving in the same direction, though less dramatically. A unified federation of private employees was founded in 1948, followed in the same year by an even larger federation which now included the State sector salaried employees. In 1950, this federation of white collar workers, together with the small group of anarcho–syndicalists which still survived, began to agitate for the formation of a new trade union federation. Simultaneously, the students were attempting to organize a united working class campaign against inflation. In 1952, the political pressure of all these sectors outside the traditional organizations and politics of the working class led to the formation of a Committee for Trade Union Unity which included the outlawed Communists and both varieties of Socialists. Finally, early in 1953, the CUT held its founding congress.

A white collar worker from the State sector, Clotario Blest, was elected the CUT's first President. He was to hold that position until 1961, when he resigned over the Communist Party's decision to call off a general strike. Blest was a revolutionary Christian and, after the Cuban revolution, a fervent Castroist. In 1965, he became one of the founding members of the MIR.

In spite of their own disastrous experience with Videla's government and the 'progressive bourgeoisie', the Chilean Communists continued to present the programme for a democratic bourgeois revolution which they had originally outlined in 1933, and with it, the old politics of a class alliance with 'democratic' bourgeois sectors. This was to remain the basis of the Communist Party programme over the next twenty-odd years: an end to the domination of international monopolies, nationalization of imperialist firms, the creation of an independent industry, agrarian reform and the democratization of the Republic – all these were to reappear in 1970.

A sector of the Socialist Party (the Socialists of Chile and their supporters) now clearly began to support the PC's programme, although it was never able to impose this line on the Party as a whole. In 1970, as in 1952, Salvador Allende represented this reformist wing of the Party.

The revolutionary sector of the Party, represented by the Popular Socialist Party in the period of division from 1947 to 1958, was also hardening its position, although its politics remained very confused throughout this period. During its period of independence, this faction moved towards a direct commitment to the principle of permanent revolution, a theory first put forward by Trotsky in relation to Russia, and which argued that only a socialist revolution could fulfil the historical tasks of the original bourgeois revolution in colonial or semi-colonial countries. This position was stated very clearly in the Popular Socialists' conference in 1953, when the party criticized the Communist position that what Chile needed was a bourgeois democratic revolution:

'. . . In the case of Chile and generally in almost all the colonial and dependent countries, reality is much more complex (than the 'stages' theory of successive revolutions would suggest). Our bourgeoisie had developed with a much more limited field for its operations, subordinated to the great foreign firms. Because it never had the power to undertake great investments, it chose not to set itself up as a rival to imperialist capital, preferring to establish a close association between its own interests and those of the imperialists, so that its interests became more or less complementary to those of imperialism itself. This factor, as well as the close association between this class and powerful rural interests, means that this class is organically incapable of fulfilling the revolutionary tasks undertaken by the bourgeoisie in the developed countries.

. . . In our countries, the bourgeoisie is not a revolutionary class. The revolutionary classes are the industrial workers, the miners, the peasants, the intellectual petty bourgeoisie, the artisans and independent workers, and all those sectors of the population whose interests are in contradiction with the established order. Within this framework the organized working class comes more and more to play the decisive rôle.'

In 1958, these two very divergent Socialist conceptions of the nature of Chile's position as a dependent country, and the tasks of the Chilean revolution, came back together again without any clarification as to what the line of the united party should be. Thus the Socialist Party continued to be a centrist party, after the *Ley Maldita* as it had been before, and continued furthermore to be a party comprising two distinct and almost independent factions. But the period of the Popular Front had left the revolutionary wing much stronger within the Socialists, if not within the working class as a whole, and finally, much clearer about its basic position. The weight of the revolutionary Socialists in limiting the extremes of class collaborationism within the coming period was to be very important.

Furthermore, the party had succeeded in shedding the extremes of personalism and opportunism embodied in the figure of Grove. After 1947, political personalities within the party were to be important because of their association with a definite political line – not because of any undefined position as a charismatic figure.

Within the working class, the revolutionaries were still very clearly a minority and they continued to be so throughout the period of Popular Unity itself. The net balance of forces for the whole of this period is probably well represented by the vote within the CUT in 1955–6, when the question at issue was whether the organized working class should attempt to bring down the government of Ibáñez through an unlimited general strike (the position put forward by the Popular Socialists and the anarchists), or whether on the other hand, it should try for a series of alliances against Ibáñez with other 'democratic' sectors like the Radical party and the nascent Christian Democrats. The implication of the latter position was a decision to limit its general strikes against the government's freeze on wages to one- or two-day affairs, on the assumption that they could be resumed if the government still refused to give in; this line was upheld by the Communists, the Socialist Party of Chile, the Radicals and the Christian Democrats themselves. At the time the CUT executive voted 14–10 against the proposals put forward by the Popular Socialists.

After this first unsuccessful attempt to persuade the CUT to adopt a policy of a quasi-insurrectional general strike, the Popular Socialists resigned themselves to the politics of elections, represented by the Popular Action Front. Here their chief contribution was their ability to prevent the Communists and their own reformist wing from extending the Popular Action Front itself into an alliance with other social sectors outside the working class, represented either by the Radical Party or by the nascent Christian Democrats. From 1958 to 1969, the Popular Action Front was clearly a 'Workers' Front' of the kind advocated by the Socialists in 1933–6: it did not include any party which, by whatever stretch of the imagination, could be regarded as bourgeois – and this in spite of the fact that throughout this period, the Communists' own policy was still based on the idea of a potential 'Democratic Alliance', which from 1952 to 1958 clearly included the Radicals and the Christian Democrats.

The existence of a force to the left of the Communist Party thus had the effect of creating an independent politics of the organized Chilean working class, which, from the point of view of the class struggle, represented a very important step forward. From 1953 to 1970, neither of the two major working class parties was involved in any presidential administration. At every presidential election, Salvador Allende stood as a candidate against the candidates of the bourgeoisie, on a programme worked out by Socialists and Communists in co-operation with the CUT. The CUT itself was not compromised in any fashion by a need to support the anti-inflationary policies of successive governments.

Thus, although the politics of the Chilean Left as they emerged from the Popular Front were still electoralist and still largely reformist (and in that sense confined by the limits of bourgeois ideology) the independent political weight of the working class within the system was nonetheless considerable throughout the period of economic crisis from 1953 onwards. The threat which this working class independence implied for the capitalist order became obvious very quickly. In 1958, Allende came within a hair's breadth of winning the presidency, losing to the principal bourgeois candidate, Jorge Alessandri, by 30,000 votes – less than the number of votes which went to a completely unknown cleric who stood at the bottom of the electoral list. In 1964, for this very reason, the Americans and a part of the Chilean bourgeoisie would choose to back a dark horse candidate standing on a programme of radical reformism and an ideology deliberately designed to compete with Marxism: Eduardo Frei and his Christian Democrat Party, propounding the 'Revolution in Liberty'.

For the bourgeoisie, the years from 1953 to 1970 were years of dangerous economic instability and even more dangerous political radicalization, as the problems of Chile's distorted and dependent economy once again brought extreme pressure to bear on the system as a whole.

Three Regimes of Social Crisis: Ibáñez (1952-58), Jorge Alessandri (1958-64) and Eduardo Frei (1964-1970)

A thumbnail sketch of the nature of Chile's political regimes and their different attempted solutions to the continuing economic and political instability of the country in the next twenty years, might run as follows: *Populism, 1952–53; Repression, 1953–1958; Free Enterprise and American Aid, 1958–64; Populism and Repression and More American Aid, 1964–1970.*

Ibanez 1952-58

President Carlos Ibáñez del Campo was elected for the second time in 1958, with a rather more honestly constructed electoral mandate than he had managed to win at the beginning of his dictatorship in 1927. His platform was pure populism. He offered repeal of the *Ley Maldita*, a minimum salary and a family allowance for workers, and a government willing to listen favourably to just wage demands. The CUT gave him its cautious support and even invited him to speak at its first May Day rally. The Popular Socialists were much less cautious, in spite of their contemporary decision not to trust the national bourgeoisie, and actually joined his cabinet, only to leave it in October 1953, when the Minister of the Interior suddenly denounced the CUT as an 'illegal organization'.

It was the beginning of five years of bitter confrontation between the government and the working class: a kind of confrontation prefigured very accurately in May 1954, when the President had Blest imprisoned for attacking the government at the CUT's second annual May Day rally, and the CUT itself organized a general strike to obtain his release (and won). Ibáñez was forced out of his populist stance by the arrival of hyper-inflation: the cost of living level rose by 71% in 1954 and 84% in 1955. The chief cause was probably the decline in Chilean copper revenues following the end of the Korean War. Ibáñez called in an American agency, Klein-Saks, to prepare a 'stabilization' plan in the hope of getting financial support both from the Americans and the International Monetary Fund, and thus was reinforced in his own determination to force the salaried classes to absorb inflation in the form of a cut in their own real wages. In September, 1955 (shortly after the Communists and Socialists of Chile had successfully won a battle within the CUT in favour of holding negotiations with the government) the government itself declared a State of Emergency, citing 'information of a new seditious plan by Communist elements determined to paralyse the most important industries in the country', and adding, 'the Government has identified 15 international agitators, Russians trained in Spain . . .' Simultaneously, the Klein-Saks programme was sent to congress for approval. Before another general strike could be called, Ibáñez had trade union leaders throughout the country arrested and brought charges against the national leaders of the CUT for infringing the *Ley Maldita* which he himself had promised to repeal.

Both in its ends and in its means, Ibáñez' stabilization policy was a success. In 1956, the rise in the cost of living from one end of the year to the other was only 32%. The CUT was massively defeated in the general strike of 9 January 1956, called to protest against the re-imprisonment of Clotario Blest and its other national leaders, which was massively boycotted by the working class itself. Ibáñez was an old master at combining repression with small local concessions, so confusing the reaction of the working class at the critical moment; while denouncing the 'Russians trained in Spain' in 1956, for example, he simultaneously offered a general amnesty to all those workers who had been imprisoned for their part in illegal strikes during the previous months. Furthermore, the politics of the one-day strike and subsequent negotiations with the government (the politics advocated by the reformist majority within the CUT) played straight into the president's hands; he was given every practical opportunity to offer concessions when the workers on strike had won a temporary victory, and suddenly when they were once again demobilized, to go back to the attack with a new and unexpected offensive. Thus eventually the CUT's call for a general strike fell on deaf ears: Chilean workers learned from sad experience that even when they 'won' such a strike, it did no good.

In spite of the temporary success of Ibáñez' policy of repression, the CUT survived. In the next election it supported the political programme and the candidate of the Popular Action Front – a decision which led the Christian Democrats within its ranks to retire temporarily. Furthermore its candidate very nearly won.

JORGE ALESSANDRI (1958–1964)

The Chilean bourgeoisie itself was not particularly happy with the results of the programme of stabilization, which had succeeded in reducing the rate of inflation at the cost of industrial growth and its own profits. In 1958, they put up a candidate who was clearly one of their own. Besides being the son of Arturo Alessandri and a member of one of Chile's leading families, Jorge Alessandri was a leading industrialist in his own right and president of the bosses' union, the Confederation of Commerce and Production.

Presidential Election Results – 1958

Jorge Alessandri	389,909 votes or		31.6%
Salvador Allende	356,493	,, ,,	28.5%
Eduardo Frei	255,769	,, ,,	20.5%
Luis Bossay (Radical)	192,077	,, ,,	15.4%
Antonio Zamorano	41,304	,, ,,	3.3%

The election results were a shock to both the Chilean bourgeoisie and its foreign allies, particularly those in the USA. A Marxist had come within a hair's breadth of winning the presidency of Chile. Clearly radical social change would soon be on the agenda unless steps were taken over the next six years to head off the Popular Action Front.

At the turn of the century, the United States began to challenge Britain's place as the dominant imperialist power in Chile. By 1958, American investment accounted for 80% of all foreign investment in Chile, and Chile had the seventh highest level of American investment in the world. Most of this investment, of course, was tied up in the copper mines – $483 million out of $736 million – but in any case, American interests were clearly directly affected by the results of the 1958 presidential elections.

Direct US Investments in Chile

	$ millions
1879	1.0
1908	31.0
1914	171.0
1953	590.0
1958	736.0

After 1945, the US had regarded Chile as one of the most 'stable' States in Latin America. The narrow defeat of the Popular Action Front forced the USA to recognize that its investments in Chile were potentially fragile. A year later, Fidel Castro took power in Cuba. The cumulative unease of the Americans led to a massive increase in technical, political and cultural 'assistance' to Alessandri.

Alessandri's government inspired great confidence among Americans during the first few years, replete as it was with competent businessmen and managers. His projected solution to the crisis of Chilean capitalism was to restore free competition within the private sector (by admitting larger quantities of goods manufactured abroad), while simultaneously reducing State intervention in the economy. Coupled with this faith in the efficiency of the free market was a touching belief that 'the real and most important cause of our problems . . . is to be found, at bottom, in a crisis of morality'. American policy-makers found this approach congenial, particularly since Alessandri believed that foreign capital should positively be encouraged to enter Chile, and a US aid agency noted (accurately enough) that if this regime were to fail, its collapse would 'almost automatically ensure a marked swing to the left'.

Alessandri himself stated that 'it is indispensable to create a propitious climate for foreign capital', for the very good reason that only foreign capital and foreign aid could prevent his own national policies from leading to massive inflation. The government was determined not to increase taxes on the wealthy (although in fact Chile's upper classes were very lightly taxed), both because taxation was politically sensitive and because increases were supposed to discourage capitalists from investing. But its economic programme depended on an expansion of State sector expenditures in the first few years, to develop an infrastructure which would persuade private capitalists to invest. There were only two methods of financing this increase in State expenditure open to the president: either a loan from Chile's own Central Bank (which would have been purely a matter of printing money to meet expenses, and thus highly inflationary) or else foreign loans. The government chose foreign loans.

Loans and foreign investment were intended to be the basis for a painless road to economic development. Between 1958 and 1964, Chile's foreign debt (public and private) rose from $569 million to $1896 million, with the bulk of the new capital coming from the USA. In many ways, Alessandri had turned back to the solution to the crisis of dependency first invented by the dictator Ibáñez in 1927–32, by finding a patron willing to bail the country out of its existing economic difficulties (while, of course, also walking off with all possible economic gains). Chile soon found itself enmeshed in a complicated debt repayment cycle, in which further loans and credits were required if the country was to pay off the original ones, and thus in a cycle of ever deeper entanglement with the USA. Many key political decisions began to depend on an approving nod from Washington, while simultaneously, the influx of private foreign capital – encouraged by favourable tax and profit repatriation treatment in Chile – linked the Chilean monopolies ever more closely with American multinational corporations. The dynamic sectors of Chilean industry began to figure as part of the planned global strategy of American corporations, thus deepening and extending Chile's dependency on the USA.

The situation which confronted Allende in 1970, his own problems with the blockade of American corporations and the renegotiation of the external debt, were in many ways a reflection of the effects of policy decisions taken by the Alessandri regime, which were clear evidence of what happened if the natural instincts of the national bourgeoisie were followed through.

For a time the president's programme of 'growth with stability' worked, thanks to the influx of American funds. But American demands on client governments in Latin America were changing. In 1961, at Punta del Este, president Kennedy made a speech announcing a new American policy towards Latin America, based on the conception of an 'Alliance for Progress'.[6] 'There is no place in democratic life', the American president declared, 'for institutions which benefit the few while denying the needs of the many, even though the elimination of such institutions may require far-reaching and difficult changes such as land reform, tax reform and a vastly increased emphasis on education and health and housing'. The considered response of the US towards the obvious effect which the Cuban revolution was having on Latin American politics, now took the form of pressure on all its client governments to stave off revolution within their own countries by granting some kind of reform.

When the Alliance for Progress was established, Alessandri put up a Ten Year Development Plan, with a request for finance to support it. To comply with the objectives of the new alliance, the government even passed an agrarian reform law of a kind. But plan and reforms were both little more than window-dressing to obtain funds from the USA. In the short term, the window-dressing was successful. Within Chile pressure for real reforms was growing, particularly after the president's counter-inflationary policy collapsed with a balance of payments crisis in 1962, and inflation once again became a serious problem. The United States now regarded reform in Chile as necessary in order to solve the existing social unrest and prevent a swing to the Marxist Left. As early as January 1963, the Americans had begun to look for a reforming capitalist alternative to Alessandri's traditional conservatism. Competent businessmen and managers were no longer a sufficient guarantee of stability: the Americans thought the alternatives were reform or revolution, and they were in no mood to make concessions.

The USA thus contributed directly to a serious split within the Chilean bourgeoisie from 1964 to 1970. Traditionally, the Americans had favoured the conservative sectors of the Chilean upper class: the commercial bourgeoisie and industrialists-*cum*-landowners like Alessandri who by now were represented in the National Party. Now they withdrew support from the political representatives of this class fraction, and set about looking for a new populist alternative capable of meeting the Marxist parties (at least verbally) on their own terms. They found this alternative in a minority party, the Christian Democrats, and a new kind of strong man with a considerable talent for political manipulation: Eduardo Frei.

In 1964, Eduardo Frei won the Presidency of Chile with a resounding majority, 56%, after the front of the united Right had been persuaded that unless it withdrew support from the Radical candidate who was also running, Allende would win.

4

EDUARDO FREI 1964–1970: 'REVOLUTION IN LIBERTY'

The roots of the Christian Democrats in Chile go back to a youth group which broke away from the Conservative Party in 1937 to form the so-called National Falange. The Falange was anti-Nazi and anti-Franco, but it did identify with some elements of Fascist ideology, particularly corporativism. Eduardo Frei was a leading member from the beginning. In the 1940s, the Falange remained an insignificant small party, although Frei himself became a cabinet minister for nine months in 1945. In the 1950s, however, the new party began to grow. In 1957, it joined forces with the small Social Christian Party, to become the Christian Democratic Party of Chile. In the presidential elections of 1958, running as a candidate for the new party, Frei obtained 20% of the national vote.

From the time of the collapse of González Videla's Radical administration in 1950, the party began to lay considerable stress on its own social conscience, and to make some appeal for support from white-collar sectors of the CUT. Basing themselves on left-wing currents within Catholic thought, the Chilean Christian Democrats evolved a loose 'communitarian' ideology which claimed to be neither capitalist nor socialist. Frei himself frequently emphasized that capital was a social asset which should serve the needs of the people – a political theme which had been good coin in Chilean politics since the nitrate crisis. In practice, however, 'communitarianism' was a cover for a modernizing reformist, pro-capitalist and pro-imperialist party whose leadership hoped that by emphasizing community participation as a solution to social injustice, could create for itself a mass base.

The cornerstone of this new attempt to mobilize mass support for a capitalist party was a highly sophisticated ideology, which allowed the party's supporters to claim that they, too, were revolutionaries. Thus in 1964, the Christian Democrats promised the electorate a 'Revolution in Liberty': far-reaching structural reforms to resolve the long standing economic and social crisis, without the danger of class war. The leading Christian Democrat economist, Jorge Ahumada, wrote a book called *La crisis integral de Chile* (The universal crisis of Chilean society). This universal crisis combined political, social, cultural and ideological as well as economic factors. The two critical factors, however, were seen by the Christian Democrats as the lack of participation by large social groups among the very poor in Chilean politics or society (the problem of the so-called 'marginals', people who were on the margins of the existing society) and, second, the lack of social justice and the evident inequalities between different social groups. It was a conception which appealed particularly to the practising Catholics within Chile, who felt that the existing order was decidely un-Christian in the weight of economic hardship and social prejudice it forced upon the poor, but who also felt that Marxism was an atheistic and dangerous ideology. Thus Christian Democracy began with a good chance of finding support among Chilean working class and peasant women, who were much more likely than their husbands to be faithful attenders at church.

The key to the Christian Democrat challenge to Marxism lay in its conception of the 'marginals' as a virtual ideological substitute for the working class. Peasants, urban slum-dwellers and the unemployed – all were now 'marginals'. The organized working class however was not 'marginal' (according to the Christian Democrats) but already incorporated into the national system, at least in economic terms. In political terms, of course, it had been captured by an 'alien' ideology. The working class was seen as a social layer which enjoyed considerable privileges within the system, and was therefore at some points opposed to the Christian Democrat programme because it would have required them to sacrifice their own interests – a neat inversion of the Leninist theory of a 'labour aristocracy' which in certain circumstances is willing to betray the interests of the whole of the working class, because it has been bought out. The existing political division between Christian Democrats and the Popular Front could thus be presented as having its roots, not in the distinction between a modernizing party interested fundamentally in preserving the bourgeois order, and a working class alliance which was not committed to that order, but as a matter of conflict of interests between those who had the care of the 'marginals' at heart, and the self-interested working class.

It was an exceedingly clever attempt to counterfeit a socialist ideology. Where Marxists would claim that the proletariat was the most important force for social change within a capitalist society, and suggest that the problems of other oppressed classes could only be solved if the proletariat took revolutionary action, the Christian Democrats claimed that the proletariat was *passé*. So was class conflict: ' "Conflict," said Marx, "is the motor of history." He forgot that history is a vehicle with two motors. The other is solidarity'.[7] The message of the communitarian ideology was that the *crisis integral* could be solved if only workers and capitalists were willing to attempt to live in harmony, through a combination of solidarity and structural reforms.

In the context of Chile's class structure, the question of the marginals was as strictly practical as it was ideologically useful. The social groups involved were numerically important in Chilean society – particularly women, and the urban poor and unemployed. The potential for large numbers of the dispossessed to join a politically independent, organized and active working class was there: at every presidential election, the Popular Front had another chance to put forward its own candidate. The need to incorporate the marginals into the bourgeois order, then, was an overriding imperative for the existing bourgeois system, as well as a matter of convenience for a political party looking for a clientele. In order to gain its base among this group, the Christian Democrats used a combination of straightforward patronage and techniques of mass mobilization more often used by the Left. Their programme offered the expansion of employment opportunities and social services – education, health, housing, social welfare benefits. Politically, they set about creating various community groups under their own control – Mothers' Councils, Sports Groups, Neighbourhood Associations of shanty-town dwellers, organized through two new government agencies: the Institute for Agricultural Development and *Promoción Popular*.

Frei was thus a model 'Alliance for Progress' candidate and he had considerable American financial backing (The *New York Times* estimated that in the months prior to the 1964 election, the Christian Democrats were receiving $1 million a month from abroad to finance their campaign.) The national bourgeoisie had been forewarned of the recurring danger of a Popular Action Front victory by the Front's success in a by-election in Curicó in March 1964. Having little hope themselves of winning with a conservative candidate, they threw their support behind the Christian Democrats to prevent the Marxists coming to power (although there were some heartaches within the more conservative elements of the bourgeoisie at having to make what they regarded as Hobson's choice). The only third party candidate to stand was Durán, a Radical, who had very little electoral success. The result was that Frei won the presidency with 56% of the vote, and the Christian Democrats proclaimed that they would be in power for the next thirty years.

President Frei's chief problems on taking office were the same as had beset the Chilean economy since the 1950s: inflation and stagnation, the inability of a country with a small home market based on wealthy consumers to provide a large enough market to make mass production efficient, and the inability of existing industry to satisfy the basic demands of the wage-earning population for houses, clothes and food. Christian Democracy had a plan to solve the basic problems created by the logic of a dependent economy: a plan to make Chile an exporter of goods to other countries in Latin America and even to Europe, and to broaden the base of the market by creating a new class of consumers among the 'marginals', particularly the peasantry.

The Christian Democrats argued seriously that economic growth would not be possible without structural reforms – a strictly pragmatic basis for the party's commitment to social justice. Its programme represented a break with all those members of the Chilean bourgeoisie who were willing to sacrifice economic growth to the preservation of the old system of landed estates in the countryside, which was inefficient, and had failed for many years to provide enough food to feed the growing urban centres, but which still remained an important feature of the life style of much of Chile's upper class. The Alessandri family, for instance, who had made their original fortunes trading in Valparaíso and now owned the country's paper company (running it in co-operation with an American multi-national), also had a landed estate not far from Santiago, and were on the whole opposed to any serious land reform. Christian Democracy derived its support from industrialists who were willing to break with this tradition and the political commitments which flowed from it, in order to encourage the efficient and cheap production of food, which would thus lessen the pressure for wage increases. In return, 'progressive' industrialists could expect substantial help from the Americans, especially since the government's programme was a classic formulation of the basic demands of the Alliance for Progress: capitalist economic growth through agrarian reform and tax reform.

Economic growth was to be based on an increased home market and the development of exports. The Christian Democrat economists had argued for some time that Chile's domestic market was too small to allow for efficient mass production: they saw this problem of the size of the existing home market as one of the reasons for the ultimate failure of the Popular Front's policies to lead to any substantial economic growth. Agrarian reform was seen as a means of increasing the size of the home market fairly quickly (while satisfying the demand for social justice), and at the same time, as a way in which the internal production of food could be stimulated, and the drain on Chile's balance of payments due to imported food, cut down. By expropriating the large and inefficient landowners and turning their land over to peasant co-operatives, the Christian Democrats hoped to increase both production and rural incomes. The new prosperity among the peasants would provide a brand new market for domestically produced manufactured goods. Eventually, the peasant co-operatives would become family farms, and a new class of small capitalist farmers would be created. Agrarian reform would thus not present any kind of threat to the existing capitalist order, at least in the long term.

Other steps were to be taken to make Chilean industry more efficient. The quality of Chile's human resources was to be raised, through a massive programme of educational expansion at the primary level and at the level of technical training. New industries necessary to a modern economy, like a plastics industry, were to be created through joint programmes with foreign capital. The infrastructure necessary to make an efficient national industry possible would be provided by increased government expenditure at every level (it was a programme which dovetailed nicely with the need for consistent and increasing government expenditure to resolve social tensions). The cost of this vast attempt at modernization could be partly financed from the profits of growth itself and the proceeds of new tax reforms, and also from the expansion of copper production which could be gained under a new agreement with the American companies, called 'Chileanization'. On the other hand, an influx of foreign investment, and massive financial aid from the USA were crucial to the government's programme.

With the shift to the left in the country at large, the Christian Democrats had been forced to adopt some kind of anti-imperialist policy, at least verbally. In 1958, Frei himself had defended American investment in copper. In 1964, however, 'Chileanization' was the Christian Democrats' proposed alternative to the full nationalization proposed by the Popular Action Front. With the agreement of the copper companies, the Chilean government bought out 51% of the shares in the Chilean mines. The companies retained control of management (subject to an agreement with the government to expand copper production) and gained new concessions from the government over taxation and the proportion of their profits which could be sent out of the country. On the whole, then, the arrangement was very profitable for the foreign interests involved. In 1969 the Anaconda Copper Company was drawing 80% of all its profits from investments throughout the world from Chile. Expansion of copper production was financed not by the companies, but by US government loans.

In its first three years, the Christian Democrat programme was quite successful, in spite of its own political problems with Chile's Right (which used its support in the Senate to hold up the passage of 'Chileanization' till 1966 and of the Agrarian Reform Law till 1967). Thanks in part to the growth in government expenditure and the consequent stimulus to consumer demand, industrialists put back into operation the industrial capacity which had not been used during two years of stagnation, and production of manufactures grew. At the same time, new productive enterprises such as a car industry, an electronics industry and a petrochemicals industry were put into production. These new enterprises were generally set up by foreign multi-nationals, sometimes in cooperation with the government, sometimes not. At the same time, American businessmen began to buy into industries which had previously been owned by Chileans. Once again, as in the years of Ibáñez' dictatorship and Alessandri's presidency, the government in power was able to give the Chilean economy a temporary boost, at the cost of increasing its long term dependence on the USA. But in the short term, even the government's counter-inflation programme was successful, and the cost of living index fell from 38% in 1964 to 17% in 1966.

Politically, during this period, the Christian Democrats were riding the crest of a wave. In the shanty towns and rural areas the party made significant advances in organizing the marginals under fairly tight control from above. The salaried middle classes were also happy: structural reforms of the economy which promised future prosperity without requiring them to sacrifice any immediate interests, were very much to their liking. In the Congressional elections of 1965, the Christian Democrats won 42.5% of the votes.

The fly in this ointment, however, was the organized working class. From the beginning, in spite of the Christian Democrats' long record of presenting a sympathetic front to trade unionists in conflict, the Frei administration favoured an authoritarian policy. The original trade union legislation passed in 1924 made a single trade union, virtually a closed shop, obligatory in every factory with more than 26 employees (while of course attempting to make it illegal for workers in different factories to join forces). The president proposed a labour code which would have made it possible to form anything up to three unions in a single plant (thus substantially weakening trade union organization), and which, furthermore, would have allowed him to order back to work any strikers who were demanding a pay rise above the legally permitted ceiling, calling upon the police or the armed forces as he chose to back up this order, and forcing the strikers to accept compulsory arbitration. The proposed labour code was justified as an attack on the 'privileges' of the working class. At the same time, Frei himself supported a bid by other sections of his party to set up a rival to the CUT – a new Christian Democrat Trade Union Federation.

None of these initiatives brought the party any joy, even within its own ranks. The majority of Christian Democrat trade unionists were opposed to the labour code, and equally opposed to any attempt to pull them out of the CUT. Their opposition eventually forced the government to withdraw its attempt to create a new institutional basis for splitting the Chilean labour movement. But Frei's own inclinations were clearly in the direction of a tough line, which quickly brought him into open and bloody conflict with the working class. In January, 1966, the El Teniente copper mine went on strike. President Frei declared the strike 'unconstitutional' and arrested its leaders or supported their dismissal, but nevertheless the strike lasted until March and the miners managed to generate sympathy strikes from other workers. When a second mine, El Salvador, came out in sympathy the government sent in the troops, who killed six miners and their wives and wounded several more. The President defended the troops' action and accused the Marxist parties of being responsible for the conflict. Once again, he came under very heavy criticism from within his own party, although the party's ideology was still sufficiently strong for its own Left to be unwilling to exonerate the Marxists of all blame.

In fact, troubles over union legislation in the first three years revealed very clearly that the Christian Democrat Party was built on an unstable base, and that it would have real difficulty in reconciling the divergent class interests in its own ranks. For the first three years of president Frei's administration, the strength of Christian Democracy and 'communitarianism' as an ideology, and the party's real commitment to modernizing Chilean capitalism (even if it cost the Chilean landed gentry some heartaches) were successful in hiding the differences of intention between the party's leadership and large sections of its base. In spite of the reforms, however, president Frei's Cabinet Ministers were drawn almost exclusively from the same social layers as those appointed by president Alessandri: corporation lawyers, managers, industrialists, and large landowners. These were men determined that the Party's reforms went just far enough to make Chilean capitalism efficient, while satisfying the necessary minimum of popular demands and undercutting the existing power of the working class.

But it was in the nature of the Christian Democrat ideology that it could also justify much greater social change, and large sections of the party had been attracted to it by its promise of social justice as an end in itself: particularly among the peasantry and radicalized white collar workers or intelligentsia. These people wanted more than a bourgeois party could give. Thus in the end, the Christian Democrats prepared their own grave as a reforming alternative to Marxism, and the party began to split.

After three years of reforms and increased public expenditure, Frei and his supporters began to be alarmed at the prospect of a rising rate of inflation. The existing conflicts within the party hardened. At the 1967 conference there were three factions: the *oficialistas*, who supported Frei; the rebels, who were slowly evolving towards a socialist position, and actually succeeded during the conference in capturing the party leadership; and the *terceristas*, who tried to find a middle position between the other two. The splits came into the open over the question of the *Plan Chonchol* (called after one of its authors, Jacques Chonchol, head of the government's land reform agency). The *Plan Chonchol* advocated increasing the weight of the State in the national economy, more social reforms, and an acceleration of the agrarian reform programme. In many of its details, it was not unlike the programme put forward by the Communists within Popular Unity. The *oficialistas*, on the other hand, were proposing a cut in public expenditure, a cut in the money supply, a cut back on the number of new foreign debts incurred, and a change in the direction of public investments so that housing and construction projects were cut back to the benefit of investments in mining, education and agriculture. The rebels won, temporarily capturing control of the party apparatus, which Frei only gained back, after a struggle, in January 1968.

At the same time, another and more sophisticated attempt by the Christian Democrats to solve the problem of the organized working class and bring it under greater government control, met with disaster. It was based on a counter-inflation policy outlined by the Minister of the Economy in 1967 (though in Chilean terms, inflation was not yet a serious problem in 1967). The Minister of the Economy presented a forced savings scheme, which the CUT treated with derision. Workers were to be given a legal wage increase equal to the whole of the cost of living during the year, but only 75% of it would take the form of cash. The other 25% would be in national savings certificates, to which the employer would contribute as much as the worker, in the worker's name. These national savings certificates would then be invested, and the workers who invested them would become 'share-owners' in the new capital which was thus created, though they would get only 5% interest on their holdings every year (a negative rate of interest in view of Chile's record of inflation) and the 'shares' could only be cashed in on unemployment or death. As a concession to the trade unions, the government offered them the right to sit on the boards which would determine the investment. As a price for this handsome deal, the government demanded suspension of the right to strike for one year.

It was a programme worthy of president Ibáñez, taking away with one hand what it was offering with the other, and demanding a *quid pro quo* at the same time. In other circumstances – like the crisis of 1924 and the Popular Front itself – this kind of 'arrangement' had successfully won over at least a section of the working class, and worked in the very substantial interests of the bourgeoisie. But the Christian Democrats were unlucky. The CUT called a general strike to defeat the government's proposals, charging accurately enough that they were an attempt to integrate the working class into the capitalist system. There were massive street demonstrations. Frei brought in the troops to break the strike, and five people were killed and over 200 arrested. Once again, the Christian Democrats showed their willingness to use violence against the working class. They lost, nonetheless. The right-wing parties also opposed the government's plan, arguing that businessmen should not be forced to contribute to a fund which would expand government intervention in the economy. The combined opposition of left and right forced two Finance Ministers to resign, and finally forced the government itself to come to an agreement with the Communists, whereby the government agreed to drop the forced savings proposal and its proposal for a year-long ban on strikes, and the Communists agreed to vote for a legal wage increase which was about 85% of the year's rise in the cost of living.

In retrospect, one could reasonably argue that the highly unstable system of alternate populism and repression which had governed Chile since 1924, was buried with the forced savings scheme. For all the sophistication of its ideology and economic programme, Christian Democracy failed to solve the problem presented by a politically independent working class. Its populism succeeded in gaining it some support in the rural areas, and much greater support among the urban poor, particularly women. But it was clearly in no position to claim to represent the majority of the population, and would clearly have to compete with a well-organized political rival on its left flank. The attempt to cement the Chilean social system together with a counterfeit Marxism and a series of social reforms had failed, and so in the end did the economic programme. In 1968 and 1969, Chile's economy slipped back into stagnation, and the cost of living began to rise again.

What the Christian Democrats did succeed in doing, by raising a programme of reforms, was in dividing temporarily the Chilean bourgeoisie. The Chilean Right has never been happy about tolerating reforms, even if in its own ultimate interests. It was certainly not happy to tolerate a reforming party which, far from reducing social conflicts and creating social harmony within the country, had in fact prepared the ground for a further radicalization of a substantial proportion of its own members and of the oppressed classes at large.

3 The Crisis of 1970: Party and Society

In 1964 the Christian Democrat Eduardo Frei had been elected to the Chilean presidency on the basis of a promise to enact far-reaching structural reforms in Chilean society. His 'Revolution in Liberty' was a model Alliance For Progress programme whose aim was to undermine the traditional appeal of the Marxist parties to the Chilean working class; as such it enjoyed the full support of the US government. The good showing of the Popular Action Front (FRAP) in the 1958 elections had surprised and unsettled the ruling class; thus in 1964 all sections of that class, including the National Party, joined forces behind Frei in order to head off the Marxist challenge.

Frei was the representative of the more 'modern', 'progressive' sector of the bourgeoisie; this, together with the rhetorical appeal of Christian Democracy to the 'marginal' sectors of Chilean society (peasants, urban shanty-town dwellers, women, youth etc.) suggested both to the ruling class in Chile and to interested foreign observers that Frei offered the best hope of eroding the traditional support of the Marxist parties. The ideology of class collaboration and 'the end of class struggle', combined with the incorporation of new, previously unorganised sections of the population into the polity would, it was hoped, have the effect of building up a popular counter force to the organized working class.[1]

However, Frei's 'Revolution in Liberty' did mean that the large landowners of Chile would have to bear much of the cost of the reforms, as well as accept a diminution of their social and political power. Thus despite the increasing dominance within the ruling class of the industrial bourgeoisie, the conflict between its interests and those of the agrarian bourgeoisie remained. This was expressed in the continuing competition between the various bourgeois parties – on the one hand, the Christian Democrats, and on the other the National Party (which in 1966 had fused the Conservative and Liberal parties) which represented the older and more established fractions of the ruling class. In 1964, the imminent Marxist threat had forced them to make some sacrifices in order to preserve bourgeois rule, even though it meant that the relative standing of the older, agrarian sectors within the capitalist class had to suffer as a result. This did not mean that they were happy with the situation, nor that they were willing to accept it without seeking to reduce the costs to an absolute minimum. It took Frei three years, for example, to push his agrarian reform law through Congress, and in the process many concessions were made to the large agrarian interests. Even so, the law that emerged proved to have quite radical implications, especially since its implementation coincided with an attempt by the Christian Democrats to organize the peasantry into rural unions. It was hoped that the beneficiaries of agrarian reform, together with the rural workers organized by the Christian Democrats, would provide an important base of political support for the government of Eduardo Frei. This was clientilistic politics at its clearest and most obvious. In return for access to the land or an improved bargaining position with the landowner, the peasants, organized paternalistically into government-sponsored unions and federations of co-operatives, were expected to provide political support and allegiance to their benefactor – the government. A similar process was expected to occur in the cities as a result of the organization of shanty-town dwellers, women and youth.

The entire model was built on the premiss that economic expansion would and could continue. Yet this, too, was to be achieved at a cost – the increasing monopolization of the economy, a rising level of foreign intervention in (if not control of) the Chilean economy and a foreign debt that, by 1970, had reached massive proportions. The crisis, both economic and political, of 1970, which was to contribute directly to the victory of UP, stemmed from the structural conditions of the Chilean economy (as we have discussed in previous chapters) exacerbated by the peculiar contradictions of the Frei regime itself. However limited his promises, it was clear that economic conditions had worsened to such an extent by 1966–67 that Frei found himself faced with a number of choices, all of which essentially required either drastic modifications of the model of economic growth and social development, or its complete abandonment.

It is clearly necessary to understand the specifically economic nature and source of the crisis that the Christian Democrat government faced in 1970, before going on to analyse the social and political expressions to which that crisis gave rise, and which in large part explain the victory of Salvador Allende in the Presidential elections of 1970.

The Chilean economy in 1970

The Chilean economy in 1970 was beset by a number of long-standing problems: inflation, stagnation, high unemployment and underemployment, balance of payments crises and very unequal income distribution and access to education, health and welfare. Popular Unity argued that it was necessary to transform some of the structural characteristics of the Chilean economy in order to tackle these problems. Pedro Vuscovic, Allende's first Minister of Economy, put this point as follows:

> The stagnation, inflation, inequality, unemployment and denationalization of the economy, existing in extreme and increasing degree, were the inevitable outcome of the kind of subordinate capitalist development that characterized the Chilean economy and society. The state itself with its tradition of

involvement in the economy of the country, was no more than an associate in the process of monopolization and dependence intrinsic to that system.[2]

Three characteristics needed to be changed: dependency on imperialism, the pivotal role of the State in maintaining the accumulation of private capital and the oligopolistic structure of the Chilean economy.

Dependency

As argued throughout this book, the external links and relationships between Chile and the world capitalist system have been of fundamental importance in shaping the structure of the Chilean socio-economic system. Chilean development has been conditioned to such an extent by its incorporation within the world capitalist system, and thus by events external to it, that this development process has been called a dependent one. From the colonial exploitation by Spain to the nitrate and copper enclave economies, the dominant Chilean economic interests have always accommodated themselves to foreign economic interests.

The dominant foreign interest in Chile is the USA.[3] Dependence on the USA is not only economic but also cultural, military and political; thus it is not just an external variable but part of a system of social relations between different classes within Chile. The strength of the ideology of capitalism among the Chilean middle classes, for example, was in part sustained by the deliberate 'aid' and other policies of the USA.

The economic aspects of Chilean dependence took a number of different forms: an increasing trend towards foreign ownership of crucial parts of the Chilean economy, relying on the USA for essential imports, e.g. spare parts and machinery, and growing indebtedness.

Foreign investors had traditionally little interest in Chilean manufacturing industry (the market was too small), but since 1967 this had changed.

Foreign Investment in Manufacturing in Chile ($m)

	1965	1966	1967	1968	1969	1970	Total
Total	9.24	5.07	9.27	30.02	42.29	45.65	141.54

Source: *Corporación de Fomento de la Producción: Inversiones Extranjeras en Chile.* May 1971.

Between 1965 and 1970, investment in manufacturing was almost the equal of that in mining, the traditional field for US investment in Chile.

Distribution of Foreign Investment ($m)

Sectors	1965	1966	1967	1968	1969	1970	Total
Agriculture	0.11	—	—	—	—	—	0.11
Mining	2.25	—	0.57	73.23	10.83	56.54	143.42
Industry	9.24	5.07	9.27	30.02	42.29	45.05	141.54
Services and others	0.35	0.01	0.02	0.57	2.47	—	3.42
Total	11.95	5.08	9.86	103.82	55.59	102.19	288.49

Source: *Corporación de Fomento de Producción: Inversiones Extranjeras en Chile.* May 1971.

By 1970 foreign interests were increasingly becoming the dominant force in the largest and most dynamic Chilean industries.

Foreign Participation in Chilean Industry (*Top 160 firms*)

Total number of firms	With foreign participation	1%–30%	31%–50%	51%–75%	76%–100%
A	B	C	D	E	F
160	82	28	17	15	22
100	61	21	12	12	16

Source: L. Pacheco: *La Inversión Extranjera en la Industria Chilena.*

That is, of the top 160 Chilean firms 82 (51.3%) have foreign participation, and in 37 of these (23.2% of the total) this participation constituted more than 50% of the capital of each. Of the top 100 firms 61 had foreign participation with 28 of these having more than 50% of the capital. If one considers that about 30% of the capital is usually sufficient for control, then 54 of the 160 (i.e. 34%) are controlled by foreign interests, and out of the 100, 40% are controlled by foreigners.

There was also a trend towards an increasing foreign participation in such sectors as insurance, banking, communications, wholesaling and retailing. Nevertheless, by far the most important USA stake in Chile was in mining.

Composition of US Direct Investments in Chile (*Cumulative*)
(Book Value in US $ millions)

	Mining & smelting	Manufact- uring	Commerce or trade	Other	Total
1929	$331	$ 7	$13	$72*	$423
1936	383	5	12	84	484
1943	215	28	15	76	329
1957	483	22	9	52	666
1960	517	22	12	188	739
1964	500	30	20	239***	789
1968	586**	66	39	271	962
1969	452	65	41	288	846

* Of which utilities and transportation were $67 million.
** Of which an estimated $320 million book value in copper. (*Miami Herald*, December 22, 1970).
*** Of which utilities were $175 million.

Note: All figures are probably gross understatements – for tax purposes. In any case, compare the total 1969 mining and smelting investment figure of $452 to the $700 million demanded by the copper companies as compensation for the 1971 nationalizations.

Source: NACLA: *New Chile* 1973, p. 92.

Apart from coal, the USA participated in all the main mining ventures in Chile: copper, iron, nitrates, iodine, salt. Of these by far the most important was copper, comprising 78.5% of the total value of Chile's commodity exports in 1970. The two major US copper companies in Chile, Anaconda and

Kennecott, laid particular store by their Chilean investments for reasons made clear in a Chilean government advertisement in *The New York Times:*

Anaconda and Kennecott
Profitability and Investments, 1969

	Investments worldwide	*Investments in Chile*	*% invest. in Chile*
Anaconda	$1,116,170,000	$199,030,000	16.64%
Kennecott	1,108,155,000	145,877,000	13.16
	Profits worldwide	*Profits in Chile*	*% profits in Chile*
Anaconda	$ 99,313,000	$78,692,000	79.24%
Kennecott	165,395,000	35,338,000	21.37
	Rate of return worldwide	*Rate of return in Chile*	
Anaconda	8.5%	39.5%	
Kennecott	15.0%	24.1%	

Source: Chilean government advertisement in *The New York Times*, January 25, 1971.

It is true that by 1970 the Chilean Government had acquired a majority share in the largest Chilean copper mines.

Major Chilean Copper Mines 1970

Mine	Foreign investor	Chilean state participation (CORFO)	Output in metric tons per year
Chuquicamatá	Anaconda	51%	180,000
El Teniente	Kennecott	51	283,000
El Salvador and Portrerillos..	Anaconda	51	77,000
La Exotica	Anaconda	25	(100,000)*
Rio Blanco	Cerro	30	(60,000)*
Sagasca	US Cont. Copper	25	(29,000)*

* Figures in parentheses are projected production figures due in mid-1970s.
Source: NACLA: *New Chile*, p. 101.

But Frei's 'Chileanization' of copper still left many important decisions to the US copper companies, as well as paying an inflated price for their shares, allowing them to triple their profits (between 1965 and 1971 Anaconda made $426 million profits in Chile and Kennecott $178 million) and to hedge against nationalization by contracting debts of $632.4 million – which Chile guaranteed – for the copper expansion programme. In 1970 copper was still the key to Chile's dependency on the USA.

The two other economic facets of dependency – the structure of Chilean imports and Chile's indebtedness – gave the USA powerful leverage to disrupt the Chilean economy if it so desired. Exports, although 90% minerals, went to a variety of countries, with the USA taking only 23% in 1968. Yet in 1968 the USA supplied 39% of Chile's imports. About 70% of all capital goods imported by Chile came from the USA and so not surprisingly the bulk of crucial spare-parts and machinery came from the USA. Chile's industrial structure was closely tied to that of the USA.

In 1970 Chile's *per capita* foreign debt, standing at about $300 per head of population, was one of the highest in the world. Its size was the result of a strategy of development pursued first by Alessandri and then by Frei, which pushed up Chile's debt from $598 million in 1960 to $3,127 million in 1970. This strategy, incidentally, had the effect of increasing the consumption levels and the expectations of Chileans, especially those of the main beneficiaries, the Chilean middle classes. In terms of the balance of payments, Chilean current export revenues nearly always exceeded total imports. The chronic balance of payments deficit largely resulted from profits remitted to the metropolitan countries, which exceeded the amount of new private foreign capital entering the country. Aid helped Chile to finance its balance of payments deficit, but at the cost of building up future interest and amortization payments. In 1965, with an official debt service charge of over 40%, President Frei had to negotiate and reschedule debt repayments. The constant need to renegotiate the debt and obtain new credits put Chile in a weak bargaining position over internal and external policies *vis-à-vis* the USA and the international financial community, the main Chilean debtors. When it came to power in 1970, Popular Unity faced a situation in which profit remittances in direct investment and debt servicing in public and private debt comprised some 30% of total Chilean exports. This gave the USA, with its power to ensure that the flow of aid and credits to Chile could cease, a powerful tool for disrupting the Chilean economy.

Economic dependency brought in its wake a series of other US activities in Chile. There were in 1970 about 80 private US institutions in Chile ranging from the Ford Foundation programme for Higher Education to the Seventh Day Adventist Welfare Service. The Chilean military received training and equipment from the USA. And in nearly all key sectors – communications, trade unions, education, community organization – there was an American organization giving advice, training and money. The American Institute for Free Labour Development, for example, spent over a million dollars trying to persuade trade unionists that it was undesirable for trade unions to be politically orientated. To break the ties of dependency meant much more than just breaking the economic chains.

The State

Chile has a long history of state intervention in the economy; particularly since the establishment of CORFO in 1938, that involvement has grown steadily. Between 1964 and 1970 public expenditure as a percentage of gross national product increased from 35.7% to 46.9%. In a series of studies the Chilean Planning Agency, Odeplan (Oficina de Planifícacion Nacional) showed that the State's role in the accumulation of capital was of overwhelming importance. Between 1961 and 1969, for example, total public investment (direct and indirect) as a percentage of gross investment in fixed capital increased from 46.6% to 74.8%, and indirect public investment, i.e. public funds transferred to the private sector via credits or capital transfers increased from 12.5% to 50.3% of total private investment.[4]

The Chilean State generally left the high profit areas to private enterprise, concentrating its investment on infrastructure and inputs to help the private sector. The State also initiated many enterprises, which were sold to private enterprise as soon as they became profitable; for example, steel, fishing, some mines, metal-mechanical industries etc. Thus the State subsidised the private sector. This is not very surprising: of the 27 Ministers in the Frei and Alessandri Governments, 20 were either corporation lawyers, managers, industrialists or large landowners and only 6 from professions not directly linked to business interests.

Popular Unity thought that this degree of State intervention made their task easier. For instead of being used to subsidise the private sector, the State sector could, they argued, be used to generate its own surplus and to direct the economy in a way conducive to a transition to socialism.

The monopolistic structure of the Chilean economy.

There have been relatively few sectoral conflicts between the Chilean bourgeoisie. The large industrial capitalist was often also a large landowner. The tendency in Chile has been for wealth to become more and more concentrated in fewer and fewer hands. The Frei Government attempted to lessen this trend, particularly in agriculture, where prior to his reform about 1.3% of farmers controlled about 72.7% of agricultural land.

Land Tenure in 1965

Size of Units		Number of units	Total size (thousands of hectares)	Average size (Ha)
1. Less than 5 hectares	..	123,636	207	1.7
2. 5–50		92,408	1,556	16.8
3. 51–200		23,959	2,284	95.3
4. 201–1000		10,158	4,310	424.4
5. 1001–5000 ..		2,601	5,495	2,112.8
6. More than 5,000	..	730	16,795	23,007.4
7. Total national ..	..	253,492	30,648	

Source CIDA: *Chile-Tenencia de la Tierra y Desarrollo Socio-Económico del Sector Agrícola.*

But although the Christian Democrat agrarian reform claimed that it was going to create 100,000 new peasant proprietors, by 1970 less than a third of Chile's *latifundios* were expropriated and only 21,000 of the promised 100,000 peasant families had received land. Popular Unity still faced the task of destroying the *latifundio* system in 1970.

In industry there was a high degree of concentration of ownership. Three large holding groups – Banco de Chile, Banco Sud Americano and the Edwards group – controlled about 70% of all Chilean capital in business corporations. And in a study in 1970[5] it was shown that 284 joint stock companies owned 78% of Chilean shares and in 60% of these the ten largest shareholders owned 90% of the shares. In Chile it was possible to pin-point the key families who dominated the industrial scene: the Alessandri, Yarur, Matte and Edwards families. Some of the holdings of these groups were as follows:[6]

(1) the Yarurs dominated the textile industry, owning the five largest Chilean textile plants and controlled the fourth largest private bank, the Banco de Crédito e Inversiones;

(2) the Alessandri–Matte group controlled or influenced sixty-nine corporations, amounting to 16.1% of the total (1960) Chilean capital investments; and

(3) the Edwards family had interests in, or controlled the following: *El Mercurio*, the largest Chilean daily newspaper (with separate editions in each major city) and the dominant printed advertising medium; Banco A. Edwards y Cia. the fifth largest private Chilean bank; the Chilean Consolidated Insurance Co.; the Chilean brewing monopoly, Cia. Cervecerías Unidas; several large *haciendas;* a 50% interest in a joint venture with Britain's Lever Brothers, in a detergent company; the Pepsi-Cola bottling plant in Santiago; a 20% interest in the Chilean subsidiary of Ralston Purina; the second largest magazine publisher, Lord Cochrane, which also had distribution rights over numerous US comic strips (such as Flash Gordon, Felix the Cat, Rip Kirby . . .); a large tool-making firm; the newspapers, *Ultimas Noticias, La Segunda;* and figured on the board of directors of Chile's steel monopoly, the Cia. Acero del Pacífico, and of IBEC. Chilena, the Rockefellers investment company.

Complementary to the concentration of industrial wealth was a trend towards concentration in banking, distribution and other activities. The problem for Popular Unity was how to take over these oligopolies, and alter the structure of the economy.

This structure and the policies which accompanied it left Chile with a number of pressing economic problems in 1970[7]. The causes and possible policies to deal with these problems are of course complex and in many cases long-term. The following illustrates some of the economic problems which Popular Unity had to face from 1970 onwards, but does not analyse them. For a long period the Chilean economy had been unable to maintain sustained rates of growth for more than a few years at a time. Since 1967 the Chilean economy had stagnated, and it was to be one of Popular Unity's main objectives to move the economy out of stagnation.

Per Capita GNP Growth

1961	1962	1963	1964	1965	1966	1967	1968	1969	1970
3.6	2.4	2.1	1.6	2.4	4.6	0.0	0.6	0.7	1.0

Source: *Odeplan: Antecedentes sobre el Desarrollo Chileno, 1960–1970.*

Together with stagnation the Chilean economy has, especially since the Second World War, been beset with one of the highest rates of inflation in the world.

Consumer Price Index: % annual increase

1960	1961	1962	1963	1964	1965	1966	1967	1968	1969	1970
11.6	7.7	13.9	44.3	46.0	28.8	22.9	18.1	26.6	30.7	32.5

Source: *Odeplan: Antecedentes . . . op cit p. 39.*

Not surprisingly, given both stagnation and inflation, the savings and investment rate was low. Thus although rural population had declined from 31.8% in 1960 to 25.8% of total population in 1970 there had not been sufficient investment in productive activities like manufacturing to absorb the increasing urban population. Unemployment in Chile was high, certainly much higher than the 1970 official figure of 6.0% for Santiago. Underemployment also remained a serious problem. The occupational structure of Chile reflected the swelling of government employment thanks to revenues from the mining sector, and reflected underemployment which in countries like Chile usually merges into the catch-all category of 'services'. The following table gives the occupational structure of the working population of Chile in 1970:

	Sector	Number	%
1.	Fishing and agriculture	738,000	21.71
2.	Mining	99,200	2.92
3.	Manufacturing industry	567,300	16.69
4.	Construction	200,000	5.88
5.	Commerce	451,500	13.28
6.	Services	965,100	28.39
7.	Transport	175,600	5.17
8.	Electricity, Gas and Water	11,800	0.35
9.	Unemployed	190,600	5.61
10.	All (including unemployed)	3,399,100	
11.	All at work	3,208,500	

Of the total 665,700 (19.58%) are self-employed.

From this table it is possible to see some of the dilemmas that Popular Unity inherited from Frei: how to win over the very large petty bourgeois and white collar sectors.

Finally if one measures income distribution in terms of the minimum wage (the minimum wage could be taken as a crude estimate of the basic subsistence level) then one finds a highly skewed distribution of income with the top 2% households getting 12.5% of total income and the bottom 30% less than 8% of total income. The poor in Chile are very poor. Frei failed to change the picture; it was to be one of the fundamental aims of Popular Unity to radically alter the existing distribution of income. To do so involved changing the structure of Chilean society in directions never contemplated in Frei's 'Revolution in Liberty'.

Distribution of Household income 1968

	Country		Urban		Rural	
	% household	% income	% household	% income	% household	% income
Less than 1 sv*	29.8	7.6	19.3	4.0	46.6	19.0
1–2	31.6	20.1	30.6	16.1	33.5	32.8
2–3	17.6	18.9	21.5	18.9	11.4	19.1
3–4	7.4	11.2	9.5	11.8	3.9	9.2
4–5	4.5	8.7	6.1	9.7	1.8	5.5
5–6	2.9	7.1	4.0	7.9	1.2	4.5
6–8	2.7	8.0	3.8	9.3	0.9	4.2
8–10	1.5	5.9	2.2	7.0	0.4	2.5
More than 10	2.0	12.5	3.0	15.3	0.3	3.2

* *sueldo vital* = minimum wage.

Source: *Odeplan Antecedentes . . . op. cit.* p. 16.

Political disillusion and disenchantment on the Right

The crisis that came to a head in 1970, then, had begun three years earlier. The uneasy passage of the agrarian reform bill left little doubt as to the fragility of the alliance between landed and industrial interests. While there was never any doubt that the PDC was a bourgeois party, the differences between the various fractions of the Chilean ruling class, both in terms of social base and economic interests, and of political disagreements between them over how to deal with the growing challenge from the working class were sufficiently great for the more conservative fraction of that class to feel the need to maintain its political autonomy, embodied organizationally in the National Party. It was natural, therefore, that when the PDC began to initiate reforms, the PN and the employers' associations should oppose these measures, which they saw as detrimental to their interests.

The Christian Democrats and the Nationals disagreed profoundly, for example, about the Agrarian Reform law, which was eventually approved after considerable debate in Congress in 1967. But it was not merely the National Party which sought to defend the interests of the landowners. As Kaufmann has pointed out,[8] the most radical centres of opposition crystallised around a coalition of the presidents of the national producers' organizations. An *ad hoc* organization calling itself the Agricultural Federation (FEDAGRI) was formed to oppose the measure. Also in opposition, though somewhat less vociferously, was the rival pressure group to the SNA (the National Agricultural Society), the Consortium of Agricultural Societies of the South (CAS). There seems to have been a clear difference of political strategy between these agriculturalists' organizations and the SNA itself. Whereas the SNA argued that a hard-line resistance to the agrarian reform could only lead to more massive reform, the agriculturalists argued that without standing firm they would face a peaceful but certain destruction. Behind this latter strategy lay the assumption, as Kaufmann points out, that a united upper class, with its command of wealth and organization, would have a good chance of emerging victorious in any breakdown of governmental authority. For a military intervention against the PDC government was not entirely out of the question.

Meanwhile, the industrial groups, such as SOFOFA, (*Sociedad de Fomento Fabril*, the Chilean CBI) had remained neutral, for it was the PDC wing of the bourgeoisie that had initiated the reform law. This split increased the chance that the moderate position of the SNA would triumph so that a policy of concession rather than one of outright opposition would prevail. Nevertheless, although the Right had not won this particular battle, they were far from being reconciled to the PDC government. In fact, the effect of their opposition had been to curtail quite severely, if not actually stop, the extent to which the Agararian Reform law was carried out (see above).

In this sense, the conciliation of interests within the bourgeoisie successfully held back one of the central political platforms of Christian Democracy – the incorporation of the rural population. The Christian Democrat programme had aimed to introduce the structural reforms necessary to widen the market, and introduce a limited redistribution of wealth and income. The agrarian reform had been essential to that programme, in that it would both stimulate agricultural production and increase the participation of the peasantry in the internal market. Other measures, such as tax reforms and wage readjustment policies, would at the same time ensure that the level of working class purchasing power was maintained. The programme for increasing popular participation and integration in the political system, together with a concern for mobilizing and incorporating previously excluded sectors of society – women, peasants and slum dwellers for example – had, furthermore, an important political basis.

It should not be forgotten that these were the initial years of the Alliance for Progress, and the fear existed that unless steps were taken to placate disadvantaged social groups there could well be another Cuba in Latin America. In many ways, the Christian Democrat party embodied the basic notions of the Alliance for Progress strategy for Latin America; one of its motivations for incorporating these 'marginal' groups into the political process was to head off any incipient mobilization by the Left.

It was clear that the political participation of the peasantry, for example, could not be postponed for much longer. If the Christian Democrats did not act, the Left would win an increasingly large base in the countryside. On the other hand, if the Christian Democrats were the first to incorporate the peasants and other marginal sectors into organized national politics, then they would have built an important electoral base for themselves. The measures of land reform (for the peasants), of 'Popular Promotion' (for the slum dwellers) and 'Mothers' Centres' (for women) would provide the organizational means for the distribution of patronage required to consolidate these new social groups as an electoral base for the PDC. Of course, these were not the only sources of support for the PDC, but their incorporation did signify an important expansion of political participation in Chile.

Such populist programmes were by no means foreign to the outlook of Christian Democracy. The ideological formulations of Chilean Christian Democracy had always stressed bringing new social groups into the political arena as a prerequisite for a new and higher level of social integration in Chilean society. Not that Christian Democratic ideology was always clear-cut and consistent: far from it. According to Petras[9] there are two distinct tendencies in the party: the populist and the corporatist. While on the one hand, the populist strain in Christian Democratic ideology focuses on the plight, the human condition, of the poor and marginal sectors of society, the corporatist elements focus on the need to organize bureaucratically, under the domination of elites and interest groups which bargain among themselves within a context of shared values. Whereas populist ideology stresses the alienation of the poor from existing society and the need for people on all levels of society to participate in political debates, the corporatist strands tend to choke societal conflict and locate the focus of policy-making within the limited circles of a few authoritative elites. The two trends, populism and corporatism, merge in rejection of a class model of society and in an attempt to recreate the nation as an organic whole, integrating the dispossessed and marginal sectors into society under the tutelage of the corporate elites.

The very ambiguities and contradictions inherent in Christian Democratic ideology make it an ideal vehicle for the obfuscation of class consciousness and for the generation of sectoral and corporate clienteles. The different components of the ideology are variously stressed and emphasized according to the nature of the audience (peasants versus businessmen) and according to the tasks confronting the Party leadership (winning an election or dealing with an economic crisis).

Thus although the PDC directly represented a sizeable fraction of the bourgeoisie, and in no sense sought to challenge bourgeois domination as a whole, the fact that it represented only one fraction within the ruling class and the salience of populist elements in its programme (and even more so in its ideological pronouncements) predisposed the older, more established sections of the ruling class to view the Frei administration with some reservation.

The economic policies of the Frei government met with a considerable degree of success in the first two years. Inflation was reduced to 20% by 1966, while production rose 5% in 1965 and 7% in 1966. Industrial production increased by 20% in those two years. But the level of savings did not rise, and the working class was able to maintain pressures on wage levels. The result was the re-emergence of inflationary pressures in 1967. From 1968 onwards, the government was forced to abandon any serious attempts at stabilization policies and simply tried to prevent the inflationary pressures from getting out of hand.

The difficult economic situation of 1967 was worsened by the fact that the rate of growth of public expenditure was drastically reduced that year, and hence no longer continued to stimulate industrial production as it had done previously. The increasing economic difficulties of the Frei government coincided with a rapid increase in the number of strikes and with a general growth in the combativity of the working class and peasantry.

The upsurge of militancy in the working class and peasantry in the second half of Frei's presidency was by no means an unprecedented phenomenon. As has been shown, the Chilean working class and peasantry have a long history of struggle against the ruling class, and this struggle was increasing throughout the decade of the sixties. But with the economic crisis of 1966–67, popular mobilization rose dramatically.

This is most clearly seen in the following table, which shows the number of strikes recorded.

Strikes 1960–69

					Total	Legal	Illegal
1947–50	..	..	..	..	121	39	82
1960..	..	..	..	..	257	85	172
1961..	..	..	..	..	262	82	180
1962..	..	..	..	..	401	85	316
1963..	..	..	..	..	413	50	363
1964..	..	..	..	..	564	88	476
1965..	..	..	..	..	723	148	575
1966..	..	..	..	..	1073	137	936
1967..	..	..	..	..	1142	264	878
1968..	..	..	..	..	1124	223	901
1969..	..	..	..	..	997	206	771

Source: Alan Angell, *Politics And The Labour Movement in Chile*, 1972, p. 76.

This rise in militancy was not confined to the urban working class. In the sixties the struggle was broadened to include the seizures of plots of urban land in order to establish squatter settlements, and saw the massive incorporation of the peasantry and rural proletariat into the political system. Within the urban working class, the methods of struggle underwent a change: the workers began to occupy the factories during industrial disputes. The following table gives figures for the number of occupations of urban lands, of factories, and of farms.

Occupations 1968–71

			1968	1969	1970	1971
Urban lands ..		..	8	73	220	175
Factories	..	..	5	24	133	339
Farms	..	..	16	121	368	658

Source: Joaquín Duque and Ernesto Pastrana, *La movilización reivindicativa urbana de los sectores populares en Chile 1964–72* in *Revista Latinoamericana de Ciencias Sociales*, No. 4, Dec. 1972, p. 268.

The response of the Christian Democratic government to this upsurge in the combativity of the working class and peasantry was to step up the scale of its repressive actions. A tactical riot squad, known as the *grupo móvil*, was created and 'United States military aid to Chile, which was pouring in at a greater *per capita* rate than anywhere in the world except South Vietnam, was increasingly oriented toward counter-insurgency and riot control.'[10]

It was against this background that the process of political mobilization essential to the 'Revolution in Liberty' began to get out of hand. The government was increasingly less able to control the political mobilization of its supporters, since it could no longer provide the material rewards it had promised without generating a growing class conflict. Ultimately the contradiction between the class nature of the Christian Democrat Party, as a party of the bourgeoisie, and its populist and reformist mobilization of marginal social groups whose overall social expectations had begun to rise as a result of early reforms, proved too much for it. The Party experienced internally the effects of this division within the bourgeoisie itself.

The growing disillusionment of the more conservative fractions of the bourgeoisie with the Frei government led them to abandon the alliance formed in 1964; consequently, the National Party named its own candidate to the 1970 elections – Jorge Alessandri. Within the PDC, the candidature of Radomiro Tomic on a left platform was an indication that, even after MAPU's split with the party, there remained sectors within the Christian Democratic Party committed to the reformist-populist political strategy.

Tomic and Christian Democracy

For a long time Tomic had been regarded as the automatic successor to Eduardo Frei. Chilean constitutional law prevents a president from succeeding himself, and consequently, Frei was not eligible to stand for re-election in the 1970 elections. The ironic fact about Tomic's candidacy was that his position within the PDC was quite different from Frei's.

On the left of the party the failure of the Frei government led to a general radicalization. In 1969, the disillusionment of some of the more progressive sectors of the party, particularly with respect to agrarian reform, had led to the formation of MAPU (the Movement for United Popular Action) led by Jacques Chonchol, which was subsequently to join the Popular Unity coalition. This left Eduardo Frei at the head of the right-wing section of the party, and Tomic, after the departure of Chonchol and MAPU, as the undisputed leader of its left wing.

If the Right had become increasingly disenchanted with the PDC under the leadership of Eduardo Frei, it was unlikely to be enthusiastic when presented with the candidature of Radomiro Tomic. Yet the continuing divisions within the PDC, corresponding to its multi-class social base, made it extremely difficult for the party to ditch Tomic and choose a hard-liner who might prove more acceptable to the Right in the National Party.

For his part, Tomic sincerely believed that his mere presence in Chile (after his return as Ambassador to the United States) would be sufficient to unite the entire Christian Democratic Party behind him in a short time.[11] Given the fact that the PDC was divided into three distinct factions – the 'officialist' wing led by Frei, the 'rebel' group (later to form MAPU), and the 'third position' group led by Luis Maira and Bosco Parra (which in 1971 became the *Izquierda Christiana*) – such a hope seems to have been rather illusory. When the MAPU group left the party in 1969, Tomic's base of support within the PDC, and hence his range of possibilities for manoeuvre, were considerably reduced.

Tomic wished to enter into some kind of electoral agreement with the forces of the left, constructing a broad Popular Unity coalition that would leave the National Party isolated and without any chance of winning the election. However, in the National Council (*Junta Nacional*) of the PDC held in August 1969, this position was outvoted and Tomic was forced, against his wishes, to stand as candidate for a Christian Democratic Party which refused to ally itself with the Left.[12] At the same time the Freista group continued to hope that they would be able to gain the support of the National Party for a PDC candidate as they had done in 1964.

With Tomic as a candidate (and possibly even with a more right-wing PDC candidate) it was not likely that the Frei group would have much success in attracting the support of the traditional right. The alliance of the PN and the PDC in 1964 was a measure of desperation in the face of a common enemy, but since then, Frei's reforming measures had seriously antagonized large sections of the landowning oligarchy.

The Left in 1970

The Frei period witnessed a general radicalization whose repercussions had been felt both within the PDC and throughout the Left generally. Yet the perspectives for the Left in 1970 seemed to many to be less favourable than they had previously been. Despite the agreement finally reached among the parties of the Left in 1958 regarding a common front, the nature of this front continued to be differently interpreted by right-wing members of the Socialist Party and members of the Communist Party on the one hand, and left-wing Socialists on the other. An impressive electoral showing in 1958, and the increasing dominance of parliamentary conceptions of the road to power within the Socialist Party led, over the years, to a gradual redefinition of the FRAP in the direction of the kind of broad front favoured by the Communists. In 1964, however, its showing at the polls was less encouraging, as it became increasingly caught up in internal debates. Inside the revolutionary Left there was developing a general feeling that the Left would never come to power via the electoral road; critical of the continuing electoral orientation of the Socialist Party, a group of socialist students split away from the Party in 1963, to form in 1965 the MIR (the Movement of the Revolutionary Left). The pessimism of the MIR with regard to the electoral road found important echoes within the Socialist Party, and increased when Radomiro Tomic emerged as the Christian Democratic presidential candidate on a platform closely resembling Allende's. Many thought that this would allow the Christian Democrats to pull off the same old demagogic trick again. But events were to prove that the leftism of Tomic was designed to recover lost ground in the face of an increasing mobilization on the left.

The Popular Unity coalition came into being in 1969, and differed somewhat from the old FRAP. Some revolutionary elements, like the MIR, had rejected the electoral orientation, but the Socialist-Communist coalition was to be strengthened by the entry of the MAPU and the Radical Party.

The return of the Radicals did not, however, mean a return to the politics of the Popular Front period. Whereas previously the Radical Party had played off the divided parties of the working class against one another, it was now much smaller and weaker, and the two Marxist working class parties dominated the Popular Unity coalition. This was by no means a guarantee of success, for the struggle for revolutionary leadership had still to be fought out. But that is the story of the political developments during the three years of the Popular Unity government. Suffice it to say at this point that the formation of a coalition based on a common programme did not eliminate the differences within the Left. The experience of government heightened and clarified those differences, and posed new problems for the Left.

The formation of the Popular Unity and the selection of a candidate

When the first initiatives towards forming the Popular Unity were made in 1969 there were a number of issues that needed to be resolved. In the first place, which movements and parties were to participate in the Popular Unity? Would the Christian Democrats, or a section thereof, join forces with the Communists and Socialists? Clearly, this would not be inconsistent with the Tomic strategy of an opening to the Left. On the other hand, there was a real concern in the Communist and Socialist Parties that the entry of the PDC, or even the entry of a substantial fraction of that party, into the Popular Unity coalition might result in a bourgeois dominance of the coalition and a simple repetition of the disastrous experiences of the Popular Front of the thirties. A similar question was raised with regard to the participation of the Radical Party.

There were also sectors within the Socialist Party who, after the experience of 1964, regarded continued participation in elections as merely sustaining an illusion and as a further step in the reformist degeneration of the Chilean Left, a view shared by the MIR, who refused to participate in the electoral campaign and considered that the UP had little chance of winning the 1970 elections. The group around Raúl Ampuero – the *Unión Socialista Popular* (USOPO) – which had earlier been expelled from the Socialist Party was not invited to join the Popular Unity coalition because of objections from the Socialist Party.

Underlying the question of which groups should participate in the coalition was the question of which social class, and what kind of politics, would be dominant in the coalition. How far could the Communist-Socialist FRAP be broadened without losing its revolutionary and working class character? This issue took concrete form in the debates around three issues: the adoption of a candidate; agreement on a programme; and agreement on the internal organization of the coalition and on the distribution of governmental positions.

When the six parties that were eventually to form the Popular Unity began discussions on a programme in October 1969, it proved relatively easy to come up with a programme on which there was substantial agreement. Nor was there a great deal of disagreement over the internal organization of the coalition and the distribution of governmental positions. It was agreed that the candidate of the UP should accept the basic programme, that the government should be a multi-party government, that a political committee of the Popular Unity should be established to consult with the president on governmental policy, that there would be no partition of 'zones of influence' within the governmental apparatus according to party lines, and that the ministers would be distributed proportionally between the various parties according to the following formula: 3 Radicals; 3 Socialists; 3 Communists; 2 MAPU; 3 API and PSD (of which 2 would be from one party and 1 from the other).

Despite the apparent ease with which agreement was reached on a basic programme and on the norms by which the campaign was to be conducted, the actual process of selecting a candidate nearly proved to be the rock upon which the entire enterprise was sunk. Five candidates were proposed. The Radicals put forward Alberto Baltra, the Socialists Allende, the Communist Party proposed the poet, Pablo Neruda, MAPU suggested the architect of the agrarian reform, Jacques Chonchol, and the API and the PSD presented the leader of API, Rafael Tarud as their presidential candidate.

Tarud was a landowner and entrepreneur (*commerciante*) of Arab origin who had first entered politics in 1952 on the populist bandwagon of Ibáñez. He later dissociated himself from Ibáñez. Tarud founded his own party – API – in April 1969. While the API remained primarily a personalistic grouping, Tarud was successful in building up a certain base amongst some ex-Ibáñez supporters (including some military and police officers), and among certain sectors of the Arab community. Nevertheless, the API remained principally a caudillistic clique representing the petty-bourgeoisie of the small provincial towns. The PSD, with a similar sort of social base, threw the little weight that it had behind Tarud's candidature.

The Radical Party's candidate, Baltra, had been nominated by his party at the convention of June 1969 as the leader of the leftist current within the party. Opposing this current was a conservative or 'recuperationist' group behind Julio Durán. At that convention the conservative faction were expelled by 582 votes to 43, and subsequently formed the Partido Democratica Radical, lending their support to the candidacy of Alessandri. In the words of a Communist

Party journalist, Baltra was 'a politician of sincere leftist convictions.'[13] Later events, (the struggle for the formation of the social property area and the splitting of the PIR from the government under the leadership of Baltra) were to pass a decisive judgement on Baltra's characterization as a sincere leftist.

It is not entirely clear why the Communist Party chose Neruda as their candidate, since he was not well known as a professional figure, even though he had been a member of the Party since 1943. Neruda was, however, well-known as a poet both in Chile and throughout the world. In choosing Neruda, the Communist Party made it clear at the same time that they would accept another candidate from one of the other parties in the coalition, thereby clearly indicating that they did not realistically expect Neruda to be adopted as the official candidate of the Popular Unity coalition.

The candidate of the MAPU, Jacques Chonchol, had achieved prominence as head of one of the land reform agencies, INDAP (Institute of Agricultural Development). Chonchol was an agronomist, and frequently claimed that he was not a politician, but a technician. He had not come into the limelight through a parliamentary career, but had become known because of his close association with the nascent peasant movement which had been encouraged by the unionization and land reform laws of the Frei administration. It was precisely this non-involvement in traditional politics which made Chonchol an attractive figure for many Chileans, and especially for the youth. An additional consideration, as far as MAPU was concerned, was their belief that Allende had come to represent and symbolize the old electoralist left, and would not provide a new dynamic image for the voters. Chonchol had the advantage of being young, untainted by a long political career, and might attract many votes away from the Christian Democratic Party.

The Socialist Party was unlike the others in that there was considerable internal dissension with regard to the selection of a presidential candidate. For many years the Socialist Party had rejected the notion of an electoral alliance with the Radical Party and had insisted strongly on the formation of a front formed by the dominance of the two main working class parties. The revolutionary tendencies within the Socialist Party had been strengthened at the Congress of Chillán in 1967 when the groups led by Altamirano, Almeyda and Sepulveda, together with the Ampuero group, had won the voting against the more moderate factions grouped around Aniceto Rodríguez and Salvador Allende. The result was a rather contradictory position. Although the Socialist Party eventually agreed to participate in a coalition with the Radical Party, the majority faction within the Socialist Party (by 1969 under the leadership of Altamirano) was unwilling to support the candidacy of Altamirano in the presidential elections. In the discussions that were carried out in the Socialist Party in August 1969, the Party was asked to choose between two candidates only: Allende and Rodríguez.

A substantial section of the party was in favour of electoral abstention. (This was also the position of the MIR). When the Central Committee of the

Socialist Party met on the 29th of August to choose its candidate, Aniceto Rodríguez withdrew his candidacy and his supporters abstained from voting. The Altamirano group also abstained. The result was that Allende was nominated by 12 votes with 13 abstentions.[14] The candidate of the Socialist Party, who was later to become president of Chile, did not gain a majority in his own party.

Having decided on five possible candidates, the six parties comprising the Popular Unity began negotiations on which one was to be adopted as the official candidate. After some weeks of discussion, it became apparent that there were two principal blocs within the Popular Unity; on the one hand the Socialist and Communist Parties and MAPU, and on the other hand, API, the PSD and the Radical Party. The first bloc supported the candidacy of Allende, and the second bloc that of Tarud. Even at this early stage, the middle class parties clearly aspired to a controlling position within the UP coalition. At one stage the dispute was so intense, and the position of the Tarud bloc so obdurate, that it looked as if the Popular Unity might be still-born. Finally the Tarud group ceded the leadership of the Popular Unity to Salvador Allende, and the election campaign began in earnest.

The elections of 1970, then, presented a very different picture from the situation six years earlier. The populist alternative represented by Frei and the Christian Democrats had been largely discredited. The working class and the peasantry were mobilized and active; Frei's mid-term crisis had forced him to reveal his true face and send the army against peasants and workers who were doing no more than exacting the realization of his election promises. The Right, on the other hand, saw that the alliance of 1964 had failed to undermine the influence of the mass working class parties amongst either rural or urban workers. Its disillusionment with the 'Revolution in Liberty' once again set the fractions of the ruling class against one another. This division within the ruling class was to prove crucial in Popular Unity's victory; and it is nowhere better illustrated than in the armed forces.

The dissatisfactions within the ruling class found expression even at the very core of the bourgeois State apparatus, among the judiciary, and even within the armed forces. Frei reduced the military share of the budget; in an inflationary situation this meant a decline in the standard of living of military officers. This, together with a fear that Frei might have set in motion a process of mobilization that would escape his control, generated and sustained a level of discontent within the armed forces. Given the minimal intervention of the military in Chilean politics since the 1930s, then, the military protests over the worsening economic situation were significant. In 1968, the officers of the War Academy and of some regiments formally presented their resignation. The Defence Minister was forced to resign and the Commander in Chief replaced. The Frei government promised to remedy the situation, and for the time being discontent in the armed forces lost some of its urgency.

Very little was done, however; by 1969, the same problems precipitated new demands (which were largely 'trade union' in character) and culminated in the *Tacnazo* of October of that year. The then Commander of the First Army Division in Antofagasta, Roberto Viaux, was asked to hand over his command and retire. Viaux interpreted this as a political reaction to his active campaigning for greater pay increases for the armed forces and an increase in the military budget.[15] Convinced that he enjoyed considerable support within the army, Viaux flew to Santiago and headed a garrison revolt from the headquarters of the Tacna Motorized Artillery Regiment. Viaux insisted that the revolt was a purely internal military affair; Frei, on the other hand, knew that Viaux had made several attempts to contact civilian political groups, and interpreted the action as a possible precursor of a coup d'etat. And it is certainly true that Viaux received messages of support from several army units, while two recently dismissed officers, Marshall and Nieraad, tried to incite the Yungay regiment of San Felipe to revolt too.[16] The upshot was the dismissal of the Minister of Defence and the Commander in Chief – and a new government assurance that something would be done.

Following the *Tacnazo*, other sectors of the bourgeois State apparatus moved to put forward their own wage demands. One such group was the judges of the Supreme Court. Like the growing momentum of strikes, occupations of farms and living plots, and mass mobilizations, these actions of the people at the very core of the bourgeois state apparatus – the Army and the Judiciary – indicate both a general process of politicization of Chilean society and a disenchantment on the part of the established Right with the incapacity of the Christian Democrat government to do what it had implicitly promised with the slogan of 'Revolution in Liberty' – that is, make Chilean capitalism safe and prosperous.

The Viaux affair was a clear indication of the gathering divisions within the bourgeoisie. The Right felt sure that a Marxist victory was a remote possibility. It was this, together with the divergences between the National Party and the PDC, which moved the former to present their own candidate to the elections of 1970. In significant ways, the Right's analysis was mirrored in that presented by the Left. Both were wrong. In the event, in the face of the inability of the ruling class to agree on a strategy to contain the growing challenge from the working class, the Popular Unity coalition won the election and Salvador Allende was elected to the Presidency with a percentage of the vote lower than he had received in the elections of 1964.

APPENDIX

1958 Presidential Election: *see chapter 2*

1964 Presidential Election

	votes cast	percentage
Frei (*Christian Democrat*)	1,409,012	55.7
Allende (*Popular Action Front*)	977,902	38.6
Durán (*Radical Party*)	125,223	5.0
blank, null	18,550	0.7

1970 Presidential Election

	votes cast	percentage
Allende (*Popular Unity*)	1,070,334	36.2
Alessandri (*National Party*)	1,031,159	34.9
Tomic (*Christian Democrat*)	821,801	27.8
blank, null	31,505	1.1

Party Vote 1925-1971

Percentage of total vote obtained by major parties in congressional elections.

	National* Party	Radical Party	Socialist Party	Communist Party	Christian Democrats
1925 ..	52.2	21.4	—	—	—
1932 ..	32.8	18.2	5.7	—	—
1937 ..	42.0	18.7	11.2	—	—
1941 ..	31.7	21.7	16.7	—	3.4
1945 ..	41.5	20.0	12.8	—	2.6
1949 ..	40.7	21.7	9.3	—	3.9
1953 ..	21.5	13.3	14.1	—	2.9
1957 ..	19.1	21.5	10.7	—	9.4
1960 (M)	29.5	20.0	9.7	9.2	13.9
1961 ..	30.4	21.4	10.7	11.4	15.4
1963 (M)	23.6	20.8	11.1	12.4	22.0
1965 ..	12.5	13.3	10.3	12.4	42.3
1967 (M)	14.3	16.1	13.9	14.7	35.6
1969 ..	20.0	13.0	12.2	15.9	29.8
1971 ..	18.1	8.1	22.3	16.9	25.7

*Before 1967 the figures refer to the sum of Liberal and Conservative Parties totals.
(M) — Municipal election.

4 *The Initial Strategy of Popular Unity*

The Chilean Road to Socialism

The initial strategy and tactics of the Popular Unity were based on two assumptions: that in Chile it was possible for the working class parties to achieve a degree of State power via an electoral path, and that they could then use this power within a framework of pluralism, legality, parliamentary democracy and non-violence to transform peacefully a capitalist society into a socialist one. It was this belief that dominated the actions of the Communist Party and the right wing of the Socialist Party, especially president Allende; and it was sufficiently powerful among the more revolutionary elements of the Popular Unity – the left wing of the Socialist Party, the left MAPU party, and the Christian Left – to prevent these parties from acting in a consistently revolutionary way. Thus, in addition to the ferocity of the Chilean bourgeoisie and its allies, and the crippling manoeuvres of imperialism, part of the explanation for the tragic outcome of the experience of Popular Unity must be sought in the initial conception of how socialism was to be achieved.[1] For there flowed from this overall conception a number of policies which, especially in president Allende's last year, inhibited actions being taken which *might* have prevented the Chilean working classes' present defeat at the hands of the military.

Many of the initial tactics of the Popular Unity rested upon an almost mystical belief in the peculiarities of the Chilean way to socialism. The parties of the Left found a Marxist justification of their programme in two short quotes: on the one hand, Marx's declaration at The Hague Conference of the First International that 'I do not deny that there are nations like England and America and if I know your institutions at all, Holland, where the working class could achieve their ends by peaceful means'; on the other, Engels' *Critique of the Erfurt Programme:* 'It is possible to imagine that the old society could evolve peacefully towards the new society in countries where popular representation concentrates into its hands all the power, and where according to the constitution they can do what they want from the moment in which they have behind them the majority of the nation'. The Popular Unity argued that Chile had to construct a socialist society in a new way, summarized by president Allende in his first message to Congress, as '. . . a revolutionary way, the pluralist way, anticipated by the Marxist classics, but never before put into practice . . . Chile is today the first nation to conform to the second model of a transition to a socialist society.' This second model was thought to supersede the bulk of the teachings of Marx, Engels and Lenin to the effect that a socialist transformation of society requires the destruction of the bourgeois State apparatus and the creation of a workers' State.

For Allende and his supporters, Chile possessed certain special characteristics which made this second road to socialism possible: the wide degree of political tolerance achieved through the long history of parliamentary democracy, the flexibility of the institutional and legal system, the constitutional and professional position of the armed forces in Chile (in marked contrast to the rest of Latin America and indeed parts of Europe) and the maturity and discipline of the working class organizations, all seemed to add weight to their perspective.

The leadership of Popular Unity recognized and repeatedly stressed that winning the presidential election was not the same as taking power, and that control of the executive branch of the bourgeois State apparatus did not in itself constitute a transition to socialism. Soon after Allende's victory the secretary general of the Communist Party, Luis Corvalán, stressed that 'the fight for power goes on in our country. The main enemies of the people, imperialism and the landed and monopolistic oligarchy still maintain strong positions, and have to be removed from them to guarantee the revolutionary development of Chile'. And the head of the National Planning Office of Chile, Gonzalo Martner, underlined the necessity 'to be clear that the programme of the Popular Unity is not yet a socialist programme; but it is a programme intended to prepare the country and the people – by increasing consciousness and extending education – to enter into the socialist stage. I would define our present stage as pre-socialist'. Although some leaders of the Popular Unity talked at times as if Chile were in a transition to socialism, most clearly recognised that Chile had not yet reached that stage. The problem then was how to win the battle for power and enter the transition.

The strategy for the power struggle involved a number of different policies. The more revolutionary elements within Popular Unity regarded the process as a dynamic one which must lead to a clear break with capitalism and the creation of a workers' State. Despite all the rhetoric about a revolutionary process, it is not clear that Allende and the Communist Party ever envisaged that a sharp break with the capitalist system might occur during the period of Allende's presidency. These differences within the Popular Unity coalition were to create strains and conflicts. The Communist Party and the Allende Socialists never contemplated the possibility that a dual power situation might emerge, and indeed did everything they could to prevent such a situation, at least until the very eve of the coup. The more revolutionary elements, whether inside or outside Popular Unity, would later assert enthusiastically that a revolutionary situation could easily emerge, although they were all very unclear about how, or under what circumstances such a development could occur.

The initial strategy for the conquest of power was manifestly reformist; the Communist Party had been proposing it for a long time, and it had been taken up by other reformist elements within the coalition. Crucial to this strategy was a view of the State as consisting of a number of 'chunks' of power: the judiciary, the executive, the legislature, the repressive forces and the bureaucracy. The bourgeois State was not seen as a totality whose ultimate justification was the defence of bourgeois interests, but as a conglomeration of bits and pieces each of which could, if captured by the Left, either be used against capitalist interests directly, or at the very least neutralized. It was for this reason that the Communist Party could argue on 12 August 1973, just one month before the coup, that 'the interests of the developing revolutionary process are not in conflict with the existence of professional armed forces in our country that operate on the basis of the constitution.' This view of the State apparatus, which incidentally accepts bourgeois ideology at its face value, was to prove fatal to Popular Unity.

Nevertheless, Popular Unity was not just another popular front. It had a much more contradictory character than previous popular front governments, precisely because the principal forces on which it rested were not those of the bourgeoisie, but a majority of the working class, together with a substantial part of the peasantry and important radicalized sectors of the middle class. Thus, although Allende and the Communist Party wanted to pursue a policy of class-collaboration and govern within bourgeois structures, sectors within Popular Unity, with the weight of a majority of the working class behind them, pushed the UP government into a series of measures which did threaten the capitalist structure itself. It is important to note that the process of political radicalization was significantly accelerated only when the Right tried to halt and push back the process—that is, when the workers realized that even a simple defence of their gains involved a direct challenge to the very structure of capitalism.

The government takeover of several major industries during Allende's first year was a basic blow to capitalist interests; the capitalists recognized this, and acted accordingly, exposing as they did so one of Popular Unity's root weaknesses. It had fallen between two stools. On the one hand it did move far and fast enough in transforming the economy to frighten the whole capitalist class, as well as the petty bourgeoisie and those sections of the middle class welded to the capitalist system. Thereafter these powerful groups did everything in their power to prevent further advances and to inhibit and hold back consolidation of the gains that had been made. On the other hand, Popular Unity's commitment to the legal road meant that, without a majority in Congress or Senate and faced with a judiciary hostile to its policies, the Government was unable to wrest control of the crucial industrial and distribution sectors from the capitalist class. It was this unresolved contradiction that condemned the initial strategy and tactics to failure.

The problem that faced Popular Unity, then, was how to tip the balance in favour of the working classes. Were they to continue with the strategy of accepting and working within the capitalist framework and attempt piecemeal changes, thus tying their own hands while the Right prepared for a confrontation on its own terms? Or should they attempt to prepare the conditions in the most favourable possible way for the working class? This was the crucial issue for Popular Unity and one that had to be resolved in the concrete circumstances of a situation that was constantly evolving.

The initial political strategy

The political strategy of Popular Unity stemmed from a central assumption that the transition to socialism proceeded by a series of stages, the first of which was winning an electoral majority. As a result, Popular Unity's programme emphasized not only the multi-party, but also the multi-class nature of the coalition which, in Allende's words, 'corresponded to the interests of all those who earn their living by work: workers, professionals, technicians, artists, intellectuals and employees . . . and small and medium sized entrepreneurs.' The emphasis on the multi-class nature of the programme was considered essential in obtaining an electoral majority. The initial strategy was posed in terms of the electoral numbers game. Once enmeshed in this game, policies were bound to be inconsistent, *ad hoc* and populist as the government strove to win, usually in an economistic way, as large a number of people as possible.

A number of important consequences flowed from this initial commitment to an electoral strategy. In terms of such a strategy, it was more important for workers to vote for UP than to organize and mobilize themselves to take over factories, houses or the land. Indeed, the effort to gain a higher percentage of the middle class vote would seem to have been better served by a relatively passive working class, since a determined and aggressive working class whose actions might pose a threat to the very structure of private property would have been likely to drive the middle sectors into the hands of the Right. Mass activity was seen by the Popular Unity government as an adjunct to legal and electoral manoeuvres; at the same time, it was important that it should not overflow those limits. Thus, the clauses of Popular Unity's programme which promised the take-over of large foreign companies, of the monopolies in the fields of finance, industry and distribution, and the expropriation of all landholdings larger than the equivalent of eighty hectares (about 192 acres) were to be carried through by legal means rather than achieved as a result of the activity of the working class.

The programme clearly envisaged that the destruction of the economic base of the main class enemies of the Chilean working class, whether foreign or national, would have the automatic result of destroying their political base. This assumption derived, however, from an economistic view of the power of the bourgeoisie, a view which seriously underestimated the extent to which the real power of a capitalist class lay in the very structures of the bourgeois State. The consequence was that important sections of the Popular Unity coalition continued to believe right up to the eve of the coup that it was possible to attack the bourgeoisie using the bourgeois State apparatus.

On the internal front, Popular Unity proposed to approach institutions like the Catholic Church, the armed forces, the judiciary and the professional organizations with great circumspection. Wherever possible these bodies were to be flattered, assured that their professional autonomy and integrity would be respected, and wooed or bribed into an attitude, if not of support, then at least of neutrality.

On the international front, the policy was to be equally cautious. Chile would establish diplomatic relations with all communist countries and join the non-aligned group in the United Nations. In its relations with the United States it would be firm, polite and non-aggressive, while at the same time making it clear to the North Americans that their hitherto undisputed hegemony over Chile had now ended.

The central factor in the whole initial strategy of Popular Unity, however, was the *capas medias*, or middle sectors. UP policy worked on the assumption that the middle sectors were a fairly homogeneous group with similar interests. Yet the group included small and medium capitalists, both in industry and on the land; the professions – lawyers, doctors, nurses, technicians, academics and schoolteachers; the middle ranges of the huge State bureaucracy and the classical petty bourgeois groups like shopkeepers, the service sector, the small transport owners and so on. Clearly it was felt that this group could either swing towards the Christian Democrats or towards Popular Unity.

Popular Unity proposed two main policies designed to win the support of the middle sectors. The first, which was pursued throughout the three years by both Allende and the Communist Party, involved talking to, and making concessions and compromises with, the Christian Democrats. After all, on paper the programme of the Christian Democratic candidate in the 1970 elections, Radomiro Tomic, was not so very different from Popular Unity's own programme. Prior to the 1970 elections, in fact, Tomic had floated the possibility of, and advocated, an alliance with the working class parties.[2] Further, the history of Christian Democracy indicated that the general process of radicalization in Chile had already caused a number of splits in its ranks. In this light it seemed possible to win the support of the left Christian Democrats once Popular Unity had shown its willingness to adhere to a moderate, legal and democratic line. This tactic did not meet with the approval of all the elements of the Popular Unity, however. Many coalition members, particularly the left wing of the Socialist Party, felt that if the price of co-operation with the Christian Democrats was to be the preservation of capitalism, in however modified a form, then the price was too high. As far as Christian Democracy itself was concerned, the right wing of the party clearly preferred an alliance with the National Party, in order to ensure that all progress towards the overthrow of capitalism was halted. Nevertheless, dialogue with the Christian Democrats was to remain a constant theme of Allende's three years in power.

The second main policy for winning over the middle classes consisted in a sustained campaign designed to convince them that their interests were not threatened by the structural changes that the regime was going to undertake. The government argued that, objectively speaking, the economic interests of the middle sectors were opposed to the foreign and native monopoly interests. They were not part of that tiny minority which controlled most of Chile's means of production, and they too suffered financially when the economy was manipulated to serve foreign or monopoly interests.

Studies had shown that the ownership of industry, the mines, distribution, banking and finance, and the land was concentrated in very few hands; and in all of these sectors, with the exception of land, the degree of foreign ownership was very high. For example, 284 companies owned 78% of the total industrial shares; 12 firms (0.5% of the total) obtained 25% of the banking credit.[3] Of the top 100 firms in Chile, 61 had foreign shareholders, and in 28 of these more than 50% of the capital was foreign-owned. Surely the nationalism of the small Chilean businessmen could be counted upon to bring them over to the side of the government in the struggle against foreign-owned monopolies.

Further, the middle sectors should not have felt threatened by any government proposal to increase the economic importance of the State. Public expenditure as a percentage of the Chilean gross national product had risen to about 47% by 1970, demonstrating the extent to which the State, given the weakness of Chilean capitalism, had taken on the task of capital accumulation through both direct and indirect public investment. Not only had the State initiated many industrial and other ventures (which were often sold to private enterprise as soon as they became profitable), but they had also subsidized the private capitalist sector through a complex set of credit policies, tax incentives, pricing policies and investments in infrastructure and inputs for the private sector.

Given the very high degree of concentration of ownership in the Chilean economy, then, the Popular Unity government felt that it would be possible to isolate and take-over the monopolists without creating too much disturbance. And given the extent of State intervention in the economy by 1970, it seemed perfectly feasible to change the direction of that intervention, and redirect State investment to the benefit of both the working class and the middle sectors. Thus the policies designed to win over the middle sectors were economistic on the one hand, making it possible for them to benefit economically from the changes introduced by Popular Unity; and on the other hand, were designed to protect the susceptibilities of the middle class with respect to law, order and the State.

Popular Unity's policies towards the working classes relied to a large extent on the trade union organizations, and especially the CUT (the Chilean Trades Union Congress), to ensure that changes, participation and mobilization took place within an ordered framework. In this way the government and the CUT would be able to impress upon the workers that participation and revolution meant a responsibility for increasing production, moderating wage demands and acting in a generally disciplined way. A large and important segment of the organized working class supported Christian Democracy, but it was the government's feeling that the process of change, a process undertaken for and in part by the working class, would convince Christian Democrat workers of the benefits of socialism.

It is a mistake to imagine that Popular Unity did not emphasize or indeed take seriously the participation of the working class in the process. Participation did not arise simply as a reaction to right-wing offensives. Popular Unity considered the active participation of the working class in the implementation of its policies as a crucial part of its initial strategy. The workers, and workers' organizations, were actively encouraged to take part in the running of farms, industries, education, health and cultural activities; and the trade unions did participate in national and regional as well as local level planning. Nonetheless the participation and mobilization of the workers were intended to remain within the confines of legality, and to have as their principal aim increased production. The programme of Popular Unity certainly did not envisage workers' participation as part of a process leading to the creation of dual power and thence to the establishment of a workers' State.

In 1970, about 760,000 people, or 22% of the total workforce, were employed in agriculture. Of these, less than 1% (or 6000 people) were *latifundistas* owning estates over 200 acres in size, and 4% owned between 50 and 200 acres of land. The rest were divided between family farms (around 9%), those who owned less than 12 acres and had to sell a part of their labour in order to survive (some 35%), some 7% on areas affected by previous agrarian reforms, some 18% rural workers on commercial farms and some 22% *afuerinos* – migrant rural labourers.[4] It was UP policy to expropriate the *latifundistas* and distribute their land to workers on the estates, on the one hand, and to win over the *afuerinos* and other rural workers on the other hand, by drawing them into the permanent agricultural labour force and encouraging their unionization. The *minifundistas* (owners of small subsistence plots) were encouraged to form themselves into co-operatives, so that favourable policies with regard to credit, for example, would win their support for Popular Unity.

Unionization was also the key to the incorporation of the unemployed and the shanty town dwellers into Popular Unity. Committees of the unemployed were to be set up, and a series of policies were formulated which would increase employment possibilities.

The electoral strategy of Popular Unity also led them to give a high priority to winning over large numbers of women. In the past more women than men had voted for the opposition parties. Popular Unity proposed to form a new Ministry of the Family which would deal mainly with the problems facing women; women were to be drawn into political life and involved in seeking solutions to problems of distribution and price control. Material supports such as nursery schools and playgroups were to be expanded, giving women more leisure to participate both in production and in political work.

Popular Unity's initial political strategy was thus a carefully balanced set of objectives designed to win an electoral majority by offering economic and political incentives to workers, shanty-town dwellers, small and middle-sized capitalists, professionals and State employees, peasants and rural workers and medium-sized farmers. The attainment of these objectives depended on a rapidly expanding economy, which would give Popular Unity the resources to satisfy all the demands that would flow from its programme. The strategy never envisaged the possibility that the activities of a socialist government would lead to a profound economic crisis, nor the probability of an armed clash with the bourgeoisie and its allies at some stage, nor did the government have any plans for preparing the workers and their allies to win such a clash.

The initial economic strategy

The Popular Unity's initial economic strategy was part of a total strategy the main aim of which was the consolidation of power in the hands of the working class. Power could not, in their view however, pass immediately into the hands of the workers; the strategy proposed, therefore, was designed to pave the way towards that consolidation, through a series of carefully planned and controlled modifications in the existing economy, while it still remained in capitalist hands. The economic perspective, in other words, was reformist; like the political programme of Popular Unity it provided for a reform of capitalism which would in its turn make possible the transition to socialism.

The main exponent of Popular Unity's economic strategy, the first Minister of Economic Affairs in the Allende government, Pedro Vuskovic, argued that 'economic policy is subordinate, in its context, shape and form, to the political need to increase Popular Unity's support'.[5] What he meant, of course, was electoral support. Thus economic strategy was subordinated from the outset to an electoral political strategy, whose key aspect was to win over the so-called middle sectors to the side of Popular Unity. And it was with the aim of extending support for the coalition among both the middle and the working classes that the initial economic strategy was oriented towards consumption. In line with an overall electoral perspective, Popular Unity emphasized the necessity of preserving a continuity with the previous economic system sufficient to sustain productive capacity and techniques. The economic strategy, therefore, was not conceived as involving a sharp break with the capitalist system, but rather as one step in a gradual process of change.

The analysis on which Popular Unity based their programme argued that the essential economic relations determining the functioning of the Chilean economy were its dependency on imperialism, the concentration of the means of production in private hands, and the type of State intervention which had obtained in the past. These were regarded as the most important long-term causes of Chilean under-development. If they were to be overcome, a significant transformation of the Chilean economy would have to be carried out which would, in their view, alter the logic of the Chilean system of production and its operation, and thence alter the functioning and distribution of benefits.

There was, however, a more immediate and urgent need to carry through a whole series of more short-term measures to deal with the situation that had arisen since Allende's election. As might have been expected, the capitalist class's reaction to the election result was one of panic. This took the form of a race to withdraw deposits from banks and savings accounts, a flight of capital abroad, journeys abroad (in September and October the Central Bank sold $31m for tourism compared to a previous average of $10.5m) and a drop in investment. The inevitable result was a decline in economic growth and a rise in unemployment. Popular Unity was therefore faced with an economic crisis which required immediate solution.

Thus in the first year the Popular Unity regarded the restoration of economic activity and the transformation of the economy as the fundamental questions, in the belief that such measures would alter power and class relations and improve the correlation of class forces. Both had to be carried out simultaneously and to some extent depended on each other: the first without the second could have strengthened capitalism; the second, without the first, would have led to a worsening of the economic situation. The problem was a difficult one: how to increase economic activity, while at the same time taking over crucial parts of the existing system.

To restore confidence and obtain rapid economic growth, the government proposed a Keynesian strategy of increasing aggregate demand to take up the slack in the Chilean economy. For the first year it was decided to use no more than the potential of the existing production system; very little new investment was envisaged. The government thought that if they changed certain key variables they would be able to change the traditional functioning of the economy. The most important of these was the concentration of effective demand in the hands of a wealthy few, needing only a limited number of highly sophisticated goods. The solution they adopted involved a large redistribution of income, especially to the poorer employed sections of society, which would increase effective demand for basic, popular goods, and have the added desirable effect of strengthening Popular Unity's support. On the other hand, an increase in demand without adequate supplies to satisfy it would be inflationary. In order to prevent such a situation, the government proposed to enforce strict price controls on most basic goods, thus reducing in effect the marginal profit rate. The assumption behind this was that in order to maintain or at least lessen the decline in total profits, the private sector would expand production and take up the excess capacity lying dormant throughout Chilean industry; this would have the additional advantage of taking up some of the unemployed labour. Furthermore, the State sector itself planned to rapidly expand its programme, especially in the construction sector.

Control of the economy was crucial. The government had either to declare that it would preserve capitalist economic relations, despite some nationalizations, and enable the capitalist economy to continue to function as such, or it had to carry out its socialization programme at maximum speed in order to ward off economic catastrophe. Of course, it is possible for private enterprise to operate efficiently within a generally socialized economy as long as its security is guaranteed. It is crucial, nevertheless, that the socialized sector should control the economy as a whole: if it does not, and the capitalist class believes its property is not secure, the result will certainly be an economic crisis.

Popular Unity recognized the political as well as the economic need to create an area of socially-owned property with the greatest possible speed. The election results had left the capitalist class in disarray and Popular Unity therefore had some flexibility to strike hard before the capitalists reorganized themselves. The intention was to take over as quickly as possible about 150 of the largest industrial and mining firms, about ten of the largest distribution firms, virtually the whole of the financial sector, about 80% of exports and 60% of imports, part of the communications industry, and all land over eighty hectares.

Obviously in a period of change and economic transformation there were going to be bottlenecks and shortages, the most important of which would probably occur in the agrarian sector. The government intended to expropriate all land over eighty hectares within a two year period, after which uncertainty would end and production return to normal. It was anticipated that production would be unable to keep pace with the increased demand for food during those first two years, so the government decided to use its foreign exchange reserves to import goods, especially foodstuffs, when serious shortages arose.

Clearly, if it was envisaged that foreign exchange reserves would be used to import goods which might be lacking during the period of change, then it was essential to plan how those reserves would be used. Yet Popular Unity never formulated a clear policy for this vital sector. Since copper accounted for about 70% of Chile's exports, the price of copper was obviously a key factor; yet it was one which the Popular Unity government could do little to control. So despite the emphasis given to the dependency of the Chilean economy on foreign capital, it was the external sector policies which exhibited the greatest lack of planning.

The dominant organizational forms in the agrarian sector were to be the Agrarian Reform Centres – large scale production units which would allow for specialization. These centres were to exist alongside the *asentamientos* of the Frei agrarian reform, the agrarian capitalist farms, co-operatives and the small, semi-subsistence farms. Various mechanisms, particularly the organization of peasants' councils, were to be devised to ensure active participation in the changes in agricultural organization. Economically, the intention was not to drain the surplus from agriculture for industrialization (as happened in the

USSR and eastern Europe), but to use the surplus from other sectors to assist agriculture. Popular Unity envisaged only a short-term decline in internal agricultural production. After the first year or so of expropriations it was planned to invest part of the surplus from mining and the social property area in the mechanization of agriculture which, together with the more just and more efficient relations of production in the countryside, would ensure the rapid expansion of agricultural production. The long-term aim was that Chile should become a net exporter of agricultural produce.

The emerging economic structure was to include three spheres of ownership: the social property area, owned and controlled by the government directly and operated with the active participation of the workers in the industries involved; a mixed or joint sector in which State and private interests operated in concert; and a private property sector. It was the crucial social property sector, however, which must predominate; it was the key to all economic strategies after the first year. The policy of increasing consumption and transforming the economy through takeovers during the first year was to be followed by a policy of production and investment in subsequent years. The investment policy, in its turn, depended on the social property area's ability to cream off the profits which had previously accrued to the monopolies and invest them in such a way as to increase productive forces. The efficiency of the social property area and its pricing policies were therefore crucial; furthermore, Popular Unity was relying on huge profits from copper to help finance their ambitious investment programme. All this, of course, was to be carried out in the context of a planned economy.

The political results of the initial strategy

The choice of Allende's first cabinet was a clear example of reformist politics in practice. Although the working class parties, like the Communist and Socialist Parties, represented the main strength of Popular Unity, while the other parties in the coalition had little real numerical strength, Allende gave as much weight to the dying Radical Party as to the Communists and Socialists. In fact, Allende went out of his way to ensure that voices representative of middle class reformist interests were accorded as much influence as working class interests. The four Socialists in the cabinet all represented the moderate, reformist viewpoint within the Socialist Party. Indeed the Minister of Economy, Pedro Vuskovic, an Independent, was probably the most radical figure in the cabinet, and he was in a very weak position since he did not enjoy the support of a political party. On choosing his first cabinet, Allende correctly stated '. . . the future government of Chile will not be a socialist government: it is unscientific to maintain the contrary. I have said repeatedly – and it could not be otherwise – that my government will be a multi-party one.'

Allende's first cabinet

Post	Party	
Post	*Party*	
Interior	Socialist	
Foreign Affairs	Socialist	4
Housing	Socialist	
Secretary to Cabinet	Socialist	
Labour	Communist	
Public Works and Transport	Communist	3
Finance	Communist	
Defence	Radical	
Education	Radical	3
Mining	Radical	
Agriculture	MAPU	1
Economy	Independent	1
Health	Social Democrat	
Land and Settlement	Social Democrat	2
Justice	A.P.I.	1

A further indication of the legal and electoral tactics that were to dominate Allende's first year came with the virtual disbanding of the thousands of Popular Unity Committees which had been formed at the time of Allende's presidential victory in order to defend and mobilize support behind him. The government made no attempt to maintain their active involvement in the battle for power once Allende's inauguration had been assured, and they withered away as a result.

Nevertheless, the first year did see a number of independent initiatives by peasants and workers, which particularly incensed the Communist Party, who argued that this kind of action would undermine the confidence in the government of the middle sectors, the *capas medias*. They tended to attribute all such initiatives to the MIR (the Movement of the Revolutionary Left), which was then subjected to virulent attacks in which the Communists accused them not only of infantile, petty bourgeois ultra-leftism, but also of acting in the interests of the CIA. Yet at the same time, Allende appointed a MIR bodyguard for a while, and praised the MIR for their help in unmasking right-wing plots. Negotiations with the MIR were conducted throughout the first year, and Allende sometimes engaged them in public debate, as he did at the University of Concepción.

It was part of MIR's policy to press for mass mobilizations, and they undoubtedly did help to organize some occupations of rural and urban lands. But their role was much less significant than was suggested by the Communists and the bourgeois media. The illegal takeovers carried out with or without the help of the MIR were immediately exaggerated and used by the bourgeoisie to attack the government for its inability to keep the political process within legal confines. The government responded, not by defending the right of the poor to occupy land and houses but by placating the bourgeoisie, condemning illegal occupations and continuing its attacks on the MIR. At one time, relations between the Communist Party and the MIR deteriorated to such an extent that a gun battle broke out during the December 1970 student elections at the University of Concepción in which one MIR student was killed.

The bulk of illegal occupations was in fact confined to one province – Cautín, where the Mapuche Indians were concentrated. For the Mapuches, these invasions constituted no more than reoccupation of stolen Indian lands; in some cases they even held titles proving their legal ownership of such land. The government, however, was frightened by opposition attempts to whip up hysteria about 'illegality and violence'. Their response was to send the Minister of Agriculture to Cautín with instructions to speed up the expropriation of land in order to make the *de facto* takeovers legal. The landowners in the area, for their part, responded by setting up 'armed vigilante' groups.

Throughout the first year, it became increasingly obvious that many parts of the bourgeois State apparatus (the judiciary for example), could not be used by the executive to carry out the programme of Popular Unity. In general terms, Allende's response to this was to try to negotiate compromises with the Christian Democrats, and these approaches usually meant concessions by Popular Unity. When the president of the Supreme Court, for example, attacked a government proposal to establish popular, neighbourhood courts, the initiative was quietly dropped.

On some fronts, however, the initial strategy seemed to be meeting with success. The Chilean Catholic Church was carefully wooed into a position of neutrality. Many priests came out in open support of socialism. In April 1971, eighty priests published a document in the name of Christians for Socialism which asserted that 'the task of our party is to contribute to the construction of socialism in Chile through the contributions of forces inspired by Christianity... We seek the revolutionary convergence between Christians and Marxists'. A survey of Chilean priests conducted by the Jesuits revealed that only 5.3% regarded Marxism as a perverse doctrine.[6] Unlike Spain, the right wing in Chile could not appeal to the Church for ideological support against the Left.

On the international level, recognition and diplomatic relations were rapidly established with Cuba, China, North Korea, North Vietnam and East Germany. With the exception of Brazil, which remained opposed to Popular Unity throughout, president Allende soon established friendly relations with other Latin American states: Argentina, Peru, Ecuador, Colombia, Venezuela and Mexico were at least verbally well disposed towards the Allende government. Bolivia, of course, did not establish relations with Chile; the government of General Torres, which would undoubtedly have provided another ally, was overthrown before it could recognize the Allende government and replaced by the right-wing Banzer regime. Chile, then, was not isolated within Latin America, and its decision to join the non-aligned group and press for a stronger

Latin American voice in the Organisation of American States raised its status considerably among Latin American countries.

The cautious policy pursued by Allende had particularly significant implications as far as one key sector, the armed forces, was concerned. Allende played to the hilt on the so-called professional, non-political tradition of the Chilean armed forces. He initially appointed a Radical, Ríos Valdivia, to the key Ministry of Defence, who clearly stated from the outset: 'I will not permit party politics to be introduced into the ranks of the armed forces under any circumstances whatsoever.' As a consequence, the attempts by the MIR to formulate and carry through a policy of infiltration and propaganda within the armed services were suppressed. The MIR newspaper, *El Rebelde* was temporarily banned after it had carried an article calling for the democratization of the armed forces. Allende's alternative was to try and buy off the armed forces: he gave them wage increases, allowed the officers full control over internal armed forces affairs, permitted the United States to continue its military aid programme and preserve its contacts with Chilean officers, and tried to integrate the armed forces more fully into the life of the nation; all of which served to increase the power and influence of the Chilean officer class.

In electoral terms, the strategy proved successful. In the municipal elections of April 1971, Popular Unity, thanks to its reforms and redistribution policies, recorded its highest ever electoral support – 50.9% of the votes.

Municipal elections results, 4 April 1971

Party	% 1969	% 1971
Communist	15.9	17.4
Socialist	12.2	22.9
Radical	13.0	8.2
Social Democrat	0.9	1.4
Christian Democrat	29.8	26.2
National Democrat	1.9	0.5
National	20.0	18.5
Radical Democracy	—	3.9
Popular Socialist Union	2.2	1.5
Popular Unity		50.9
Opposition		49.1

A socialist victory in a congressional by-election offered further confirmation of the growing popularity of the government, on the strength of which Allende began to speak of the necessity of replacing Chile's two-chamber legislature with a single-chamber Assembly of the People, and of formulating a new socialist constitution which 'at an opportune moment, we shall submit to the sovereign will of the people'. That decision was postponed, however, and instead of launching an offensive, Popular Unity interpreted the electoral results as a vindication of their cautious, reformist path.

The successes of Popular Unity, however limited, were nevertheless sufficient to bring together the two capitalist parties, the Christian Democrats and the Nationals. In June 1971 these opposition parties formed an electoral pact. The Christian Democrats and the National Party agreed to present a single candidate in the coming by-election in Valparaiso, which was won by the right-wing candidate. This pact effectively marked the end of Christian Democracy's role as a reformist party. The open alliance of the Christian Democrats with the Nationals so alienated sections of the Christian Democratic youth move-ment and a left-wing group in the party that 20% of the youth and 13% of the general party membership, including eight deputies, left the party and formed the Movement of the Christian Left. Radomiro Tomic and his followers, however, stayed within the Christian Democrat party, although despite some rhetorical flourishes they had little power within or outside the party. For its part, however, Popular Unity, in its determination to sustain a dialogue with Christian Democracy, continued to act as if the left-wing of the Christian Democrats remained powerful within the party.

On the land the implementation of the Frei Agrarian Reform law created problems. The agrarian capitalists with land between forty and eighty hectares felt threatened by illegal takeovers and by the growing demand among the Popular Unity parties, other than the Communist Party, for the expropriation limit to be lowered from eighty to forty hectares. Many of the beneficiaries of the Christian Democrat land reform had managed to build themselves a rela-tively privileged position in the countryside; some had become employers in their own right, and these people sometimes regarded the policies of Popular Unity as a threat to their new found privileges. The problem in the countryside was very complex. Both the unionization policy of Popular Unity and the policy of dismantling the *latifundios* had been very successful. Yet many con-tradictions remained, contradictions which could not be solved within the framework of the Christian Democrat Agrarian Reform law. It was crucial for Popular Unity's economic strategy that production increased in agriculture. The policy of allowing the previous landowners to retain part of their land as well as their machinery and equipment still left them in a powerful position, which they used to oppose Popular Unity. Many of the rural workers demanded a more radical reform, and pressed for the seizure of land: this provoked a number of clashes in the countryside. Agricultural production did increase during the first year, nonetheless, but at the end of 1971 it was becoming clear that many crucial problems remained unsolved.

By the end of 1971 the principal political strategy of Popular Unity – that of winning the middle sectors – was bankrupt. The government's policy of giving generous credit terms, tax concessions and other incentives to the small and medium capitalists had failed to convince them, and a proposed bill defining the division of the economy into three areas – a social sector, a mixed sector and a private sector – did nothing to assuage their fears. Why, then, was it that Popular Unity's programme failed to win over the middle sectors, despite the fact that it went out of its way to improve their material conditions? Ideological and political factors were clearly paramount; however much Popular Unity tried to buy the middle classes, years of strident anti-socialist propaganda had left many of them very little disposed to support a socialist government, however mild and cautious its policies. During its first year in power, Popular Unity failed to launch any ideological offensive against the still dominant bourgeois ideology. There had been no attempt on the government's part to mobilize support, or to increase participation in implementing government policy. As a result, the bulk of the middle class was left to move *en bloc*, particularly when shortages occurred, into the bourgeois camp. Marx pointed out that 'a whole superstructure of feeling, ways of thinking, conceptions of life arises above the different forms of property'. By posing the problem at the ideological level, the Right was able to develop a massive campaign about supposed threats to democracy, liberty, the rule of law (and of course, private property) which proved more successful in winning the middle sectors to its ranks (even before economic problems began to affect them) than was Popular Unity, with its anti-imperialist, anti-monopolist and anti-oligarchic policies.

When Allende proposed that there should be fixed maximum incomes, for example, both the National Party and the Christian Democrats supported all claims by professional and technical groups designed to protect their income differentials. In July 1971, the College of Lawyers protested, with the support of the Right, that they too should be included among those groups who were entitled to an income higher than the fixed maximum. And any attempt to reform the professions and make them more responsive to the needs of the people was virulently opposed by the professional associations – again with right-wing support. Any such move was condemned as an insult to the dignity of the professions. In the end, the right-wing parties persuaded a majority of professionals to form a united front against Popular Unity – the United Chilean Confederation of Professionals – whose aim was described as 'to secure respect for the freedom to work'. Popular Unity responded by forming a left-wing association of professionals, which probably covered about one quarter of the lawyers, doctors, nurses, engineers, supervisory staffs and academics in Chile.

The professionals became some of the most vociferous opponents of Popular Unity. For many this was understandable, as they depended for their wealth on the unequal distribution of income which Popular Unity was pledged to change. Doctors with wealthy private practices were directly affected and some, like the lawyers, depended on the very existence of the market economy to sell their skills. It is important to emphasize here the ideological aspects. The professions were jealous of their corporate privileges and status. Popular Unity's proposals to restructure the organization of professions, however mild, were met with fierce rejection. In November 1971, for example, the left-wing dominated council of the University of Chile proposed a new university structure. The rector of the University, Edgardo Boeninger, feared that the proposals would strengthen the power of the Left and suspended the council. The ensuing row led to a series of violent clashes between left and right-wing students. What is of interest is the ideological portrayal of what was in many ways a minor organizational proposal. Boeninger and his supporters formed a University Front to defend, as it was claimed, a free, critical, pluralist and democratic University. Law, medical, dental, veterinary and commerce students occupied their schools 'in defence of democracy'. The law students and lawyers were particularly incensed at the proposal that the Law Faculty should fuse with a new Faculty of Juridical, Economic and Social Sciences. The very suggestion that law was an aspect of social science was treated by the Right as an attack on the rule of law. The rule of law, *El Mercurio* proclaimed, is the basis of the foundation of Western civilisation, and to make law a social science is to end the autonomy of legal science and hence of society.

Popular Unity's initial strategy depended on the assumption that the interests of the petty bourgeoisie and the small and medium capitalists were opposed to the large foreign and native monopoly groups. Objectively this may have been the case, but the actual economic policies of Popular Unity failed to convince these groups. Generous credit and fiscal incentives did enable some small and medium capitalists to expand production and increase profits, but an overall policy of increasing wages and holding prices probably hit the small and medium capitalists harder than the large capitalists who could, given the high ratio of capital to labour in their enterprises, absorb the wage increases more easily.

The policy of a 'transaction to socialism', as it was derisively called in Chile, meant that the government compensated or even bought up directly the owners of capital. The circulation of liquid cash in the Chilean economy rose rapidly, and holders of this cash tended to try and buy dollars or goods on the black market. Faced with an expanding black market, the government proposed to centralize foreign exchange activities in the hands of the Central Bank to allow firms and individuals one bank account only, to end the secrecy of the banks, and to launch a campaign against the black market. Some of these measures are, of course, normal in advanced capitalist economies, but in Chile the Right launched a major propaganda offensive against the proposals accusing the government of totalitarianism, of threatening economic, social and political freedom.

As supplies grew scarce, and the black market expanded as a result, the government was forced to intervene in distribution in order to ensure that supplies continued to reach the working classes. Rationing would have been the logical step; in the first year, however, Popular Unity did not anticipate problems of supply; thereafter, the government felt that rationing would lead irrevocably to the loss of middle class support.

The working classes, too, increasingly wanted to take initiatives on distribution as their solution to the shortages. The black market was, of course, profitable for those shopkeepers, such as butchers and poulterers, who were able to sell to the rich. To prevent this the government had to step in and enforce price controls on butchers and other distributors who infringed the law.   As the *Juntas de Abastecimientos Popular* or JAPs, People's Supply Committees, increased their power and influence over distribution, Popular Unity came into conflict with private retailers and wholesalers who felt that they were being bypassed by the JAPs.

Needless to say, the Right used every opportunity to publicize conflicts between Popular Unity and the petty bourgeoisie and small and medium capitalists.   Their campaign was highly successful, and as early as December 1971, before supplies had really become short, a 'Front of the Private Area' was formed under the auspices of the Confederation of Production and Commerce.   This front, controlled by the National Party and the Christian Democrats, in effect linked together the big capitalists, the small and medium capitalists, and the petty bourgeoisie, under the slogan that all private property was sacrosanct.   In this way, the attempt by Popular Unity to drive a wedge between the monopoly, imperialist, latifundist interests and those of the small and medium capitalists and the petty bourgeoisie had failed.   As it became increasingly difficult to obtain essential imports because of the foreign exchange crisis and the 'informal' blockade imposed by the United States, the standard of living of the *capas medias* fell.   They naturally blamed the government, and identified their struggle with the Right, whose ideological offensive had increased in strength among the middle sectors, which now moved into open opposition against the working classes.

The working classes themselves remained solidly behind Popular Unity, although, as the CUT elections showed, the Christian Democrats managed to maintain hold over some sections of the working class, particularly the white-collar workers.   The Right had yet to launch its major offensives.   Nevertheless, the coyness about mobilizing the workers on a large scale in the first year did give the Right the opportunity to regroup and build a strong position which provided a pole of attraction for the middle sectors, as well as a strong base from which to launch an offensive.

The Economic Results: Transformation of the Economy

One of the first and most popular moves to transform the economy was the nationalization of the American copper companies, which received the unanimous approval of Congress and Senate, and was not openly opposed by any group in Chile.   Allende agreed in principle to the payment of compensation but only after the deduction of all profits in excess of 12% over the previous fifteen years.   This meant that virtually no compensation was paid.   The Chilean government did agree, however, to honour the debts the American copper companies had incurred in their expansion programme, despite the fact that the programme had been financed almost entirely by loans from the USA.

The Nationalization of Copper

Of the three United States corporations which controlled about 80% of Chilean copper production, Anaconda, Kennecott and Cerro, the Controller General of Chile estimated that after appropriate deductions had been made from the book value of the mines, Anaconda owed Chile $68 million, Kennecott $310 million and Chile owed Cerro $33 million plus $3 million in interest for its investment.

Since 1910, when US capital first invested in Chilean copper, several billions of dollars have been transferred to the USA as profits. Between 1953 and 1968 US mining and smelting concerns in Chile made a profit of $1,036 million, of which only $71 million were reinvested or returned as new investments. The 'Chileanisation' of copper under President Frei meant that the US copper firms sold 51% of their Chilean holdings to the State and were granted tax reductions and a relaxation of restrictions on profit remittances in return. As part of the deal the US copper companies agreed to double production between 1966 and 1972. However, 75% of the expansion programme was financed through Export–Import Bank loans (guaranteed by the Chilean Government), 23% by contributions from the Chilean Government and less than 2% by capital from the companies themselves. In the six years of Frei's Presidency, Anaconda made profits of $426 million and Kennecott of $178 million. In 1969 Anaconda received profits on investments in Chile of 39.5% and Kennecott of 24.1%. Not surprisingly the American copper companies were not displeased with Chileanisation: as the Kennecott 1967 annual report put it 'Kennecott voluntarily and enthusiastically entered into an agreement with the Chilean government'.

The American copper companies had taken billions of dollars out of Chile; done little to refine and fabricate copper in Chile, exporting only raw or partially refined copper; manipulated the price of copper to suit their own interests and not that of Chile; and run the copper mines to maximize their profits, and not for example to expand employment and domestic ancillary industries. When the American copper companies finally pulled out of Chile they left the mines in such a state of disrepair that a French consulting firm estimated that it would cost millions of dollars to get the mines into shape for production.

It was much more difficult to take over other parts of the Chilean economy. Congress and Senate were dominated by the opposition parties who made it impossible to pass legislation for expropriation. To get around this legislative block, Popular Unity lawyers unearthed some legislation from the short-lived Socialist Republic of Marmaduke Grove in 1932 – legislation which had never been repealed. Law number 520 of August 1932 and its various subsequent modifications allowed the State to intervene in industries under wide-ranging conditions, for example stoppages because of labour disputes, price speculation, holding back supplies or not maintaining normal production.

Using this law the government took control of or bought up a large number of firms. Within its first year Popular Unity increased the State share of gross domestic production by almost 20%, and gained almost complete control of the production of nitrates, iodine, copper, coal, iron, steel; about 90% of the financial and banking sector; almost 80% of exports and 55% of imports; as well as a substantial part of the textile, cement, metal, fishing, soft drink, electronics, and part of the distribution industries.

The legality or otherwise of many of the interventions and nationalizations became a source of bitter legal wrangles. Régis Debray described the activities of Popular Unity's first year thus: 'From top to bottom of the administrative hierarchy, from one end of the country to the other, the front of the stage is occupied by an interminable legal wrangle.'[7] Behind those wrangles, however, lay a real battle for power which in the end could only be resolved by force. In some cases Popular Unity's efforts to extend the social property area were defeated. The attempt to buy up the important *Cía. Manufactureros de Papele-y Cartones* (the largest paper firm in Chile), for example, was defeated when the private sector overbid the government and bought up a majority of shares. In many cases the powerful and conservative Controller General of Chile (a sort of guardian of the constitution, who decided whether presidential decisions contravened the constitution), declared the takeovers to be illegal. Nevertheless, by a variety of means, including intervention, nationalization, requisitioning, stock purchase and workers' seizure, the social property area was gradually extended.

Major Interventions and Nationalizations in the first year of Popular Unity

Action*	Date	Company	Rationale for Action and Form of Compensation
R	11/70	Largest woollen textile firm, Fábrica de Paños Bellavista Tomé, owned by Yarur interests and W.R. Grace. 1,350 workers.	Operated below capacity.
I**	11/70	A subsidiary of Northern Indiana Brass Co. (NIBSA), the major producer of brass fittings and valves.	Production dropped and the firm laid off its 280 workers. In June 1971, CORFO purchased NIBSA's 50% equity for $.3 million.
I	11/70	A subsidiary of Ralston Purina.	Had imported depreciated machinery instead of the reported new machines. The firm was also undercapitalized.
SP	12/70	Cía. Acero del Pacífico (CAP), Chile's largest steel producer.	Nationalization of vital industries; to be the base of a new national metallurgical complex. CORFO purchased the 45% of CAP's stock still remaining in private hands for $90.6 million payable over 3–8 years. CORFO now owns 100%.
N	1/71	Carbonífera Lota Schwager, Chile's major (and Latin America's largest) coal producer, accounting for 85% of Chile's coal output. 9,800 workers.	Recovery of basic resources; government purchased 51% of stock and contracted for 100% of ownership in the future.
SP	1/71	Private Chilean commercial banks.	The Central Bank began buying stock in the commercial banks. By September 1971, it controlled 19 banks of the 22 private Chilean commercial banks.

Major Interventions and Nationalizations – contd.

Action	Date	Company	Rationale for Action and Form of Compensation
N	1/71	Lanera Austral, textile plant.	Allende announced the formation of a State textile concern, based on the two large expropriated firms, Bellavista-Tomé and Lanera Austral.
N	1/71	INESA, cement plant.	Nationalization of vital industries.
—	2/71	—	Chile announced sale of copper directly to China.
SP	2/71	Zig–Zag, largest publisher in Chile (publishes *Ercilla*.)	Purchased stock because firm was on the verge of bankruptcy, having not paid its 900 workers for 4 weeks. State plans to base a publishing company on it.
SP	2/71	R.C.A.	Gaining control of distribution; CORFO purchased a 51% equity (it previously held 33%) forming the first firm in the new "mixed" sector.
—	3/71	The three largest copper mines, Chuquicamata, El Teniente & El Salvador (belonging to Anaconda & Kennecott).	'Delegate directors' were sent to the mines to investigate mismanagement.
SP	3/71	Bethlehem-Chile Iron Mines, one of the largest iron ore producers.	Recovery of basic resources; CORFO purchased Bethlehem's two mines and related facilities for $25 million to be paid over 17 years beginning July, 1973.
SP	3/71	ARMCO Chile, leading producer of grinding balls for the mining industry.	Nationalization of vital industries; the government-owned Cía. Acero del Pacífico purchased 35.7% of ARMCO's equity. The government plans to acquire the majority of the stock of all steel manufacturing firms – INDAC, RODINSA, ARMCO, COMPAC, SOCOMETAL, and INCHALEM – to build a major integrated metallurgical complex.
—	4/71	Anaconda Sales Corp.	Gaining control of distribution; the State Copper Corp. (CODELCO) took over the sale of copper, but met serious international pressures when setting up sales agencies abroad.
N	5/71	5 large Yarur textile plants.	Placed under State jurisdiction – to be used as base of the new State-owned textile industry.
WS	5/71	Ford Motor Co. plant.	Workers occupied the plant after the company had announced the layoff of 400 workers (out of a total of 600).

Major Interventions and Nationalizations – contd.

Action	Date	Company	Rationale for Action and Form of Compensation
SP	5/71	LIPIGAS and SERVIGAS, 2 private liquid gas producers.	Nationalization of vital industries; the state oil agency, ENAP, formed a subsidiary ENADI, to handle the distribution and sales of liquid gases, combustibles, lubricants and petroleum by-products.
-	5/71	—	State agency, GASMA, is formed to construct and operate pipeline for natural gas from Punta Arenas to major Chilean cities.
—	5/71	Kennecott's El Teniente copper mine.	Minister of Mines delegated 8 government-appointed administrators to operate the mine after production fell.
WS	5/71	14 textile mills.	Workers simultaneously seized 14 textile mills. The seizures were followed by State requisitioning to maintain production.
SP	5/71	Anglo–Lautaro Nitrate Co., controlled by the Guggenheims, accounts for nearly 80% of nitrate production.	Recovery of basic resources; CORFO purchased stock for $8 million payable in 10 years.
SP	6/71	Bank of London and South America (BOLSA) with 10 branches.	Nationalization of banking; State took over the first foreign private commercial bank, with compensation to be paid over 5 years.
I	n.a.	El Melon and Cerro Blanco, the 2 largest cement producers, which in 1964 accounted for about 87% of industry's capacity.	Intervened because of falling production, thus endangering the construction industry.
SP	7/71	Bank of America, with 8 branches.	Nationalization of banking; State purchased the B of A assets for $2.5 million.
SP	n.a.	Cerro's Río Blanco mine (4th largest copper mine in Chile).	Recovery of basic resources; The Cerro Corp. agrees to sell its Río Blanco mine for $55 million, *if* the government will take over its $56 million debt to the US Eximbank.
N	7/71	All major copper mines. (Anaconda, Kennecott and Cerro subsidiaries).	Recovery of basic resources; Constitutional amendment for the nationalization of the copper mines passed unanimously by the Chilean Congress.

Major Interventions and Nationalizations – contd.

Action	Date	Campany	Rationale for Action and Form of Compensation
—	7/71	Kennecott.	Gaining control of distribution; CODELCO took over sales of copper produced at El Teniente.
WS	8/71	Cervecerías Unidas, the brewing monopoly (an Edwards interest); and INSA (with General Tire equity), the largest producer of tires and batteries.	Workers occupied the two large plants, charging mis-management.
—	8/71	Ford Motor Co. plant.	Result of workers seizure (May, 1971) and part of nationalization of the auto industry. Fiat will operate the plant and assemble 3,000 trucks annually.
N/SP	9/71	I. T. & T. telephone Co. which provided most of the country's service.	Nationalization of basic services. I. T. & T. claims its assets are worth $153 million while Chile claims they are worth $24 million.
SP	9/71	General Motor's truck assembly plant in Arica.	G.M. desires to sell out by December 1971 because of 'limitations' imposed on it by the Chilean government.
I/N	9/71	General Tire's Chilean subsidiary, INSA, largest producer of tubes and tyres.	Nationalization of vital industries. Government seeks to create a tyre monopoly by combining INSA with MANESA (a former Firestone operation taken over by the government).
N	9/71	MADECO, largest maker of copper products. Owned by General Cables Corp. (of N.Y.) and Fiat (of Milan, Italy).	Plants were intervened to avoid supply shortages in the industry.
N	9/71	First National City Bank's 8 Chilean offices.	Nationalization of banking. The assets worth $3.5 million (book value) are to be sold for $4.55 million to the Chilean government.
N	10/71	E. I. Dupont explosives plant, largest in South America.	Nationalization of vital industries.

* Abbreviations: I – Intervention; N – Nationalization; R – Requisitioning; SP – Stock Purchase; WS – Workers' Seizure & Requisitioning.

** A law passed in 1932, under President Carlos Dávila's administration allows the government to send officials (*interventores*) to oversee production should a private firm operate below capacity.

Source: NACLA. New Chile 1973

What remained unclear, however, was the direction that the economic trans-formation was to take. The declared intention was to establish a planned mixed economy, in which the private sector was subordinate to the planned social sector. Yet although the government planning agency, Odeplan, had devised numerous plans on paper (the 1971–6 Development Plan consisted of 16 large volumes of national and regional plans), the translation of theory into reality remained as difficult as ever. For the success or otherwise of planning depended on the outcome of the political struggle, on whether Popular Unity could gain control of the economy. Even in those sectors which were under government control there was no clear operational conception of what the relationship was to be between effective planning, workers' participation and the market mechanism. The result was that the social property area continued to work inefficiently even though it was clearly essential to the government's economic strategy that it should operate in the most efficient way possible.

By the end of 1971, two problems posed by the existence of an area of property under social ownership remained to be solved: (1) how would the area be run and administered? and (2) how could it exert its control over the economy as a whole? The latter question, which was directly linked in its turn to the question of whether Popular Unity should consolidate its gains or continue the advance, led to internal divisions within the coalition. The architect of the initial economic strategy, Pedro Vuskovic, was led by the logic of his strategy to the conclusion that it was essential that the social property area control the totality of the economy. This did not mean the take-over of the small and medium sized units, still less the take-over of shops, but it did require effective control of the industrial and distribution sectors. By the end of the first year Popular Unity controlled only about 20% of total industrial production. The government proposed that 253 firms with a capital and reserves of more than 14 million *escudos* should be incorporated into the social property area. The opposition counter-attacked by putting forward a proposal of their own – the Hamilton-Fuentealba project – which would have crippled any further efforts at nationalization, since it proposed to revoke the legal basis for government interventions in private firms, and to deny the government the right to buy private firms without reference to congress. The bill was in fact passed by congress, and then vetoed by the president. The battle over this bill was to become part of the long political fight between congress and the president, a symbol of the struggle between the working class and the bourgeoisie. In the end, the working class largely solved the problem in their own way: by a massive takeover of factories during the October strike of the bosses and in the aftermath of the failed coup of 29 June, 1973. Yet Popular Unity never settled the problem. In June 1972 Vuskovic was replaced at the Ministry of Economy by a Communist, Orlando Millas, who pursued the Communist and Allende policy of limiting the size of the social property area in order to placate the middle sectors and the Christian Democrats.

Efficiency within the social property area became a major problem. Shortages of raw materials and spare parts held up the production process. The government in an effort to hold prices stable tried to keep down the prices of the social property area. However, the result was that the social property area, instead of producing surpluses which could then be invested for productive purposes, ran huge deficits. And even in terms of controlling inflation, of redistributon to the poor and of an advancing process of nationalization, the complexity and number of price controls led to some bizarre results, for example petrol, most of which was imported, remained incredibly cheap. All too often the price of public utilities and of the nationalized industries were below costs of production. This necessitated subsidies, financed through further money creation, which in turn stimulated inflation.

The government planning agency, Odeplan, and the CUT drew up a new plan for the organization of firms within the social property area. The plan gave the workers greater participation in the running of the factory while at the same time giving them an interest in maintaining production and making it more efficient.

Organizational structure of a firm in the Social Property area

Administrative Council

↑

Trade Union ⟶ Coordinating Committee ⟵ Divisional Production
of the Workers Committee

↑ ↑

Assembly of all the Divisional Assembly of
Workers the workers

↑

Departmental Production
Committee

↑

Departmental Assembly
of the Workers

↑

Sectional Production
Committee

↑

Sectional Assembly of
the Workers

The Administrative Council consisted of a president, appointed by the government, five representatives of the State, and five representatives of the workers. It was therefore a structure which gave the workers of the firm full participation in the running of that firm, but not control.

These structures did function fairly well; yet they too were unable to solve the problem of efficiency. The general political climate always prevented the new norms of participation from having their full effect in terms of productivity. In order to counteract the right-wing offensives, workers had to spend much of their time in demonstrations, meetings and political activity, all of which necessarily cut down on working time. Lightning strikes by bus owners made it increasingly difficult for workers to arrive at work on time, and labour discipline probably declined as well. All these were minor factors, however, compared with the problem of bureaucracy. Popular Unity used a 'quota' system of appointment to maintain the balance of political parties within the coalition. In ministries and the management of industry this sometimes led to internal disputes which made it impossible to implement policy, particularly in those cases where the parties of Popular Unity had different policies. In the State bureaucracy, the problem was accentuated by a Christian Democrat law which made it impossible for the government to dismiss public employees. In many ministries a Popular Unity Minister and his assistants had to contend with an administration hostile to the policies it was supposed to administer.

The Economic Results: Economic Growth

To reactivate the economy the government redistributed income to the wage and salary earning sectors. This was part of a policy of increasing effective demand. They gave a *reajuste* (the yearly pay increase to compensate for the past year's inflation) above the 1970 34.9% inflation rate to the poorer employed groups. In addition the trade unions bargained for and obtained a substantial wage and salary increase. These measures together with the raising of the tax exemption limit, free distribution of some goods and services, for instance milk to the poor, and government expansion of housing, all substantially increased the demand for goods and services. The increase in aggregate demand, combined with other changes, produced a number of chain-reactions throughout the economy.

On the positive side, Popular Unity which had been faced initially with a stagnant economy, high unemployment and attempts by the bourgeoisie and US interests to cause economic panic and chaos, did manage to restore economic growth, reduce unemployment, reduce the rate of inflation, redistribute income and increase the level of consumption of the poor.

Economic Growth

Source: ODEPLAN: Analysis of the Economy in 1971

MAGNITUDE OF MACRO-ECONOMIC VARIABLES IN 1970 AND 1971
(In thousands of millions of escudos of 1970)

	1970	1971 (a)	% Variation
Gross domestic product	92.2	100.0	8.5
Personal consumption	64.9	72.3	12.9
Government consumption	12.5	13.1	4.6
Gross domestic investment	14.5	13.3	−7.7
Exports	14.8	15.6	5.7
Imports	14.4	15.3	5.7

GROSS DOMESTIC INVESTMENT
(In thousands of millions of escudos of 1970)

	1970	1971	% Variation
1. Construction	7.6	8.6	12.5
2. Variations in stock and equipment (national)	1.7	.5	−71.3
3. Imported machinery and equipment	5.2	4.3	−16.8
Total:	14.5	13.3	− 7.7

LABOUR FORCE, EMPLOYED AND UNEMPLOYED

	Annual average		December (a)	
	1970 (000's)	1971 (000's)	1970 (000's)	1971 (000's)
Labour force	3,189	3,270	3,234	3,323
Employed population	2,994	3,140	3,000	3,194
Unemployment	195	138	234	129
Rate of unemployment	6.0%	4.2%	7.2%	3.9%

(a) Estimated figures

PURCHASING POWER OF SALARIES AND WAGES

	Index of Salaries and wages 1968=100 (A)	Index of Consumer Prices 1968=100 (B)	Index of Purchasing Power of wages and salaries 1968=100 (C)*
1968 October	100	100	100
1969 October	135	127	106
1970 October	206	172	120
1971 October	297	192	154

Source: National Institute of Statistics; Index of Salaries and wages and consumer prices.

(*) $C = \dfrac{\text{Index 'A' } (1968=100)}{\text{Index 'B' } (1968=100)} \times 100$

Many of these 'success indicators', however, were purchased at a high price. Although the government had planned to increase its revenues to help to pay for some of the benefits it was providing, congress refused to allow the government to pass legislation to bring this about – it refused, for example, to accept an increase in taxation which would have helped to raise the revenue necessary to finance these economic policies. Popular Unity was obliged to find funds to meet the increase in public sector wages, to buy up banks, factories and land, to pay compensation for some of the units that had been taken over (even though such compensation usually proved to be minimal) and to pay for increased government expenditure. Popular Unity solved the problem by borrowing from the Central Bank, with the result that the supply of money increased by more than 100%. The government's fiscal and monetary programme bore little resemblance to the programme proposed at the beginning of the year. Government income was less than anticipated, whilst government expenditure exceeded estimates: the result was a fiscal deficit 71% greater than planned.

In a capitalist market economy which was functioning normally, an increase in purchasing power, a large fiscal deficit and an increase in the money supply of such magnitude would have resulted in a substantial increase in prices. Instead, the consumer price index fell from the 34.9% increase of 1970 to 22.1% in 1971. The main reason for the fall was the enforcement of price controls which in some cases, including that of the public sector, meant that prices fell below costs of production. In many instances profits fell drastically, and with them any possibility of increasing private investment.

Yet production in most sectors did increase in the first year; industrial production increased by about 12.1%, copper by about 4% and even agricultural production by about 5.8%.[8] But all these increases were accompanied by a decline in total investment. So where did the increased supply come from? In some cases, textiles for example, it came in part from the increased efficiency and enthusiasm of the workers in the new relations of production. There were, however, four main sources of this increase in supply: the use of underutilized industrial capacity; stocks and inventories; a decline in investment which released extra resources for the purchase of consumer imports, and the use of foreign exchange reserves to import consumer goods and inputs for the production of those goods. To increase supply from these sources in effect implied mortgaging the future.

In retrospect, it is clear that earlier government predictions fell short of the actual increase in demand and failed to foresee the problems of supply that did arise. Thus even the seemingly sensible strategy of utilizing that part of existing industrial capacity which was not being used created problems for the immediate future. Odeplan had estimated in 1970 that about 75% of industrial capacity was being used. Within the industrial sector, however, the use of capacity was unevenly distributed, and used capacities varied; in the crucial intermediate goods sector, for example, used capacity was 85.5% This meant that if nearly all of the economically viable capacity were used up immediately, there would be little left to meet future demand. Similarly, the running down of stocks and inventories, of foreign exchange, together with the failure of private capital to reinvest surplus, meant that unless large amounts of foreign exchange became available for imports, Popular Unity had left itself with virtually no economic leeway with which to meet increases in demand. This was bound to result in shortages, and, as the government carried on with its expenditures, in rampant inflation.

Moreover, Popular Unity's initial strategy did not arise in an international vacuum. From the very beginning, the USA worked to undermine Popular Unity; the structure of the Chilean economy, which was one of extreme dependence on the USA, enabled it to do so to devastating effect.

For many years the management of the Chilean balance of payments had depended on the entry of foreign capital. This was not because Chile had a trade deficit (Chile always exported more goods than it imported) but because Chile had witnessed a massive outflow of capital:profit repatriation, interest and amortization payments on past debts, payments for invisibles such as insurance and shipping, and the expatriation of capital by Chileans into bank accounts abroad.

In 1971, although the expropriation of North American companies reduced the outflow of profits, there was a huge deficit because, as the 1972 Inter-American Committee of the Alliance for Progress report concluded 'approximately two-thirds of the total deficit was determined by the behaviour of financial factors': i.e. there was an outflow of autonomous foreign capital without a corresponding inflow, as there had been previously.

Chilean Balance of Payments 1970-1971

	(*Millions of Dollars*)	
	1970	*1971*
Trade		
Exports	1,272 (61¢)*	1,146 (50¢)*
Imports	1,202	1,270
Trade Balance	+ 71	—122
Financial Services	—129	— 90
Paid to Foreigners	186	126
Profits	97	38
Interests	90	88
Paid by Foreigners	57	36
Autonomous Capital Movements	+149	—103
Balance of Payments Total	91	—315
Reserves	344	30

* Copper price per pound in US cents.

Source: Interamerican Committee of the Alliance for Progress (CIAP/541), 'Domestic Efforts and the Needs for External Financing for the Development of Chile', 1972, Table V-6; and *Republica de Chile, Dirección de Presupuestos, Folleto No. 122*, Orlando Millas, Minister of Finance, *Exposición sobre la politica económica del gobierno y el estado de la hacienda pública*, November 15, 1972.

When the United States stopped aid and investment to the Allende government, the results were crippling for the Chilean economy. From the point of view of North American capitalists and hence the US government, however, it was a logical response. It is unrealistic for any anti-imperialist government such as Popular Unity to expect aid and credits from the USA and its allies. Chile did receive some credits and aid from China, the USSR, Eastern Europe, Sweden and some Latin American countries. In the first year, a stand-by credit was even obtained from the International Monetary Fund. In addition, Popular Unity renegotiated and postponed for a short time the huge debt repayments it had inherited from previous governments. Yet none of these sources of finance could fill the gap left by the 'informal blockade' maintained by the USA.

After the first year Chile was faced with a constant balance of payments crisis. In addition to North American policies on aid, trade, credits and investments, a number of factors increased balance of payments difficulties. Popular Unity's policy of maintaining a fixed exchange rate throughout the first year did not help, since the effect of this policy was to subsidize imports and, to a limited extent, penalize exports. Exports were only slightly penalized because, other than minerals, they were few and some in any case received tax concessions to overcome the exchange rate policy. The subsidy on imports, on the other hand, was considerable; most of these imports were used to meet the increased demand for consumer goods, especially food and drink (the imports of machinery and spare parts actually declined – an indication of the fall in investment). The original tactic of increasing consumption helped to use up Chile's foreign exchange reserves very rapidly; given Chile's dependence on the foreign sector, this was very short-sighted.

Two other factors which lay beyond Popular Unity's control also contributed to the balance of payments crisis. The first was the world-wide increase in food prices. The rapid expropriation of land meant that the government relied on the import of foodstuffs to meet the increased demand for food during the period of expropriation. The increase in world food prices increased the foreign exchange costs of these imports. The second factor was more crucial: the fall in the price of copper. In the first year of Popular Unity the price of copper fell from an average of 61 US cents per lb. to 40 US cents, causing an estimated loss in foreign exchange of $200 million. Hence the severe balance of payments crisis which Popular Unity faced at the end of its first year, a crisis exacerbated, furthermore, by two problems that had become endemic by the end of 1971 – inflation and shortages. These problems in their turn, fed and were fed by the political crisis.

Conclusions

The initial perspectives of Popular Unity were based on a false hypothesis: that it is possible to create peacefully a workers' State simply by using the bourgeois State apparatus.

This is not to argue that the initial tactic of contesting and winning elections is a mistaken one. Only an intransigent dogmatist would deny that having left-wing parties in control of part of the bourgeois State apparatus was a major and historic victory for the Chilean working classes.

Many important gains were made during the first year, but politically and economically the initial strategy had a number of crucial weaknesses which were to persist throughout the three years of Popular Unity. Many, and probably the majority on the left, did not expect the victory of Salvador Allende. Thus in contrast to the detailed plans of action that had been prepared for the elections of 1958 and 1964 the Popular Unity had come to the elections of 1970 with little more than an electoral programme. Therefore, although the overall reformist strategy was clear, particular decisions tended to be taken in a very *ad hoc* way during the first year.

The initial economic perspective was excessively oriented towards consumption. In retrospect the government's projections had failed to anticipate either the extent of the increase in demand or the problems of supply. The income distribution policies, whilst laudable in their aims were too indiscriminate in their benefits. A more controlled and precise redistribution from the rich to the poor would have been politically more effective, and less destructive of potential productive capacity. In the end, however, the crucial economic factor was the failure of Popular Unity to gain overall control of the economy. The capitalist class remained in a sufficiently powerful economic position to enable them to prevent further advances by the government. It was thus difficult to maintain the initial increases in production within a basically market economy or to plan the economy as a whole.

Politically the crucial issue was the battle for power. The initial strategy and tactics were in both the short and long run unsuitable for winning such a battle. In an effort to win over the middle sectors, Allende and the Communist Party tried to put brakes on working class mobilization and initiatives. The working classes were not prepared for a confrontation, but were instead lulled into false expectations about the role of the armed forces. The point here is not that Popular Unity should have had the arming of the workers as one of its slogans; in the first year it was likely that such a slogan would have been suicidal, and indeed the bulk of the workers would probably not have supported it. But it was necessary to have a series of policies that warned and prepared for confrontation, and which left the workers in the best possible position in such a confrontation. Such policies would, of course, include a series of steps designed to split the armed forces. The roots of the failure to achieve either an adequate preparation of the workers or to split the armed forces lay in Popular Unity's initial strategic conception; for although it was abandoned, at least partially, by important segments of Popular Unity, crucial segments did cling to the heart of that strategy – an assumption that the bourgeois State apparatus could provide sufficient power and basis for the transition to socialism.

5 Strategy and Tactics of the Right

When the Popular Unity coalition won the presidential elections of September 1970, and Allende assumed the presidency in November of that year, there arose a situation in which a coalition of working class and middle class parties had captured, by peaceful means, a part of state power.

It is crucially important to recognize, however, that when Allende assumed power the bourgeois State apparatus was intact. There had been neither a civil war nor a revolution, nor any crisis within the ruling class such as might result from a major war or civil disaster. The bourgeois social order, the bourgeois parties, the armed forces and the capitalist economy all remained intact. The task facing Popular Unity, therefore, was to challenge or undermine the hegemony still enjoyed by the bourgeoisie as a result of their uninterrupted control of all these institutions. Unless it were able to successfully erode the very basis of bourgeois State power, the government would find itself facing a situation in which the ruling class still called the tune, retained the initiative in political terms and was thus in a position to provoke a series of crises designed to bring about the downfall of the popular government.

The government, however, did have an initial tactical advantage. In 1970 the Chilean upper classes were divided over how to respond to the growing challenge from the working class and the peasantry; as a result, it was some time before they were capable of any effective action against the new government. The strategists of Popular Unity hoped that these differences within the ruling class could be exploited to the advantage of the new government. In many ways their initial strategy was designed to maintain the split between the various fractions of the ruling class and win over wavering elements from the middle classes. This initial strategy failed – as it necessarily had to; and coincidentally with the failure of UP's strategy for the first year, the opposition – both internal and external – moved increasingly into an aggressive attack upon the government.

Early moves by the opposition

The divisions within the Chilean ruling classes in 1970 impeded the development of any coherent and unified bourgeois strategy for some time after Allende's victory. Initially, in fact, the dominant groups exhibited a notable disunity. On the one hand, there were attempts to prevent Allende from assuming the presidency at all, by trying, with American support, to organize a military coup which would annul the elections. These attempts led to a plan to kidnap the Chief of Staff of the Armed Forces, General René Schneider, who was widely known for his support for the constitutionally elected government. The kidnapping backfired, however, since Schneider resisted and was killed in the ensuing scuffle. As a result, in part, of this incident, such *golpista* tactics were discredited – at least for the time being.

On the other hand, there were large sectors of the bourgeoisie and the middle strata who were unwilling to overthrow bourgeois constitutionality without first using all the means at their disposal in an effort to limit the new government's freedom of action. In this way, they felt, UP could be kept in harness to the classic pattern of social democratic reformist government. After all, the basic nature of the bourgeois state remained unaltered and the bases of bourgeois power (in the last resort the army) remained untouched. The first step in this process was to demand that Allende sign a Statute of Guarantees in return for the support of the Christian Democrats in the parliamentary vote that would confirm him as president.

> Statute of Guarantees
> 1. The continuation of the existing political system together with constitutional guarantees of individual freedom.
> 2. The existing legal system should remain.
> 3. The armed forces and police should continue to guarantee democracy.
> 4. The independence of the educational system from ideological orientations, and the autonomy of the universities should be guaranteed.
> 5. The continuing independence of the trade unions and social organizations.
> 6. The press and the mass media should be free from State intervention.

Chile's long and continuous bourgeois-democratic tradition had permitted the growth and development of a deeply-rooted ideology of legalism and respect for the constitution which permeated important sectors of the working classes and some strata among the middle classes. Indeed, some of the parties forming the UP coalition – such as the Radical Party and the API – were profoundly committed to these ideological positions; it was their belief that the 'mature' Chilean working class would combine with the large number of middle class elements already incorporated into the State apparatus to facilitate the transformation of a Marxist challenge into a social-democratic reformist adaptation remaining well within the confines of a bourgeois State and a capitalist economy.

From the opposition's point of view, then, there were two central issues: firstly, bourgeois institutions and the bourgeois order had to be defended.[1] The campaign began by defending the 'independence' of the judiciary and was later extended to cover questions like the 'defence of democracy' and 'freedom of expression'. Secondly, the defence of private property, in particular of small and medium property, was to be the means whereby the bourgeoisie would mobilize the broad masses in its support. In the first instance, therefore, the plan of counter-attack devised by the bourgeoisie bore a striking resemblance to Popular Unity's own strategy for winning over the middle sectors, limiting itself at this stage to a purely electoral perspective. From the point of view of the bourgeoisie, what was at issue was clearly the maintenance of a hegemonic bourgeois ideology whose institutional expression was the separation of powers. The question for the government, on the other hand, was how to break the dominant ideology without losing its legitimacy in the exercise of power.

From the very beginning, a fierce attack was launched in the bourgeois press denouncing the arbitrary acts and transgressions of the Constitution supposedly perpetrated by the UP government. The Christian Democrats (PDC), on the other hand, claimed throughout the first year that it was a legitimate reforming party; in this way it set itself more or less directly against the UP, presenting itself as a rival for the support of the middle sectors. In marked contrast, the National Party (PN) repeatedly called for a united front of the bourgeoisie capable of toppling the government. The PDC's position was that the revolution in Chile could be made in two ways; either in a violent and ultimately totalitarian way represented by Popular Unity (insofar as it was a coalition dominated by the Marxist parties), or a democratic road represented by a PDC recombined with certain elements of the UP coalition. This initial position of the 'progressive' wing of the Chilean bourgeoisie may be contrasted with the position later assumed by the PDC under the leadership of Frei, when it came out openly in favour of a military coup.

As events unfolded, however, and the militancy of the working class increased, the political agents of the bourgeoisie closed ranks. Their first major offensive was ideological; for if the institutions of bourgeois society were to remain intact it was clearly a matter of priority to maintain the coherence of bourgeois ideology within the camp of the bourgeoisie itself, and to propagate it among the proletariat and its allies. It was at this level that it became clear in the first place that the possibility of compromise between Popular Unity and the bourgeoisie was growing more and more distant, as the owning classes launched their sustained ideological assault on Popular Unity.

The mass media

One section of the Statute of Guarantees had stipulated that Allende ensure the freedom of the press and the mass communications media. During all the three years of the Allende government, indeed, the opposition continued to publish a considerable number of newspapers, magazines and books (seven new magazines appeared during the first months of 1971 under the imprint of the big newspaper monopolies) and to control a large number of broadcasting stations. The opposition, of course, did not have a monopoly over the mass media; the government and the parties of Popular Unity also controlled several newspapers, radio and TV stations as well as the State publishing house, Quimantú. Throughout the UP period, both sides struggled to extend their control over the mass media. The TV station owned by the University of Chile, for example, was the object of a series of occupations and legal battles between pro- and anti-government factions within the University.

The means of mass communication controlled by the opposition attacked the government systematically, continually and savagely. By publishing alarmist headlines, they contributed directly to maintaining social unrest, and even played their part in the general economic sabotage by artificially creating shortages of consumer goods. *El Mercurio* might announce for example, quite out of the blue, that a shortage of detergents was just around the corner; their readers would then rush out and buy up whatever detergents they could find, thereby depleting stockpiles and creating an artificial shortage. (It should be pointed out, in fairness, that this tactic was used only during the first two years, when shortages were irregular and apparently random. When scarcity became generalized, there was no longer any purpose in continuing the campaign.)

From time to time, when papers had published libellous articles or when a state of emergency had been declared, copies of newspapers were seized and newspaper offices or radio stations closed down by the government for a few days. These defensive measures were invariably greeted with howls of hysteria from the rest of the opposition media, and the old nonsense about totalitarianism was always dragged out for the occasion. Nevertheless, it is difficult to comprehend the extreme reaction of the bourgeois press and radio stations to the actions of the Allende government, unless it is remembered that (rightly or wrongly) the UP was perceived as a serious threat by the bourgeoisie. They claimed – with what degree of sincerity or self-delusion it is impossible to say – that the actions of the government were part of a plan hatched in Moscow, Peking or Havana whose object was to subvert the foundations of bourgeois society and impose on the freedom-loving people of Chile a totalitarian dictatorship along Soviet Russian lines.   It was also claimed that hordes of extremist workers were being armed and were preparing to surround Santiago. The hysteria of the bourgeoisie was unbounded.

This extraordinary daily barrage of lies and distortions had the desired effect of intensifying opposition to the government and magnifying the alarm of the middle classes. It also had the effect of instilling into the bourgeoisie and those sectors of society open to bourgeois influence a profoundly distorted perception of the actual situation in Chile; in this sense they fell victim to their own propaganda. It is this savage propaganda campaign that explains in part the ferocity which the soldiers exhibited in the fighting following the coup. They had been led to believe in a systematic way that they were going to face a well-armed working class.

But the reality was very different; the working class was not in a position to offer any serious resistance; yet the soldiers attacked the factories and workers' districts with a level of violence quite disproportionate to the armed response from the workers. The effectiveness of this sustained propaganda may also explain, insofar as it also reached a civilian audience, the effectiveness of the campaign of denunciations instituted by the military junta after the coup.

Education

The ideological offensive, of course, embraced other levels too. From the beginning, the bourgeoisie had seen education as a key field of ideological conflict; it too had been one of the 'untouchable' areas stipulated in the Statute of Guarantees. Like the mass media, education was one of the bastions of bourgeois influence; it was vital, therefore, that they preserve their dominant position in education from any influences from the Left.

In fact, Popular Unity had done very little by way of educational reform. The educational system was left very largely as the government had found it in 1970; there had been some reorganization in the universities, but of little more than an administrative character. Nevertheless, the opposition brought the issue of education to the forefront as early as September 1971, and it had increasingly become a focus for opposition attacks on the government.

Despite these harbingers of trouble, the UP government responded to the need for educational reform by introducing, in April 1973, a plan which differed very little from the programme that had been put forward by the teachers in the 1920s. Clearly educational reform had been on the agenda for a very long time, and was long overdue. The plan proposed by the Ministry of Education was known as the Plan for a Unified National School (ENU).[2] Basically, the reform aimed at making Chilean education more technical and vocational, gearing it more closely to the needs of an under-developed country. One of its provisions, for example, was to offer students the opportunity of experiencing a variety of work environments before leaving school, with the object of helping school leavers in their choice of future occupation. Similarly, there was to be provision for those already at work to attend evening classes, thus raising the general educational level of the work-force.

In line with these organizational changes, the content and curriculum of teaching were to be overhauled. Furthermore, those schools that refused to accept the provisions of the new reform would not receive government recognition. The proposal immediately became the target for a massive campaign in the opposition mass media. There were a number of demonstrations against the plan by schoolchildren from the well-to-do districts, many of which involved a degree of violence and disorder, thus adding fuel to the opposition press campaign.

The principal charge made by the opposition was that the proposed reform opened the way for increasing State control of the content of education, so that under Popular Unity schools would become nothing more than centres of Marxist propaganda. Clearly, the opposition felt that the reform threatened directly one of the key bastions of its ideological power. Nor were the political parties of the bourgeoisie the only sectors to protest; the Church asked that the project be delayed while they studied it in detail, and the officer corps of the army held a number of meetings to discuss the plan. In the end, the government was forced to back down, and the proposal was effectively shelved. That round in the class struggle was a clear victory for the bourgeoisie. Yet although the reform never reached congress, its fate says much about the political character of the Popular Unity government. The irony is that the reform was in no sense revolutionary; on the contrary, it was an attempt to democratize education and at the same time to give a greater emphasis in the curriculum to technical subjects and areas. In a real sense, it was a reform that could have brought immediate benefit to a capitalist economy. And yet, given the high level of consciousness among the working class, it is clear that the bourgeoisie saw in the democratization of education the dangerous seeds of future subversion.

Congress and the institutional struggle

The opposition assault, of course, was in no sense confined to these ideological levels. It combined offensives at a series of points within the system, the most sustained of which was undoubtedly the political campaign within those institutions of the State apparatus which remained firmly under bourgeois control: parliament and the legal system.

During the period of Popular Unity, the Right in congress consistently used its majority to obstruct and impede government legislation, and had frequent recourse to impeachment proceedings to prevent Allende from forming a stable cabinet. There was one battle which lasted throughout Allende's three years, and which serves as a clear and typical example of the kind of attack which the opposition unleashed and maintained from the beginning of the Popular Unity government.

Some time after Allende had assumed office, two leaders of the Christian Democrat party in Congress – Senators Juan Hamilton and Renán Fuentealba – introduced a bill in the form of a constitutional amendment. The purpose of the bill was to define through a specific law procedures for the nationalization of industry, restricting the powers enjoyed by the Allende government to expropriate, requisition or intervene in a considerable number of industries. The law, furthermore, was to be backdated and retroactive in its application. The Hamilton–Fuentealba amendment contained three basic provisions: 1) it defined three sectors of the economy – the Social Property area, the Mixed Property area and the Private Property area – this was in accord with UP's economic programme; 2) no industry could be designated as part of either the social or mixed property area without specific congressional approval; 3) it provided for enterprises in the social property area to be organized as 'workers' enterprises'.

The first provision, the demarcation of the economy into three sectors, did not run counter to government intentions. As far as the second clause was concerned, the government was willing in principle to accept it; in practice, however, it disagreed with congress as to the size and composition of the list of industries for inclusion in the social and mixed property areas that was to be drawn up. The government was opposed in principle and in practice, however, to the third proposal on the grounds that the establishment of workers' enterprises introduced a form of profit-sharing and decentralization which conflicted in principle with the need to organize a centrally planned economy, in which the enterprises were not the private property of the workers who happened to be employed in them, but were social property. Of course, the notion of workers' enterprises was essentially demagogic; the PDC in no sense wished to abolish capitalism – it hoped merely to rationalize and modernize Chilean capitalism by taking over some of the monopolies, thus heading off workers' demands for control by introducing a form of profit-sharing.

After many months of drafting and discussion in congress, the Hamilton-Fuentealba amendment was approved and sent to the president in early 1972. Allende, acting within his constitutional rights, vetoed some of the provisions of the bill and sent it back to congress for reconsideration.

Congress now had to consider whether to accept or reject the presidential veto of some clauses of the bill. At this point there arose a constitutional conflict as there was disagreement over whether congress needed a simple or a two-thirds majority to overrule the presidential veto (the opposition parties, it should be remembered, held only a simple majority). On this procedural issue, then, hung the important substantive question of whether congress would be able to pass a constitutional amendment which severely limited the government's ability to create a viable State sector. At the same time, a conflict of powers between the presidency and any other branch of government was fraught with dangers for Popular Unity since it brought with it the spectre of military intervention against the presidency under the guise of resolving a constitutional stalemate.

Negotiations now began between UP and the PDC. The talks focused on two questions: the list of industries to be nationalized and the question of workers' enterprises. After lengthy argument the UP agreed to compromise over the issue of workers' enterprises and allow some to be set up on an experimental basis. The attempt to reach agreement on the list of enterprises to be nationalized, however, ended in failure. In the end, the whole matter came to hinge upon the paper industry, a monopoly which the UP wanted to nationalize despite the vociferous objections of the PDC, who claimed that this would pave the way to totalitarianism by enabling the government to cut off supplies of paper to the opposition press. As negotiations over this crucial industry became bogged down in their turn, the left wing of the Socialist Party and the hardliners in the PDC – notably Frei – each took initiatives to call off the discussions. The constitutional amendment was allowed to proceed on its course.

For some time it lay dormant in congress; but it raised its head again in 1973. The same procedural–substantive issues arose, only this time there were no grounds for compromise and few ways of delaying the inevitable institutional conflict. The issue was supposed to be resolved by the *Contraloría* (which, together with the Supreme Court, ensures that presidential decisions do not contravene the Constitution); predictably enough, it decided in favour of the interpretation given by congress. The deadlock between the president and the congress had clearly reached a point of crisis. This is not to suggest that the constitutional conflict was of itself sufficient to bring about the overthrow of Popular Unity; it formed one more level of the general economic and political crisis that had been steadily building up during the preceding months. The underlying factor in the crisis was the emergence of demands stemming directly from the working class and its organizations, demands which sought to go beyond the reformist conceptions of the Allende government. UP's inability to respond to these demands, because of its continuing adherence to its initial reformist strategy, served only to deepen the economic crisis; at the political level, a sharpening class struggle was reflected in Allende's failure to form a stable cabinet which would govern the country and effectively implement new policies. The opposition was never slow to exploit and exacerbate the crisis; in congress they repeatedly held up government legislation, in particular the tax and wage readjustment bills, on which rested the whole economic policy of the UP. By consistently obstructing and underfinancing these and similar bills, the opposition-controlled congress went a long way towards ensuring that the financial crisis which it had predicted would come to pass. At every level, then, the crisis was defined and advanced by the refusal on the part of the bourgeois parties to come to terms with the government; they decided, on the contrary, to issue a series of calls directed at the armed forces, and designed to encourage them to prepare to 'act to save the nation'. In this process, then, the constitutional conflict is best seen as an integral part of a many-sided ideological offensive whose object, in this particular arena, was to reach the situation where the government could be pronounced unconstitutional and a military coup against it given the necessary legitimacy.

Since they had a majority in congress, the opposition parties were able to engage in systematic harassment of the Allende administration. Congress could impeach any minister or *intendente* by simple majority vote, and demand his replacement. What this meant was that congress could, potentially, exercise a veto on the formation of the cabinet. In practice their power to do this was slightly limited by the need to prove unconstitutional behaviour on the part of the relevant minister; but given this proviso, the opposition made considerable use of their power to impeach government officials, particularly towards the end of the UP period.

The first such impeachment proceedings were instituted against the Minister of the Interior, José Tohá, in January 1972. Allende reshuffled his cabinet and reappointed Tohá as Minister of Defence. Thereafter impeachment proceedings mounted in tempo and forced Allende to reshape his cabinet several times during the last eighteen months. The net result was a disturbing lack of continuity in the formulation of government policy and a tendency for government to become increasingly less effective. By 1973, the opposition was using the threat of continued impeachment of whoever Allende appointed as Minister of the Economy as a means of exerting constant pressure on the government to radically change its economic policies.

The Legal System

In the complex set of checks and balances within the Chilean Constitution, the ruling classes controlled the judiciary as well as the legislature. This control was exercised at a number of levels: at the lower levels, the ordinary courts and the agrarian tribunals showed their class bias by consistently ruling in favour of the interests of property and against the interests of the working class and the peasantry. Dozens of peasants were imprisoned during the Allende regime for the occupation of farms, and workers were arrested and jailed a number of times after political demonstrations or factory occupations. At times the police and army were used to dislodge peasant occupants from farms they had seized. This is not to say that the Allende regime consistently or consciously permitted the law to be used against the interests of the working class. On the contrary, and with the exception of attempts by the reformists to persuade the workers to return factories to their 'rightful' owners, the Allende government always sought to restrain the police. In general, although there was reluctance to support farm and factory occupations (especially during the initial period), the government refused to repress them once they had occurred. Since control of the law courts remained with the bourgeoisie, however, the government could not stop the local representatives of bourgeois interests from seeking to apply the law in order to restrain the actions of workers and peasants. When forty-four farm workers occupied a farm in the Melipilla area which was scheduled for expropriation, for instance, the local judge had them arrested and incarcerated. In this case (though not in all), however, extensive popular mobilization did secure their release.

The action of local courts was not confined merely to arresting 'trouble-makers'. The agrarian tribunals consistently decided in favour of the landlords whenever a dispute arose about awarding a reserve of land to the former land-owner. In this way, the agrarian tribunals acted to preserve the economic base of the agrarian bourgeoisie. As time went on and the Allende government came under increasing pressure from the propertied classes, the picture grew even more gloomy for the working class. The police and the army were used with increasing frequency against the workers. And as control of the situation slipped progressively from the hands of the reformist government, both the police and the army tended to revert to their traditional role of defenders of the bourgeois social order, and began to act on their own initiative and independently of the government[3] – which did very little to stop them.

The control exercised by the old ruling classes over the local judiciary was equally secure at the national level, where both the Supreme Court and the *Contraloría* acted in a consistent way to place obstacles upon or block entirely the way forward towards any profound institutional transformation of Chilean society. In mid-1973, for example, both these august institutions ruled that the government had contravened the Constitution – and thus set the seal of doom upon an administration which was already inextricably caught in a gathering crisis. From April 1973 onwards, the bourgeoisie moved entirely on to the offensive; and in this move they could assume the continuing support of their allies outside Chile.

Imperialism

From the very outset, the United States attempted to intervene in Chilean politics and engineer the overthrow of Allende. The range of options open to US policy makers, however, was limited; a direct military invasion like the invasion of the Dominican Republic, while not entirely out of the question, would have proved immensely costly in Chile and might well have backfired. A better alternative as far as the US was concerned was to work together with the Chilean bourgeoisie in a joint effort to overthrow the government.

At the same time, the US was able to take actions on its own behalf which would help to bring about a situation in which Popular Unity found it increasingly difficult to control the economy and maintain a wide base of support among sectors of the middle class. These actions took two forms: 1) gaining the support of various groups in Chile and 2) initiating an economic blockade whose long run effect was to vastly increase the economic difficulties faced by the UP government.

The reason why the US was able to exert such considerable pressure was because the underdeveloped capitalist economy of Chile was heavily dependent on the United States for imports of raw materials, spare parts and machinery; at the same time it had great weight in decisions made outside Chile about the refinancing of Chile's burden of heavy debt repayments. United States investments in Chile were huge and distributed throughout the economy: copper mines, manufactured foodstuffs, petrochemicals, textiles, office equipment, paint, cement, radio and television, construction, motor vehicles, pharmaceuticals, telephones, banking and hotels.[4] Obviously the US was vitally interested in protecting its massive investments in Chile, on the one hand, and on the other in preventing Chile's example from being followed anywhere else in Latin America.

There were differences between the various American interest groups about the appropriate policy to pursue in the Chilean situation, especially during the initial period. Some multi-national corporations, such as ITT,[5] began independent action to oppose the Chilean government; official US government policy, on the other hand, was initially rather more cautious. According to David Eisenhower and Dale Johnson,[6] from September 1970 until July 1971, the United States government officially pursued a 'wait and see' policy, while moves were made to encourage other Latin American nations to enter into some kind of joint action with the US. As it became clear that this was not going to happen, the US began to tighten the screws on Chile. The deliberate application of stiff economic sanctions against Chile did not emerge as a clear policy until January 1972; but from that time forward the pressure was on and remained on in earnest.

Significantly, the adoption of the tough line followed hard on the heels of two important events. One was Fidel Castro's visit to Chile in November and December of 1971, during which the March of the Empty Pots was held – a demonstration of middle class women against Allende which indicated a clear polarization of the political situation and the end of the relatively tranquil first phase of the Popular Unity government. The second major event was the announcement of the terms of compensation for the expropriated copper companies. Chile claimed that after allowance had been made for the excess profits shipped out of Chile by the copper companies, little or no compensation was due to them. It was these, the virtually confiscatory terms of compensation, rather than the nationalization itself which drew the ire of the copper companies and the US government.

There were a number of ways in which the US could exert pressure. Almost immediately following the 1970 elections new investment in Chile stopped completely, and there was a considerable amount of capital flight; a situation of economic panic and chaos was deliberately engineered by big capitalist interests inside and outside Chile. Following this immediate step, the US began to cut credit to Chile (much of it came from the US-controlled Export-Import Bank). Loans from the Agency for International Development (AID) were stopped, even though Allende was saddled with a huge repayment problem from AID loans to the previous (Frei) administraton. Under US pressure, both the Inter-American Development Bank and the World Bank stopped their loans, and the major US banks followed suit, cutting all credit to Chile.

Thus Chile was faced with a situation in which new loans were extremely difficult to come by; at the same time it was necessary to repay the immense foreign debt accumulated by the Frei government. In November 1971, Chile declared a moratorium on its debt repayments to the United States and other countries, and asked for a rescheduling of its remaining 1971 debts and of the estimated $414 million due in 1972. At the Paris Club meeting in early 1972, the US sought to block the re-negotiation. Eventually the US was forced to back down, and repayment terms were arranged.

The US government was not alone in seeking to apply economic sanctions to Chile. The copper companies, too, took action on their own behalf. The Kennecott Copper Corporation, previously the owner of the El Teniente copper mine, took legal action to have copper from that mine embargoed. Kennecott claimed that since they had not been given adequate compensation for the nationalization, they were still part owners of the copper produced in the El Teniente mine. In September 1972, Kennecott asked a French court to block payments to Chile from the sale of copper about to be unloaded from a ship recently arrived in Le Havre. The aim of the exercise was to pressure Chile into opening negotiations about compensation. By January 1973, the Kennecott strategy was having a certain degree of success and Chilean copper sales were declining.

It should not be assumed that US opposition to the Allende government was limited solely to economic sanctions (many opposition groups and leaders were directly financed by US sources, among them the leader of the truck-owners strike, León Vilarín). The most obvious case was the plot by the ITT corporation, exposed by the journalist Jack Anderson, to create a situation conducive to Allende's downfall. While there is no evidence to support the contention, it seems reasonable to suppose that ITT was not alone in giving direct aid to the opponents of the Popular Unity government.

United States imperialism acted consistently to defend its interests, just as it has done and will continue to do in other parts of the world. But it must be stressed that while the US played an important role in creating the conditions for a military coup and even directly aided the Chilean bourgeoisie in its efforts to overthrow Allende, it did not by any means act alone. The Popular Unity government was overthrown by its own bourgeoisie (and its political agent, the armed forces) when it became clear that there was a real threat to bourgeois society. In view of the prevalence of conspiratorial views of imperialist intervention in underdeveloped countries, it should be stressed that the principal reason why the Allende government was overthrown by the Chilean bourgeoisie was because there existed the threat that the working class would make a socialist revolution, despite the reformists in the Popular Unity. This is not to underplay the role played by US imperialism in aiding the Chilean bourgeoisie; it is merely to point out to those who still cling to manifestly erroneous theories, that the bourgeoisie in underdeveloped countries, when faced with a revolutionary working class movement, is not progressive in any sense whatsoever. It is profoundly reactionary. Whenever they felt they could benefit from it, for example, the political agents of the bourgeoisie turned from their institutional assaults on the Allende government to more direct forms of action. They organized street demonstrations, strikes, lockouts and sabotage; they conspired at every level to make Popular Unity government inoperable.

Direct action

Despite its reactionary character, it is still possible for the bourgeoisie to develop a considerable mass base among the petty bourgeoisie and even among some sections of the working class, as we have tried to show elsewhere in this chapter. This mass base was first brought out into the streets in December 1971 for the so-called March of the Empty Pots. These demonstrations by the opposition women, whose declared object was to draw attention to supposed food shortages, precipitated a great deal of street violence; so serious did the situation become in fact, that Allende felt constrained to call in the military, through the declaration of a state of emergency, in order to control the situation. (Allende was to have increasing recourse to military intervention in order to control opposition-inspired social disorders.) One thing should be clear, however; the marchers with the empty pots in their hands were predominantly middle and upper-middle class women who were very far from suffering food shortages. The poorer sections of society, on the other hand, the women of the working class, did not go on these demonstrations.

It is true that most consumer goods became increasingly scarce; it grew more and more difficult to come by toothpaste, butter, detergents, sugar, oil, cigarettes, rice and meat. At the same time, an enormous black market was developing where those who had the means could buy their food and household items. Naturally it was not the working class women, but the families of the middle and upper classes alone who could afford to buy their goods at inflated black market prices. But the picture was not entirely one-sided; towards the end of 1972, there was a growing number of relatively low income petty bourgeois families who were experiencing a drastic drop in their standard of living. Furthermore, this group was neither organized into People's Supply Committees, as were the workers, nor did it possess the financial resources of the middle class which would have enabled them to participate fully in the black market.

The most significant direct challenge to the government of Popular Unity came, however, with the employers' strike of October 1972. This offensive, like that of July 1973 which was to be a significant factor in bringing down Allende, brought the bourgeoisie face to face with the government in a direct confrontation.

The October strike did not come out of the blue any more than did the coup of September 1973; it was preceded in fact by two months of intensive organizational effort on the part of the opposition. In August the shopkeepers of Chile went on strike in protest against alleged government interference in free trade – in other words, a crack-down on the black market. As usual, extremist elements in the ranks of the opposition, like the thugs of Fatherland and Freedom, sought to create accompanying social disorder, as a result of which Santiago was once again declared an emergency zone. This particular threat blew over, however, due largely to lack of organizational strength on the part of the shopkeepers. It was followed in September, however, by widespread rumours of the existence of a plan to spread disorder sufficient to spark off a military coup; the atmosphere grew very tense, but the government was able to step in quickly enough to pre-empt a planned coup by enforcing the retirement of general Canales, who was to have played a leading part in it, and restoring the situation to a relative normality.

Nevertheless in October 1972 the bourgeoisie initiated a general strike which lasted until the middle of November. It was the first massive and serious assault by the bourgeoisie at this level, and led to a series of important changes in the Chilean political situation. The first step in the attack was a strike by lorry owners in the southern city of Punta Arenas. A recently nationalized factory had cancelled its contract with the (private) lorry owners' association and intended to purchase its own transport fleet. The displaced lorry owners struck in defence of their short-term economic interests, but strove to present the issue as one of free enterprise verses State interference. Within a matter of a few days, the strike became nationwide. The alacrity with which other sectors of the bourgeoisie and the middle classes lent their support to the strike clearly suggests that the strike was seen to involve questions of crucial significance. From the point of view of the Chilean bourgeoisie, the strike offered the opportunity of putting into action the strategy of exerting mounting economic as well as political pressure on the government. The aim was either to over-throw the government of Popular Unity or at the very least to hamstring its future activities and restrict the ability of the revolutionaries within UP to advance their policies.

In fact, the 'strike' was a lockout by the bulk of the capitalist class in Chile. Shopkeepers closed their stores, factories closed their gates, transportation ground to a halt as petrol became scarce, and the thugs of Fatherland and Freedom patrolled the streets searching out and browbeating those shop-keepers who had still not joined the strike. The government was facing its most serious crisis to date.

Of course, some sectors of society were hit harder by the strike than others. Many shops which were supposedly on strike opened their back doors to admit their bourgeois customers; middle class families, for example, simply increased the amount of goods they bought on the black market. The organized working class, on the other hand, responded by occupying many of the factories where lockouts had occurred and continued production. This was not always easy, since many of the technical personnel refused to return to work. Nevertheless in the majority of cases production returned to near-normal levels – an elegant testimony to workers' control of industry.

The strike of the shopkeepers, however, continued to be the central problem. The slowness of legal methods – the use of government inspectors to force shopkeepers to reopen their shops – could not answer the urgent need for supplies. So the organized working class again took the initiative by establishing parallel systems of retail distribution under democratic control. The possibility of a rising level of working class mobilization always remained in the back-ground, constituting a threat which the opposition, and particularly the military, had to take into account. One of the reasons why some elements within the military were unwilling to organize a coup at this stage may have been their reluctance to take on the working class in a direct confrontation. The mere presence of a working class waiting in the wings was a sobering consideration for many elements within the military. As a result, the trump card of the military coup was held back until other options had been exhausted.

As the strike dragged on, then, it became apparent that the bourgeoisie was not going to succeed either in toppling the government or in provoking a military coup. The issue now was what kind of concessions could be wrung from the government. Allende's anxiety to preserve national unity at any cost led him to make major concessions to the lorry owners at this crucial time. He acceded to their demands that no striker should be victimized (some among them who were public employees had been fired), and agreed to guarantee the rights of the small and medium bourgeoisie, conceding further that industries that did not form part of the monopoly area would be returned to their previous owners. In the light of these concessions, it was a simple matter for the lorry owners to present the outcome of the strike as a victory, or at least to claim that they had emerged undefeated.

At the same time, Allende accepted the inclusion of the generals in the cabinet; this had been one of the key demands of the opposition parties, supposedly in order to ensure a return to normality and to guarantee that the congressional elections of March 1973 would take place in an orderly way. Given the Allende government's commitment to the electoral road, of course, it was inconceivable that the elections should not have taken place in the proper manner. The real reason for the opposition insistence on the inclusion of the military was to provide a safeguard and a guarantee of some kind that UP would slow down the process of social transformation and act more like a normal social democratic government. In fact, the entry of the military into the cabinet in November 1972 did coincide with a period of relative political quiet and retrenchment.

1973 : **The final phase**

The March elections were clearly seen by all sectors of Chilean society as a decisive test for the regime. Should the opposition be able to increase its representation in congress to two-thirds of the seats it would then be able to impeach president Allende and legally overthrow the government. Even if this objective were not achieved – and as the election drew near electoral studies indicated that it would not be – the opposition contended that the election results could be construed as a sort of plebiscite, a popular judgement on the performance of the UP government. Within the ranks of the opposition, the PDC was concerned to see whether it was losing ground to the National Party by not taking a sufficiently hard line; any such indication would strengthen the right wing within the Christian Democratic Party.

As it turned out, the UP won 44% of the vote – a result far exceeding most expectations whether on the right or on the left. Although the opposition had received more than half the votes, the election was clearly a victory for the UP, indicating that the UP had maintained and if anything increased its support amongst the working class and peasantry. Consequently, the Right did not gain a two-thirds majority in the congress and the constitutional stalemate continued.

Throughout most of this chapter we have referred to the opposition and the bourgeoisie as if these were homogeneous entities. In fact, the bourgeois opposition to the Popular Unity government was organized into a number of political parties and organizations of professionals and employers. The political positions of these parties diverged in a number of important ways since they frequently represented different fractions of the ruling groups. The National Party, representing the old established oligarchy, enjoyed strong support from the great landowners, and generally took a more intransigent line than did the PDC, which represented more 'modern' sectors of the bourgeoisie. However, the actions of the various oppositional organizations tended to dovetail together and complement one another. Each organization has necessarily to take cognisance of the political positions adopted by the others and could not move too far politically without running the risk of losing some of its base to other parties. This was particularly true in the case of the Christian Democratic party, which was seriously constrained in any move towards rapprochement with the UP by fear of losing ground to the National Party. Consequently the PDC had continually to move to the right as Chilean politics polarized so as not to lose to the National Party its predominance within the opposition. To the right of the National Party stood a number of Fascist and neo-Fascist groups of considerable political importance. In some cases members of these organizations held dual membership in the National Party.

Fatherland and Freedom (*Patria y Libertad*) was quite clearly the largest and most influential of the various Fascist groups in Chile. It first came to public prominence during the demonstrations against Fidel Castro's visit in November and December 1971, and played an important part in provoking the street violence that followed those demonstrations. Fatherland and Freedom had an explicitly corporatist view of how the State should act and regarded itself as a movement for 'national regeneration'. Unlike the classic European Fascist movements, it did not have a sizeable following among the unemployed and the *lumpen*. It was by no means a mass party, and thus could never pose the question of the seizure of State power as the culmination of its own activities. It must be seen, then, as the most reactionary wing of the bourgeoisie. Nevertheless, it did employ Fascist methods in its daily political action; its paramilitary forces provided the shock troops for the mass demonstrations of the bourgeois parties, while operating at the same time as a small band of men dedicated to essentially conspiratorial ends: terrorism and sabotage. Its influence in the armed forces is hard to estimate, but there can be little doubt that it did have an influence quite disproportionate to its numerical strength. There is overwhelming evidence that it was deeply implicated in the uprising of 29 June

1973; several of its militants were involved in the actual rising itself as snipers in the area of the presidential palace, and its leaders fled to foreign embassies as it became clear that the attempted coup had failed.

Fatherland and Freedom's most important activities were the organization of gun-running from Argentina and the organization and training of military units in the south of Chile and in Bolivia. It seems clear, furthermore, that they had close ties with the large landowners in the South. In the cities, it was extremely active in the campaign to organize the middle-class neighbourhoods into self-defence units on a block by block basis. This form of organization was called PROTECO; its primary aim was to organize neighbourhood defence against a supposed left-wing threat. The fact that the left-wing parties had no intention of ever conducting a pogrom of any kind in middle class areas did not prevent Fatherland and Freedom from whipping up a level of hysteria which led to the formation of a number of PROTECO committees in several upper- and middle-class suburbs of Santiago. In the event, their main functions were to compile lists of politically unreliable people in the neighbourhood and to keep watch on the movement of strangers in the locality. In a word, PROTECO represented the organization of the bourgeoisie and petty bourgeoisie on a war footing.

There existed in addition to the overtly political organizations of the opposition, a number of professional and employers' associations which were to play a significant role in the events of the final months. In Chile these organizations are known as *gremios*. The *gremios* organized a wide range of business interests. At one level they grouped together numbers of small businessmen in trade associations whose prime economic function was interest group representation in bargaining with the government and trade unions. At another level the *gremios* grouped together important sections of the Chilean ruling class to articulate common economic and political interests. These include the National Agricultural Association (SNA-*Sociedad Nacional de Agricultura*) and the Association for Industrial Development (SOFOFA-*Sociedad de Fomento Fabril*). These *gremios* represented the interests of big business and the large landowners and were the equivalent of a chamber of commerce. From the point of view of the opposition, the utility of the *gremio* system is that it facilitated the development of a sense of the identity of interest between small businessmen and professionals on the one hand, and the large industrialists and wealthy landowners on the other.

In addition, the PDC had a certain following among sectors of the working class and peasantry. This provided the basis for a demagogic campaign to unite these disparate class segments into a syndicalist movement with clear corporatist overtones. Behind this corporate-syndicalist front the opposition was able to claim that it represented a non-political movement of all sectors of society aimed at overthrowing the totalitarian menace of the UP. The movement was, of course, little more than an employers' organization, representing the interests of the bourgeoisie and weighted by professionals and petty-

bourgeois groups. Despite the class bias of the oppositional syndicalist movement, it did provide some kind of mass base for the employers' strikes of 1972
and 1973, as well as an excellent ideological cover to obfuscate the defence of the
class interests of the bourgeoisie.

Both Fatherland and Freedom and the National Party had come out openly
in favour of a military coup early in 1973. *El Mercurio* of 17 June – i.e. before
the attempted coup of 29 June – reported that the official position of the
National Party was that Allende was no longer the constitutional president of
Chile because the Constitution had been broken, and drew the conclusion that
'no-one is obliged to respect or obey a government which had ceased to be
legitimate'. And under the right-wing leadership of Aylwin and Frei the
Christian Democratic Party was not far behind in deciding that the only
solution would be a military one.[8]

Already in June 1973 the PDC had formed an Armed Services Group with
the express intention of organizing its supporters within the military. But like
the National Party, it was necessary for the PDC to demonstrate that the
Allende government had in fact seriously infringed the Constitution. For the
Christian Democrats the key issue was the fate of the Hamilton-Fuentealba
constitutional reform. Early in June the party gave notice that unless Allende
passed the constitutional reform in its entirety into law the Christian Democrats
would regard the Constitution as having been broken and the government as
illegal. According to reports in *El Mercurio* and *La Prensa* for 1 June, a partial
promulgation would be regarded by the Christian Democrats as unconstitutional.

As Allende temporized and played for time, the attitude of the PDC leadership hardened. By mid-July the president of the PDC, Patricio Aylwin, was
reported by *El Mercurio* as saying that 'in Chile there exist armed groups, and
the laws and Constitution are broken'.

From then on it was only a matter of time as the denunciations piled up.
By 22 August the Chamber of Deputies (dominated by the Christian Democrats and the National Party) had openly called on the armed forces to leave the
cabinet and to take action to 'ensure the essential bases for democratic harmony
(*convivencia*) among the Chilean people'. The events after 11 September were to
show what the armed forces understood by that call to do 'their patriotic duty'.

Throughout this chapter we have tried to show how the Chilean bourgeoisie reacted to the popular victory of 1970 and how it increasingly came to
favour a military coup to overthrow Popular Unity. Unless Allende completely capitulated to their terms, the bourgeoisie would, and did generate the
conditions whereby a military coup was on the order of the day. When the
crunch came, the bourgeoisie knew that it could count on the military to defend
bourgeois society. In this complex historical process, American imperialism
played an important role. Nevertheless, this role was, in its most fundamental
aspects, a subsidiary one. The struggle in Chile was between socialism and
capitalism, between the working class and its allies and the bourgeoisie and its

allies. Any other way of looking at the events of those three years fundamentally distorts reality. To view the overthrow of the UP government, for example, as a result of the meddling of US imperialism in the constitutional affairs of a sovereign nation, while correct as far as it goes, fails to account for the widespread resistance of the Chilean bourgeoisie and the mass base they were able to develop amongst sectors of the middle classes. For this opposition of the bourgeoisie and middle classes would have occurred anyway, irrespective of what US policy had been. The lesson is an old and a very simple one. 'No ruling class in history has ever willingly surrendered its privileges.'

6 The Economic Crisis

Introduction

There can be no doubt that the profound economic crisis which beset Chile in 1972 and 1973 was a contributory factor to the coup of 11 September, 1973. The widespread shortages, the necessity to queue for hours for certain basic goods, the frustration of not being able to obtain crucial spare parts and repairs, the frequency of strikes, and an uncontrollable inflation – all these helped to create a climate propitious for a military intervention to put an end to the 'chaos'. The aim of the Chilean Right was, of course, to produce precisely the sort of 'chaos' which would encourage a military coup. In this they succeeded. It is impossible to deal with the Chilean economic crisis as if it were something amenable to a technocratic solution. The roots of the crisis were political, and the solution to the crisis could only be political. It is only international agency and banking reports which try to pretend otherwise.

Nevertheless, although a primary cause of the economic crisis was the right-wing offensive, UP's own economic strategy and tactics were bedevilled by problems of economic mismanagement and inconsistencies. It is true that any society which attempts a radical transformation of its structure must expect some economic disorder. For example, all major historical reforms of the land tenure structure have, during the period of reform, led to a decline in marketed agricultural production. The Chilean agrarian reform, although not unsuccessful from the point of view of maintaining production, was no exception to this historical rule. And in general to end the economic irrationalities of capitalism involves in the short run a destruction of a production system which cannot be replaced quickly. In addition, the new organizational forms struggling to replace the former capitalist organizations inevitably suffer from the inefficiencies of new and untried forms of organization. Cuba, for example, fifteen years after its revolution, is still struggling with these problems.

It is important to note that economic policy making under Popular Unity had to play a peculiar role. In all those countries which are generally called socialist, the seizure and consolidation of power came prior to the formulation of an economic strategy for transforming the economy. In such cases the formulation of economic policies prior to power was relatively unimportant. But under Popular Unity short-term economic policies had to play the role of the spear-head of the attack for the battle for power. This logically flows from the overall strategy of a peaceful, parliamentary road to socialism. For if mass mobilization and a direct, if necessarily armed, assault on the citadels of bourgeois power are excluded, then control of the direction of the economy is a crucial first step in weakening the power of the bourgeoisie. If the capitalists maintain effective control of the economy, then the State sector is likely to become increasingly subordinate to their overall interests. The British Labour Party in power is a striking confirmation of this.

In Chile economic policy making formed an integral part of the battle for power. Any analysis which ignores this as an objective of Popular Unity and applies conventional economic performance criteria misunderstands the role economic policies were meant to play. Given the policy of isolating and defeating only a part of the bourgeoisie – the monopolist, foreign and *latifundista* interests – the crucial economic policies were thought to be to extend the State control of the economy and to enlarge the support of the UP, particularly by winning over the 'progressive' bourgeoisie, the petty bourgeoisie and the middle sectors, many of whom had voted for the opposition parties. It was also considered necessary to cement the support of the Chilean working class and peasantry, not all of whom voted for Popular Unity, but the majority of whom made up the bulk of UP supporters. Hence the UP tried to satisfy the demands of all these groups in its first year. But the redistribution and consumption policies of the UP could only be short-term, for in a poor country like Chile the amount of resources available for redistribution for immediate consumption are limited. Such a policy could only make sense if it altered the correlation of class forces in favour of the working class, and allowed the workers to move towards winning the battle for power.

So what happened? As analysed in Chapter 4 the initial economic strategy of income redistribution as a means of stimulating production and winning political support had a number of unintended effects. The Keynesian reflation of the economy via an expansion of government expenditure, employment creation, and an increase in wages, boosted effective demand. There is no doubt that the increase in demand was greater than intended. Large sectors of the organized working class expected the advent of Popular Unity to herald the occasion for a much higher level of real wages. Faced with a weakened capitalist class and a government which felt that it had to satisfy some of those expectations, the share of the wage and salary earning sector in the national income increased by about 24.6%. The 'boom' of Popular Unity's first year also favoured all other sectors of the population except those being taken over or faced with effective price controls. Nevertheless, there was a clear crisis of confidence on the part of the capitalist class. Their expectations *qua* class were that Popular Unity heralded an attack on them: the take-overs and the decline in profit rates were a signal of worse to come. They were therefore unwilling to invest. They were not, however, unwilling to consume. 1971 was then a year of increased consumption for nearly everyone. The increase in consumption was met partly from increased production, especially from the taking-up of excess capacity, but it was mainly met from imports and from stocks and investment funds. So, during 1972 consumer demand no longer worked towards stimulating growth as unused capacity and stocks were fully utilized, for very little new investment appeared, and there was a shortage of foreign exchange to import machinery and spare parts. Instead there were bottlenecks in production and distribution which inhibited the translation of demand into increased production, resulting in inflationary pressures and shortages.

From 1972 onwards Popular Unity faced a precarious political and economic situation. Workers clearly did not expect the rate of increase of wages to continue, but what they would resist were attempts to reduce their real wages in an effort, a necessary effort, to increase the rate of investment. The middle classes, whose standard of living had also increased in 1971, but who found that a few items were becoming scarcer as a result of the increased consumption of the workers, were also opposed to any attempt to make them pay for an increase in the rate of investment. And the Right, sensing that UP had failed to win these sectors, mounted a political and economic offensive which, as economic difficulties increased, would successfully turn many of the middle sectors into a mass base for a frontal assault on Popular Unity. Meanwhile, the bourgeoisie got its funds as quickly as possible out of Chile.

In economistic terms the crucial problems were to increase the domestic supply of goods to match demand, to increase the supply of foreign exchange, and to achieve an orderly functioning of the production system. But behind these economistic phrases lay deep political problems. To increase supply required a steady flow of spare parts and repairs and an increase in investment. However, it was unlikely that the capitalist class would channel their savings and profits into increased investment, unless UP gave up its programme and satisfied them that the capitalist mode of production would remain intact. To increase the supply of foreign exchange – a necessity if spare parts, repairs, and new machinery were to flow in to increase production – required either an increase in export earnings, a decrease in imports, or an inflow of foreign capital. However, the nationalization of copper and the general anti-imperialist stance adopted by Popular Unity meant that foreign capital from the hitherto main source, the USA, was likely to cease. Alternative sources of foreign capital, the socialist bloc and other countries, were unlikely to adequately fill the gap left by the withdrawal of US capital. The distribution policies of the first year had led to an increase in food consumption, whilst the implementation of the agrarian reform law meant that agricultural production would be unlikely to be able to satisfy that demand. To reduce imports would in effect have meant reducing the imports of foodstuffs and thus adding to the shortages resulting from the increase in demand. To increase export earnings basically meant that either the price of copper increased (something outside UP's control) or the production of copper increased. But, although the latter was part of UP's plan, the nationalization of copper had led to a shortage of certain technical and managerial staff and other problems which meant that in the short run increased production was unlikely. Thus, after the first year, to keep the economy growing without inflation required a number of very difficult political and economic decisions. These decisions would have had to be taken even if the working class had won the battle for power. The decisions were made doubly difficult by the fact that the battle for power was unresolved.

Contrary to the bleatings of international bankers, the 'harsh' decisions required did not include restoring 'labour discipline' by imposing a rigid hierarchical order on labour, ('labour discipline' in terms of production seems to have been highest in those firms which had the greatest degree of participation and political consciousness), but they did involve 'rationalizing' the production and distribution system: balancing supply and demand, using 'prices' to reflect priorities, reducing total consumption (this did not necessarily mean reducing the consumption levels of the poor) so as to increase the surplus available for investment, and reducing the money supply and the fiscal deficit. But, as pointed out, the first year policies had only marginally altered the balance of class forces. Important and significant inroads had been made into the power of the capitalist class, both foreign and Chilean, but their basic institutions remained; they were still a major force within the economy, and after the initial confusion and weakness they had united and built up a considerable mass base which could be used to launch an offensive against the UP. Faced with the dilemma of a powerful opposition and an expectant working class, Popular Unity seemed incapable of imposing any coherent economic policy. It was not that they were unaware of the need to increase production. This need was the main focus of the Communist Party's campaign ('Production is also Revolution' as their poster put it) even when it became clear that the Right was planning and encouraging a coup. It was not that UP lacked competent economists able to devise technical solutions. It was that the UP lacked the power to implement its policies. As a consequence, at a time when firm and decisive policies were needed, the economy simply drifted.

Government Proposals for the Economy

Frequent attempts were made by the government to stop the drift into economic chaos; none succeeded. As in the political sphere, there emerged two divergent strategies within Popular Unity on how to deal with the economic problems. The Cordillera Regional Committee of the Socialist Party summed up these two strategies in March 1973 as follows:[1]

> The revolutionary tendency considers that the present economic problems are the result of a struggle against imperialism and the sharpening of the class struggle, and that scarcity of goods, the black market and speculation must be fought by establishing a war economy (which would entail rationing certain articles of mass consumption) and by popular organizations taking control over supplies for workers. On the other hand, the reformists believe that existing problems can be solved through greater efficiency in production, reorganizing the public finances, and regaining the confidence of the national bourgeoisie in order to give the capitalist dynamic new life.

The revolutionary tendency argues that it is necessary to extend the socialized sector of industry, this being a question of life or death, as it implies the passing of real power into the hands of the workers. The reformists argue that to extend nationalization of industries beyond the original list of 90 monopolies can only provoke a crisis in the whole Chilean process, by alienating medium-sized producers. . . .

In periods of relative social calm the reformist strategy generally won out. But in the periods when the workers had to defend their gains from right-wing attacks, the revolutionary strategy generally came to the fore as the workers often occupied their factories and demanded an acceleration of the process. By September of 1973, the capitalist dynamic had not been given new life, but neither had the production system been reorganized under anything remotely resembling a rationally planned economy. The economy had drifted into chaos.

Popular Unity was slow to realize and even slower to admit that it was in the midst of an economic crisis. The speech of Américo Zorilla, the Minister of Finance, in November 1971 outlining the government's objectives for 1972 gave little indication of the problems the government was to face. And it was not until December 1971 that the government indirectly admitted that something was wrong with its economic policies. The policy of a fixed, overvalued exchange rate throughout 1971 had encouraged imports. In December 1971 the government in effect devalued by creating six exchange rates ranging from food and petroleum to luxury goods. Nevertheless, although food imports had increased very rapidly in 1971, the government still kept the exchange rate very low on the imports of food – in effect subsidizing food imports and encouraging their consumption.

In February 1972 the government again promised immunity from expropriation for the 35,000 or so small industrial firms in Chile unless they went bankrupt or closed. But at the same time the Minister of the Economy, Pedro Vuskovic, advocated the need to take over as rapidly as possible the large industrial firms. In this he was supported by the Socialist Party; but the Communist Party, although in favour of the takeovers of the industrial monopolies, began to urge caution, particularly as the economy was running into bigger and bigger problems. In June of 1972 Allende changed the two ministers who had been in charge of economic policies since the beginning. The changes – Pedro Vuskovic was replaced by Carlos Matus as Minister of Economy and Américo Zorilla was replaced by Orlando Millas as Finance Minister – were widely regarded as a victory for the more moderate, cautious policies advocated by the Communist Party.

By the middle of 1972 it was clear that the two main economic problems facing Popular Unity were shortages and inflation. As argued earlier, one consequence of the economic policies of the first year of UP was a monetary demand in excess of available supply. In a belated effort to increase the supply of goods and to cut back demand the government raised the prices of most goods except foodstuffs in the beginning of August, and raised the price of foodstuffs, on some items by over a 100%, on 18th August. But this, of course, created a dilemma for UP. To raise prices without increasing wages is to cut the standard of living of the workers. In a capitalist economy it also increases the profits of the capitalists, and if, as in Chile, there were serious doubts whether the capitalists would invest to expand future production, then such a policy creates an even bigger dilemma. Elections were not far off, and with the Christian Democrats demogogically demanding higher wages for the workers and attacking the government, UP felt that it had to compensate the wage and salary earners immediately for the increase in prices. A 700 escudo bonus was awarded on 18 September, the Chilean National Day of Independence holiday, the *reajuste* – the annual readjustment of wages and salaries to compensate for the year's inflation – was brought forward to October, giving a 100% readjust-ment to all except the higher income scales, and prices were frozen until the congressional election of March 1973. Although politically understandable, the increase in prices followed by a corresponding increase in wages did nothing to solve the economic problems facing the country: all it did was to fuel inflation.

For a brief moment it looked as if the attempt by Kennecott Copper Corporation to embargo payment on a shipment of Chilean copper through a French court had provided the opportunity for tough economic measures to counter the economic crisis. In a speech in Valdivia, President Allende claimed that he was going to put the economy on a 'war footing' to counteract Kennecott's actions, and to deal with the deteriorating situation in the Chilean balance of payments and the agrarian sector. Allende pointed out that because agricultural production was not keeping pace with demand, the government had to import $350 million worth of foodstuffs – the size of the balance of payments deficit. Many observers took Allende's speech to mean that the government would shortly introduce rationing as one of the measures for putting the economy on a 'war footing'.

But the October 1972 general strike of the bourgeoisie intervened before anything could be done. Economically the effects of this strike were to turn a deteriorating economic situation into a catastrophic one. The Chilean working class, however, emerged from the strike better organized, well-disciplined, confident that they could run the economy, and putting forward demands that were not for higher wages but for a series of measures to deal with the economic crisis. Lamentably, the government largely ignored these demands, and, with the military in the cabinet, pursued a policy of 'social peace' by, in effect, freezing the situation. The economy then just continued its downward drift.

However, demands for rationing did become more persistent. In November the Christian Left issued a sharp statement criticizing the government for not introducing rationing, and arguing that rationing was both inevitable and desirable and that food imports should be cut. In January a government report urged Allende to introduce rationing. The report argued that the amount of food available had increased by 27% in the two years of Popular Unity, and that nevertheless food stocks available in the shops had declined because of inadequate infrastructure – transport, storage, etc., the large and uncontrolled increase in demand, hoarding, and the emergence of a black market which, according to the report, halved the amount of goods available through the official distribution network. Partly in response to the report the new Minister of Finance, Fernando Flores, introduced a plan for the state monopolization of the distribution and marketing of agricultural production, i.e. a form of wholesale but not retail rationing. The Right mounted a massive campaign against the plan as destroying democracy, as 'political control via the stomach', and tried to turn the plan into a major election issue. In fact, the government already controlled a large part of the distribution and selling of foodstuffs. The real problem was that of implementing the official controls, and wiping out the black market. Flores's proposal that the private producers should legally be obliged to sell their products to government agencies, if enforced, would have helped to weaken the black market. But without rationing at both the wholesale and retail stages, the black market would continue. And the Government never felt politically able to introduce an effective form of rationing.

It was not really until after the March elections that the Popular Unity government returned to the problem of defining and implementing a coherent economic policy to deal with the serious economic situation. Not surprisingly the Communist Party placed strong emphasis on the need for a sound economic policy to ensure victory in the 1976 presidential elections. Shortly after the March elections the Communist Party proposed a series of measures to deal with the economy. Among these measures were plans to secure the profitability of the state enterprises, aiming at making them self-financing, to link wage increases to productivity increases, and to use a mixture of material and moral incentives to increase production. Greater participation by the workers in the management of the economy was also emphasized – though the report made it clear that it considered this should be mainly confined to the plant level.

Given the extent of the economic crisis, and the way in which the crisis was adversely affecting the political position, it is surprising how little was done between the March elections of 1973 and the attempted coup of June 1973. In his presidential message to congress on 21 May, Allende described the main economic objectives of the government as (1) to establish a single and centralized direction for the economy, (2) to ensure that the economy functioned in a planned way, (3) to guarantee the greatest democratic participation of the masses. An anti-inflation programme was outlined involving higher taxes, especially on property, a limit to the money supply, and a more realistic price policy, but in general the parts of his speech dealing with the economy consisted of vague generalizations and in no way amounted to a coherent policy.

Clearly all the parties of Popular Unity and the economic ministries were involved in detailed discussions and the drawing-up of economic plans to deal with the economic crisis. Both the Communist and Socialist Party criticized the wage policies whereby wage and salary earners received a readjustment for the increase in the cost of living index every four months or so. The Communist Party advocated a return to annual wage readjustments, and the Socialist Party wanted wage policies to be linked to production. Detailed investment plans, the planning of foreign exchange, plans for the delivery of seeds and fertilizers to farmers and so on, were prepared. But it seemed to take the attempted coup of 29 June to prod the government into announcing a new economic plan to deal with the situation. The plan, which consisted of sixteen detailed points covering pricing policy, wage policy, distribution, planning, financial controls in the social property area, was the first overall coherent statement on economic policy since the initial economic strategy. But it came too late. Through the months of July and August the tempo of the right-wing offensives increased. The government was never given the opportunity to see if its emergency plan would work. And it was left to the military junta to implement its 'free market' solution to the economic crisis.

What Happened to the Economy?

The above sections outlined some of the difficulties encountered by Popular Unity in adopting and implementing policies to deal with the economic crisis. This section is intended to give a very general survey of some of the main features of the Chilean economy from 1970 up to 1974. Only two sectors, agriculture and the foreign sector, and one problem, inflation, will be dealt with in any detail. The agrarian sector will be analysed in some detail mainly because it has not received much attention elsewhere in this book and because agricultural production is crucial for an understanding of the economic crisis; the foreign sector because of the emphasis often placed on the 'informal blockade'; and inflation because of its political importance. Although the presentation divides up the economy into neat little boxes, it should be emphasized that the economy is a totality in which each part influences the performance of the other.

As many statistics will be presented it is worth emphasizing that these are probably more unreliable than the already unreliable statistics encountered in any developing country. The rate of inflation in Chile made any accounting difficult; there was a large black market, much of whose produce did not appear in official statistics; and given the political tensions, both sides, the Left and the Right, had an interest in presenting what was happening to the economy in a way favourable to themselves. The figures used in this chapter are mainly ones given officially after the coup of 11 September. They have not been checked for accuracy, and should therefore be treated as no more than rough guides of probable trends. They are not a definitive statement on the performance of the Chilean economy.

With these provisos, the following table summarizes the main economic indicators for 1970 to 1973. All the figures for 1973 are officially provisional.

Chile: Overall Economic Indicators 1966-1973

GROSS DOMESTIC PRODUCT

	percentage variation			
	annual average 1966-70	1971	1972	1973c
1. Total GDP	3.7	8.3	1.6	—5.7
2. Sectoral GDP				
a. Agriculture and Livestock and Fisheries	2.5	5.1	—3.6	—16.1
b. Mining	5.0	1.7	—6.5	0.6
c. Industry	3.3	12.9	3.1	—8.4
d. Construction	1.4	9.5	—10.6	—28.1
e. Other sectors	4.1	7.9	4.6	—1.7

CONSUMPTION AND INVESTMENT

1. Total consumption	3.1	14.7	0.9	—2.4
2. Gross fixed investment/GDP (coefficient)	15.5	14.3	13.6	11.4

COPPER

	1971	1972	percentage variation	1973	percentage variation
Production (thousands of m.t.*) ..	708	717	1.6	746.8	4.2
Large-scale mining (thousands of m.t.)	571	593	3.09	615.9	3.9
Small- and medium-scale mining (thousands of m.t.)	137	124	—8.0	130.9	5.6
CIF Price – Electrolytic (c per pound)	48.5	47.8	—1.4	80.8	69.0
Exports (value in millions of US$)	695	647	—7.3	1125.0	73.8

*m.t.= metric tons.

INTERNATIONAL FINANCE

	balance in millions of US$			
	1970	1971	1972	1973c
Trade balance	138.7	—110.4	—497.8	—318.7
Net financial services	—196.1	—89.8	—116.6	—85.0
Balance on current account ..	—57.4	—200.2	—614.6	—403.7
Net movements of autonomous capital	148.5	—103.5	295.7	150.5
Balance of payments	91.1	—309.0	—318.9	—253.2
Foreign exchange reserves ..	343.2	34.5	—293.6a	—547.0b
Exchange rate (E° for one US$) ..	11.55	12.41	19.53	94.2c

FISCAL SITUATION

			real variation		
		1972	1973c	1971-2	1972-3
		(In millions of E°)		(%)	(%)
1. Current revenue	.. ..	38.4	154.0	—15.0	—40.7
2. Total expenditures	.. ..	65.0	328.0	—5.7	—25.3
3. Deficit:					
i. Absolute value	.. ..	26.6	174.0	12.8	—3.1
ii. Ratio to expenditures	..	40.9	53.0		

MONETARY SITUATION

	percentage variation			
	annual average			
	1966-70	1971	1972	1973c
1. Money in the private sector ..	40.0	113.8	151.8	365.1
2. Public sector money in circulation	62.2	111.8	276.3	
3. Quasi-money (general total) ..	46.1	68.1	119.8	120.1

PRICES, WAGES, AND EMPLOYMENT

1. Consumer prices: annual average	26.0	20.1	88.8	575.3
December of each year	—	22.1	210.6	681.6
2. Wholesale prices: annual average	29.6	17.9	70.0	n.d.
December of each year	—	21.4	143.3	n.d.
3. Wages and salaries: April of each				
year	38.1	53.0	40.3	176.1
October of each year	—	51.9	121.2	340.8
	1970	1971	1972	1973
4. Rate of unemployment in Greater Santiago: December of each year	8.3	3.8	3.6	n.d.
5. Share of wages and salaries in national income	54.9	65.8	59-63c	n.d.

a. Excludes renegotiation of external debt US$152.4.
b. Excludes renegotiation of external debt US$168.7.
c. Preliminary figures.

Sources: National Planning Office (ODEPLAN), Central Bank of Chile, National Institute Statistics, Budget Office of the Ministry of Treasury, CODELCO, Institute of Economics of the University of Chile, and the OAS Secretariat.

The above figures give some indication of the extent of the economic problems between 1970 and 1973; a decline in production, investment, consumption and foreign exchange; an increase in imports, the money supply and the cost of living index. The only bright spot in the 1973 economic horizon was the increase in the price of copper. A closer look at some of these indicators will help explain the complexity of this economic crisis.

Manufacturing

Chilean manufacturing increased rapidly in 1971, increased slightly in 1972, and declined in 1973.

Manufacturing Production

					percentage variation		
Month					71–70	72–71	73–72[1]
January	..	..	..	..	—2.2	19.9	—2.3
February	..	..	..	..	1.4	19.3	1.4
March	..	..	..	..	6.9	12.8	3.1
April ..	..	..	..	..	1.3	14.6	—7.7
May ..	..	..	..	..	17.1	6.1	—6.2
June ..	..	..	..	..	9.8	4.6	—8.7
July ..	..	..	..	..	7.8	2.9	—9.3
August	..	..	..	..	17.2	1.0	—
September	..	..	..	..	30.2	—8.8	—
October	..	..	..	..	21.1	—8.3	—
November	..	..	..	..	30.8	—8.8	—
December	..	..	..	..	31.3	—6.2	—
Year ..	..	..	..	..	14.7	2.8	—8.0[2]

1. Provisional estimate.
2. Projection as of 30/7/73.

Source: National Institute of Statistics.

As can be seen from the above table the rate of growth of manufacturing production had declined by May of 1972, and dropped substantially by September of 1972.

By September of 1972 it seems that most spare industrial capacity had been utilized, and available stocks consumed. For industrial production to pick up it was necessary for capacity to be increased with new investments, and for existing industrial capacity to be renovated with the import of spare parts for machinery and equipment; neither happened. With profit margins continuing to be cut, with fear and uncertainty over government policies, and with the intention of creating economic chaos to bring down the government, private industrialists refused to invest or replace existing machinery. The social property area (which controlled about 22% of industrial production) failed to compensate for the decline in private sector investment. In fact, the social property area, retarded by investment problems and by the increasing difficulty in obtaining spare parts and replacing antiquated machinery due to the chronic shortage of foreign exchange, generated increasing deficits instead of surpluses.

From October of 1972 onwards the class struggle was intensified as the Right launched a series of major offensives. These offensives, general strikes, partial strikes, short-stoppages, bombings, killings, and sabotage, were very effective in disrupting production. Not surprisingly, given the state of uncertainty, nobody in the private sector was willing to risk new investment.

In the face of these offensives, particularly during the October 1972 strike and after the attempted coup of June 1973, the workers took over large numbers of factories, some of which were later returned to their former owners. During the first eight months of 1973, for example, the number of industries 'taken over' rose from 202 to 508.

The effects of take-overs on production is not clear; some were a response by the workers to prevent economic sabotage by the capitalists and the right-wing, and as such it is likely that production would have declined even further without the take-over. One of the few studies on production and productivity in the social property area claims that worker productivity increased or remained steady in 32 out of 40 socialized factories surveyed, and that production and productivity were positively correlated with the degree of worker participation.[2] Nevertheless, taken as a whole it is likely that the immediate effects of the take-overs in 1973 was to reduce production.

Mining

The success of much of UP's financial programme depended on an expansion of copper production and a continuing high level of copper prices. The assumption was that the nationalization of the US copper companies without compensation would save Chile some hundreds of millions of dollars in profit and other remittances, and would not seriously disrupt either the production or marketing of copper. The surplus from copper was to be used for much-needed investment in agriculture and other sectors of the economy.

Production of copper did increase over the three years of Popular Unity, although that of other minerals products, notably iron and coal, decreased in the 1972 to 1973 period.

Mining Production

Mineral	1970	1971	1972	1973*	1972-3	Changes 12 month Average Sept. 1973
		(in thousands of metric tons)				
Copper	691.6	708.3	716.7	746.8	4.2	
a. Large-scale mining ..	540.5	571.3	592.5	615.9	3.9	—2.8
b. Medium and small-scale mining	151.1	137.0	124.2	130.9	5.3	—0.4a
Saltpetre	669.3	832.2	709.2	676.1	—4.7	—12.0
Iodine	2.2	2.6	2.1	2.2	4.8	9.2
Iron	11264.9	11227.6	8630.9	9314.2	7.9	—1.7
Coal	1509.8	1622.9	1457.7	1303.4	—10.6	—12.6

*Provisional figures.
a. June 1972.

Source: Central Bank of Chile.

But production was much less than envisaged. The 1967 copper investment programme, for example, envisaged a production of 900,000 tons of copper in 1972: the actual figure was 717,000 tons. By 1970 it was already clear that the projected production figure would not be reached. And not surprisingly, in the short run, the nationalization of copper under Popular Unity did affect production. Some skilled technicians left, the size of the labour force increased and labour discipline declined, and workers complained that some of the newly appointed supervisory staff were inefficient and appointed more for political reasons than their technical or administrative skills. There were also technical difficulties resulting from the destructive way in which the US copper companies left the mines, and from difficulties in obtaining machinery and spare parts from the USA. But paradoxically, the most disruptive factor in production was probably strikes, particularly the crippling El Teniente strike of 1973. However, the three years of Popular Unity did show that Chile could both produce and market her copper without the US mining companies.

As well as the failure to achieve the anticipated production levels, UP was hit by the fall in the price of copper – a factor over which Chile has no control. The price of copper fell from 57.7 US cents per lb. in 1970 to 48.5 cents per lb. in 1971, to 47.8 cents per lb. in 1972. Codelco, the Chilean copper agency, estimated that the fall in the price of copper cost Chile about $500 million in 1971 and 1972. Although the price of copper increased in 1973 to 80.8 cents per lb., the benefits of this increase accrued more to the military junta than to Popular Unity, because of the crippling effects on production of the El Teniente strike and other disruptions.

Overall, the results in the mining sector were less than had been anticipated, but at least a secure foundation had been laid for the main wealth of Chile to remain in the hands of Chile. Not even the extreme Right in Chile would want to reverse that.

Agriculture

The rural situation has not received detailed analysis elsewhere in this book because, although there were important developments in the agrarian sector, the fate of the Chilean revolution was determined primarily by the developing class struggle between the urban working class and the bourgeoisie, and by the response of the armed forces to these developments.

Chile after all is not a country with a massive peasantry. Only 25.8% of the population were in agriculture in 1970 (compared with 47.5% in 1940). The contribution of agriculture to G.N.P. was low, only about 7.5% in 1970. Production *per capita* in agriculture had actually declined by about 5% between 1940 and 1970; and whereas Chile exported agricultural produce worth $16.2 million and imported $21.2 million in 1940, it was by 1970 exporting only $32.1 million and importing $178.2 million. Thus, although there had been a trend towards the commercialization of agriculture which resulted in the steady proletarianization of the peasantry, agriculture still remained inefficient, and a major criticism advanced by progressive sectors of the bourgeoisie was that the relative backwardness and inefficiency of the *latifundia* system of agriculture was a major obstacle to the development of a dynamic capitalism in Chile.

At the same time, the progressive proletarianization of the Chilean peasantry was eroding the political and social control exerted by the large landowners over their workers, and the ruling class feared that it might face increasing peasant discontent. The forms of this discontent varied: ranging from the demands of the Mapuche Indians in the south for the return of their rights to land taken from them by the spread of agrarian capitalism, to the right to form trade unions and bargain for higher wages.

In order to meet this economic and political challenge, the Christian Democrat government of Frei had passed a land reform law in 1967 making it possible to expropriate the large *latifundias* and turn them into peasant co-operatives, *asentamientos*. After an initial period as co-operatives, the peasants were to be allowed to divide up the land into individual parcels if they so wished. This, together with the unionization campaign initiated by the Christian Democrats would, it was hoped, create a political clientele and a stable class of small peasant proprietors which would furnish a powerful social base for Christian Democracy as well as modernizing agriculture.

Certain provisions of the land reform law, which was explicitly designed to safeguard the interests of the efficient landowners, were intended to ensure both the modernization of agriculture and the containment of the growing peasant movement. These provisions were as follows:

(1) the minimum ceiling for expropriation was set at the equivalent of 200 acres of good irrigated land. This left untouched several thousand farms of between 100 and 200 basic irrigated acres (or its equivalent, allowing for variations in soil quality, etc.) which formed the base for the medium-sized agrarian bourgeoisie.

(2) unless it could be shown that the farm to be expropriated was cultivated inefficiently, the landowner could be awarded a 'reserve' of land of up to 200 acres, which would remain in his possession. This reserve was frequently the best part of the farm.

(3) all the animals and machinery were to remain in the landowner's possession, and he was to be compensated in cash for all recent improvements in the farm.

(4) the expropriated landowner was to be compensated with government bonds and up to 10% of the tax value of the farm in cash.

(5) the government was not required to expropriate all *latifundias* above the minimum ceiling; the law could be enforced selectively.

The Christian Democrat aim had been to distribute land to some 100,000 families, to increase agricultural production, to increase the standard of living of the rural workers, and to foster the growth of *campesino* organizations.[3] By 1970 1,412 *latifundias* out of a total of 4,800 had been expropriated and organized into 826 *asentamientos* containing about 21,000 families. But agricultural production which had increased by about 4.6% p.a. between 1965 and 1968, stagnated from 1968 to 1970 partly as a result of a severe drought. The efforts to organize the peasantry were more successful. Prior to Frei the agrarian workers were virtually unorganized. By 1970 (out of the 700,000 workers and peasants who were estimated to be potentially organizable in rural unions) the various rural unions had 140,000 members and another 100,000 peasants had been organized into various cooperative committees. The Christian Democrats had also increased substantially the wages in the rural sector, especially of those in the *asentamientos*.

The application of the agrarian reform law up until 1970 had preserved much of the highly stratified internal class structure among the various types of rural workers. The organization of the *asentamiento* even created a new privileged group of peasants, the *asentados*, who it was hoped would form the base of a small land owning class opposing a more radical land reform. In addition credit facilities, a favourable pricing policy, and new facilities for importing machinery together with the threat of expropriation had encouraged *latifundistas* to divide up their estates and become commercial farmers alongside the medium sized farmers.

The application of the agrarian reform and the rapid institutionalization of the rural union movement led very quickly to combative actions on the part of the rural workers. The number of strikes increased from 693 in 1967, 648 in 1968, 1,127 in 1969 to 1,580 in 1970 and in spite of the fact that the Christian Democrat government forcibly evicted any peasants who seized lands, land seizures, *tomas*, increased from 9 in 1967, 26 in 1968, 148 in 1969 to 456 in 1970. The Popular Unity government was thus faced with an increasingly organized, mobilized and aggressive peasantry.

The Christian Democrat reform law which UP inherited did allow for the expropriation of all *latifundia*. The problem for Popular Unity was to overcome the negative aspects of the law, organize the poorer strata in the countryside – the *afuerinos*, the *minifundistas*, native communities and others – extend unionization, widen the beneficiaries of the process, and increase production. The last was important and to some extent contradictory with the other aims. The peaceful transition to socialism as envisaged by Popular Unity entailed among other things a redistribution of income which in its turn implied a large increase in demand for foodstuffs. It was imperative that internal agricultural production increase to meet that demand, otherwise the government might be forced to use its invaluable foreign exchange to import foodstuffs instead of using it to import machinery and equipment essential for growth.

By the end of 1972 Popular Unity had completed its expropriation programme which gave the agrarian reform area about 33% of agricultural production, about 20% of the total rural labour force, and about 50% of the irrigated land of the country. The *latifundia* system had seemingly come to an end. But the new organizational system to replace it remained unclear.

UP was very aware that the *asentados*, the beneficiaries of the Frei agrarian reform, were a new privileged class: about 30% of the rural labour force still remained without land and a minifundista had on average about one tenth the amount of land of an *asentado*. The complicated set of rights and privileges of belonging to an *asentamiento* led to the *asentados* becoming new employers of wage labour. Not surprisingly the Christian Democrats had developed strong support among this group.

The expropriation of land by UP had been accompanied by a doubling in unionization, and by a dramatic rise in more direct forms of peasant mobilization – in 1971 there were 1,758 strikes and 1,272 land seizures. These strikes and occupations were only rarely directed against Popular Unity. For example, a third of the strikes in 1971 were solidarity strikes, and the bulk of the *tomas* were designed to speed up the expropriation of the farm. The *tomas* in 1971 were mainly confined to the Mapuche regions, and regions in which few expropriations had previously occurred. A predominant feature of these *tomas* was that they were organized by the peasants themselves, and involved those rural classes previously untouched by the agrarian reform. Also, and importantly, about half the land seizures were on farms of less than 200 acres. This created a problem for UP as it brought to the fore the question of the class struggle on farms of less than 200 acres, and the question of legality.

Popular Unity tried a number of new organizational forms in the reformed agrarian sector, in an effort to counteract the limitations and inequalities of the *asentamiento*.[4] The first organizational form proposed was that of the *Centro de Reforma Agraria* (Agrarian Reform Centre – the CERA) which brought together a number of farms to form large scale production units. The idea was that the *Ceras* would encourage specialization, economize on the use of infrastructure and machinery, and incorporate the landless labourers and even in some areas *minifundistas*. All members of the *Cera* were to have equal rights. However, the permanent workers of the expropriated *latifundio* often opposed the *Ceras*, so the government compromised with the *Comité Campesino* which was a more egalitarian *asentamiento*, but still leaving out seasonal labourers and *minifundistas* if the permanent labourers so insisted. Farms of a more agro-industrial nature, e.g. breeding and forestry, were organized as State farms, run by technicians and the agricultural workers, both paid a fixed daily wage. Some farms were just 'intervened' and run by an *interventor* until either the dispute had been settled or it became legally expropriated.

Finally, alongside these and the already existing organizational structure, Popular Unity established peasant councils which were to group together the various peasant organizations at local, regional and national levels. As these councils excluded all those not yet organized, and as the Christian Democrats had a majority among the already organized rural groups, the MIR and the left-wing parties of Popular Unity pushed for and formed another type of peasant council which included the non-organised peasantry. These latter councils were never recognized by the Christian Democrats. And although numerous peasant councils of both types were set up the majority of them failed to function regularly and effectively. The peasant councils never became the organizational expression of peasant power.

Popular Unity then tried a number of organizational forms in the countryside in an effort to increase production, and shift the correlation of class forces in their favour. They achieved much, especially in comparison with the historical experience of agrarian reforms elsewhere and within Chile, but in neither of their main aims were they really successful: perhaps three years was too short a time. The opposition always remained powerful within the countryside. Although the traditional *latifundista* organization, the SNA, declined in importance, this was largely replaced by a new employers' union, CONSEMACH (the Confederation of Agricultural Employers), which represented the new rural bourgeoisie which emerged from the reformed *latifundistas* and the existing middle-sized rural bourgeoisie. This union, together with the CAS (the Confederation of Farmers in the South) were powerful organizations opposing the extension of agrarian reform and the peasant movement. The rural bourgeoisie still controlled most of the capital in the agrarian sector. They also had the contact with the commercial middleman which, as the black market grew in importance, placed them in the position of being able to buy produce from the reformed peasantry and sell it, at a large profit, on the black market.

The more proletarian and potentially radical groups in the countryside (*voluntarios*, some of the rural wage earners, and *afuerinos*) never became effectively organized and always remained a minority in the reformed sector. As a consequence the reformed sector acquired an increasingly petty bourgeois tendency, and in some cases (for example, the Federation of *Asentamientos*), linked up with employers' organizations to oppose government policies on certain specific occasions.

Partly because of lack of time, and partly because of having to work within the Christian Democrat agrarian reform law, many of the government policies encouraged petty bourgeois tendencies in the reformed sector. The UP continued the Christian Democrat practice of paying an *anticipo*, a monthly advance payment on future profits. In practice as profits were small or non-existent, the peasants began to regard the *anticipo* as a right, as a wage, regardless of the skills, efforts, or hours expended on the collective. Consequently, there was no real economic incentive for working on the collective farm, unlike the private plots which could be used for selling the produce to the black market. Also the differential pricing system between official prices which the collective received from the State marketing agencies and the black market prices was probably one of the most powerful incentives for producing on the private plots.

Popular Unity rightly assumed that the destruction of the *latifundia* system would in the short run lead to a decline in agricultural production. It assumed that the short run would last about two years, the expropriation period, and thereafter agricultural production would start to increase steadily. The deficiency in supply would, it was thought, be met by using the foreign exchange reserves to import the needed foodstuffs. UP was correct about the last point: imports of agricultural and livestock products increased dramatically.

Imports of Principal Agricultural and Livestock Products

	1970	1971	1972	1973
	(In thousands of tons)			
Wheat ..	200.4	367.1	745.0	950.6
Barley ..	—	—	11.0	6.8
Oats ..	—	—	—	15.0
Rice ..	36.8	19.8	58.4	98.1
Corn ..	163.6	76.8	465.0	462.4
Potatoes	21.5	7.0	59.6	144.8
Onions ..	—	—	15.0	23.0
Oil ..	33.7	75.2	49.5	67.7
Sugar ..	81.7	171.4	228.6	263.1
Tobacco ..	1.5	1.3	2.7	3.7

Source: ODEPA.

This increase in imports of agricultural and livestock products represented a tremendous burden on the Chilean balance of payments, and a restriction on the capacity to import essential supplies for the rest of the economy. Imports of foodstuffs increased from $165 million in 1970 to $245 million in 1971, to $383 million in 1972 to $619 million in 1973: this represented an increase from $17.3 per inhabitant in 1970 to $54.3 per inhabitant in 1973. The main cause for the increase in imports was the increased demand which resulted from UP's redistribution policies, but undoubtedly an important reason for the increase in imports was due to the decline in agricultural production. This decline was particularly steep from October of 1972 onwards.

Agricultural and Livestock Production, 1970-73

Product	1970	1971	1972	1973	percentage change 1972-73
	(in thousands of tons)				
AGRICULTURAL					
Wheat ..	1306.9	1368.0	1195.1	746.7	—37.6
Oats ..	110.6	112.0	111.3	109.1	—2.0
Barley ..	97.4	113.6	139.0	107.4	—22.8
Rye ..	10.7	12.3	12.4	8.5	—31.5
Corn ..	239.1	258.3	283.0	294.0	3.8
Rice ..	76.2	67.1	86.3	55.0	—36.3

Beans	..	..	..	65.6	72.2	82.9	65.0	—21.6
Lentils	..	..	..	11.2	12.0	10.7	9.8	—8.5
Peas	..	..	..	7.4	8.5	10.7	8.8	—17.8
Chickpeas	..	..	..	5.4	7.2	9.3	4.1	—56.0
Potatoes	..	..	..	683.8	835.8	733.1	623.6	—15.0
Beets	..	..	..	1655.1	1390.7	1201.6	855.9	—28.8
Marigold	..	..	..	28.2	20.3	19.9	13.5	—32.2
Rapeseed	..	..	..	69.9	82.1	78.0	40.0	—48.8
Wine(a)	..	..	..	400.5	525.1	670.2	536.2	—20.0

LIVESTOCK

Beef	..	..	..	150.1	129.6	137.0	113.8	—17.0
Sheep	..	..	..	29.5	26.6	25.2	24.1	—4.4
Port	..	..	..	48.5	49.7	55.1	49.6	—10.0
Fowl	..	..	..	52.5	58.3	61.3	37.8	—38.4
Milk	..	..	..	895.1	940.0	935.0	931.0	—0.5
Eggs (b)	..	..	..	1168.5	1052.6	1169.8	840.7	—28.2
Wool	..	..	..	19.8	18.1	16.2	15.8	—2.5

a. In millions of litres.
b. In millions of units.

Source: ODEPA.

The above figures, particularly those for 1973, are probably not an accurate indication of agricultural production. Nevertheless, the figures do show that the production of nearly all items, with the important exception of wheat, increased between 1970 and 1972, i.e. the increase in imports in this period, again with the important exception of wheat, can be primarily attributed to the increase in demand. Production may not have been as high as planned for 1970 to 1972; but nevertheless, in a period of rapid expropriation and all the political and economic problems which accompany expropriation, overall production did not decline.

The decline in agricultural production really began with the 1972-3 crop year. However, although the decline in agricultural production was severe, it was probably less than the official 1973 figures indicate. For if the amount of farm produce going into the black market is taken into account then the official production figures undoubtedly underestimate total production. Some observers have put the amount of farm produce going onto the black market as high as 50% in 1973, but this and other estimates can only be guessed. Nevertheless, although the decline in agricultural production was less than that indicated by official figures, production of nearly all farm produce, and particularly of such items as wheat, potatoes, beets, marigold and rapeseed decreased substantially.

The following table gives some indication of the decrease both in area planted and in yield per hectare for 1972-1973, a decrease which continued throughout 1973.

Changes in Area Planted and in Crop Production, 1972-73, and Changes in Prices prior to Planting (1971-72) and at the time of Marketing (1971-73)

				prices	
		area planted	yields cwt./ha.	1971-72	1971-73a
			(in percentages)		
Wheat	.. ..	—25.0	—10.6	—40.2	—11.0
Corn	.. ..	2.2	0.0	—34.4	65.4
Oats	.. ..	—9.7	—10.7	—29.3	—11.7
Barley	.. ..	—4.8	—4.2	—36.0	—12.4
Rye	.. ..	—31.5	—2.2	—40.1	—5.6
Rice	.. ..	—28.0	36.6	—39.4	17.9
Beans	.. ..	—14.5	1.0	—40.4	27.2
Lentils	.. ..	—12.6	—10.6	—11.3	54.0
Chickpeas	..	—23.6	2.2	—35.6	9.1
Peas	.. ..	—10.7	—3.6	—28.9	0.1
Potatoes	..	—15.8	—11.3	—5.0	203.2
Beets	.. ..	—26.8	—3.4	—35.4	70.2
Marigold	.. ..	—19.6	1.5	—39.0	—4.5
Rapeseed	.. ..	—45.1	—16.3	—32.7	—11.9

a. The prices used were deflated on the basis of the price index for agricultural and live-stock products; base 1968 = 100.

Source: Central Bank of Chile, Research Department.

A number of factors combined to produce the above results: the low level of agricultural prices, delays in the provision of seeds, fertilizers and insecticides due to transport strikes, the bottlenecks caused by administrative confusions and foreign exchange constraints, and the general climate of uncertainty arising from the bitter class struggles in the countryside and from the confusions over rural property ownership. There is little evidence yet available to determine which of the above factors was the most important. What is clear is that the combination of them all from October 1972 onwards led to a rapid decline in agricultural production.

Generally, the responsiveness of agricultural producers to price changes is slow, and taken by themselves and not in combination, for example, with the pricing of inputs and credit, price indicators can be misleading. However, the pricing policy of the government must have discouraged investment of both capital and labour in agriculture. This policy was, of course, very much affected by other objectives, e.g. redistribution of income and the attempt to control inflation. But in terms of both the timing and the extent of price changes the policy followed by the government was inept. For example, the government improved the relative prices of most agricultural prices in 1972 in an effort to stimulate production, but did not make the changes in time to influence the 1972-1973 crop sowing. This was probably one cause for the decline in the area planted in 1972-1973. Likewise, the relative decline in prices of most agricultural goods widened the discrepancies between official and black market prices, and helped fuel the black market and smuggling abroad.

The transport strikes of October 1972 and July 1973 were particularly effective in preventing basic inputs reaching agricultural producers and in preventing foodstuffs going officially into the towns. Again, it is difficult to estimate the extent of the loss of production due to these strikes, but undoubtedly it was high. Likewise the shortage of foreign exchange hindered the flow of essential inputs to increase agricultural production.

The bureaucracy administering agriculture was a large and overlapping one, as each successive government when dealing with an agrarian problem tended to create a new department or institute to tackle the problem. Popular Unity did not create new institutions, but as many of the personnel dealing with agrarian reform were Christian Democrats the number of bureaucrats was increased. It has been estimated that about one third of the Ministry of Agriculture's budget went on salaries and other expenses for its personnel. The administrative confusions were also greatly increased by the policy differences within UP over agrarian policy.[5] Policies in general within UP depended on the complex and changing balance of forces within the coalition. The implementation of these policies was also complex as Popular Unity mixed the chains of command in the State bureaucracies. It was not unusual to find a head of a local office to be a member of one political party, the area office another party, the zonal office yet a third party, and with even the minister being changed from one political party to another. This would not have mattered so much if the UP had an agreed agrarian policy, but in fact the parties in UP and also the MIR had different analyses of the class conflict in the countryside and what policies should be pursued.

These conflicts came to the fore over a number of different policies – peasant councils, *tomas*, organizational structures, and the agrarian reform law itself. All these uncertainties reflected themselves in declining production. This was perhaps particularly the case with the uncertainty over the expropriation limit. All on the Left agreed that there was a tremendous heterogeneity of class interests in the Chilean countryside. But, simplifying their positions considerably, President Allende and the Communist Party stressed the technical and purely economic aspects of land reform, based on the view that to increase production it was necessary to eliminate the semi-feudal *latifundia* but not the agrarian bourgeoisie; whereas the Socialist Party, MAPU and the MIR regarded the problem basically as one of attacking the big agrarian bourgeoisie. As the Socialist Party put it, the problem of production is not just a 'technocratic affair' but is 'an aspect of the class struggle in the countryside'[6] – for which it was necessary to expropriate all farms over the equivalent of forty irrigated hectares together with infrastructure and livestock. The resulting uncertainty over rural property ownership may have adversely affected agricultural production – particularly as the bulk of marketed agrarian production came from those farms of between forty and eighty hectares. But it is likely that the agrarian bourgeoisie would have opposed UP whatever happened, particularly as conflicts and tensions mounted in the country as a whole.

Distribution

The problems of distribution, both political and economic, emerged as one of the key areas of the class struggle in Chile. Politically, the attempt to control distribution widened the rift between Popular Unity and the petty bourgeoisie, accentuated middle class resentments as they saw goods which they themselves had difficulty in obtaining going to the the JAPs in the shanty-towns (the neighbourhood organizations controlling prices and supplies) and led to clashes between the armed forces and the JAPs. The political effects of this and the role of the JAPs have been analysed elsewhere; here it is intended to show the difficulties the government had in dealing with distribution problems.

The main problem facing the government in the area of distribution was its lack of effective control over it. About eighty per cent of agricultural production was commercialized privately and not through the State Commercial Agricultural Agency, ECA. Even sections of the agrarian reform area, due in part to organizational problems, tended to by-pass ECA and sell direct to the private sector which had the advantage of often paying more for the produce. In the towns State distribution agencies and the JAPs probably controlled no more than one third of the urban distribution system.

As shortages became endemic and as the government tried to fix the price of a number of basic goods, a thriving black market emerged. It was a constant temptation not only for the private sector, but also for people working in the social property area and people who received goods at the official prices to sell or resell them through the black market for a much higher price.

One policy which the UP government could have tried to deal with the distribution of goods in short supply was rationing. But the UP allowed itself be boxed in over rationing. It had been part of the right-wing campaign that a transition to socialism meant a transition to shortages and the introduction of rationing. During the first year the UP felt that rationing was not needed, and thereafter felt that to try and introduce rationing would be politically very unpopular. Instead it decided to use Dirinco, the State Industrial and Commercial Institute, to fix prices, enforce these prices, and to requisition goods in the case of hoarding, black marketeering etc. Dirinco, in fact, initiated the establishment of JAPs as a way of dealing with the distribution problem. These grassroots organizations were fairly successful not only in ensuring a fair distribution of basic products, but also in enforcing the official prices.

By 1973, when shortages were more serious, the government considered a number of more radical solutions. In mid-January the Minister of Finance, Fernando Flores, proposed the expropriation of all distribution and the imposition of *contratos de exclusividad* in which private producers would be compelled to sell their production to a government agency at official prices. In addition, a State wheat monopoly was created which was only partially successful in capturing total wheat production. There was also a lot of discussion about establishing a *Canasta Popular* (a popular shopping basket which would contain about 30 essential items), in effect a form of rationing.

None of these proposals were really implemented. The government knew it would not win support from the opposition controlled congress and senate for a more effective form of rationing. And already the JAPs had become a fierce bone of contention between the UP and the opposition, and within the UP between the moderates and the radicals. The PDC mounted a campaign against the black market, blaming Government agencies for its existence. It proposed as an alternative to the JAPs the establishment of CAPs (Committees of Prices and Supply) under the control of the *juntas de vecinos*, the neighbourhood committees set up by the Christian Democrats. The proposal was designed to try and ensure that a share of government controlled supplies went to middle class areas. But the CAPs never really got off the ground, although some supermarkets, e.g. the Unicoop, did introduce their own version of the *canasta popular*.

For the radicals within UP the JAPs represented a good example of people's power in action, a form of popular control which they wished to see extended. The moderates, however, wishing to assuage middle class fears, opposed extending the power of the JAPs. In the end the moderates won out, and the government set up a National Distribution Agency headed by a general of the air force, Bachelet, which weakened the power of the JAPs.

Problems of distribution were never solved by Popular Unity, and in fact, no policy could work effectively unless linked to the problems and control of production.

Employment and Income Distribution

The creation of full employment and the redistribution of income were basic among the objectives of Popular Unity. All commentators agree that under UP unemployment fell. The sample survey of the *Instituto de Economía y Planificación* of the University of Chile shows that in the Greater Santiago area those without work fell from 6.6% in December of 1970 to 2.5% in March of 1973, and the unemployed (those without work plus those looking for work for the first time) fell from 8.3% in December of 1970 to 3.8% in March of 1973. Also based on Greater Santiago the National Institute of Statistics gives a figure of 4.1% of the labour force as unemployed in August/September of 1973. Thus in spite of all its economic difficulties, Popular Unity kept its promise of creating what in an underdeveloped country can only be regarded as near full employment. It was no mean achievement. Since the coup, the military junta whose policies have been the reverse of Popular Unity's, in that mass unemployment has been deliberately created as part of 'national reconstruction', has tried to disparage UP's achievement by arguing that the UP increased the ranks of the employed at the cost of increased production. There undoubtedly was some 'over-manning' in the social property area and government service, but hardly anyone went hungry under UP because they were not allowed to work.

The fall in unemployment under Popular Unity is clear. What happened to income distribution is much less certain. The Inter-American Committee on the Alliance for Progress (CIAP) calculated that after the initial increase in wages and salaries in 1971 real wages and salaries fell in both 1972 and 1973.

Changes in Real Wages and Salaries, 1970-73

	1971	*1972*	*1973*
Changes from December to December	24.6	—17.4	—54.8
Changes between averages for the year	26.2	—2.8	—42.7
Index number, base 1970=100	126.2	122.6	70.4

Source: OEA/Ser.H/XIV CIAP/650

The changes from December to December are somewhat misleading as the readjustment for the increase in the year's inflation usually came in January. The figure for 1973 also includes the nearly four months rule of the military junta whose deliberate aim was to reduce real wages in order to restore the functioning of an efficient capitalist market economy. But even taking this into account the decline in real wages and salaries must have been substantial.

There are as yet no reliable figures on income distribution for 1970 to 1973. Popular Unity did have a policy of redistributing income from the higher to the lower paid, and its full employment policies must also have contributed to a more equal distribution of income. There probably was a fairly substantial redistribution of wealth and income under UP – particularly if the increase in social benefits, and the ability to obtain goods through the JAPs etc., are taken into account. Nevertheless, real wages and salaries seem to have fallen in 1972 and 1973, an indication that the economic policies of 1971 made little sense over time even in terms of income distribution – and made even less sense if one considers that in 1972 and 1973 the workers showed they did not need immediate increases in consumption to commit them to a transition to socialism.

Inflation and the Structure of Prices

In both 1972 and 1973 Chile achieved the unwanted distinction of having the highest rate of inflation in the world. Inflation is notoriously difficult to measure: the figures presented here are the official working class cost-of-living or consumer price indices as given in the Bank of London and South America Review (BOLSA). This Review correctly comments that 'the unrepresentative nature of some of these indices, imperfections in the weighting systems and incomplete coverage of items priced, limit their usefulness; nevertheless, they give a crude measure of recent movements in living costs'.[7] In Chile itself the figures were subject to much controversy: and there is some reason to believe that with black market prices considerably higher than official prices the indices underestimate increases in living costs.

Cost of Living Index: Santiago

	1971 Dec.	1972 Dec.	1973 Sept.*	1973 Dec.
Base= 100 (Dec. 1969)	164.8	434.1	1271.1	2640.0
% change on previous year	22.1	163.4	192.8	508.1

* % change on previous December.

Source: Bank of London and South America Review.

For many on the Right the rate of inflation alone justified the military intervention. Robert Moss, in his book *Chile's Marxist Experiment*, even goes so far as to suggest that the increase in the rate of inflation was part of the Marxist conspiracy, providing, together with shortages, 'the Marxist parties in Chile with the pretext to impose a system of rationing that gave neighbourhood committees (or JAPs) considerable scope to supervise the daily lives of ordinary citizens', with the final goal of 'the concentration of political power in the hands of a narrow ruling group'.[8]

But, such simple-minded conspiracy views aside, there is little doubt that the rapid increase in the rate of inflation in Chile increased the tensions and hardships in what was in any case a tense and difficult period. Economically and politically this rapid increase in inflation did tremendous damage to the Popular Unity government. It contributed towards the mobilization and organization of large sectors of the middle class by the Right against Popular Unity. It was also a major factor in working class strikes against the government. For example, the crippling El Teniente copper strike was sparked off by a disagreement over a complicated wage readjustment to compensate for the increases in the cost-of-living index – something which probably could have been avoided if inflation had been kept within reasonable bounds.

Inflation played havoc with the government's economic policies. In keeping with situations of high rates of inflation there was an increase in speculative activities, a capital flight, a reduction in savings, and a reduction of exports and an increase in imports. These might have occurred without the rapid rate of inflation; but inflation accentuated them. In addition, the government found that inflation eroded the real value of its income, and so it resorted to increasing credit to itself in an effort to maintain its position. More importantly, a combination of high rates of inflation plus price controls led to a situation where the system of relative prices became neither efficient nor socially just. The social property area, most of whose prices were controlled, produced massive deficits instead of the planned surpluses. The prices of some products were not adjusted for inflation, and ended up bearing no relation to costs or, indeed, social priorities. The failure to adjust in time the prices of most agricultural products contributed to the fall in agrarian production. The price structure became increasingly irrational.

Why then, when inflation was harming its political and economic programme, did the Popular Unity government not take drastic steps to control it?

To answer this question, it is necessary to analyse briefly the background to inflation in Chile, the main causes of the inflationary spiral in 1972 and 1973, and the policy alternatives open to UP.

Chile is not unaccustomed to high rates of inflation. Since the 1880s Chile has been plagued with persistent increases in the cost-of-living index, the highest increase before 1972 and 1973 being the 83.8% increase in 1955. So persistent have been these increases that Chile became the model for a new theory of inflation – the structuralist theory of inflation.[9] This theory argued that to understand the basic or structural causes of inflation and hence to be able to suggest appropriate policies to deal with inflation, one must go beyond the propagating factors such as the increase in money supply and the public sector deficit, and look more at the structural factors such as the land tenure structure and its effect on agricultural production, the mono-export base of the foreign trade structure, the tax system and the distribution of income and power. Chile became in many ways the testing ground for two ideologically opposed views on how to control inflation. On the one hand the 'monetarists', associated principally with the policy views of the International Monetary Fund, concentrated on the demand side, advocating the need to cut the money supply, devalue, balance the budget, and restrain or cut wages and salaries. On the other hand, the 'structuralists', associated with the United Nations Economic Commission for Latin America, argued that it was necessary to take a long-term growth perspective and concentrate on the supply side, that the 'monetarist' proposals were only palliatives and that structural and institutional reforms were needed.

This debate and the actual Chilean experience with IMF-style 'stabilization programmes' left a deep imprint on the UP. It was argued that the two major IMF-style 'stabilization programmes' of 1956 to 1958 and 1958 to 1961 cut the rate of inflation at the cost of a reduction in the standard of living of the workers (enforced by defeating, with the help of repression, the trade union movement), an increase in unemployment, an increase in dependence on foreign capital, and harm to the prospects of long run growth.[10] Many regarded the cure as worse than the disease, and as 'bottling-up' the problem for a short time rather than solving it. This background helps partly to explain the reluctance of UP to implement a traditional stabilization programme to deal with inflation. Popular Unity regarded structural reforms, the pursuit of growth and full employment as higher priorities than the control of inflation. At some time a stabilization programme would be required, but the UP was clearly hoping first to have sufficient power to ensure that such a programme would not be on the lines advocated by the IMF.

But why did inflation get out of hand in 1972 and 1973, after a reduction in the rate of inflation in 1971? As with many other facets of the economic crisis, the immediate roots of the inflationary spiral lie in the economic policies of UP's first year. One of the consequences of those policies was an increase in overall demand without a corresponding increase in productive capacity to meet that demand. Consumption increased and investment fell. The result of the 1971 policies was a series of imbalances throughout the economy; imbalances which led to inflationary pressures. These pressures were translated into increases in the consumer price index by the passive monetary policy of the Government which just printed money to satisfy the demands made upon it.

The money supply in Chile increased by 114% in 1971, 173% in 1972 and by 365% in 1973. The main cause of these increases was the creation of credit for the public sector, the deficit of which is the key factor in explaining the growth in the money supply. The public sector deficit as a percentage of total public expenditure increased from 21.5% in 1971 to 30.2% in 1972 to 47.0% in 1973.

As can be seen from the following table, fiscal income failed to keep pace with the growth in fiscal expenditures:

Evolution of Fiscal Income and Real Expenditures, 1970-73

	1970	1971	1972	1973
CURRENT INCOME	100.0	103.2	87.7	55.8
a. Taxes	100.0	103.0	87.0	57.9
i. Direct taxes	(100.0)	(85.3)	(57.8)	(36.5)
ii. Indirect taxes	(100.0)	(115.7)	(108.1)	(73.4)
b. Non-tax Income	100.0	106.4	99.1	17.1
FISCAL EXPENDITURES	100.0	136.0	129.1	84.2
a. Current expenditures	100.0	143.1	145.9	89.5
i. Operations	(100.0)	(123.9)	(129.6)	(101.0)
ii. Transfers	(100.0)	(159.5)	(159.7)	(79.8)
b. Capital expenditures	100.0	122.6	91.4	72.2
i. Direct investments	(100.0)	(102.3)	(113.2)	(93.2)
ii. Transfers	(100.0)	(146.6)	(99.3)	(85.5)
iii. Amortization of debt	(100.0)	(109.6)	(37.6)	(9.1)

Source: OEA/Ser. H/XIV CIAP/650

But why did fiscal income decline and fiscal expenditure increase to such an extent? The bulk of government revenue comes from taxation, and in the high inflationary situation of 1972 and 1973 the government found that the real value of its tax receipts declined as by the time it collected its revenues the value of the revenues was down. Moreover, the nationalization of copper had led to a decline in copper taxes, a major source of tax revenue. There also seems to have been an increase in tax evasion and the non-payment of taxes (the growth of the black market, for example, made indirect taxes particularly difficult to collect). The government was aware that the tax system was not bringing in enough revenue nor being sufficiently flexible or efficient. But all efforts to reform the tax system – by increasing taxes on the rich, increasing estate duties, introducing a wealth tax and tax surcharges – were rejected by congress, and so the government in an effort to keep up with inflation and cover its expenditures increased its means of payment by printing money.

Whilst fiscal income remained more or less constant in 1971 and declined in 1972 and 1973, fiscal expenditures increased rapidly in 1971, fell slightly in 1972, and then fell below the 1970 level in 1973. Within fiscal expenditures, current expenditures rose the fastest: by a massive 43% in 1971, remaining at the 1971 level in 1972, and then falling in 1973. Two factors were mainly responsible for this increase in public sector expenditures: the transfer of current resources to the social property area and the increase in wages and salaries.

The UP government did, of course, expand the size of the state sector. As a consequence the share of fiscal expenditures as a percentage of Gross Domestic Product increased from 23.9% in 1970 to 30.3% in 1971 and 30.1% in 1972 and then fell to 20.2% in 1973. Not only did certain welfare provisions increase, but more importantly, numerous enterprises were brought under state control. It had been UP's plan that the social property area would generate a surplus for new investment to increase productive capacity. Instead, virtually the whole of the social property area ran at a huge loss, requiring massive credit financing from the State. The total deficit of the social property area rose in current escudos from 21.9 million in 1972 to an estimated 175.8 million in 1973 which was the approximate size of the 1973 fiscal deficit. By far the most important cause of the deficits in the social property area was the pricing policy followed by that area. Pricing in the social property area never kept pace with the rate of inflation. In addition, as more and more factories were taken over by the workers in response to the threats from the right, it was difficult in this situation for Popular Unity not to pay the wages demanded, or in the tense political atmosphere to insist on the importance of labour discipline to increase production.

The government promised that wages and salaries would keep pace with the rate of inflation. In fact, if black market prices are taken into account, then this promise was not kept. As shortages grew, some goods were almost only obtainable in the black market, e.g. toothpaste and soap, and the differential between the official price and the black market price of some goods was enormous – in 1973 a quintal of flour with a controlled price to bakers of 150.6 escudos would fetch 2,500 escudos in the black market. But, with the exception of higher wage and salary earners, wages and salaries were adjusted to keep pace with the official increases in the cost-of-living index. This was a great drain on fiscal expenditures, and with fiscal incomes declining, was an important factor in the growth of the fiscal deficit.

As inflation accelerated, the government, instead of the customary yearly readjustment for inflation, began to give periodic readjustments. Suggestions for a National Compensation Fund financed through a capital gains tax, real estate taxes, etc., or for major reforms of the tax system to finance the readjustments were rejected by congress. Congress even opposed proposals by the government to discriminate against the higher paid by giving them less than a 100% readjustment for inflation. After the March elections of 1973 various proposals were put forward within UP to tie the readjustment for inflation to increases in production and productivity, and to revert back to the yearly readjustments. It is likely that such a proposal would have been introduced. But the whole problem of wage and salary structures was a major, and largely unresolved problem for the UP.

Popular Unity did try to tackle the problem of inflation. But its problem was how to do this without sacrificing its whole programme. The government proposed major reforms of the credit system: the credits to the social property area would be more tightly controlled; credit to the private sector would be granted only if the government were satisfied it would not be used for speculative purposes; special credit provisions for agriculture were drawn up; production plans which required credit had to be submitted a year in advance. Price controls were more strictly enforced; penalties against the black market and speculation were increased; the powers of the State over distribution were increased; changes in the wage and salary structure and readjustments for inflation were proposed. And so the list could go on. But inflation continued. The implementation of a much more drastic plan was required to deal not only with inflation but with the whole economic crisis.

The Balance of Payments and the Informal Blockade

In an important speech to the General Assembly of the United Nations on 4 December, 1972, President Allende made the following claim:[11]

> From the very day of our electoral triumph on 4 September, 1970, we have felt the effects of a large-scale external pressure against us which tried to prevent the inauguration of a government freely elected by the people, and has attempted to bring it down ever since, an action that has tried to cut us off from the world, to strangle our economy and paralyse trade in our principal export, copper, and to deprive us of access to sources of international financing.
>
> . . . This aggression is not overt and has not been openly declared to the world; on the contrary, it is an oblique, underhand, indirect form of aggression, although this does not make it any less damaging to Chile.

Allende then went on to list the forms which the 'informal blockade' took. These included the cutting off of finance by international finance organizations, such as the World Bank and the Inter-American Development Bank; the ending of loans from the US government (not unexpected); the withdrawal of most short-term credit facilities from private US banks; the ending of supplier credits, and credits normally granted by the Export-Import Bank, forcing Chile to pay in advance for its capital goods; the suspension of disbursements of loans granted to previous Chilean governments, forcing Chile to pay in cash for imports from the USA to keep in continuation projects already started; and the creation of a climate which hampered normal financial transactions with Western Europe.

11

Alongside these indirect forms of aggression both the International Telephone and Telegraph Company and the Kennecott Copper Corporation initiated direct actions to try and topple the Popular Unity government. The 'ITT Memos' (consisting of internal memos of ITT personnel) revealed the attempts by the ITT to strangle the Chilean economy, sow panic and foment social disorder in order to encourage and create the opportunity for the armed forces to step in and replace Popular Unity.[12] The Kennecott Copper Company attempted, through the courts in France, the Netherlands and Sweden, to place an embargo on the Chilean copper exported to those countries. This action by Kennecott not only placed in jeopardy millions of dollars worth of foreign exchange earnings to Chile, but also, by creating uncertainty, hindered the flow of credits and other financial operations with West European Banks.

These, of course, were not the only actions undertaken by the USA to ensure the defeat of Popular Unity and prevent Chile's transition to socialism. Probably the most effective actions were ones taken years before Popular Unity came to power. After all, the USA had helped create armed forces not only in Chile, but also in virtually the whole of Latin America, whose purpose was to defend the interests of the US corporations and the Latin American bourgeoisie in the name of 'anti-subversive activities'. And the USA had likewise during its many years of domination in Chile, helped to build up an ideological and economic structure which made the tasks of Popular Unity that much more difficult. Aside from these more structural considerations there is evidence, some firm and some circumstantial, that the USA actively aided and abetted the Chilean Right in its opposition to the UP and helped bring about the coup of 11 September.

But in the absence of a detailed account of the USA's role in the three years of Allende's government, it is difficult to judge the importance of the USA in the events leading up to the coup of 11 September. It could be that some future researcher will unearth convincing proof that the USA's role was the over-whelming factor in the coup. Since the coup rumours have circulated that the Central Intelligence Agency was directly responsible for planning the military take-over. *Le Monde*, for example, published statements by Chilean exiles referring to a 'Centaur Plan' drawn up by the CIA, two years before 11 September, and claiming that after the March elections of 1973, Dr. Kissinger, the American Secretary of State, took over responsibility for dealing with Chile and authorized the implementation of a plan to topple Popular Unity.[13]

It was subsequently confirmed by William Colby, the CIA Director, in a secret session to the U.S. Senate subcommittee that the CIA spent eleven million dollars between 1962 and 1970 to help prevent Allende from being elected, and that it spent, with the authorization of Dr. Kissinger, eight million dollars, between 1970 and 1973, to "destabilize" the economy, including money for right-wing strikes, to bring down the Allende Government.

Two publications of the North American Congress on Latin America, *New Chile*, and *Chile: The Story Behind the Coup*, analyse in some detail the evidence of US complicity. Along with all the evidence concerning the informal blockade, and the actions of the ITT and Kennecott, they point to the continuation of US military aid to the Chilean armed forces throughout the period of Allende's government and the continuation of links between Chilean and US military, to the increase in finance for the operations of the American Institute for Free Labor Development in Chile (the AIFLD conducts training programmes and other activities to encourage 'free trade-unions'), to the personnel in the US embassy in Santiago, ten of whom were known CIA agents, to the evidence that US dollars were financing some of the right-wing strikes, particularly that of the truck-owners in October 1972, to the decline in the price of the dollar on the black market in October 1972, indicating an influx of dollars, to the visit of the US ambassador in Chile to Washington a few days before the coup, and to the Nixon administration's admission of prior knowledge of the coup. But contrary to the interpretation given by many, particularly Communist Party writers, none of these indicate that the prime mover in the coup was the USA. It would be a mistake to underestimate the role of the USA in defeating the Chilean working class, but to place the major emphasis here is to go against the bulk of available evidence. The coup would probably have occurred even if the USA had remained strictly 'neutral'.

However, it is true that the effects of the 'informal blockade' were damaging to the Chilean economy. The US maintained its blockade, until the coup of 11 September, 1973. President Nixon described the US position on 19 January, 1972 as follows:

> Thus, when a country expropriates a significant US interest without making reasonable provision for such compensation to US citizens, we will presume that the US will not extend new bilateral economic benefits to the expropriating country unless and until it is determined that the country is taking reasonable steps to provide adequate compensation or that there are major factors affecting US interests which require continuance of all or part of these benefits.
> In the face of the expropriatory circumstances just described, we will presume that the United States government will withhold its support from loans under consideration in multilateral banks.[14]

In the case of Chile this position meant a number of concrete steps designed to cripple the Chilean economy. The first step was that by the Export-Import Bank of the USA, which refused in early 1971 a Chilean request for a $21 million loan to purchase three Boeing passenger jets. And in August of 1971 the Export-Import Bank announced that Chile could expect no loans or guarantees. Since 1945 Chile had received about $600 million in credits from the Export-Import Bank, and had made use of the Bank's insurance and guarantee programmes. The latter were very important if a foreign government wished to obtain credits from private banks, and suppliers' credits. In fact, in 1972, only $35 million of short term credits were obtained from private US banks compared to the average $220 million of past years. And all suppliers' credits were suspended. The US aid agency, the AID, immediately cut off all aid to Chile from the moment of Allende's victory, and even refused to disburse loans signed with the previous Chilean government.

The USA also successfully exerted pressure within multilateral banks. Since 1959 the Inter-American Development Bank (IDB) had granted Chile $310 million in loans. All requests from the Allende government to the IDB for loans were refused – with the exception of a $7 million loan to the Catholic University of Santiago, and a $4.6 million to the Austral University, in the south of Chile: both opposition-controlled universities. The World Bank, which had loaned Chile $235 million since 1944, refused all requests for loans from Chile during the Popular Unity period. The head of the World Bank, the former president of the Ford Motor Company and US Secretary of State for Defence, Robert McNamara, even went so far as to state publicly that 'the primary condition for bank lending – a soundly managed economy with a clear potential for utilizing additional funds – has not been met. The Chilean economy is in severe difficulty'[15] – thus knowingly damaging Chile's ability to obtain credit elsewhere.

There was an 'informal blockade' by the USA. But what effect did this have on the Chilean economy? Chile, which used to import about 40% of its total imports from the USA, found itself importing only about 15Æ in 1972. Some alternative sources of supply were found, but for some parts of the Chilean economy there were problems of specification and thus no readily available alternative spare-parts, replacements and machinery. With an industrial structure dependent on supplies from the USA, many industries had to cut back on existing production and halt new construction, some of which was already in process. For example, the Chilean Steel Company, CAP, which had obtained a $25 million loan from the US Export-Import Bank in 1969 for expansion, had to halt that expansion because the Export-Import Bank refused to disburse the remaining $13 million of the loan. In the transportation sector, NACLA reported that a Chilean source estimated that about 30% of the private buses, 21% of the taxi-buses, and 33% of the public buses were out of use because of lack of parts or tyres.[16] (The bulk of Chilean vehicles were made by US firms.) The shortage of parts and tyres was one of the causes of the truck owners' and transport strikes.

Some commentators have seen the effects of the 'informal blockade' in Chile as confirmation that the 'low profile' policy of Nixon (which holds that after Vietnam the USA will have to achieve its aims through means other than military intervention) was successful. For, after all, did not the USA put into practice the ITT proposal of creating economic chaos in Chile so that Popular Unity would be overthrown? And did not the majority of the Chilean middle classes mobilize against Allende when the economy ran into problems? But this viewpoint is to over-emphasize the importance of the USA's 'informal blockade'. That blockade did, as indicated, cause some damage to the Chilean economy, but the effects of the blockade were somewhat mitigated by the UP finding alternative sources of supplies, aid and credit.

The following table gives the evolution of Chile's external debt between 1970 and 1973.

Evolution of the External Debt, 1970-73

Group of countries or institutions	(in millions of US dollars)				percentage variation
	1970	1971	1972	1973	1970-73
1. Multilateral agencies ..	349.0	381.4	435.6	483.4	38.5
2. Paris Club	2020.0	2060.0	2094.3	2159.3	6.9
3. Socialist bloc..	14.0	6.6	37.6	40.0	185.7
4. Other European countries and Latin American countries ..	9.0	18.9	65.2	149.8	1564.4
5. Capital contributions in the form of credits	111.0	111.0	111.0	111.0	0.0
6. Total external medium- and long-range debt	2526.0	2577.9	2743.7	2943.6	16.7
—Annual growth (%) ..	—	2.1	6.4	7.4	
7. Short-term credits	78.0	90.5	353.0	478.0	512.8
—Annual growth (%) ..	—	16.0	290.0	35.4	

Source: Central Bank of Chile.

Between 1970 and 1973 the medium and long term debt increased by 16.7%, and the short-term debt increased by a staggering six fold. (The figures for 1973 include debt contracted after the coup of 11 September.) The overall picture is that of the UP obtaining aid and credit to replace that lost due to USA policies, although the financial terms were harsher than in the past. These came from a variety of sources: $90 odd million dollars from the Socialist bloc; $148 million in 1971 from the IMF in compensation for the fall in the copper price and from Chile's normal allotment of drawing rights; in 1972 $32 million from Brazil; in 1973 $100 million from Argentina, and the bulk of the short-term lines of credit from Europe and Latin America, particularly France and Argentina.

Also in November 1971 Chile declared a moratorium on its foreign debt repayments. Given its balance of payments crisis, the Chilean government requested a rescheduling of its remaining 1971 debts and of the debts due in 1972. The USA tried to win support among the other debt-holders, mainly European, that renegotiation should be conditional on adequate compensation for expropriated companies, and the acceptance by Chile of an IMF 'stand-by' agreement (in return for a 'stand-by' loan from the IMF a government often has to agree in a 'letter of intent' to a series of monetary, fiscal, foreign and public sector policies negotiated with the IMF). Eventually the USA's position was defeated. And at the Paris Club meetings in April 1972, about 70% of the debt service payments falling due between November and December 1972 were rescheduled. All of the members of the Paris Club bilaterally negotiated their terms of the rescheduling, except the USA which only reached an agreement for their $130.5 million debt after the September coup, in December 1973. An arrangement to hold a further meeting to discuss the possibilities of extending further the period of payments was postponed throughout 1973, which meant that about $328 million of debt payments were not paid in 1973. At the beginning of 1974 the military junta seemed to have little difficulty in renegotiating the external debt service payments due to be paid.

Thus, although the 'informal blockade' played a part in the economic crisis, the main cause of that crisis must be sought elsewhere. In any case, something like the 'informal blockade' must have been expected, and, one assumes, taken into account when making policies. Perhaps not all of the US policies were anticipated, particularly the cutting off of suppliers' credits and the drying up of private credits. But there is nothing in the history of US relations with Latin America to suggest that it would continue to supply aid and credits to a Latin American government which expropriates US property and attacks US policies.

In reality the main factors in the balance of payments crisis were the rapid increase in the demand for imports, especially for foodstuffs; the increase in the price of imports, again particularly foodstuffs; the decline in the price of copper (with the exception of 1973) and the decline in exports in general; and the foreign exchange rate policies which contributed to imbalances in the economy. The following table summarizes the overall position of the Chilean balance of payments, 1970 to 1973.

Chile: Balance of Payments, 1970-73

		1970	1971	1972	1973a
		(in millions of US dollars)			
1.	MERCHANDISE EXPORTS	1130.3	986.2	853.7	1367.1
	a. Mining	984.4	819.7	734.9	1233.4
	—Copper	877.7	695.1	647.4	(1125.0)
	—Others	106.7	124.6	87.5	(108.4)
	b. Agricultural and fishing	32.1	29.4	19.3	24.3
	c. Industrial	113.8	136.1	99.5	190.4
2.	MERCHANDISE IMPORTS	—1020.0	—1052.0	—1323.0	—1651.8
	a. Consumer and raw material for foodstuffs	—173.0	—328.0	—441.0	—683.0
	b. Other semiprocessed goods	—537.0	—479.1	—590.0	—683.8
	c. Capital goods	—310.0	—244.9	—292.0	—285.0
3.	NON-FINANCIAL SERVICES (net)	28.4	—44.6	—30.0	—32.0
4.	NON-MONETARY GOLD	n/d*	n/d	n/d	2.0
5.	TRADE BALANCE	138.7	—110.4	—497.8	—318.7

6. FINANCIAL SERVICES AND				
DONATIONS	—196.1	—89.8	—116.8	—85.0
a. Paid abroad	n.a.*	—125.7	—141.0	—89.0
b. Received from abroad ..	n.a.	35.9	24.2	4.0
7. CURRENT ACCOUNT				
BALANCE	—57.4	—200.2	—614.6	—403.7
8. AUTONOMOUS CAPITAL ..	148.5	—103.5	295.7	150.5
a. Revenue..	n.a.	n.a.	318.8	262.5
b. Outlays	n.a.	n.a.	23.1b	112.0
9. BALANCE OF PAYMENTS ..	91.1	—303.5	—318.9	—253.2

* no date   † not available
a. Tentative.
b. A deduction has been made of US$297.9 million resulting from the renegotiation of debt, adjustments in the payment schedules with certain countries members of the Paris Club, payments pending with the US and renegotiation of uninsured debts with countries members of the Paris Club.

Source: 1970-72: Banco Central de Chile; 1973, Banco Central de Chile and the OAS Secretariat.

The outstanding feature of the above table is the very rapid increase in merchandise imports, and within imports the increase in foodstuffs. Between 1970 and 1973 the import of consumer and raw material for foodstuffs almost quadrupled, reflecting a large increase in internal demand, a decline in internal production and the increase in world food prices. The only imports to decline were capital goods, reflecting the overall decline in investment throughout the economy. Non-mineral exports fell throughout the three years. This was partly caused by the general decline in production in the economy, but it also reflected the growth in internal demand which consumed the exportable balances of some products. Mining exports declined in 1971 and 1972, mainly as a consequence of the fall in the price of copper; the increase in the value of copper exports in 1973 was due entirely to the increase in the price of copper.

So, whereas in the past Chile usually exported more merchandise than it imported, under Popular Unity the reverse occurred. Not surprisingly, without a massive increase in foreign capital, Chile used up its international reserves.

International Reserves 1970-73 (million of dollars)

	October 1970	December 1970	December 1971	December 1972	September 1973
1. Central Bank of Chile	344.7	332.7	89.0	—113.8	—216.3
2. Commercial and State Banks	—4.5	—10.5	—54.7	—179.8	*
3. International Reserves (1 & 2)..	340.2	322.2	34.3	—293.6	*

*information not available.

Source: Central Bank of Chile.

Given the emphasis placed by the UP on the importance of its dependent relationship with the international economy, particularly with the economy of the USA, it is surprising how little foresight and planning there was in relation to the foreign economic sector. Popular Unity did eventually begin to plan its foreign sector policies through the *Secretaría Ejecutiva de Relaciones Económicas Exteriores* (SEREX) which was specifically established in 1972 to plan the use of foreign exchange and foreign commerce in general. But the planning efforts of SEREX, although of use, arrived too late to alter the deteriorating situation in the balance of payments.

The problems of the balance of payments must lie to a large extent with the UP's own balance of payments policies, particularly those of 1971. For example, the exchange rate policies bore little relation to changes in internal and external prices or shortages of foreign exchange. In its political programme the UP promised to 'put an end to the continual shameful devaluation of the escudo'.[17] And throughout 1971 the Popular Unity maintained the escudo at a fixed overvalued rate of exchange thereby encouraging the inflow of imports and discouraging, to a small extent, exports. And in December of 1971 when the government devalued and established multiple fixed exchange rates, then and in subsequent devaluations, it persisted in maintaining the escudo rate for imports of foodstuffs and oil products considerably overvalued. Now it was UP policy to keep down the price of foodstuffs (food after all is the major item in a working class budget), and from the point of view of trying to dampen down the rate of inflation, restrain wage demands and redistribute income, a case could be made for subsidizing foodstuffs. But the particular method of subsidy (overvalued exchange rate plus price controls) only increased the demand for food (food imports increased by $80 million in 1971, and with agricultural production stagnant in 1972 and declining in 1973 food imports had to increase then in any case), was indiscriminate in its benefits, and encouraged smuggling into the neighbouring countries of Argentina, Peru and Bolivia. Why petrol was subsidized is not clear (this subsidized car owners among others): perhaps this was considered a way of keeping down increases in the official cost-of-living index.

But in the end it could be that the Popular Unity government was relying on an increase in the price of copper and an upturn in agricultural production to help it overcome the balance of payments problem – in much the same way as successive British governments have, for short periods, borrowed themselves out of balance of payments problems on the assumption that North Sea oil will later enable them to repay. In fact the price of copper did increase in 1973 and 1974, and there were indications of an increase in agricultural production. So meantime Popular Unity seemed willing to run through the foreign exchange reserves, borrow from abroad and overvalue the escudo to help it in its immediate overall economic and political strategy. It did not succeed.

Conclusions

By September 1973, Chile was in a state of economic confusion. Whoever won the battle for power, a realistic programme of austerity would have been required.

The question was, whose realism? Whose austerity? After the coup of 11 September, it was the capitalist class which imposed its programme of recovery on Chile, through the armed forces. The programme won the warm appreciation of the *Bank of London and South America Review:*

> Thanks to the rise in copper prices, the resumption of the foreign financing inflow and, above all, to the more realistic methods of economic management undertaken by the military government, short- and medium-term prospects for Chile are much improved, though it will take a long time to remove the distortions imposed on the economy by the Allende regime.[18]

But what were these realistic policies? The junta called its programme a programme of 'national reconstruction', by which it meant the reconstruction of a capitalist mode of production dominated by foreign interests. The essence of its programme was the dismantling, not only of the elements of State interference introduced by Popular Unity, but of a tradition of State intervention in the market going back for over fifty years. The economy was to be 'freed'.

There was of course one exception. The workers were not 'freed': on the contrary, the introduction of a free market economy required complete suppression of working class organizations, and in places, the reintroduction of forced labour.

Prices were 'freed', with the result that the cost of basic consumption goods rose to astronomical levels. By June 1974, the price of a kilo of bread had increased twenty-two fold, that of a litre of cooking oil twenty-five fold, milk seventeen fold. Wages were held down, increases being given reluctantly when it became obvious that even a capitalist mode of production would not work unless people had a minimal power of consumption, with which to buy goods. Price increases became the preferred form of rationing, in which the needs of the wealthy had top priority and the well-being and even the health of the poorer classes was put firmly at the bottom of the list. The *Financial Times* reported a popular new Chilean dish, *pantucras*, flour mixed with water.[19]

Admiral Merino put the junta's basic perspective concisely when he commented, 'no country dies of unemployment'. There were massive dismissals of politically suspect workers, followed by further redundancies among workers whose bosses could no longer employ them, because of the crisis of underconsumption. In the spring of 1974, the junta announced that Chile's basic problem was a parasitic State sector, and declared its intention to cut State employment back by 20% by the end of 1975. Those dismissed were to be given an opportunity to buy some of the State's cars, so that they could set up in the private sector as taxi drivers.[20] Meanwhile expenditures on the armed forces increased substantially.

That, in practice, was how the armed forces attempted to deal with the economic crisis – perhaps not altogether rationally, from a strictly economic perspective. A working class solution would have been different. First and foremost, it would have had to be an advance towards socialism: towards a planned economy, in which goods in short supply were rationed according to need. Chilean socialism would not have been able to offer abundance. But it would have been a solution which maintained full employment, in which a man could work, have a house and be fed, see his children educated and take part in the democratic organization of his society. Better the socialism of poverty than the misery and rank horror of Chilean capitalism.

The dilemma of Popular Unity was that the introduction of a socialist solution to the economic crisis would have required political initiatives which its leadership was no longer capable of taking.

7 Crisis in Popular Unity and the Emergence of 'People's Power'

Towards the middle of 1972, the political strategy of Popular Unity went into undeclared bankruptcy. It was no longer possible for the government to entertain hopes of 'buying off' the middle classes, when faced with the joint determination of national capital and imperialism to create economic chaos as an excuse for bringing Allende down. The coalition itself was divided. One section wanted to call the Chilean 'experiment' to a halt, consolidating the gains which had been made, in the hopes of preserving social peace by reaching an agreement with the Christian Democrats and the national bourgeoisie. A second section wanted to push forward towards socialism, in the hope of winning the inevitable confrontation. 'Consolidate' or 'Advance without Compromise': these were the slogans advanced as alternatives. President Allende clearly supported the first slogan. In the year and a half to come, he would do everything in his power to prevent civil war, but little to prepare the working class to confront it. 'Consolidation' was also the slogan of the Communist Party, the largest single political organization in Popular Unity. At the same time, a majority in Allende's own Socialist Party clearly supported the second, revolutionary alternative.

Divided between 'reformists' and 'revolutionaries', with the reformists in control of the State apparatus but unable to impose any kind of discipline on their revolutionary partners, still less a repression of the revolutionary Left as a whole, Popular Unity passed into a year and a half long phase of internal and external crisis.

This was the setting for 'people's power'. In that year and a half, for the first time in their history, the oppressed classes of Chile began to solve their problems directly through self-organization. The organizations of Popular Unity's political base which had been set up in the first year were revitalized: assemblies of workers in the factories, People's Supply Committees in the *poblaciones* (poor or working class suburbs, often shanty towns erected on land taken over illegally), Peasants' Councils in the rural areas. Committees of action sprang up uniting these local organizations into bigger units: committees of all the factories in a given municipality, the so-called industrial cordons, and joint committees of industries with neighbourhood organizations, the community commands.

Gradually, certain basic demands emerged from these popular organizations. The government was supposed to represent the people; in that case, it should put into operation the policies the people were demanding, rather than try to muffle those demands. Bureaucratic control of the workers' movement was unacceptable. It should be replaced by workers' control, in the factories, on the farms, in the *poblaciones*. The distribution of goods should be organized by the government, so that the needs of the people were satisfied. If the bourgeois legal system and parliament stood in the way of these demands, then they must go.

The oppressed were not interested in consolidation, or in preserving the government's constitutional purity, particularly if that meant a continuation of the old system of class abuses or delivering new weapons into the hands of the Right. What they wanted could only be achieved by a socialist revolution. But they were not yet capable of demanding that revolution as something completely distinct from the People's Government they had elected in 1970. In spite of growing friction, they were still dependent on Allende for leadership. Characteristically, in the month before the coup, the united demand of the working class was for the government to take 'a hard line with the Fascists', a demand which the government, rapidly losing all control over the State apparatus, could not possibly fulfil.

For the Right, the emergence of 'People's Power' posed a very grave threat. They were acutely aware of the growth of special mechanisms of distribution in working class areas, and resented them as a direct attack on their own privileges of distribution and on the market system on which those privileges were based. But they were also aware that 'People's Power' could be an even more fundamental danger: even if only in embryo, dual power was emerging in Chile, and it posed a threat to the bourgeois constitutional order itself. There could not be two sources of executive power within the framework of the bourgeois State. (Only the left wing of the Christian Democrats was prepared to see an equivalent danger in the growing executive power of the armed forces and of independent Fascist movements like Fatherland and Freedom: dual power is only a threat to the bourgeois order when it is in the hands of the working class.)

For Allende, 'People's Power' was an embarrassment, both as a source of demands from the working class which his government could not possibly satisfy and as a serious impediment to his chances of reaching an agreement with the Christian Democrats. The middle classes reacted bitterly to all forms of working class self-organization, and would certainly not be reconciled to the government unless these were suppressed. Furthermore, 'People's Power' posed a threat to Allende's own capacity to lead and control the popular movement. Traditional institutions which supported his strategy were being superseded. The CUT, controlled by the Communist Party, was now at best following in the wake of the working class and at worst, confronting a serious rival in the shape of the industrial cordons. During 1972 the Communist Party itself began suffering from competition at the base, challenges from other political tendencies about the specific actions to be taken in the day-to-day crisis organizations of the class. There was severe pressure on its own militants from their comrades at work to move toward the Left.

For the revolutionary currents inside Popular Unity, 'People's Power' presented an opportunity to build up the popular basis for a new socialist State and to push the movement forward on the path toward real socialism. All these groups – the left Socialists, the MAPU and the Christian Left – gave open encouragement to 'People's Power': throughout the country, their militants encouraged the organization of similar institutions in new areas. So did the MIR, although its hopes for the new committees of action seem to have been more cautious. At the same time, all these organizations – not excepting the MIR – suffered from a common inability to develop a clear alternative to Allende's government. In a sense, they were caught in a trap of their own making. The Socialists, the MAPU and the Christian Left were all still members of the Popular Unity coalition. Their main perspective for political action still took that government as its point of departure, aiming to prevent it from backsliding into a successful collaboration with the bourgeoisie, and if possible, to force it to accept the results of independent working class organization. It was not and could not be a programme for smashing the State of which Allende was the titular head.

So when the final confrontation came, the organization and policy of the revolutionary Left was essentially defensive. It could not move against 'the legal government': so it had to wait, in effect, for the generals to move first. Militarily, that position would be fatal. Politically, the Left had to move in support of a government which had seriously demoralized key sectors of the vanguard and confused many more of the working class, and which, furthermore, had been losing control over the armed forces for several months; it was not ideal ground for a confrontation

The failure in Chile in 1973 was obviously and clearly a defeat for the 'parliamentary road to socialism'. But it was also a defeat for Chile's revolutionary Left. There was a working alliance between revolutionary tendencies in Popular Unity and the MIR from the first months of 1972. This alliance was consolidated semi-formally in 1973, when the MIR offered public support to the Socialist Party in the March elections. For the revolutionary Left, the alliance was a necessary practical condition for work: necessary to protect the MIR from attacks from the Communist Party (and thus by extension, revolutionary politics within Popular Unity), and also necessary as a means of reinforcing the weight of all those groups who supported 'People's Power'. It could have become something more – the basis for a revolutionary party capable of leading the working class by organizing all its demands into a drive for power. But the revolutionary party was never formed.

The failure of all the revolutionary currents to consolidate their tactical alliance into a clear alternative leadership for the Chilean working class is one of the saddest aspects of the defeat that class suffered in September 1973.

Crisis in Popular Unity, 1972

'People's Power' first emerged during Popular Unity's long moment of truth in the first six months of 1972.

In January 1972, the coalition failed to win two critical by-elections in Linares and Colchagua, both predominantly rural areas where the government had expected a victory on the basis of its consistent programme of agrarian reform. These by-elections would eventually cost it the support of the one remaining sector in Popular Unity which could be said to represent the interests of the small and medium bourgeoisie. In December, 1971, a section of the Radical Party split off to form the Left Radical Party. This faction was worried by the emergence in Linares and Colchagua of a new programme for agrarian reform, supported by Popular Unity's own local parties and the MIR: the new programme demanded that the limit on farms which could be expropriated be lowered from eighty hectares to forty hectares, and that all rights of the previous owner to keep 'his' farm machinery and movable property should be done away with, in the interests of preserving the expropriated farm as a productive unit, i.e., one with machinery, animals and tools. For the Left Radical Party, this new programme constituted a threat to the interests of 'middle class' farmers in the agricultural areas, and by extension, to the interests of the middle class as a whole. They were also worried by the increasing numbers of 'illegal' take-overs of agricultural property, for which the MIR was popularly supposed to be responsible, and by the government's failure to take action against the MIR. In the spring of 1972, they left the government and joined the opposition.

The government's capacity to reconcile the middle classes was obviously diminishing. The economic boom of 1971 had receded. As the class struggle intensified in agriculture and industry, shortages began to appear. Meat supplies grew more and more scarce: in 1972, the government spent costly foreign exchange importing supplies of beef from Argentina, but in the face of a growing balance of payments crisis, this could only be a short term policy. Furthermore, the redistribution of income had meant a drastic increase in working class demand for meat: total demand was shooting skyward as available supplies declined. There were temporary shortages in other basic goods, which were often the result of industrial sabotage or the deliberate hoarding or wastage of goods. The black market became the basic source of supply for those middle class families who could afford it, while those who were not rich enough to pay its price faced an abrupt decline in their standard of living as queues grew, inflation reappeared with a vengeance, and the government refused to increase their salaries to a level which matched either the rise in the cost of living or the increases going to the bulk of the working class. In 1972, inflation reached 163% over 1971 cost of living levels, spurred on by the black market. In 1973, before the coup, it would reach 190%, over cost of living levels in 1972.

In the first six months of 1972, Popular Unity held two political conferences to decide its future tactics, one at El Arrayan immediately after the elections, and a second at Lo Curro after its failure to reach an agreement at El Arrayan. Allende put forward a policy for reconciling the middle classes which had the complete support of the Communist Party and perhaps of rather less than half of his own Socialist Party. The basis for this conciliation was to be an agreement between the government and the Christian Democrats on a limited version of Popular Unity's own programme, which could pass through Congress with Christian Democrat support and thus finally become the law of the land. Popular Unity was to offer to limit its nationalizations to 91 key monopoly firms, rather than taking the 264 firms which had had a capital of more than 14 million escudos (about £400,000) in 1970, and which would have to be taken over if its original election manifesto were followed through.

If this concession was to have any real political significance, however, the government had to call a halt to the host of technically illegal initiatives already taken by workers and peasants in occupying their factories and farms. In the spring of 1972, the Communist Party launched a bitter campaign against the MIR for sabotaging the programme of Popular Unity with this kind of illegal action: the MIR was accused of 'playing the game of the bourgeoisie'. The campaign never went further at the national level than a battle of words and failed to spark off any generalized government offensive against the MIR, although there were local clashes between the Communist Youth and *MIRistas* which resulted in one death. At this conjuncture, official repression was impossible, because the majority wing of the Socialist Party was itself moving much closer to the politics of the MIR. (In any case, the accusation that the MIR was behind all these illegal initiatives was almost certainly an exaggeration of its real political weight; most illegal actions were the result of spontaneous initiatives by local peasants or workers against local oppressors. No one needed to convince the Chilean oppressed to act illegally, once they felt that the government was on their side, and might even give them some protection against the accustomed fury of the law.)

The majority of the Socialist Party had in fact developed a programme of its own, calling for the reaffirmation of Popular Unity's original commitment to nationalize the whole of the monopoly sector, and for greater worker participation in the nationalized sector, as well as demanding that the government solve the crisis in parliament by replacing the existing bourgeois system with a 'Popular Assembly', as it had promised in the original electoral programme. At the same time, the Socialists adopted the agrarian programme put forward jointly by the bases of Popular Unity and the MIR in Linares and Colchagua. The Socialists were proposing an offensive strategy; there was to be no conciliation with the Christian Democrats. They were throwing overboard not only Allende's hopes of persuading the Christian Democrats to agree to a limited number of nationalizations, but also the hope of maintaining their support for the agrarian reform law which the Christian Democrats themselves had initiated, and which was the foundation of the party's considerable support in the rural areas. By the same token, there was to be no conciliation of the middle classes, no concession to their faith in the existing legal framework and institutions, no repression of the working class movement in their interests. The Socialist Party systematically refused to join the president's denunciations of 'illegal' or 'inappropriate' popular initiatives, and took as one of its principal slogans, 'The task of the moment is to destroy parliament.'

The Socialist Party's answer to Popular Unity's apparent loss of popularity in the elections of Linares and Colchagua was thus to be radicalization of the original programme, and a turn away from the representatives of the 'small and medium bourgeoisie' within the coalition (like the Left Radicals and the Radical Party itself) towards the MIR. One can argue that this tactic would not have broadened support for Popular Unity: since it was never the tactic favoured by the president, and thus was never tested in practice, the argument is impossible to disprove. But on one minor point the Socialists gained a clear victory. After the by-elections, the opposition had made great play of demanding a plebiscite, on the ground that they had proved that Allende no longer had the support of the country. The Right argued briefly that there should be a general vote to determine whether the people wanted this government or not, and if not, Allende should resign. The Socialists counterposed a demand of their own for a plebiscite to be held not on the question of support for the President, but directly on their own new programme. Faced with this kind of challenge, the opposition backed down, and the demand for a plebiscite ceased to figure in right-wing propaganda.

Meanwhile Popular Unity struggled on. Allende continued to put into operation his policy of dialogue with the Christian Democrats, but the results of every concrete negotiation were consistently vetoed, by his own Socialist Party from within the coalition and by the right wing of the Christian Democrats on behalf of the bourgeoisie as a whole. In effect, the government was not in any position to suppress popular mobilization, and the risks of giving Allende 91 key industries far outweighed any benefits the bourgeoisie might reasonably expect from him. But the charade went on: the negotiations were picked up, vetoed, to be picked up again, vetoed again and picked up once more. Two participants had an interest in preserving the facade that agreement between the Christian Democrats and Popular Unity on a programme of radical reforms was still possible: Allende, because the 'legal road to socialism' could only work if the Christian Democrats agreed to it, and the left wing of the Christian Democrats, because their image as a revolutionary party capable of representing the interests of the working class also depended on it. Christian Democracy had originated as the party of the 'Revolution in Liberty': in the elections among trade unionists for CUT offices in 1972, the party had campaigned on a programme that called for Yugoslav-style socialism, one run by workers' co-operatives and not by that substitute employer, the State. During the campaign, ex-president Frei had pointedly toured Eastern Europe, as though to confirm his own understanding and sympathy for a socialized economy.

What both the left Christian Democrats and the right wing of Popular Unity failed to realize, however, was that Chile had entered a process of radicalization in which the politics of rhetoric and limited reform would no longer work. Frei himself had already realized it. While still on his tour of the East, he made an urgent telephone call from East Germany to block the first attempt at an agreement. The middle classes, petty bourgeoisie and salaried professionals, were becoming conscious that a real revolution would mean a loss of power and prestige on their part, and that it could not be realized without a substantial cut in their personal standard of living. They were not prepared to accept a revolution with costs. The working class and the urban poor who had supported Christian Democracy were also becoming conscious that their practical interests were not opposed to those of their class brothers who supported the government. In July 1972, for instance, a judge in Concepción ordered the return of a textile factory which the government had nationalized, to its legal owners. Christian Democrat workers joined those who supported Popular Unity in a demonstration with one fundamental message: under no circumstances would the factory be returned.

The Emergence of People's Power

The first independent working-class initiatives came over distribution. By late 1971, the government had set up local organizations called People's Supply Committees, or JAPs, in the *poblaciones*. Essentially, these were intended to supply the government with a new mechanism for enforcing price controls. They were committees of local shopkeepers, housewives, and trade unionists or party militants, with the duty of keeping an eye on prices and the right in turn to make demands on the government's own distribution agency, DINAC. Thus as well as supervising local prices, in practice they were in a position to exert some kind of control over distribution within the *población*. From the point of view of Popular Unity, part of their function was to ensure that enough goods reached working class areas to satisfy the growing working class demand.

From the beginning, the JAPs were a key point of friction in the relationship between working class and middle class, and a key issue between government and opposition. The relationship between the committees and local shopkeepers was a great problem: however much propaganda the government put out in favour of the friendly local shopkeeper, it was still the case that many such local shopkeepers were now in a position to make several times the official price on the black market. One of the functions of the JAPs in every *poblacion* was to control the leakage of goods from working class consumers to the black market. Obviously, their interests were at loggerheads with the principles of free enterprise, and many a local butcher was nationalized after being denounced by his JAP. Thus in its practice, the government's distribution policy quickly came into conflict with its policies for reconciling the small and petty bourgeoisie.

Not only were the JAPs attacking free enterprise as practised and understood by the petty bourgeoisie; more fundamentally still, they were challenging the privileged position of all middle class consumers. For the goods which were

12

funnelled into the *poblaciones* were being taken out of the stores which catered for the middle class: where there was not enough to satisfy everyone's demand, the working class was to get more than its customary share, and the middle class was to get less. Redistribution of income and consumption was a cornerstone of Allende's own preferred policies. It was not surprising, then, or should not have been surprising, that the right-wing press consistently denounced the JAPs as 'totalitarian'. One of the most common charges made was the charge that the JAPs were being used to penalize the government's enemies in the *poblaciones*. It seems to have been a false charge, at least as far as government policy had any control over the local JAP – considerable political efforts were made initially to persuade shopkeepers who supported the opposition to distribute goods for their local JAP. Nevertheless, in a global sense the charge was quite accurate: the government was deliberately favouring its potential working class supporters, at the expense of the existing privileges of the middle class.

In March, 1972, a JAP in one of the Valparaiso *poblaciones* introduced meat rationing. It was a wholly logical step. There was not enough meat to go round, so it was unreasonable that some people should be able to stock-pile it, providing they had money and a refrigerator, while others further down the queue got less than their fair share. It was even more unreasonable that people should be able to buy meat at the JAP's carefully supervised official price and then sell it for several times that amount on the black market. But the right-wing press reacted to this initiative with horror, and the government capitulated, forcing the local committee to withdraw its makeshift ration cards (although in 1973, as supplies of all goods grew more scarce, makeshift local rationing was to appear again).

January 1973: People's Supply Committee No. 22

Chile Hoy interviews the President of the People's Supply Committee in Neighbourhood No. 22 of San Miguel. 12 Jan., 1973.

This Committee was created about a year ago as a sub-committee of the Neighbourhood Association. All those people who were members of the original Neighbourhood Association were automatically also members of the People's Supply Committee, and had the right to get their supplies from the Committee. At the same time, we distributed leaflets to all the neighbours explaining what the People's Supply Committees were, who could belong to them, lists of prices, and so on. At first only people who supported Popular Unity joined, but after people discovered that it was not a sectarian organization, but completely open to everyone, many of those who were opposed to the government also joined.

There are 500 families in the area, of whom 300 have voluntarily put their names down for the Committee. Four of the six shopkeepers in the area have joined, as well as the only butcher operating in this area. Only one of these shopkeepers is a supporter of Popular Unity. What the shopkeepers have to do to join the Committee is promise to sell all their products at official prices.

At first it was the job of the president and another member of the Committee to get supplies from DINAC (the government distribution agency) and others directly from the organizations which distributed them. They used the president's taxi. The task was a bit much for two people, but they managed to get a good many things. They got something or other every day: sugar, chickens, butter, cheese, coffee, cooking oil, and so on. And so what happened was that every day, the people who were members of the People's Supply Committee had to queue in order to get a number, which would tell them to go to one of the shops to pick up their supplies. Every shopkeeper would get a certain number of litres of oil, for instance, and then he would sell this oil to those who came to the shop with a certain number from the Committee.

About a month ago this committee changed its organization. We held an assembly, in which we discussed the need for the people to participate more in the Committee and take a greater share in the work. The youth section of the Popular Unity League asked that they should be put in charge of the Committee. The assembly was very pleased to let them do it, because we knew the dynamism and the responsibility of these young people.

The young people immediately made two changes. Firstly, they set up various commissions to get hold of the different products that were needed . . . coffee and powdered milk from CHIPRODAL; sugar, tea, oil and soap from DINAC; vegetables from SACOP; potatoes from ECA; chickens from ENAVI; meat from SOCOAGRO; textiles from CCU; and butter and cheese from Dos Alamos.

The new President of the People's Supply Committee is a second-year law student; he reports that only DINAC will deliver to this area 'but you have to get out there and throw yourself on top of the truck to make sure the supplies don't continue on through'. As for the rest of the products, they go looking for those in the jeep belonging to the School of Graphic Arts, where the People's Supply Committee meets.

The second step they took was to call assemblies of the People's Supply Committee every fifteen days where people could give their opinions, criticize what was being done, and suggest new initiatives. That was how the idea of a supply card came up. People were tired of having to queue up every time a product arrived.

What was this supply card?

The People's Supply Committee registered all the families in the area which belonged to it. On the card, they listed the address, the number of people in the family, and the grocery, butcher's and greengrocer's where they would be buying things. This card had a number. When a particular product arrived, let's say 200 litres of oil when there were 300 families to be supplied, they wrote up on a blackboard the numbers of all those families who could come to buy some. The next time oil came, the rest of the families were listed. This absolutely eliminated queuing, both for numbers and for buying the goods in the shops. People knew that their supply would be kept for them and that they could go along and get it whenever it was convenient.

At the same time, the assembly decided to ask a dietician to join the Committee, who would decide how much was necessary for each family according to its nutritional needs. Up till then, the committee had been giving the same quantity of products to a large family as it was to a small one.

In June, 1972, a much more important popular initiative was taken with the formation of the first industrial cordon in Cerrillos-Maipú. Cerrillos is an industrial suburb of Santiago, with the biggest concentration of industries in Chile – 46,000 workers in 250 factories. Maipú, a farming area, lies on its borders. Once again, 'People's Power' grew out of concrete problems. At the time the cordon was formed, there was a major confrontation over bourgeois justice developing in nearby Melipilla. Forty-four peasant leaders had been arrested for attempting to take over a large farm in the area marked for expropriation. The judge took the side of the landowner against what, from the peasants' viewpoint, was government policy. There were demonstrations outside the courthouse where the judge was hung in effigy, and even an attempt to take him hostage in his office, and more people were arrested. Peasants and farm-workers in the area occupied more than 150 farms and called for the nationalization of all farms in the province of Santiago.

Simultaneously, there were strikes or other conflicts in three factories in Cerrillos itself, for which workers in the area were busy organizing pickets and donations. A small chicken-processing plant had been taken over by the government because its owner was selling the chickens on the black market, and stubbornly refusing to move out. There were labour conflicts in two other factories, in both of which the workers were demanding that the government intervene and nationalize the industry. A factory owned by the textile monopolist Yarur, but not on the government's list of factories to be expropriated, was being occupied by workers because Yarur had refused to honour his agreement to give the workers a share of the profits and better housing. A food-processing factory which was largely foreign-owned was on strike.

The result of all these struggles was a joint demonstration between workers in Cerrillos and the command of Maipú workers. Its target was the Ministry of the Interior: fundamentally, the workers involved were denouncing the continued existence of class justice to the so-called People's Government and demanding that it should take action on their behalf. The demonstration was not wholly a success. The Minister of the Interior did meet the demonstrators personally, but he publicly interpreted the demonstration as nothing more than a gesture of personal political solidarity as he was currently being impeached by parliament.

Cordón Cerrillos had organized, however, and put forward its own political programme:

(1) Support president Allende's government in so far as it interprets the struggles and mobilizations of the workers.

(2) Expropriate all monopoly firms and those with more than 14 million escudos capital (£400,000), as well as all industries which are in any way strategic, all those which belong to foreign capital, and all those which boycott production or do not fulfil their commitments to their workers.

(3) Workers' control over production in all industries, farms, mines and so on, through delegates' councils, delegates being recallable by the base.

(4) Salaries:
An automatic rise in wages with every 5% rise in the cost of living.

Fixing of a minimum wage and a maximum wage in every factory, by the workers' assembly of that factory.

Creation of a National Council of Salaries, elected by the bases.

(5) Repudiate the bosses and the bourgeoisie, who have taken refuge in . . . the courts and parliament.

(6) Take possession of all farms which have been marked for expropriation.

(7) Peasants' and farmworkers' control over all the agricultural bureaucracy, over bank credits, and the distribution of materials and machinery, through delegates' councils.

(8) Creation of a State Construction Firm controlled by the urban poor and unemployed and construction workers, delegates' councils.

(9) Immediate solution to the housing situation of those who live in temporary camps and squatters' settlements.

(10) Expropriation of all urban or non-agricultural land (for new housing) with the participation of the urban poor and unemployed, through delegates' councils.

(11) Set up the Popular Assembly to replace the bourgeois parliament.

It was a programme far in advance of anything proposed by the Socialists and far more concrete than anything suggested by the MIR. The working class was suggesting a strategy of its own: a revolutionary alliance between itself and other oppressed groups (not with the middle classes) under one key slogan: workers' control. What is most amazing is the workers' concrete awareness of the problems facing other oppressed sectors, for instance of the significance of the construction industry as a source of jobs for the lumpenproletariat, a source of jobs which could not be left completely in the hands of those already at work without threatening those who were still unemployed. Joint workers' control by the workers and the unemployed, in the State Construction Firm!

Cordón Cerrillos' programme is the clearest possible evidence of the revolutionary consciousness of the Chilean working class, and it posed the question of socialism for Popular Unity and all the parties involved in it in a way which they would never have posed for themselves. But politically, Cerrillos' programme still had two vital weaknesses. One of them was president Allende. The second was the problem of what to do with the bourgeois State.

The workers were clear that they only supported Allende as long as he 'interpreted the struggles and mobilizations of the working class'. But in the long run, that richly-deserved caution toward the man they had elected president would not be enough. Cerrillos needed an alternative political leadership, not one which expressed the workers' own immediate needs, but one which could translate those needs and the independent actions of workers into a political force capable of dominating the country. Allende himself was not capable of providing that kind of leadership; whether by temperament or as a matter of policy, he was completely entangled in the politics of the constitutional system which in practice, the workers were already being forced to go beyond. But there was no clear alternative to Allende. The revolutionary currents which were sympathetic to the demands of the workers, and might have provided the leadership necessary (as in a local sense, they did provide it – for instance, within each industrial cordon) were not willing to set themselves up as rivals to the Popular Unity coalition to which most of them belonged.

In the same fashion, the workers of Cerrillos and Maipú were very well aware that parliament and the existing judiciary were tools in the hands of the bourgeoisie. It was part of their practical experience. But they could not see the mechanism of the State as a whole, as part and parcel of bourgeois power, because the presidency itself was supposedly in the hands of a people's president. There is no hint in the programme put forward by Cerrillos-Maipú that the fundamental difficulties of the working class could only be solved through a violent confrontation between themselves and the armed forces standing behind the State. Allende's good faith, and the internal dynamics of Popular Unity itself stood between the working class and any real suppression of its organizations (as opposed to a simple frustration of their demands). But simply because of this good faith, the existence of the people's president obscured the real political situation in which the working class found itself: a situation in which it was challenging the fundamental basis of the bourgeois order, and exposing itself to a very grave threat from the bourgeoisie. In effect, the workers of Cerrillos-Maipú were entangled in the most dangerous of all illusions: the illusion that Allende as president and the parties which supported him and were officially in power could provide their supporters with the political means to erect a socialist order out of the resources of the bourgeois State.

In October 1972, the organization of 'People's Power' took a leap forward, paradoxically because of more active opposition from the Right. Throughout 1972, the strategy of the Right had been to use its control over the judiciary, police and parliament to harass the Popular Unity government and prevent it from making further gains over the means of production. In October the Right resorted to its penultimate weapon, a strike by the capitalists and their allies among the petty bourgeoisie. The strike began with the lorry owners. From the very first the aim of the strike was either to bring down the government or to force Allende to retreat on his commitment to make significant inroads into the capitalist system. To this end every section of the bourgeoisie was mobilized in support of the lorry owners.

On the whole the government's response was weak. The army was called out to patrol the streets while Allende negotiated with the lorry owners over economic demands which, for them, were certainly not the central issue in the strike. At the same time, the working class mobilized in a fashion previously unheard of to keep industry running, prevent sabotage and overcome the lorry owners' and shopkeepers' blockade. Many factories whose owners tried to sabotage production were taken over by the workers. New industrial cordons sprang up in all the major industrial suburbs around Santiago, with a number of clearly defined practical tasks in view: keep supplies moving, protect truck drivers who were still working against the threat of fascist violence and maintain production.

Similar organizations sprang up in the *poblaciones*. There local shopkeepers who were not on strike also had to be protected and there too an answer had to be found to the key problem of obtaining supplies. There were essentially two ways in which this bottleneck could be broken. One, which was adopted by the government, was to use a legal provision which empowered the *Dirección de Industria y Comercio* (DIRINCO) to reopen any shop illegally on strike and force the owner to sell his stock at official prices. The DIRINCO officials could count on police protection to do this; but given that there was only a small number of such inspectors, the procedure was slow and limited in its effects. On its own, it could not solve the problem.

The alternative method, advocated by the revolutionary groups, was to mobilize the population to take over shops that were on strike and set up a parallel system of retail distribution under democratic control. In some areas, an alliance sprang up between local industries with trucks at their disposal and local JAPs, now suddenly themselves being transformed into mass organizations as consumers moved into them to defeat the threat to their own lives posed by the bosses' strike. A new type of organization was spawned, the community command, with the same kind of structure as the cordons – delegates' councils elected by the factories and JAPs – but a new basis.

The inventiveness of the Chilean working class was largely responsible for the defeat of this first capitalist initiative. Workers emerged from the strike as a much more obvious source of power in their own right: as people who were capable of running the economy on their own behalf, and of making sure that it continued to run in the face of the worst the opposition could invent. But it was not the workers' task to find a political solution. That was the prerogative of president Allende. The president's own response was to reform the Popular Unity cabinet, bringing in two of the CUT's elected executive, and the three heads of the armed forces. On 2 November, for the first time in many years, active officers of the Chilean armed forces were appointed to cabinet posts; General Prats González took the politically important Ministry of the Interior.

It was a classic example of a parliamentary compromise. The representatives of the CUT (its president, Luis Figueroa, a Communist, and its secretary-general, Rolando Calderon, a Socialist) were there to guarantee to the working class that their interests would be represented in the government and that the Chilean revolutionary process would go forward. Calderon, a left-wing Socialist, was even put in charge of the Ministry of Agriculture: one of the most sensitive areas in the conflict between Popular Unity and the middle classes. At the same time, the three generals entered the cabinet to make possible a mutually agreeable settlement with the lorry-owners, by reassuring the middle classes that their interests would now be represented in the government: order and discipline and respect for law would be preserved, and, by implication, the revolutionary process would not go forward. The two halves of the cabinet were bound to find themselves at loggerheads, unless one of them ceased to press forward its claims.

Allende himself was now engaged in trying to preserve the cohesion of the country when it was obvious that the splits within it had become fundamental and were leading in the direction of civil war. In his anxiety to conciliate the middle sectors he accepted the entry of the generals into the cabinet and made a political bargain with the striking lorry-owners, promising the return of industries taken over during the strike and agreeing to leave retail trade in the hands of local shopkeepers rather than allowing distribution to become the responsibility of the JAPs. In this way, Allende allowed the lorry owners to claim a victory; they emerged undefeated from their strike, assured that the government would not penalize them for the immense damage they had done to the economy. On the contrary, their strike was merely 'suspended' until the government had fulfilled its side of the bargain. This, however, the government could not do. It did make an attempt to hand back to their original owners all those factories not officially part of the monopoly area. This was the so-called Plan Millas, presented to parliament by the Minister of the Economy, Orlando Millas (a Communist). The Plan Millas represented a resurrection of the government's old hope for a deal with the Christian Democrats: a deal by which parliament would agree to the legal nationalization of the firms in the monopoly area, if the others were returned. Once again the deal fell through. The Socialist Party, the MAPU and the Christian Left all refused to support the Plan Millas, and the Socialists forced their own representative in the Ministry of the Economy (the sub-secretary) to resign in protest. A big demonstration was mounted against the Plan in Montt-Varas Square, with the participation of all the left of Popular Unity, the MIR, and more important still, of the cordons around Santiago.

Once again the government was forced to compromise, this time with its own followers. Some factories were given back as the Plan Millas had promised (mainly those with foreign owners, though a number of small electrical firms in the northern city of Arica were also returned). But the great majority of firms remained in the hands of the workers who had taken them over. The Minister of the Economy made what amounted to a public recantation, suggesting that those factories which had been taken over and were not wanted for the social property area, should become workers' co-operatives. It was a compromise which in form should have satisfied the demands of the Christian Democrats (who after all were the most prominent advocates of 'worker-owned firms'). But in practice, of course, it made any arrangement with them impossible. Compromise with the working class had perforce taken precedence over compromise with the bourgeoisie and the petty bourgeoisie. It was proof for all to see, that the bargain which the lorry-owners and their leader, Vilarín, had struck with Allende's government was not one which the government could carry through.

Power does not come through giving back factories

(from *Chile Hoy* 29 June 1973)

A woman worker kept the flag for the takeover hidden for six months before the takeover, waiting for the right moment. Perhaps at that time, she was the only person who would have thought of such an idea. Sunday the first of July, 48 hours after the first, unsuccessful attempt at a coup, a group of 20 women headed by María Sandoval, 49 years old, took the El As Clothing Factory. Moments before the decision was taken, the flag was put out in front of the industry. Only days after the event did the male workers in the plant find out who put it there.

Seventy women, the majority of them less than 21 years old. The President of the union in the factory, a Christian Democrat: the union of white-collar workers in the hands of the bosses' 'friends'. No one would have thought the factory could be taken over; no one, but the women who kept the flag hidden.

Friday the 29th, hours after the attempted coup, the peaceful workers in El As Clothing Factory took over the factory in obedience to the orders of the CUT, and began organizing turns at watch. That day (in spite of their normal punctuality) the bosses did not turn up.

The Sunday shift was made up of 20 women. María Sandoval, a 49-year-old worker, led the group.

'I was already thinking about it, turning it round and round in my mind, unable to decide. Then I began to discuss things with the comrades. They paid us a pitiful amount. They treated us humiliatingly. They insulted the government. They sold things on the black market. We talked about it among ourselves. On every shift there was a comrade who tried to convince the other women.'

At three o'clock on Sunday morning, the workers decided: the El As Clothing Factory, which supplies the army with combat uniforms and makes other clothes, was taken over by its workers. María Sandoval, who led the movement, adds:

'We thought that the comrade who is president of the union, who is a Christian Democrat, was not going to join us. All the women were going to be involved, even those who were Christian Democrats. But to our great surprise comrade Fuentes was with us all the way and even put himself at our head. Now he is one of the most determined.'

At the present moment, there is a court order against María Sandoval and the union President. The 70 women and a few white-collar workers are remaining inside the factory. They want it nationalized.

'The following day . . .' added Marcos Fuentes . . . 'an army general came by. We thought we would have trouble with them, but he told us not to worry, but please would we continue making combat uniforms. You know, there are no problems with that – except that the bosses took away all the keys to the equipment, and we have still not been able to break open the locks!'

The El As Clothing Factory has six workshops and uses material from nationalized industry, to make blue jeans which used to be sold on the black market as American jeans. Now it belongs to Cordón O'Higgins. One of the women workers in front of the factory told *Chile Hoy*:

'Afterwards we received support from the Cordon. We even got a comrade coming from the Central Station Communal Command, to offer us all the solidarity of his sector. We are only a few, but we are not alone: that's what we say! This factory is not going to be returned to the bosses for any reason. Not even if the bosses come back with a few of their police friends to threaten us with guns, as they did on the day after the takeover.'

Before the 29th June, politics was never talked about in El As. The majority of the women are supporters of the Christian Democrats, and the few women who are left wing, did not discuss things any more actively. Today, a few weeks after the take-over, the workers are organized in committees and in vigilance brigades, and are discussing the CUT's statements and disagreeing with them. The women who were passive only a few weeks ago, are planning and participating in decisions about the future steps to be taken, in the event of an attempt to eject them forcibly.

María Sandoval, with the CUT's statement in her hand, explained:

'Look, this statement here is a betrayal of the working class. The CUT's solution is to talk with the bosses and to reach an agreement with them, giving them back the factories, that's what it's all about. I was never very much one for mixing in politics, we never talked very much about the Process (the process of moving towards socialism), but now we're all involved and we know what it means, and all we can say is that this statement is a betrayal of the working class. Perhaps this is a small factory (the government's argument was that only important factories should be nationalized), but at the bottom what's important here is political and not economic: if we workers want power, we shall never get it giving back factories, however small they may be.'

The president of the union read the statement and added: 'I'm not in agreement with it either, even if I am a Christian Democrat. (Not that I'm with Frei, of course, he's fighting to maintain his privileges!) But we here think, even the majority of the Christian Democrats that are here, that this statement of the CUT is not a good thing. If we take a factory, or if workers occupy their centres of work, these cannot be given back, not even by reaching an agreement with the bosses. Imagine us sitting down here with the owners of this factory, whom we know very well indeed, reaching an agreement! That would be a real loss of dignity!'

Our discussion with the workers of the El As Factory was interrupted when the president of the union received a telephone call. When he returned he was looking thoughtful:

'Look, comrade, they have just told me that in Vicuña Mackenna, the police attacked workers who had set up barricades. This thing is developing . . . We have been burning our bridges night after night, so that in the end the government could retreat!'

Nevertheless, in spite of the temporary victory of the cordons over 'Plan Millas', the level of mass mobilization visibly declined during the next few months. The presence of three generals in the cabinet gave added weight to the reformist wing of Popular Unity, a tendency which was reinforced by the temporary absence of Allende himself (on tour in Mexico and making a well-publicized visit to the UN). While the president was out of the country, general Carlos Prats was legally the head of the government, as Minister of the Interior. He was a much more formidable figure to challenge. Prats himself publicly emphasized the effects on the armed forces of the 'responsibility' shown by workers during the bosses' strike.

In any case, everyone, Right or Left, was marking time in the hope that a solution to the crisis could be found in the next parliamentary elections, to be held in March. The military themselves had let it be known that they were in the cabinet until Chile had a chance to vote on the president's programme. Left and Right now divided themselves into hostile blocks on traditional political lines, with the principal concern of winning a majority. The Left temporarily saw its own unity as an overwhelmingly important matter –

divisions might lower the vote. The major point at issue from the perspective of the opposition, which felt certain it could win the elections, was the question of whether Allende could be forced to guarantee an honest election. It was a time of increasing political tension, a time when the traditional political divisions of the country hardened and became bitter enough to make civil war seem a real possibility. But it was not a time for political innovation.

The cordons continued to meet regularly, as delegates' councils, but their relevance to the immediate needs of the working class diminished once the bosses' strike was over, and they served principally as a focus of support for the politics of the Left within Popular Unity and for the activity of all the different revolutionary tendencies. In January, 1973, the Left mounted a new campaign to reinforce the strength of 'People's Power' in distribution, with the full co-operation of both the different revolutionary tendencies in the coalition and the cordons. But this time, the campaign ended in defeat. Its basic aim was to increase the power of the People's Supply Committees or JAPs in order to cope with the headlong rush of inflation, by giving the JAPs a retail outlet where they could guarantee that goods would only be sold at official prices, the so-called 'people's supermarkets'. Coupled with the demand for 'people's supermarkets' went a new demand for rationing. In January, the left-wing press carried reports that People's Supply Committees were issuing ration cards (this time in the *poblaciones* around Santiago), and the incumbent Minister of the Economy, Fernando Flores (a MAPU militant) spoke openly in favour of the introduction of rationing on a national scale.

Not surprisingly, the project met with vigorous reaction from the Right. Flores was forced to recant his statement. A government project which would have introduced rationing at the wholesale level but not at the retail level (i.e., not in competition with local shopkeepers) was thrown out by congress. Once again, Allende brought in the military, this time to take over distribution. The president was hoping perhaps that generals would be able to enforce some kind of discipline on the private sector of the economy. But the immediate effect of this new turn to the armed forces was to squash any existing tendency to let the people of the *poblaciones* solve problems through their own organization. The socialist militant who had been in charge of organizing 'people's super-markets', Jorge Inostroza, was fired. He made a public statement, saying that a distribution policy which had been agreed upon by Popular Unity as a coalition could not be changed so easily simply by removing a single bureaucrat. But the air force general who had arranged his resignation was not interested in setting up people's supermarkets. Recognizing a victory for its own class, the right-wing daily *El Mercurio* produced a triumphant headline: 'MILITARY YES. PEOPLE'S SUPPLY COMMITTEES, NO! The left wing of Popular Unity committed to support the platform of Popular Unity as a whole in the hope of winning a respectable proportion of votes in March, was not in any position to challenge the administration.

The results of the congressional elections in March came as a surprise to nearly everyone. Despite the growing shortages, inflation and the opposition's bitter press campaign, Popular Unity won 44% of the vote. Any hopes the opposition may have entertained of increasing its representation in congress were dashed as the working class demonstrated that it would defend Allende's government against the attacks of the Right.

The immediate effect of the vote was two-fold. On the one hand the government was encouraged by the election result and took some important initiatives: the military left the cabinet, a decree was issued nationalizing forty-one firms, and the ENU educational reforms were proposed. On the other hand the opposition realised that if Allende could not be voted out of office, his removal would necessarily have to be engineered by other means.

On the legal front, the National Party declared that the government was henceforth illegal, while Christian Democracy investigated alternative legal offensives. The bourgeosie did not, of course, confine its actions to the legal and verbal. Towards the end of April it instigated a wave of violent demonstrations protesting against the proposed educational reforms. This was followed in May by the El Teniente miners' strike; originally conceived as a wage dispute, it was encouraged by the opposition as a repudiation of the Allende government, and continued until the end of June. At the same time the opposition continued its street demonstrations in Santiago and launched a number of unco-ordinated and short-lived strikes. Throughout May and June the government was in a constant state of near crisis, and was unable to exert effective control without recourse to military support through the declaration of a state of emergency.

On 29 June, there was another national emergency: an attempted coup. The coup was easily crushed, with the participation of General Prats himself, but it succeeded in calling forth a massive mobilization of the working class to defend the government. The same day, people from all over Santiago gathered around the presidential palace to demonstrate their support for Allende against those who wanted to overthrow him. For the first time in many months, the CUT clearly took a lead, putting out an immediate call for workers to occupy their factories when the news of the attack on the presidential palace first came. Even factories which had not previously been notably political responded to this call: several hundred factories were taken over in Santiago, some of them on the government's list, most of them not. For once, the CUT and the cordons were united. The feeling was widespread that the crunch was on its way, and that the working class and its allies must prepare by launching a massive attack on all property which remained in bourgeois hands. In some rural areas, peasants began to plan the takeover of all unreformed lands. The CUT itself argued for the next ten days that the working class must be prepared to defend itself, and stood out against government pressure to hand back the factories, in spite of pressure from Allende himself to return to the methods of conciliation with the Christian Democrats and the small and medium capitalists.

But on 10 July, the CUT capitulated once again to reformists in the coalition, this time perhaps even against the will of the Communists on its own executive.

A directive was put out, calling for the 'normalization of production'. Another compromise had been reached: of the 100 or so factories which workers were still refusing to hand back to their previous owners, the government agreed to take half into the Social Property area, while others were to be organized as workers' co-operatives. It was a concession, from Allende's point of view, but not one which did much to relieve the feeling of defeat among the working class, which had after all thrown everything into support of his government, only to see it rejected in favour of an old 'dialogue' with the opposition which looked now less than ever like a permanent solution. In a sense, the temporary fusion of cordons and CUT on the 29th was now a disadvantage. The cordons had put their faith in the bureaucracy, however temporarily; they were now demoralized and no longer posed a clear alternative leadership for the working class.

Once again, there was a clear right-wing offensive. But this time the attempts of the working class to meet it and overcome it were hamstrung. The truck-drivers were once again on strike, as they had promised, and with them many other professionals and technicians including many in the health service. The military had begun systematic searches for arms in factories up and down the country, and their mode of operation showed clearly enough that they were not just interested in arms: they were determined to terrorize workers in factories which were thought to be militant, and to prevent the formation of cordons or force those in existence to break up, wherever the local political context allowed them a virtually unrestrained use of force. Local government officials were under exceedingly heavy pressure from their counterparts within the State repressive apparatus to suppress any kind of 'disorder'. Many spontaneous demonstrations on the part of the working class were broken up by police. When the government ordered police and soldiers to help with the requisitioning of trucks from strikers, and the CUT made a last attempt to organize workers nationally through its local branches to carry out the requisitions, the police and the armed forces in many areas refused to support such action, and even attempted to disperse workers who had been mobilized by the CUT. The State apparatus was rapidly slipping out of Popular Unity's control, especially in the regions.

This was the moment which President Allende chose, willingly or un-willingly, to bring the armed forces back into the Cabinet. From the point of view of the working class, the result was complete confusion. The political and economic situation was so bad that many people were prepared to hope that the reappearance of generals in office meant that the government was going now to take a 'hard line with the Fascists', as so many of them had been de-manding. Among the ranks of those without any long-standing political education or any very clear conception of what was happening to them, this seemed the only explanation. But for the vanguard of the working class – those who had organized the cordons, those who were most aware of the damage created by the armed forces in their search operations up and down the country –

this last move of Allende's was deeply disturbing. For the first time, the question of whether the government would betray them was posed concretely in the working class.

The Parties should tell their Bases what is going on

(*Chile Hoy* interviews workers on a demonstration organized by the CUT, 9 August 1973).

Chile Hoy: What do you think of the new cabinet?
Socialist militant from Cordón San Joaquín (a member of the executive committee):
   My personal opinion is that this cabinet is a result of the dialogue with the Christian Democrats, but not a result which gives them everything they wanted, because they wanted middle ranking officers in the administration as well as generals in the Cabinet.
   I think President Allende's hand is behind this cabinet. I don't think it's a betrayal. I think we need now to analyse the situation in which we find ourselves, when it may be necessary for the proletariat to take a few tactical steps back to allow it to continue gathering forces around it, and to prepare itself for a greater crisis on the road to taking power. Without entering into a justification of this Cabinet, we think that it is a tactical step which has been taken with the idea of accumulating forces to allow us to answer the reaction, tomorrow, with a much firmer organization.
   But the fundamental task of this govenment has to be to take a firm line with the sectors which provoked the strike, and pseudo-trade-unionist sectors which are acting against the workers.
Chile Hoy: And what about the searches, and the fact that the military are now being integrated into the cabinet?
Socialist militant from Cordon San Joaquín:
   As a Cordón, we have asked for the law which enables them to search factories for arms, to be repealed.
Chile Hoy: What do the majority of the comrades in the cordon think of the new cabinet?
Socialist militant from Cordón San Joaquín:
   We have not discussed it yet. But certainly people are very confused. In fact, the demonstration today lacks a sense of combativity, there is no common purpose, and there are no clear slogans. One can see that the masses don't look on the incorporation of military men into the cabinet with much sympathy. There is no clarity. The parties should tell the masses what their reasons are for choosing this road. Neither Calderón nor Figueroa (both leaders of the CUT, and ex members of the government, the first Socialist, the second Communist) filled this need in their speeches. And it would have been difficult for them to do it, in this climate of agitation.
The president of Cordón Vicuña Mackenna, where the movement to take over factories after June 29th was strongest:
   We saw this cabinet as a betrayal of the working class. It shows that the government is still vacillating and has no confidence in the working class. The generals in the cabinet are a guarantee for the capitalists, just as they were in October, a guarantee for Vilarín (leader of the striking lorry owners) and not for the working class. We've already been through this solution: More tyres and trucks for Vilarín . . . the same thing again. For this reason, we think that the situation is quite dangerous, because we think the army's searches will continue and we believe that many of those now fighting will fall, including those of us who are at this moment struggling for People's Power.

That was the opinion of the whole cordon, meeting before the demonstration; 45 unions, and some representatives from the CUT, have passed a resolution repudiating the new cabinet. We wrote out a statement which we asked the CUT to read out, but they didn't, and they wouldn't let us speak as representatives of the cordon.
CUT official from the municipality of Macul in Santiago:
The people are very dispirited over this new cabinet. We don't know why the military have come back in. This can be seen in the demonstration. The people are disoriented.

What we would demand from this new cabinet, is that it take a hard line with Vilarín and his lot, really put them in their place, so as to satisfy the majority of the workers who are demonstrating in support of the government.

It's going to be the same as the cabinet in October . . . We weren't ready in October, but now we are ready for any emergency.
Chile Hoy: Are your people ready to confront the coup?
No, not to confront the coup.
President of Cordón Cerrillos:
We haven't yet met to discuss the cabinet, but the meeting will follow the demonstration.

I think this step has produced disunity and disorganization among the workers. They feel that their demands are being frustrated, and for this reason the demonstration has been like a march of corpses. The people have come, but they are very demoralized.
A construction worker:
I will wait to see what this cabinet does, before I pass judgement. I came to the demonstration to repudiate this strike, which is anti-Chilean and in favour of the coup, and to defend the government which represents the workers, because the transport owners want to starve the workers out.

The first thing the cabinet must do is to stop the coup and then solve the strike, so that construction materials arrive . . .
A woman from the *poblaciones:*
Fantastic. At last we are going forward, once and for all. The government will take a firm line, this circus which is ruining the country will be over. I have confidence in the generals . . .
Chile Hoy: In spite of the searches for arms?
But we have been talking with the soldiers. Not all of them are the same . . . I don't know if I am wrong.
Another member of the executive of Vicuña Mackenna; a trade unionist from a milk processing factory:
We're here on the CUT's orders, but as a Cordon, because in truth what we want is a revolution, we don't want reformism, we want people's power once and for all in Chile. We don't want generals in the new cabinet, because we think they want to stop the Revolution.
Chile Hoy: And what do you expect from the new cabinet?
The only thing we want from this cabinet is that it should not come asking us to give back industries we've taken over. Also that it should force the lorry-owners back to work.

Allende may not have been consciously trying to betray his supporters, but his actions over the next month suggest that he was himself extremely confused. For a time, even the reformist sector of Popular Unity lost control over the president. The fragmentation of the different parties inside and outside the coalition was in many ways at its worst: even the revolutionary Left, the

Socialists, the MAPU and the MIR, were at loggerheads over the role to be played at this conjuncture by the cordons. MAPU's last weekly paper to appear before the coup (at the beginning of September) reported that for two weeks, the different cordons in Santiago had not met to discuss the co-ordination of their defence efforts – and this in spite of the fact that the Socialist Party itself had created a 'Co-ordinator of Cordons', a kind of super-cordon covering the province of Santiago which was now publicly calling on workers to organize defence committees in every block of houses and factory, and to integrate these with the existing network in preparation for the confrontation to come. At the critical moment before the coup, the working class lapsed into passivity. It was only a momentary lapse. Faced with the armed forces' action of 11 September, many of the shop-floor militants came out fighting in defence of the government, either from within their factories or as snipers trying to pick the soldiers off from convenient roofs. But for far, far too many of them, that last struggle was as suicidal as the battle put up by president Allende himself within the presidential palace. The best weapon in the hands of any resistance movement is its own organization and co-ordination. Co-ordination was the one ingredient that was totally lacking in the battle which the working class of Santiago put up against the coup.

The Parties and People's Power

When the confrontation came, none of the parties of the Chilean Left were able to make any effective use of that immensely strong layer of working class organization involved in 'People's Power'. Neither the Communist Party, with more than 60,000 militants among the Chilean proletariat, nor the much smaller but also much more clearly revolutionary MIR, proved able to turn people's power into a force capable of making the Chilean revolution. That is the key to the historic failure of Popular Unity itself.

It is still too soon to advance any definitive theory about the reasons for that failure. All that is possible within the scope of this book, is to give a very brief account of the parties' public policies and actions, and speculate about the reasons behind them. But without some analysis of the parties' different interpretations of people's power, this account would be incomplete. For the organizations of the Chilean working class were not somehow politically immune from contamination by the broader politics of Popular Unity. They did not grow out of a vacuum, but out of a political context dominated very clearly by certain political lines. Their internal development was pushed forward or retarded by the activity of militants from all the different tendencies, working inside the cordons, the people's supply committees, and the community commands. For all the independence of people's power from Allende's government, its strengths and its weaknesses in those last two years were the mirror of the strengths and weaknesses of the different parties of the Chilean working class, and their different political aims.

After the formation of a number of cordons besides Cerrillos-Maipú during the strike of the bosses' in October, their very existence became a source of severe strain within the Popular Unity coalition. The cordons were organizations which had developed outside the framework of the CUT and which, on the whole, operated independently of its political leadership. Their leaders were elected from the shop floor – not appointed by the government – and could be changed very quickly if their political line did not please the base, simply by a decision of the workers' assembly in any factory to change its delegate to the cordon. Meetings of the cordon itself were completely open. Anyone who wished to could attend them and speak, although only delegates could vote. For all these reasons, the political 'quota' which worked in the government, guaranteeing each party a certain political representation according to its overall weight in the coalition, could not operate within the cordons. The cordons were centres for a changing, more flexible politics. They were open to *MIRista* penetration. They were also open to public competition between the different political tendencies in Popular Unity itself.

Although during the October crisis, the CUT itself had sent out a call for the formation of workers' defence brigades, many of its leaders saw the continued existence of the cordons as a threat to their existing position within the movement, a threat to substitute a new form of organization in the place of the CUT. The Communist Party supported this interpretation; its militants accused the cordons of being parallel organizations, usurping the functions of the CUT, and refused at first to have anything to do with them.

So the cordons quickly became an excuse for internecine warfare within Popular Unity, for a battle between the two giants in the coalition, Communist Party and Socialist Party, between the line calling for 'consolidation' and the line calling for 'advance'. It was Socialist Party policy to give the cordons every possible kind of support. Their militants were actively involved in keeping the cordons alive in 1973. In the absence of the even stronger Communist Party, Socialist Party militants dominated the assemblies and executive committees of the cordons, together with a smaller representation from the MAPU and the MIR.

This particular dispute began to resolve itself after 29 June when, realizing the imminent danger of a confrontation, the CUT called for all workers to co-ordinate their activities through the cordons. Regional representatives of the CUT began to attend cordon meetings. At the same time, Communist Party militants who had stood outside this particular form of people's power also began to join in. There was no public directive from the Party, and the actual integration of Communist militants and the CUT with the existing cordons was far from trouble-free. In some places, Communist party militants with a strong factory base set up alternative organizations to the cordons which had been formed the previous October – parallel cordons! In others, particularly in rural areas, the Communists themselves seem to have taken initiatives to secure the participation of the MIR. The cordons were to become unified organizations of the working class, to confront any future attempts at a coup.

For a while, it was mooted by the Communist Party that the cordons should also become a new, and effectively much more democratic, form of organization of the CUT itself. But this plan was shaken very severely in July, when the CUT gave in to government pressure and called for the return of some factories taken over after 29 June. Once again, the conflict between revolutionaries and reformists broke out within Popular Unity; once again, the CUT was in open conflict with the cordons. The leadership of the cordons called a joint meeting in late July to set up a co-ordinating body for all cordons in the Santiago area. The question of the cordons was posed as a question of dual power: they were to be 'complementary organizations to the people's government, which could bring new life to the existing organizations of the working class, but under no circumstances organizations dependent on the government'. They would defend the government, in so far as it represented the interests of the workers; and meantime, they were to take charge of 'pushing forward the process and increasing the force of class contradictions'.

This was Socialist Party policy; at the time, all the presidents of the cordons seem to have been Socialist Party militants. As far as the aims of 'people's power' were concerned, it was policy which Altamirano himself had made clear in an interview given to *Punto Final* (the MIR journal) in February. But the Socialist Party's new focus on the cordons as organizations of dual power now brought it into a temporary conflict with the MIR, which did not want the cordons to become the key organizations (although MIR's representatives in the cordon committees did attend the initial co-ordinating assembly). In fact, *MIRistas* now publicly began to support the idea that the cordons were a form of 'parallel CUT', a position which had previously been the monopoly of the Communist Party, and the best solution to their existence would be to integrate them as democratic bodies at the CUT'S base. The MIR argued, very strongly, that 'people's power' was best embodied in the Community Commands, which represented not just the working class, but the working class in conjunction with its urban allies. They also argued, strongly, that it was a mistake to form a provincial co-ordinating body for the cordons. The only provincial co-ordinating body should be the one which had functioned the previous October, during the strike in which all bodies of 'people's power' had participated.

One can find several different rationales for this last sectarian conflict. One reason is obvious, though it may be unkind. The Socialist Party effectively controlled the cordons, because of its existing strength among the proletariat. The MIR lacked that kind of strength (although its forces within the working class were growing). The last *MIRista* 'front' organization to be formed was the Front of Revolutionary Workers, as late as 1972 (following the Front of Revolutionary Students, the Movement of Revolutionary Peasants, and the Movement of Revolutionary *Pobladores*). On the other hand, the MIR was strong among the urban poor and unemployed, and to that extent would be stronger in the Community Commands than in the Cordons.

A kinder interpretation of the MIR's position would be that the MIR were already conscious of the fact that, in the face of a coup, the organization of the working class to defend its factories could be fatal. A factory is no place from which to mount a guerrilla operation: the guerrilla politics of the working class have to be based on the organization of the working class at home.

Whatever explanation one finds for these different positions, Communist, Socialist, and MIR, it is clear that all the disputes meant a dispersal of efforts in Santiago, at the very time when militants in other areas were doing their utmost to push forward the organization of 'people's power' against the coup. These conflicts may explain some of the lack of co-ordination in Santiago in the face of the coup. On the whole, it is the Socialist Party and the MAPU – the left of Popular Unity itself – which seem to emerge with most credit from those last months. They were at least coherent, and public, and bore some relationship to the situation. The left of Popular Unity was prepared to organize people's power as far as possible as a defence against a coup. Where the Socialist Party was concerned, this organization for defence was also seen in some sense as the organization of the working class for revolution. The Socialists saw the different organizations of people's power (but at first particularly the cordons) as the potential basis for a new socialist State, which could replace the old bourgeois State, given that the workers could win the coming confrontation. They called for the formation of defence committees 'in every block, in every industry, in every school'. By the end of August, the emphasis on the cordons had shifted towards an emphasis on organizing everyone under the aegis of community commands, the better to co-ordinate defence efforts. But the meaning of the organization was the same: to fight the coup, defend the government, and so further the revolution. Politically that strategy did nothing to solve the problem posed by Allende's disintegration as a leader for the working class, or the demoralization being caused among the working class by his actions.

Thus Popular Unity limped along for almost two years in the face of an ever-increasing threat from the Right: its reformists determined to follow their original path of conciliating the bourgeois parties, its revolutionary wing equally determined that there would be no compromise with the interests of the working class, and neither wing sufficiently powerful to impose its politics on the coalition as a whole. Between 1972 and September 1973, the gravest failure of the Chilean Left was its inability to take any consistent political action whatsoever. In order to reconcile the Christian Democrats, Allende had to repress the growing mobilization of the working class. But he could only have done so at the cost of repressing half his own party into the bargain, thus creating a final split in both the Socialist Party and the coalition. The politics of the united front were too deeply ingrained in the president's personal history and in the history of the Chilean working class as a whole for him to be able to take that kind of decision.

Carlos Altamirano, secretary general of the Socialist Party, faced a very similar choice, and similarly failed to take any consistent decision. It was impossible for the revolutionary wing of Popular Unity to offer a decisive leadership to the working class as a whole while remaining in the coalition. But it was also impossible for revolutionaries to leave the coalition, without suffering all the costs of a split within the Socialist Party and a temporary weakening of the working class movement as a whole in consequence. In March 1973, the issue was posed concretely when the MAPU split into a majority, revolutionary wing and a minority wing which supported the Communists and Allende. The split created intense bitterness between the two groups, who became proverbial for a time for being more interested in attacking one another than in attacking the Right, and it caused some of the party's militants to leave in disgust. But in the summer of 1973, the left-wing MAPU was in a position to take a decidedly more independent line towards the government, at a time when such a line was becoming increasingly necessary. In the spring, Altamirano and his supporters were strongly rumoured to be considering a similar split within their own party: in the end, they decided not to risk it.

In these two years of internal crisis, the revolutionary consciousness of the Chilean working class revealed itself very clearly, and Chilean workers again and again showed an amazing capacity for developing their own new forms of organization in a fashion which mirrored the socialist society they were hoping would soon come into being. One can see such organizations as being in part a response to the failure of leadership and organization from above, especially in moments of political confrontation – the bosses' strike of October 1972, the attempted coup of June 1973. But self-organization at the base could not in the end provide a substitute for some resolution of the political crisis within the working class parties. In the end, when no clear leadership and no alternative strategy emerged from the debate within Popular Unity itself, the working class itself became demoralized. Not surprisingly, the moment of its demoralization was also the moment chosen by the forces of reaction for a final coup.

8 The Army Moves In

The 'Constitutional' Armed Forces

One consequence of Chile's increasing class polarization was that by 1972, civilians on both sides were pressuring the armed forces to intervene and resolve the crisis. Whatever the ambivalence of Christian Democracy, the rest of the Chilean Right was calling publicly for a military coup. But Allende himself was also attempting to use the weight of the armed forces as legal guardians of 'law and order' against the emerging terrorist bands of Fatherland and Freedom and increasingly disruptive strikes organized by the whole of the opposition.

For almost three years, President Allende maintained that the Chilean armed forces had always respected the constitution and would support the 'legal' government. Obviously, he was wrong. And it is easy enough to prove that he was falsifying history (for it was the Chilean armed forces themselves who invented the constitution, in a series of military dictatorships between 1924 and 1932, mounted to resolve an earlier social crisis caused by world-wide depression), and to find evidence which suggests that for more than 20 years, the armed forces had been steadily becoming less 'Chilean' and more of a local police force for American imperialism.

The Chilean Armed Forces and the USA

There are 75,000 men in the Chilean armed forces: 50,000 of them in the army, navy and air force, and another 25,000 in the carabineros or paramilitary police. For the size of Chile's population, about 10 million, it has one of the largest armed forces in South America. Where Argentina has 5 men in uniform for every thousand of its population, Chile has 7.5.

The army is the largest of the three conventional forces, about 26,000 strong, and by reputation the least reactionary: many of the ranks are conscripts. The air force has 8,500, and the navy about 15,000. The navy is traditionally the most conservative of the three forces; in September 1973, it was the one which initiated the coup. The Chilean navy was modelled on Britain's, and still has ties with the British navy: currently this country is building two submarines and two destroyers to satisfy its needs, and other frigates are under repair. The new Chilean ambassador to Britain is an ex-admiral.

But most of the officers in the Chilean armed forces have been trained in the USA or in Panama if they have gone abroad at all. Since 1953, the Americans have been contributing an average of 10% to the cost of Chile's defence budget, in aid and credits for equipment. Military aid to Chile jumped after the Cuban revolution. It continued during Allende's presidency, even when all forms of economic aid from the USA or the international agencies under its control were cut off. The Americans refused a Chilean government request for credits to buy a Boeing 707 for passenger use, in 1971, but they were quite happy to supply credits to the Chilean air force for the purchase of 12 supersonic F.E.5's.

Other forms of contact with the American military also continued under Allende's government. The American navy put its battleships into Valparaíso harbour in 1971 for a special 'open house' to the Chilean public, and in March 1972, General John Ryan of the US Air Force paid a visit to Santiago at the request of the Chilean air force, and met President Allende.

In December 1972, the US Defence Department announced that it planned to offer Chile $10 million in military aid in 1973. This was double its usual commitment: Chile and Venezuela topped the Department's list of beneficiaries in Latin America.

The coup itself took place when the American navy and the Chilean navy were supposed to hold 'joint manoeuvres' off the Chilean coast – manoeuvres which provided cover for the Chilean navy's own preparations for the coup, and protected the military from any help to the existing government coming from outside the country. There were published reports after the coup that Washington had had 48 hours notice. One explanation given by government officials was that the Chilean forces had told their American contacts, but these cool men had treated the story as just another piece of gossip. There may be a grain of truth in that. In December 1971, in the middle of the Chilean Right's first big mobilization, the White House Press Officer put out a public statement saying that Allende's fall was 'inevitable'. In Chile at the time, it was widely believed that he was announcing a coup in preparation. The second time, Washington waited for the *fait accompli* before announcing the news.

Nevertheless, the 'constitutional' traditions of the armed forces were real enough, and it took the Right and the Americans three full years to prepare the Chilean military for the coup. The evidence suggests that when Popular Unity came to power, the armed forces were divided into two factions: those who supported traditional 'anti-communism' and those who were prepared to accept reform of the developmentalist kind advocated by the Christian Democrats. Allende's ability to make use of these divisions was obviously of immense importance. For right-wing elements were in favour of military action to resolve the country's growing radicalization, even before he was elected.

Allende's belief in the 'constitutional' role of the armed forces was not just a case of personal naïvety. When Popular Unity came to power, most of its militants were well aware of the dangers. There was a saying that Allende himself spent 23 hours out of every 24 worrying about the army. *'Constitutionalism' was a tactic: an attempt to use the ideology of the bourgeois State against the apparatus itself, to restrain those elements in the armed forces who wanted a coup.* As a tactic, it reflected vividly Popular Unity's worst blind spot, its inability to understand that the structures of the bourgeois State were not some kind of neutral territory to be captured by the working class, but a basic element in the system of bourgeois domination, an active force on the side of the bourgeoisie. But this appeal to bourgeois ideology only became the dominant tactic when events made it seem the easiest way of keeping the armed forces under control, that is, when the Right committed the tactical error of murdering the reformist and emphatically 'constitutionalist' General René Schneider, Chief of Staff of the Armed Forces, after Allende had been elected in 1970 but before he could take office. In 1970, it was obvious that the armed forces were one of the biggest threats to the new government. The illusion that they were really 'constitutionalist' and represented some kind of neutral force within the country only penetrated Chile's Left when more than a year went by without the Right showing enough strength in the armed forces to make it look probable that they would intervene.

Allende consecrated Schneider's death as the corner-stone of Popular Unity's own policy towards the armed forces. Schneider became the martyr who had died to preserve their constitutional purity. It was a superb piece of opportunist politics, making the maximum use of the very real sense of shock within the armed forces following Schneider's death. But three years later, after democratic politics had led the country into a situation of pitched class conflict, after many civilians had died and the armed forces themselves had put down one coup at the cost of the lives of some of their own NCOs and soldiers, their officers were less wary of the risks that a coup might shed some military blood. Then 'constitutionalism' would prove to be Popular Unity's greatest weakness: for it meant that in the preceding three years, the coalition had tied its own hands on the question of reform within the armed forces. The Chilean military remained an island of bourgeois hierarchy and discipline in the face of a collapsing bourgeois order – which meant that its forces emerged virtually intact to make the final coup.

'Constitutionalism' implied a *quid pro quo*. The armed forces would not intervene in politics, so long as no one challenged the pre-eminent role of the existing State apparatus, and in particular their own monopoly over the means of violence. The appearance of Fatherland and Freedom as an active force did not really pose any threat to the existing order: after all, its militants claimed to look towards the military for leadership and were calling openly on them to take control. As far as the neo-Fascists were concerned, the armed forces could afford to be ambivalent about asserting 'law and order'.

But it could not afford to be ambivalent about any similar moves towards independent action on the part of the working class. For three years, the right-wing media did everything within their power to keep alive the myth that Cuba was supplying the Marxists with arms. Unquestionably, by 1973, the armed forces were convinced that their monopoly over arms was being challenged from the Left. And this belief had some justification, however much their fears may have been exaggerated by right-wing propaganda. Faced with the appearance of armed fascist thugs supporting and defending right-wing strikes, the Chilean working class could not afford to keep its end of Allende's bargain. Committees of self-defence were organized, along with all the other elements of 'People's Power'. When party headquarters were being attacked and bombed by Fatherland and Freedom, with the police seemingly incapable of controlling terrorism by the Right, it was logical that they should take some measures to defend themselves. Bourgeois 'law and order' does not guarantee the safety of revolutionaries: when they organize to guarantee their own safety, they pose a threat to that very 'law and order'.

'People's Power' itself was also fundamentally unacceptable to the armed forces, as it was to the Christian Democrats, and for much the same reason. When the workers began taking political initiatives in their own right, initiatives over which the government had no control, then they posed a fundamental threat to the world of hierarchy and discipline on which the armed forces were founded. 'People's Power' in Chile was never sufficiently strong to become a real alternative to the State apparatus: but the Christian Democrats, and the army, were vividly aware that it could play that role. Allende's own political position made it impossible for him to suppress the rival. As soon as this became clear, the coup was inevitable.

The coup of 11 September revealed just how damaging Allende's policy of 'constitutionalism' had been. For this policy meant in practice that, for three years, the ranks of the armed forces had been insulated from the political process which was transforming the country outside their barracks: they missed three critical years of class education. 'Constitutionalism' committed Allende to preserving the existing order of discipline within the armed forces, just as it was when he was elected. In the three months preceding the coup, the officers were thus able to pick off or identify soldiers and NCOs who were sympathetic to the Left. It seems at least likely that Popular Unity (or its various parties, independently) and the MIR, had been trying to infiltrate the armed forces. Without reforms in the internal structure of the military, such infiltrations were worse than useless. During the coup, soldiers in Concepción wiped out a whole school of NCOs who were thought to be *MIRistas*. There was no 'trade union' or other independent organization of the ranks to give them some basis for protecting their own men.

'Constitutionalism' also meant that right up to the last moment, Allende himself could not come out and openly denounce the armed forces for the preparations they were making to overthrow him, or order his supporters among the generals (four generals out of twenty-two) to move whatever forces they could lay their hands on to support the working class. When the coup was on the cards, Allende supported the right-wing navy hierarchy in its arrest and torture of a number of serving ratings whom the officers were accusing of 'subversion': subversion which seems to have amounted to their informing left-wing politicians of the preparations for a coup. At the same time, he was forced to accept tamely the resignation of one after another of his four supporters, including Prats, the Chief of Staff. After all, for three years, both he and these same supporters had been stressing that unity must be preserved through a doctrine of 'constitutionalism' and 'apoliticism'. Faced with a real threat of civil war, they could not suddenly turn their backs on that position for one of mobilizing whatever forces were under their control to fight a bloody, political battle on Popular Unity's behalf against the majority of the officer corps. When the coup came, Prats was not in any position to bring out the troops for Allende: he too was committed to being 'constitutional'.

And above all, 'constitutionalism' functioned in the end to keep the working class and its leaders under the worst of all illusions. For three years, even those elements within Popular Unity who had always claimed that some kind of confrontation was inevitable had not been preparing the working class to meet it. The arming of the Chilean working class was carried out hurriedly, inefficiently, probably over the last two months. There was not even adequate provision for an 'underground' set of communications: to destroy the fighting unity of the Left, the army had only to take over the government's official radio stations. Allende always claimed that he would do everything in his power to avoid civil war. The ultimate result of his commitment to this gentle road to socialism was that the Chilean working class met a military coup without any kind of adequate preparation, and was massacred.

Unconstitutional Origins

Even before Allende was elected, there were persistent rumours in Santiago of a military plot to overthrow the previous, Christian Democrat, administration. The rumours followed an army mutiny in October 1969 led by General Viaux, who was later to become a key figure in Fatherland and Freedom. Ostensibly, the mutiny's motivations were all economic: President Frei had neglected to raise the armed forces' salaries to keep pace with inflation. The mutiny was put down, salaries were raised by some 80–100%, new military equipment was purchased and the affair came to an end. But in March 1970, the government announced that a seditious group of army officers had been plotting to over-throw the administration. Many of these officers were pensioners (a retired general was named as the ringleader) but 'serving soldiers' were also involved. The plotters, it seemed, had planned to assassinate members of the administration and senior officers unsympathetic to the coup, take power, muzzle the unions (the CUT had called a general strike against the October 1969 mutiny) and mount an offensive against the MIR.

The plot was probably nothing more than a prolonged piece of self-dramatization, motivated by officers' grievances against the infiltration of 'left-wing' ideas by the Christian Democrats into the traditionally anti-communist leadership of the armed forces. After the October 1969 mutiny, President Frei had retired the existing Chief of Staff and replaced him with General Schneider, popularly supposed to be a supporter of Tomic (the left-wing Christian Democrat who was to run for president in 1970). Schneider was certainly a 'constitutionalist' and publicly took the position that the armed forces had no right to decide political questions. At the same time, he allowed younger officers to use the official journals to attack the abuses of 'anti-communism', particularly its use as a blanket justification for military inter-vention on behalf of the privileged classes, whenever their interests were threatened by reform.

But when in September 1970 Allende won a plurality of the vote, General Viaux and other retired and serving officers from all branches of the services, together with civilian sympathizers, set about plotting in semi-earnest. They plotted a mutiny in Concepción to be timed to coincide with the kidnapping of 'constitutionalist' officers: Schneider, Prats, Pinochet, and Schaffhauser. They expected an uprising by forces of the Left if Alessandri were confirmed as president by congress (as they hoped he would be, and as he could have been under the existing constitution which, when no presidential candidate got an absolute majority, allowed congress to take the final decision). If Allende was confirmed as president, they planned to stop him taking power by a coup.

The plan backfired with the attempted kidnapping of General Schneider, its first step. Unexpectedly, Schneider fought back against the kidnappers, and was mortally wounded by the exchange of fire (he died in hospital, three days later). The serving officers who had been party to the plot received a rude shock. It was the first time in living memory that the military had killed one of their own officers – in spite of all the faction fights and the succession of coups between 1924–1932, when the military ruled the country, military leaders had never spilled one another's blood. Those who were implicated actually supported the government's State of Emergency, and were later allowed to resign (among them, the commanders of the Santiago and the Concepción garrisons). The Right was temporarily discredited within the armed forces as it was in the country. Popular Unity sent its own investigators to join the military in the search for Schneider's murderers, and before his term came to an end, President Frei appointed still another 'constitutionalist' to replace Schneider as Chief of Staff of the Armed Forces, General Prats González. The myth of 'constitutionalism' was born.

The End of Reforms

In practice, 'constitutionalism' resulted in an immediate modification of Popular Unity's own original electoral platform. There, the various parties in the coalition had specified that the constitution would be reformed to give NCOs and serving soldiers the right to vote, thus ending in principle their political isolation. The Left had also agreed that the armed forces were not to 'participate in activities of interest to foreign powers', and promised them access to technical training and modern military science, but only 'as deemed convenient to Chile and in the interests of national independence and of peace and friendship among peoples', in clear reference to the intimate connections which existed between the Chilean armed forces and the American armed forces, who not only provided much of the technical training but also footed 10% of the Chilean defence budget. The armed forces were to be reoriented towards making a practical contribution to development – running literacy courses, making roads. And finally, they were to have a 'just and democratic system of remuneration' and a better system of internal promotion to allow soldiers to move from the ranks into the officer class.

It was a vague programme in many ways, but one which could have been used as the basis for far-reaching internal reforms and which did point to the dangers of subversion by the Americans. The time to put these reforms into operation was clearly the government's first year in power, when the assassination of Schneider had temporarily weakened the position of the Right within the armed forces. Instead, almost all of the concrete proposals in the electoral platform were abandoned. NCOs and serving soldiers were not given the right to vote. Connections with American imperialism continued (and were to continue even during 1972 and 1973, when the USA was doing its best to mount an economic blockade against Chile, and publicly saying that Allende's government could not last). The only proposal which was implemented was the involvement of the armed forces in 'development', along lines already pioneered by the Christian Democrats. Meanwhile, the government made

---

EL REBELDE

The people say:

We Demand the Immediate Democratization of the Armed Forces and Police

The right to vote.

An end to internal discrimination.

One salary scale for officers and men.

Integration of professional schools belonging to the different branches.

The right for the ranks to meet freely and discuss their problems.

Their right to read and have copies of all kinds of magazines within the barracks.

A just wage.

An 8-hour day, in practice, with any overtime being paid for.

The right to participate in mass organizations, like all workers.

We demand the right for all soldiers and policemen not to be used any more as a force of repression against the working class.

The right to disobey officers calling for a coup.

The right to join with the people in their struggle against the capitalist class.

every effort to keep the forces happy with high wages and other social benefits, like preferential treatment for the building of houses.

In September 1971, the MIR brought out its own programme on the armed forces in its weekly paper, *El Rebelde*, and distributed leaflets carrying the same message around Santiago (see page 193).

The MIR's programme would have lessened officer control over the ranks and guaranteed their right to free access to political ideas, political discussion, and political organizations. But Popular Unity was absolutely consistent in its new programme of taking the same attitude to such attempts at reform as was likely to be taken by the officers themselves. The government removed that issue of *El Rebelde* from the newstands and laid a charge against its author, Andrés Pascal Allende. He happened to be a nephew of the president. After a few weeks, the charge was quietly dropped. But the point had been made: no political interference would be tolerated in the armed forces. The army was to remain under the officers' control.

The Armed Forces as Arbiter in the Class Struggle

In the next year, paradoxically, it was Popular Unity itself which did most to bring the armed forces and their officers into politics, as an 'impartial arbiter' in the class conflict and a political weight on the side of the legal government. This increasing involvement of the military began in December 1971 with the March of Women with Empty Pots – an attempt by the Right to create the kind of detonator which had been used successfully in Brazil in 1964 to bring on a coup. In Brazil, the women and the Church together had taken to the streets claiming that 'all that was most sacred' and the very bourgeois family itself was being endangered, and the armed forces responded.

In Chile, the Right was given a nasty shock. Instead of moving to overthrow the government, the police and the armed forces moved to support Allende. The women coming into the centre of Santiago were dispersed with tear gas bombs after a violent clash between their 'guard of honour' (supplied and armed by Fatherland and Freedom, and the Christian Democrat youth brigade) and some construction workers, well before the march had reached the presidential palace. Many young men of wealthy families and right-wing sympathies were arrested during the demonstration and held incommunicado for a number of days. In the days which followed, a State of Emergency was declared in Santiago, an army general was in control of the city, and soldiers patrolled enforcing a curfew in the city's wealthiest suburb. There was even a shooting incident: a young member of Fatherland and Freedom was accosted by soldiers after curfew driving through the suburb, and refused to stop (as it turned out, his car was carrying arms). In the skirmish which followed, the soldiers shot him in the leg. The right-wing press was bitterly indignant.

The events of December marked the beginning of a new right-wing campaign against the armed forces – a campaign which centred on denouncing them as cowards, traitors, men who were weakly supporting the Marxists in government when their first and foremost duty was to defend the nation against the totalitarian threat, people who had 'sold their country' for the price of a slightly higher wage and a few extra privileges. This campaign continued throughout 1972 and 1973, reaching its culmination in May and June 1973, when officers began receiving white feathers through the post – the universal emblem of cowardice. It alternated in slightly schizophrenic fashion with demands from the Right that the military be used to 'guarantee' the government's behaviour in key conjunctures – such as the period from the bosses' strike of October 1972 to the March 1973 elections.

These right-wing attacks on the military gave the government and its different parties a sense of security. With so much venom being expended on the armed forces by the Right, it seemed unlikely that they would move practically to support their denouncers. In March 1972, the police and the armed forces came to the government's rescue again in a situation very similar to that of December. A massive 'March for Freedom' had been organized by the opposition, and the government got wind of a plot by Fatherland and Freedom to make it the occasion for a massive outbreak of violence, and establish connections with some officers to make the violence an excuse for a coup. Another State of Emergency was declared in Santiago, with a general in charge, this time lasting almost three weeks. Police raided the Fatherland and Freedom headquarters and posed for news photos a wide and frightening assemblage of weapons, and hand-lettered placards with slogans like 'Women March for Chile'. The pattern seemed to be confirmed: in case of an offensive from the Right, the forces of law and order would support the legal government. Officers were brought in to Chuquicamata to help the management, because Popular Unity was having increasing difficulty there with the miners (many of them Christian Democrats). There were already rumours that the military might be brought in to the cabinet. It was assumed that they were in favour of a programme of limited reforms. But in essence, so was the Communist Party: the call to 'consolidate the process' seemed to be one which the army and the right wing of Popular Unity might well share.

Two incidents during 1972 should have warned the government that the repressive apparatus of the State would be at best a dangerous ally. In March 1972, after the Santiago State of Emergency was over, the Right called a similar March for Freedom in Concepción. Once again, there was evidence that Fatherland and Freedom were preparing an orgy of violence. The CUT, the MIR, and most of the local party organizations (with the single exception of the Communists) planned a counter-march to attack the Fascist offensive. Permission for this second march was refused, with the president himself intervening to call it off, but the march of the opposition was allowed to proceed. In the event, there were two marches, one of the Right, one of the Left, and the police were brought in to prevent a clash.

In this situation, the police attacked the left-wing march. One student was shot and killed. Forty people were injured, including a fisherman, a MAPU militant, who was chased by the police up into an apartment building and pushed out of the window. His back was broken and he was paralysed for life. The scale of the violence was obviously not consonant with a restraining action.

The second incident came in August, in Santiago, and it involved a MIR stronghold, a *población* called Lo Hermida. The police wanted to search the *población* for a known ultra-leftist, not a *MIRista*, but a member of the more extreme 26th of July Movement. According to their story, they asked the *población* to hand over the man, and its leaders refused. So they came back the next morning with 400 men in plain clothes and uniforms, and went in shooting. One inhabitant was killed outright, and another was mortally wounded: other leaders were arrested and badly beaten up. The incident caused a great stir within Popular Unity. President Allende himself felt called upon to make a public apology to the *población*, and the Central Committees of the Socialist Party and the MIR jointly headed the funeral procession for the victims. The chief and the deputy chief of the Chilean CID were both fired (both of them were Popular Unity militants, one Socialist, one Communist).

Lo Hermida vividly illustrated not only the ferocity of the repressive apparatus even when nominally it was under left-wing control, but what was perhaps more important, a fundamental political stalemate. In the existing Chilean context of mass mobilization and radicalization, Allende could only 'protect' the foundations of the bourgeois State at the cost of systematic police repression of the masses. The whole of Allende's own strategy and that of the Communist Party led logically towards the systematic repression of 'extra-legal' forms of political action. If the police and the armed forces were to be reconciled permanently to the government, this policy had to be followed through: politically and in practice, the repressive apparatus of the State would not allow the mass movement to flout legal norms and would meet all its 'excesses' with a bitter and violent resentment. But Allende himself could not allow them to make this kind of attack on the movement; politically, a policy of systematic repression would have resulted in the coalition breaking up and, more important, in the alienation of Allende's only political base, the working class. In 1971 and 1972 police frustration was relieved by the persecution of those left-wing groups in the country without real political allies, the various super-Castroites and militarists who stood to the left of the MIR. When in 1971 one such group assassinated a previous Minister of the Interior who had ordered the armed forces in to repress a group of squatters (resulting in 12 deaths), Allende introduced a new statute making political assassination a crime punishable by death. In 1972, a similar but less extreme group was subjected to consistent torture with the excuse that they might have been plotting to assassinate the president. But these were tiny minorities within the country, without real political support. The same could not be said for the MIR, the Christian Left, the MAPU, or the Socialist Party.

Meanwhile, two critical elements in Popular Unity's policy towards the armed forces were quickly being eroded. As shortages grew, the policy of 'buying them off' became less effective. It was still possible to keep their wages higher than they had been under previous administrations, high enough to match official figures of inflation. But it was no longer so easy for the armed forces themselves to translate this increased money into goods, for black market prices were very high, and goods supplied from official sources were becoming scarcer. The armed forces began to share the general middle class resentment of popular organizations and of the government's erosion of their privileged position as consumers. In the two months before the coup, when Allende's control over the military vanished completely, this resentment was to become overt.

The People Demand that an Officer be Dismissed

On 21 July 1973, the people of San Antonio published an open letter '*To the workers, peasants, urban poor, students and soldiers in San Antonio and throughout Chile, to the Government of Salvador Allende and the commanding ranks of the armed forces*'. The letter was signed by more than 100 trade unions, Mothers' Unions, neighbourhood organizations, and special groups like the Patriotic Front of Retired Soldiers, Christians for Socialism, and the Revolutionary Front of Doctors and Lawyers. It also carried the signatures of 700 local activists, the municipal headquarters of the CUT, and the local headquarters of the Socialist Party and the MIR.

'*As organizations of the people of San Antonio, as revolutionary parties, as political leaders, we think it is our duty to denounce the arbitrary actions and the reactionary arrogance of the Commander of the Military Engineering School at Tejas Verdes, Lieutenant Colonel Manuel Contreras Sepúlveda.*'

They published a list of examples:

A. **Aggression against Popular Organizations:** *The Executive of the People's Supply Committee in Tejas Verdes was arrested for not giving products to the families of military men, who are supposed to receive their supplies from the regiment. These goods arrived in just the necessary quantity for the members of the People's Supply Committee, which the military families have not joined.*

B. **Threatening a Small Shopkeeper:** *The shopkeeper was put under pressure to sell goods to the military which were intended for the families belonging to the People's Supply Committee.*

C. **Breaking and Entering;** *Searching a grocery for cigarettes which belonged to the People's Supply Committee.*

D. **Taking over Powers which he does not have:** *He stopped public and private transport from using the High Street in Tejas Verdes.*

E. **Being Responsible for the Death of a Child:** *Again taking over powers which did not belong to him, he refused to allow an ambulance to pass which was carrying a gravely ill child. Because of the delay the child died.*

F. **Sabotaging Agricultural Production:** *On Mucalem Farm he appropriated farm machinery and the houses of the farm workers.*

G. **Boycotting Trade Union Organizations:** *The CUT sent the Army Supply Depot 1,800 pieces of slate, to be kept for them, which the army are now refusing to hand back.*

H. **Expelling a Left-Wing Militant from his Home in the Barracks:** *On Wednesday 11, the Commander wrote to NCO Figueroa ordering him to remove his son from the house within the 24 hours. Figueroa's son is a MIR militant. The Commander threatened that if the son was not thrown out, Figueroa's position in the armed forces would be reconsidered.*

I. **Infiltrating Reactionary Politics into the Regiment:** *He allows reactionary officers to pass insults against the Government of President Allende, the revolutionary parties, and the new organizations of People's Power, day after day. This is happening all the time in classes given for the soldiers, in the refectory and in the courtyard of the regiment.*

J. **Persecuting the Revolutionary Press:** *He has repeatedly tried to stop the programme of the Revolutionary Workers' Federation going on the air on Radio Sergeant Aldea. On Wednesday 13 July this radio station was invaded by military personnel, demanding the closing down of the Revolutionary Workers' programme, among other things. The Director of the station was arrested and the military demanded the station's books for future charges and imprisonments.'*

'*We call upon all organizations of the workers and the people of Chile to express their solidarity with those who suffered aggression at the hands of reactionary officers, and to denounce these officers publicly, and demand their dismissal from office. The whole of the municipality of San Miguel is on the alert and will mobilize when necessary in order to carry out this just demand.*

'*If the voice of these organizations is not heard, we will mobilize ourselves for a municipal strike which will join in a national general strike to notify those who are in favour of a coup, and the bosses, once and for all, that this country will be Socialist!'*

At the same time, 'constitutionalism' was increasingly becoming a weapon for the Right as much as a weapon for the Left, as the class struggle grew fiercer, the opposition of parliament to Allende's programme more intransigent, and the independent action of the working class much more obvious. In 1972, there were several instances of conflict between the government and the judiciary: local judges who were also local landowners, inevitably sided with their class against peasants who were trying to take over farms which had been 'legally' expropriated. One instance in Melipilla near Santiago was so clear that the government itself felt forced to denounce it as an instance of 'class justice'. And obviously, in doing so, it was attacking the judiciary. The same kind of conflict was obvious in parliament, which Popular Unity had threatened to abolish in any case (it was to be replaced by a Popular Assembly): there the majority was clearly committed to forcing Allende to hand back all but a very small minority of the firms which had been taken over. This he could not do, not only because it would have involved an ultimate betrayal of the programme and the workers would not have accepted it, but because the bosses in many industries in which there had been intervention were committed to sabotaging production. The government was in a cleft stick. It could and did refuse to take any action to solve the basic conflict over power which was at the root of all these difficulties. But in the circumstances, even its failings, even its random gestures, were bound to be capable of interpretation as 'unconstitutional'.

In effect, all parties in Popular Unity were guilty of consistently misunderstanding the position of the military in the face of a dramatic social change. For the diagnosis of the Right was largely accurate. There was a sizeable conservative wing within the forces, as the Schneider assassination should have shown, willing in principle to plot against the government but not willing in practice to take on the mass movement. It was a question of nerve. A successful coup would require the armed forces to kill some of their own people: officers like Schneider, who were in sympathy with reforms and would not have supported a dictatorship, and men in the ranks with stronger convictions of class solidarity and perhaps even ties with Popular Unity itself. It would require a willingness to submit Chile to a rule of terror much bloodier than the battle which was then going on in Uruguay, much more vicious than the rule of torture in Brazil. Preparation of that kind of nerve in an army which had never fought a battle took time.

In retrospect 1972 might be christened Popular Unity's 'Year of Illusions'. These illusions came to a climax with the bringing of the military in to the cabinet in early November, to 'solve' the bosses' strike. During the strike, the police and the armed forces had once again patrolled the upper class streets of Santiago: confirmation from the point of view of the government, that they would support it in a crunch. When Allende named his new cabinet on 3 November, with three generals in it, including Prats, the Chief of Staff of the Armed Forces, as Minister of the Interior, he gave as his justification that 'it has been the workers on the one hand, and, on the other, the Armed Forces who have upheld the regime . . . these sectors which have been defending the Constitution and the law'. Thus both trade union leaders (two members of the CUT's national executive) and generals belonged in a cabinet which was supposed to provide a political response to the right-wing offensive.

The prospect of military men in the cabinet caused an internal battle in the Socialist Party. Its official weekly, *Posición*, produced an editorial harshly criticising the government for taking this step and predicting that military participation would 'put brakes on the process'. There were even rumours that the Socialists had considered staying in the coalition, but leaving the cabinet. That line was overcome, with the token gesture of a Socialist militant from the CUT being placed in the Ministry of Agriculture, as a guarantee that 'ultra-left' policies would continue, and the following edition of *Posición* carried a pointed speech by Altamirano himself lauding the military for their patriotism and declaring that their integration into the Chilean process was necessary and good. But in the event, *Posición*'s first prediction was correct: the net result of military involvement in government was to freeze the class struggle and retard the development of working-class organizations, perhaps in some areas (such as distribution) noticeably pushing it back.

MIR consistently opposed the inclusion of the generals in the cabinet. For the Communist Party, they were not a problem. For both sides, it was thought, were now looking for a 'consolidation' of the process.

14

At the end of November, General Prats himself gave two public interviews (one to a left-wing journal and one to a right-wing journal) which substantially strengthened the illusions of the Left about its support within the ranks of the armed forces. He claimed that being 'nationalistic and patriotic', the military were in favour of the government's stand against imperialism and the monopolies. He commented that for the armed forces, the strike of the bosses had been a revelation. 'By and large, it was a strike of professionals and businessmen. In previous governments it was the workers who struck against their employers,' he said. 'The country's workers have given an example of great social responsibility during the development of the strike movement, and their social conscience, their sense of order, and their desire to maintain production merit the respect of the armed forces.' It might be considered a slightly backhanded compliment to workers whose 'sense of order' had led to massive development of independent organizations. At the same time, Prats projected once again the picture of a military machine which was unwilling to pay the price of repressing the workers' movement. 'The day the rule of law is broken in this country,' he replied when asked about possibilities of a military coup, 'there will be a state of subversion in this country ten times worse than that which confronts Uruguay with the *Tupamaros*.' The armed forces would have to turn themselves into a specialized military police: this they were not willing to do.

But Prats' public stance as a reformist concealed a more fundamental reason for military participation in the cabinet, the reason which the united opposition had put forward in October in the middle of the bosses' strike, when they demanded that the military join the government to guarantee free elections in March. For the Right, and for large sections of the armed forces as well, military participation was a means of ensuring that Popular Unity would meet 'honestly' an electoral test which they hoped it would lose. From the outset of the strike, ex-President Frei had put forward the position that the coming parliamentary elections were a kind of plebiscite, a time when the nation as a whole could vote whether or not to continue with the government's programme. More optimistically, the Right were hoping that these 'free elections' would give them enough of a majority in parliament to throw Allende out legally (a hope which they seem to have shared with the USA). For one aspect of the Chilean constitution was a provision that given a two-thirds majority of both houses, parliament could impeach the president. The Right in parliament had just under the necessary two-thirds.

Prats himself was careful to keep his public statements of support for the government within the limits set by this electoral perspective. The country had voted to go forward with this programme, and as a soldier, he said, he would support them in carrying out the programme: but the country would have another chance to consider the programme in March.

Thus from 2 November 1972 to 4 March 1973, the military remained in the cabinet, while the country divided ever more clearly into two distinct and bitterly opposed camps, but neither side was able to take any action to increase its own strength. In the end, Popular Unity and its supporters took 44.33 % of the vote: enough actually to increase the government's support in parliament, though not to give it the majority. The Christian Democrats were shocked, once again: they had won the 'plebiscite', but with a much lower percentage of the vote than would have been expected on normal electoral predictions of voting strength of Chile's different parties, and they suddenly faced the prospect that by the time of the presidential elections Popular Unity and its supporters might gain a clear majority of the vote.

The Armed Forces Prepare For War

After the elections, Allende once again asked the commanders-in-chief of the armed forces to join the cabinet. This time he had strong opposition from the Popular Unity coalition itself, which temporarily felt strong enough to do without a military prop. But at the same time, the commanders-in-chief were growing much tougher: they proposed apparently four conditions which Allende could not accept. It was the first clear sign that the military were moving into opposition: as one admiral put it to a cocktail party in the wealthiest suburb in Santiago, it was now a matter of waiting for the politicians to discredit themselves completely.

At the same time, the armed forces began to take initiatives on their own to deal with potential threats from the working class. Using the Law for the Control of Arms, which the opposition majority in parliament had passed, giving them the right to conduct all searches for illegal weapons, they began to raid factories and other likely caches for the Left. At first these raids were few and far between. They picked up speed very rapidly after the troops themselves put down an abortive coup on 29 June, at the cost of some of their own men's lives and the lives of twenty-two spectators. The searches seem to have had three objectives.

Obviously, the military were genuinely looking for arms in some places, convinced that the Left was arming itself systematically with help from Cuba and Communist countries in Europe – a belief which had been carefully fostered for a year and a half by the right-wing press. But the officers were also trying out their soldiers: trying them out to see if they would take this confrontation with their class brothers, as a whole, and to identify the individuals who were reluctant to engage in such actions and could be picked off as possible infiltrators from Popular Unity or the MIR. Furthermore, quite clearly, they were trying to terrorize the working class and force it into retreat.

Punta Arenas is an Occupied City:
— report from *Chile Hoy*, August 17 1973

The raids are continuing, and the working class continues to be the principal victims of these searches for 'illegal' arms. Workers are being abused and humiliated: the

Law for Arms Control is only being used against the Left. Antofagasta, Valparaíso, Talcahuano, Santiago, Puerto Montt, Punta Arenas. Only the city or the industrial district is different: the people who are affected are the same. The experience of Punto Arenas on August 4th is proof that the section of the armed forces behind these raids is not looking for arms.

The 'war operation' laid on by the military in Punta Arenas cost the life of one worker, Manuel González. An examination of the circumstances shows that the search for arms was only a pretext. The real aim was to terrorize the workers to prevent them from forming industrial cordons, and to find out who were the leaders of the cordons.

Since the attempted coup on June 29th, this city has been under virtual military occupation. The streets are patrolled by an impressive number of soldiers, who stop and search pedestrians and workers who happen, by some coincidence, to be all supporters of the Left. Ten days before their attack on the factories on the 4th of August, the three provincial commanders of the different branches of the armed forces made a public statement, advising the working class that any attempt on their part to form industrial cordons would be stopped immediately, and that as MIR was behind the cordons, *MIRistas* would also be searched very carefully for illegal arms.

When the provincial CUT called on the workers to organize cordons, searches of working class homes were stepped up. The culmination of this offensive was the operation on the 4th. During this operation, the officers forced individual workers to submit to an intensive interrogation at the point of a machine gun. They demanded the names and addresses of union leaders, their political sympathies, and the names of the 'instigators' of the cordons.

In Punta Arenas, a city of about 70,000, the military garrison is about 7,000 strong. [Editor's note: this exceptionally high ratio would be due to the city's proximity to a border which is in dispute between Chile and Argentina.] On the morning of Saturday 4th August, some 800 of these men surrounded the industrial sector. They came without any of the usual marks of rank, wearing dark glasses and calling one another by pseudonyms like 'Tiger', 'Lion', 'Panther', and so on. For a search operation involving eight factories, they brought tanks, sub-machine-guns, and fixed bayonets. An air force plane flew back and forth over the district. Below, Commandante Manuel Torres de la Cruz directed the operation.

The result: one worker murdered, one more seriously wounded, and many beaten up. The soldiers found no arms, but they were able to obtain the name, the address and the political sympathies of every union leader. Damages in only one of the factories raided that Saturday amounted to 250,000 escudos, for broken doors, shelves, plates, and windows.

The reason for this whole brutal show was that the three commanders of the armed forces in Punta Arenas did not want any industrial cordons to be formed. Its result was completely the opposite: the day after the operation, the first industrial cordon in the province of Magallanes was formed, and it included the eight factories which had been searched. The commander-in-chief of the 5th Division of the army, Manuel Torres de la Cruz, was determined that the workers should not organize. A few hours after the attacks, the provincial CUT called a 24-hour strike, and after the funeral of the murdered worker, two more industrial cordons were created in Punta Arenas, the Central District Command, and the Prat District Command.

The young airman who opened fire on the murdered worker was taken to a Santiago hospital suffering from shock. Today, other soldiers with machine guns are mounting a permanent guard over the homes of some of the officers in Punto Arenas. This was the result of the kind of operation which other Torres de la Cruz are setting up in other industrial districts throughout Chile.

The working class refused to be terrorized: instead, it turned to the government, calling for a 'firm hand' against the Fascists on strike and against what were popularly supposed to be a minority of officers in favour of a coup. Its courage in the face of this kind of terrorization may well have made the repression that much more ferocious, as it encouraged the officers to fear for their own lives.

It is clear that, for some time, the officers had been conducting a kind of propaganda campaign of their own inside the armed forces, a campaign designed to vilify the government and all the parties inside and outside Popular Unity, and to convince the common soldier that if he did not act against the workers, the workers would murder him in his bed. In August, officers in the navy were openly discussing preparations for a coup. Serving sailors and subofficials in Valparaíso and Talcahuano who objected publicly to these preparations, tried to organize themselves to oppose them, and tried to get information to left-wing public figures like Senator Altamirano, were arrested for 'subversion' and submitted to a barrage of tortures to get them to implicate the three major left-wing figures in the 'crime' of preparing an armed uprising: Altamirano of the Socialist Party, Garretón of the MAPU, and Miguel Enríquez of the MIR.

The incidents in Valparaíso and Talcahuano were to be President Allende's most inglorious hour. At first, he himself denounced the 43 men who were under arrest as 'ultra-lefts' who had been preparing an armed uprising, and supported the navy. When evidence began to accumulate that the only crime of these men of the ranks was their public opposition to a coup, he kept silent. When the navy itself moved to charge the three left-wing political leaders with subversion, as well as the sailors, he still kept silent. The 'People's Government' was completely unable to support people in the ranks of the armed forces who were trying to preserve it against the officers' preparations for a coup – it was left to the different parties involved, the Socialists and the MAPU and MIR, to denounce the tortures and lies and bring as much public pressure as possible to bear on the navy to let them go. In the end, Allende refused to give public support even to Popular Unity's own Political Committee, when it brought out an official statement condemning the actions of the navy and the charges laid against Altamirano and Garretón. He thought it was tactically wrong.

There could be no clearer instance of the bankruptcy of 'constitutionalism'. On a key issue of power within the armed forces, whether it should lie with the ranks who supported the Left or the officers who were preparing a coup, Allende gave his tacit support to the officers, and he did so at just the time when the threat of action by the armed forces to overthrow him was at its height, and his need to rely on the common soldiers' class consciousness was greatest. The arrests in Valparaíso and Talcahuano were a clear indication that Allende's policy was madness. On 11 September, the armed forces intervened, united, to defend their officers' own class privileges and the bourgeois order on which those privileges were based.

9 *Preparations for the coup*

The build-up

The results of the March elections were a considerable blow to the Right; they had anticipated that Allende's vote would be less than the 1970 level, and that the combined votes of the parties of the opposition would provide the two-thirds necessary to impeach Allende and bring down the government. Instead, the Popular Unity vote increased.

The Congressional Elections of March 1973

Composition of Congress before and after the March elections.

| | Senate | | Congress | |
	Before	After	Before	After
Opposition	32	30	93	87
Popular Unity	18	20	57	63

Popular Unity increased its percentage of the votes cast from the 36.2% in the presidential elections of September 1970 to 43.4% in March of 1973. For the Right, which had presented the election as a plebiscite, the election results were a defeat.

Until March, the strategy of the Christian Democrats had revolved around two points of attack. On the one hand, economic sabotage continued and was extended; on the other, the campaign of parliamentary obstruction held back many of the socio-economic initiatives planned by Popular Unity. Clearly, the objective was to maintain an atmosphere of crisis which would create disillusion and demoralization among the working class; the result, as it was envisaged, would be a decline in electoral support for the Allende government. Despite their growing involvement in extra-legal opposition to Allende, then, the guiding perspective for the Christian Democrats until March 1973 remained that of a political party seeking to reconquer institutional, or rather executive, power. From March onwards, however, all pretence at legality was set aside; the watershed had been reached, and in the months to come the Christian Democrats were to espouse every initiative or tactic which offered a possibility of bringing down Popular Unity. The left wing inside Christian Democracy were, relatively speaking, inclined towards a more conciliatory posture, but the wing of the party dominated by Frei (which retained a majority in the party) became increasingly intransigent in the course of the year. Nevertheless, their position always remained much more ambiguous than that of the National Party, whose line after March clearly led towards insurrection. Although the two organizations sometimes struck tactical alliances, and were equally adamant in their total opposition to the government of UP, their perspectives were different, particularly with regard to what it was that should follow Allende. The National Party's sole concern was the restoration of capitalism and the social relations of capitalism; Christian Democracy, on the other hand, placed a greater emphasis upon the return to power of its own party after the overthrow of Allende. At crucial points, then, its ambiguous attitudes towards the extreme Right (particularly Fatherland and Freedom) indicated the need to retain and extend their political support. This should not detract, though, from the brutal fact that the imperative which overrode all others was to halt the process which Popular Unity had begun and return to the capitalist road.

For Popular Unity, the extent of their support in the March elections was unexpected. The immediate result was a series of moves by government which indicated a clear recognition of working class demands. Despite economic difficulties and the vast propaganda campaign of the Right, the working class had once again put its strength behind Allende; but its support was coupled with growing demands for a faster and more determined advance towards socialism – demands, in short, for clear revolutionary leadership from Popular Unity. That at least was how the victory was interpreted by the revolutionary Left. The Communist Party and Allende himself, on the other hand, regarded the electoral victory as a licence to advance the programme of reforms, but at the same time insisted that it offered a clear vindication of the reformist road.

At the end of March the military, which had formed part of the cabinet since November 1972, left the government. Allende's new cabinet was composed entirely of civilians. At the same time, the Millas project (the plan to return most of the factories to their original owners after the workers' take-over of October 1972), which had caused such deep divisions between UP and the workers' independent organizations, was abandoned, and the government published a list of a further 45 enterprises which were to be nationalized. This still fell within the framework of a reformist policy, however, and in no way satisfied the demand of the revolutionary Left to the effect that revolution should advance and expand in the coming period. MAPU, for example, which was now the third largest party in the UP, having received 100,000 votes in March, split only three days after the election as a result of an ideological dispute in which one side supported the Communists while the other leaned towards the left of the Socialist Party.[1] The issue for the Left now was the formation of a truly revolutionary leadership; fatally, such a leadership was never formed, despite the hopes expressed in the post-election period. Thus while the elections had united the right-wing parties in their struggle against Popular Unity, they had simply deepened the divisions within the Left between reformists and revolutionaries.

The decision by the right-wing parties to employ every possible means to overthrow Popular Unity began to make itself felt very quickly. The Christian Democrats intensified their attacks at the level of parliament, acting in concert with PN congressmen to defeat the legislation which the Allende government required to carry forward its programme. The budget, for example, was severely reduced as a result of right-wing pressure; the effect was to immediately reduce the finance available to the expanding State sector, and to force Allende to use deficit financing to carry through his social programme – which effectively guaranteed a rising rate of inflation. A bill to continue the redistribution of income by giving higher wage rises to lower paid workers, and vice versa, was thrown out, and an attempt to impose heavy sanctions on hoarders and black marketeers was given no truck by congress.

The struggle of the reaction was not, of course, confined to parliament. In the streets, demonstration followed demonstration, and Left and Right clashed violently as the campaign of provocation and assault by the Right got under way. The National Party called openly for civil disobedience and insurrection, while its neo-Fascist wing, Fatherland and Freedom, began to organize openly for armed confrontation with the government. Well-armed and disciplined, and enjoying impressive support from the Right both within and outside Chile, it rapidly became one of the best organized groups in the country; its insistent calls for a rising against Allende were to culminate, bloodily, on 11 September. For Fatherland and Freedom, and for the National Party, the only alternatives, as a headline in the former group's newspaper proclaimed, were 'Nationalism, *Gremialismo* and the Armed Forces'. The response of Christian Democracy to the rise of Fascism was, naturally enough, equivocal. They charged the Fascists with 'irresponsibility' and meekly asked, in a newspaper article, 'Do they believe, can they seriously imagine that the armed forces would carry out an armed coup in Chile? And if they do, then do they seriously believe that it will be done on behalf of their movement?'

The Left, of course, did not stand idly by. In April, a series of street confrontations had culminated in a number of attacks by the Right on the headquarters of left-wing political parties, left-wing newspaper offices, the homes of left-wing leaders and even on the presidential palace itself. The CUT called a workers' demonstration to protest at the growing power of the Right. The response was massive. The workers took to the streets; but as they passed the headquarters of the Christian Democrat Party, shots rang out leaving one worker dead and seven wounded. This incident produced further and more violent clashes; on 4 May, four leaders of Fatherland and Freedom were killed in Santiago, and in Concepción, a right-wing demonstration to protest at the death of a local member of the same organization brought Christian Democrats and Fascists out in unity.

Faced with this radicalization of the Right, the working class took its own measures to resist. The dearth of goods caused by hoarding and black marketeering found its response in the cordons, as workers took direct action to solve the problem of food distribution. The illegal takeovers of land continued, and the workers were not slow in defending themselves against the constant assaults of the Right when these interfered in any way with the work of the cordons. Allende's reaction was hesitant. In his May Day address, he exhorted the people to produce more, since 'only the devastating force of the people can detain the Fascist threat by producing more, working harder and showing a greater total effort'. The Communist Party, through its General Secretary Luis Corvalán, insisted that a moderate posture could still win a majority of the middle sectors to the side of Popular Unity, and condemned the MIR for its support of direct action, claiming that the illegal actions of workers and peasants were merely provocations designed to divide the country. By mid-May, however, the situation had become so tense that Allende declared a state of emergency in Santiago province, whose most immediate effect was a revocation of all civilian gun permits and a ban on all unauthorized public meetings. In the event, this served to strengthen the Right who were, curiously, left relatively unscathed by the arms searches. The same was to be true in July and August, when the army made no attempt to hide the fact that its searches were directed almost exclusively against the working class areas.

The Right and the strike at El Teniente

Throughout April and May a series of strikes testified to the tense political situation. Some clearly had straightforward economic objectives, while others were more overtly political. The employees of the Public Works Ministry, for example, not only demanded higher wages, but also called for State intervention in sectors of the building industry not already in public hands, and for an end to the practice of awarding between 50% and 60% of the public works budget to private contractors. Here the political issues reflected activity within the working class, both in the cordons and within the Left. Other strikes, however, while they too posed economic demands, presented a political aspect which was much less clear.

As far as the Right was concerned, the areas of conflict were urban transport on the one hand, and the copper mines on the other. On the 13 May the Christian Democrat Party had decided at a National Assembly to adopt an attitude of intransigent opposition to Popular Unity; the strikes in the mines and in urban transport seemed once again to provide the opportunity to organize a general strike of key sectors to bring down Allende.

The strike at El Teniente began on 19 April, and was to last seventy-four days. In 1943, after a series of strikes, the workers of El Teniente had won the right to an automatic 100% wage readjustment tied to the monthly increase in the cost of living index. This automatic readjustment was cut to 50% in 1959. In September 1972, the government passed a bill which would give a 100% wage readjustment tied to the increase in the cost of living between January and October 1972, to all workers. What the bill failed to make clear, however, was that this increase was not to be added to the miners' individual wage escalator agreement; thus the increase of 41% that the miners had already received from their own readjustment in the course of the year was to be deducted from the 100%. At the time, the workers accepted this decision pending a discussion on whether or not to allow the 41% deduction. The Right, of course, grasped the issue with both hands and repeatedly told the workers that UP had sold them short.

At the end of 1972, the Controller General was asked to adjudicate; in February 1973, he declared himself incompetent to decide. The miners' unions then turned the case over to the Mining Conciliation Board; its decision, delivered on 17 April, supported the government's interpretation of the bill. The Christian Democrats and the National Party had campaigned throughout in favour of the maximum possible increase; now theirs were the loudest voices in the demand for a strike against the government. On 19 April, the El Teniente union leader Guillermo Medino, whose sympathies lay with the Christian Democrats, declared a strike.

For Allende, the strike posed a very serious dilemma. The stated policy of the government was to narrow the gap between income levels, redistributing income in favour of the low paid workers. The miners, however, already earned something like four times the average industrial wage. The government therefore offered a productivity bonus, but refused the additional readjustment.

The right-wing parties could hardly contain their delight; an important, if not crucial sector of the working class was now engaged in a direct confrontation with the Government. There could hardly have been a better opportunity to exploit the differences within the government coalition, and the mass media controlled by the Right moved quickly to add their support to the miners, calling for action against Popular Unity. Nothing could have been more calculated to sow confusion and disillusion among the workers.

In the end lengthy negotiations achieved a settlement and the majority of the El Teniente miners returned to work. A hard core – mainly white collar and skilled workers – persisted in their strike. The government tried a show of force against this rump of strikers, but succeeded only in provoking new clashes. On 10 May a State of Emergency was declared in the province; the strikers, however, sustained by right-wing support, and supplies of food from right-wing farmers brought in by truck owners hostile to the UP, refused to move. On 14 June the remaining strikers (a minority of the total work-force, it should be remembered) marched on Santiago. Those who reached the capital engaged in violent confrontations with the police and government supporters. It was during this period that the source of support for the remaining El Teniente strikers was seen at its clearest. The Christian Democrat party headquarters became a refuge for the strikers, and the support of right-wing congressmen and Senators was expressed at a ceremony held in the congress itself; the elegant ladies of Santiago, who had last taken to the streets with empty sauce-pans in their hands, now rushed to collect funds for the strikers and to offer them food and hospitality. The opposition was determined that this strike should destroy the government.

The following day, Allende, ignoring the express wishes of both Communists and Socialists, agreed to negotiate with the strike leaders. The talks failed, as the Right was determined that they should, and during the next two weeks the opponents of Popular Unity laboured hard to raise the strike to the level of a general and widespread political challenge. Many doctors, teachers and students went on short-period strikes in support of the El Teniente strikers. The Christian Democrats called for a general mobilization of their peasant organizations, the National Party called for 'civil resistance' and Fatherland and Freedom stepped up its campaign of violence and terrorism, organizing a series of violent confrontations throughout the country. Despite a supposed government ban on its activities, there were 77 bomb attacks throughout the country in the week of the 17 to the 24 of June alone.[2] One student died and more than a hundred people were injured in these confrontations. The campaign sustained by Fatherland and Freedom extended to harassment and threats against leading left-wing politicians, officers sympathetic to UP and even General Carlos Prats, who was publicly harassed in a manner that many members of Popular Unity interpreted as a threat upon his life. Ominously, a few white feathers began to arrive at the homes of officers of the armed forces who had not taken an open stand against Allende.

There could no longer be any doubt that the Right was preparing for a showdown. The Supreme Court warned Allende that he was bringing the country to the verge of a breakdown in the rule of law. The National Party took a full page advertisement in *El Mercurio* to state its conviction that the government had now gone beyond the bounds of the Constitution and the law, while the PN president, Senator Jarpa, declared that 'civil war is the price we have to pay for overthrowing a dictatorship'. Ex-President Frei, too, hurried to add his voice to the general chorus, publicly accusing the government of bringing the country to a state of desperation. The Communist Party, for its part, continued its campaign of collecting signatures 'saying no to civil war'!

The attempted coup of 29 June

This carefully orchestrated right-wing offensive on all fronts against Popular Unity culminated on 29 June, when the tanks and armoured cars of the Second Armoured Regiment, under the command of Colonel Roberto Souper, attacked the presidential palace and the Ministry of Defence. In retrospect, it seems clear that Souper moved precipitately, and perhaps in reaction to his own imminent arrest. There can be little doubt that this was to be one of a number of risings throughout the country, supported by the parties of the Right and actively organized by Fatherland and Freedom. A week before, however, the plot had been discovered and exposed, and the coup postponed as a result, as many implicated officers were arrested and a State of Emergency declared in Santiago on 28 June. In the event, no other army units joined Souper – in fact only some 150 men out of the total of 900 men comprising the Second Armoured Regiment actually participated. If further evidence of direct right-wing involvement were needed, it was given by the five leaders of Fatherland

and Freedom who took refuge in the Ecuadorean embassy immediately after the failed coup, and asked for political asylum. Many other leaders of the coup followed them there, among them Souper's brother. As they left for exile in Ecuador, they published a bitter denunciation of other sections of the armed forces which, they claimed, had agreed to support the coup, only to withdraw at the last moment. 'Marxism,' they complained, 'is only maintained in power in Chile because the armed forces have decided to sustain it . . . We would never have thought that soldiers would open fire against their fellow-soldiers, nor that the armed forces would contribute to the maintenance of tyranny.' The president of the National Party, Senator Jarpa, was at the airport to see them off. Ex-President Frei who, as president of the Senate would succeed Allende in the event of the latter's death, made no comment.

Letter from a comrade: the attempted coup of 29 June

4 July 1973

Dear Comrade,

Just received your letter. Well I think the most important news I can tell you is about the failed *coup d'état* against the Allende government. The Friday of last week was an historic day in Chilean history and clearly breaks a tradition of the Chilean armed forces since 1932. Nobody expected the coup and it took everyone by surprise. The description of the events you probably know, so I will speculate a bit on the projections of the attempted coup. First lesson: the military today are a clear political force and will have to be considered as such by the government and the opposition. Second lesson: this is only the beginning of future attempts at coups. Third lesson: the question now is who rides the tiger, the working class or the military? The political struggle of the left-wing parties now has to link their political action with paramilitary preparation of the working class. The stronger and better trained (and hopefully armed) the workers are, the less likelihood that future coups will occur, or at least that in the ensuing civil war the workers might win with, and only with, of course, the support of what is called by the Socialist Party – the 'patriotic soldiers'. The military who are pro-UP might in case of civil war give arms to the workers.

The military are today divided in three factions: one group wants openly to topple the government (encouraged by Patria y Libertad, and Partido Nacional and perhaps also the Poder Judicial as all these groups have since about a month started a campaign in which they attack the government as being unconstitutional), the other group – perhaps the majority – has a centrist position and is headed by Prats, and the third group is pro-UP and is led by Bachelet. The Prats faction is constitutionalist and in turn is split in two groups – one leaning more towards the PDC and the other to the UP. The mere fact that today we are doing this political analysis of the armed forces reveals that they no doubt have reached a great politicization, breaking the myth about their professionalism and revealing also on the other hand the growing polarization and politicization of every echelon of Chilean society. The only institution which had not taken publicly a political position so far in Chilean society had been the military. They are quickly catching up and although the coup failed utterly and was too precipitate, it revealed the political power of the armed forces and made the point that people's power is rather insufficient to sustain a government if compared with the power of the gun. The situation might be different if our working class were armed, but it isn't. Therefore even a left-wing solution to the problem of power will have to get the support and full backing of a group of the military – they have the guns.

Last Friday we marched in support of the government after the situation was dominated by the military loyal to the government. We are quite well organized now, and formed two brigades which have a leader. Our brigades belong to a section which in turn has a chief and is integrated into the sections of the *coordinadora educacional* (secondary students and university students of our area) and this *coordinadora* is integrated in turn into the *comando communal* to which industries, JAPs and *pobladores* of the *comuna* belong. X also came with us on this occasion, and I must confess we all felt a bit frightened – although only for a moment – as rumours circulated that fascists would try to provoke us and above all that snipers were still hidden and shooting from some buildings around the Moneda. Allende's speech and that meeting were historic and the chiefs of the army and of the police were presented at the end of the speech by Allende *para que reciban el saludo del pueblo* (to receive the greetings of the people). We cheered them and shouted *soldado, amigo, el pueblo está contigo* besides *a crear, a crear poder popular* and *la izquierda unida que pase a la ofensiva* (soldier friend the people are with you; create, create people's power; a united left must go onto the offensive). There were also shouts of closing congress.

6 July 1973

Well yesterday at last the new cabinet was announced. Originally I wanted to continue the letter referring to the difficulties which Allende had in forming the new cabinet. First he said the new cabinet would be announced on Tuesday, then it was Wednesday, but only on Thursday did it come out. Apparently the military put certain demands forward to enter the cabinet and this was not accepted by the PS and the PC. Then Allende wanted to include some internationally known personalities of the independent left so as to bring certain social peace (which I think would be ineffective) but they did not want to join. Names like F. Herrera, Hernan Santa Cruz and the Rector of the Catholic University of Chile, Fernando Castillo Velasco. People who would be able to listen to the PDC or other centrist parties. Well you must know the new Cabinet through the English press. The tension has been relieved a bit, but my impression is that at this stage of affairs this Cabinet is of little relevance and the basic conflict is still there and has not been resolved, not even partially. Therefore it is likely that future attempts at a coup might occur or at least clashes between government supporters and opposition in the streets. The CUT and the masses are quite radicalized and have taken over various industries as a result of the failed coup and have no intention whatsoever of returning them. So the revolutionary process continues and has not been stopped yet. Therefore one cannot say yet that our way to socialism is finished, but only that the Chilean road, i.e. the legal way is exhausted.

I include some clippings of newspapers during our week of *estado de emergencia* in which press censorship was introduced to an unaccustomed Chilean readership. Today it sounds anecdotal, but a few days ago it was disturbing as we didn't know exactly what was going on and rumours circulated widely. *La Prensa*, the PDC paper, did not come out for two days and when it finally did was half in white, i.e. censored. Even a comic strip of Don Memorio was censored! And Chile seen from abroad too! So in those days you might have been better informed than we were. (*Ultima Hora*, the PS evening paper, did not appear one day because it was so greatly censored by the military that they preferred not to print it).

On the day of the attempted coup, the parties of Popular Unity met and agreed to distribute arms to the workers. In a radio message on the same day, Allende called on the workers to take over farms and factories, and announced the arming of the workers, 'should the situation necessitate such a move'. That situation, however, had not yet arisen in Allende's view; he felt confident, he said, of the loyalty of the armed forces. Indeed the prompt response of General Prats in putting down the coup, seemed to vindicate his assertion. The coup was put down without difficulty, leaving some 22 dead and a number of wounded.

The reaction of the working class and its organizations was determined and speedy. The CUT called for an immediate occupation of factories and offices, reinforcing Allende's call. The response was a massive occupation by workers of factories, and the reorganization of the cordons and 'community commands' with the object of defending the gains of the working class against this renewed assault from the Right. Once it was clear that the coup had not been successful, however, Allende immediately moved to stabilize the situation. Characteristically, he turned in conciliatory mood to the Christian Democrats and sought a compromise. In a revolutionary situation as this was, his response was inexplicable. The working class had taken control of many sections of industry, and was more united and highly mobilized in the aftermath of the coup than ever before; it remained on the offensive, awaiting a revolutionary lead for the next stage in the struggle. In the massive demonstration which took place outside the bullet-scarred palace of La Moneda on 30 June, the workers chanted their demand for people's power, for the creation of a society in which the power remained with them. The Left must unite and go on the offensive, they said, and the government, at this moment, must show a firm hand, a firm hand!

Allende, however, ignored the strength and preparedness of his own base among the workers and turned instead to the armed forces, as he had done in all previous emergencies, to 'restore law and order'. The last time the armed forces had entered the cabinet, in November 1972, their aim had been to prevent further advances by the working class, restore law and order and ensure that the March elections took place legally and democratically. No doubt many members of the armed forces had shared the Right's conviction that the election would end in a defeat for Allende. They had been wrong then, and this time there was a marked reluctance on the part of most of the upper ranks in the armed forces to participate in Allende's government, unless he first accepted a series of conditions which would have entailed that Allende relinquish the programme and aims of Popular Unity itself. The Communist and Socialist Parties totally rejected these conditions; in any event, it is probable that the heads of the armed forces felt that their freedom of manoeuvre would be restricted by membership of the government, and that they preferred to remain free of such trammels.

Allende turned to a series of internationally known personalities, asking them to join his government and thus enable him to negotiate with the Christian Democrats; all his nominees refused the offer, however. Allende then turned to the left-wing of Christian Democracy; there he found a sympathetic response, and gained the agreement of one of its members, the rector of the Catholic University, Fernando Castillo, to enter a 'peacemaking' cabinet. The Christian Democrat leadership, however, stepped in to veto any such move – the Party's attitude remained clear. There would be no conciliation until Allende agreed to return to the established legal and institutional framework, renouncing any further advances along the road towards socialism. Whether or not Allende realized it, the Christian Democrats were very clear about where the real threat to the bougeois order lay. A public statement from the PDC singled out their anxieties over the illegal arming of the workers, 'the *de facto* establishment of people's power' which was directly 'incompatible with the rule of law . . . the essential foundation of our democratic system'. The price of reconciliation could not have been clearer. And yet Allende still held to a conciliatory posture, appointing a cabinet of technocrats which in no way reflected the real class struggle that was being waged outside the cabinet room. Both Allende and the Communist Party stuck fast to the reformist illusion, blind to the lessons that had been learned both by the workers, and by the armed forces, for whom the failed coup of 29 June had provided a dry run for the full scale assault of 11 September.

The attempted coup left matters much clearer. It was evidence that the armed forces were no longer in any sense 'above politics'. As one agricultural technician put it to *Chile Hoy*, shortly afterwards: 'What we think is, it would have been very silly for a section of the armed forces to come out alone like that, very strange. We cannot understand why Allende does not explain the real situation to the people.' A week after the attempted coup, the Socialist paper *Aurora* carried an article discussing Allende's public promise that if necessary, the workers would be given arms by loyal troops.

> We stopped to think about that promise – all those of us who were not members of the armed forces, who took over factories and services that morning, all those civilians who rushed over to the area round the Presidential Palace that morning. It was with sticks and bits of iron that workers took factories over. It was with empty hands, with no weapon but their own pure gall, that workers mobilized to defend the Presidential Palace.
>
> It was with hissing and shouts that our comrades confronted the tanks. When the tanks levelled their weapons against that unarmed mass of people, the people ran away. But they regrouped and came back again, hissing and shouting in a desperate attempt to defend the government with their simple physical presence, with pure nerve, with their own decision to fight . . .
>
> The President of the Republic, the party leaderships, the loyal forces within the military, should consider the situation very carefully. Can the next attempt at a coup be stopped by loyal troops, acting alone? Yes, or No?
>
> If they make the wrong judgement, and move too late to arm the people, as happened in Bolivia, if Fascism imposed itself upon this country, they will be assuming a dreadful responsibility before the tribunal of history. In all those cities in Spain where the armouries were opened up to the trade unions. the Fascist uprising was crushed within the space of a day. But in those cities where the authorities found it impossible to give the civilian arms, Fascism was victorious, and from those centres it spread to the rest of the country.
>
> If our authorities are wrong, if they make the same mistake made by Torres in Bolivia and the Spanish Republicans in Spain, what a sad evaluation history will make of them!

But the armouries were not opened. Worse, the government brought pressure on the CUT to renege on its original refusal to allow factories that had been taken over to be returned. It took Allende until the end of July to persuade the CUT to agree, and even then it was never carried out, since in many instances, the workers themselves would not agree to turn them over. Still, the decision was a great blow to working class morale. As a Christian Democrat worker who had been involved in taking over his own textile factory put it – 'We have been burning our bridges, just so that the government could retreat.' The lessons drawn by Popular Unity's supporters by 29 June were not to be reflected in the president's actions. There was to be no firm hand.

The final stages; run-up to the coup

In the aftermath of the failed coup, the El Teniente strikers went back to work. The strike had cost between $70m. and $100m. in lost production. Popular Unity was given no respite, however; when the government tried to draft emergency legislation to deal with the economic crisis, an inflation rate of over 200% and a decline in both industrial and agricultural production, the Right was intransigent. The government plan involved further extension and rationalization of the social property area, guarantees for the protection of small and medium-sized firms, increased labour discipline and centralization as well as further participation by the workers in the running of industry. In effect, it also introduced the rationing of certain basic goods – which was immediately denounced in Congress as a herald of totalitarianism and economic dictatorship. The important thing, however, was that all these measures failed to touch the real roots of the economic crisis, which were political; similarly, its solution was a question of power – the conquest of state power alone could ensure it. But Allende chose instead to pursue the course of conciliation. Many of the occupied factories were returned to their original owners, and the commissions appointed to run the remaining factories included no representatives from the cordons, the organizations created at the grass roots by the workers themselves: all in the cause of avoiding civil war. Allende had warned that 'every citizen should be aware that the nation is on the verge of civil war, which the government is pledged to avoid'. The Communist Party newspaper *El Siglo* continued to carry headlines saying 'No to civil war', while Luis Corvalán replied thus to accusation that the workers were beginning to arm themselves: 'Because the workers took some immediate security measures against the recent attempted coup, and maintained these precautionary measures, some reactionaries have begun to raise a storm, in the belief that they have found a new issue to use to drive a wedge between the people and the armed forces. They are claiming that we have a policy of replacing the professional army. No sir! we continue and will continue to support keeping our armed institutions strictly professional.'[3]

The workers were less reluctant to act; they were in militant mood, and made it very clear that they thought the factories in the hands of the workers should remain in their control. Both the CUT and the PC agreed, and there emerged for the first time a breach between them and the right wing of the Socialists. The central question for the Left, then, was that of power, particularly as far as strengthening the cordons and the community commands was concerned. It was imperative that the workers too be rearmed in preparation for a conflict to come. As the right-wing offensive proceeded, the Left saw its power as lying in the cordons and their commands; Allende, meanwhile, vacillated and leaned always towards collaboration and conciliation.

The Right was clearly aware of where the real conflict would unfold. Factories had already been searched for arms before 29 June; three days after the attempted coup the armed forces renewed and extended these raids. Their legal rationale was the existence of the Law for the Control of Arms, which enabled the armed forces to search freely for arms. Originally passed during the Bosses' Strike of October 1972, this law suddenly became the most important on the statute book; a godsend for the Right, the Left soon came to regard it as the new *ley maldita* (evil law), a reference to the law of 1946 for the Defence of Democracy which had served as a justification for large-scale repression of the working class movement. When the 1972 law was originally passed, the representatives of Popular Unity had abstained; Allende, in an unforgiveable lapse, had failed to use his veto. Perhaps he was afraid that any open confrontation with the Right on this issue would fuel right opposition propaganda that the Left was preparing to impose a Communist dictatorship. Perhaps he felt that any veto would imply a dangerous questioning of the 'constitutional' status of the armed forces. In any case, hesitation on this issue was to prove disastrous. With this law as a pretext, the armed forces throughout Chile entered factories, schools, universities, working class districts and the headquarters of left-wing parties and organizations, ostensibly in search of illegal arms. In theory, of course, the law was supposed to apply to Right and Left; yet although it was well-known that Fatherland and Freedom were heavily armed, only isolated forays were ever made against them. The armed forces, at least, were very clear as to where the enemy lay.

The Working Class and the Military

The following is a summary of an interview with the president of the Central Industrial Cordon of Osorno, a small city in the agricultural south of Chile, which appeared in *Chile Hoy* on 7 September 1973. The president's own words are italicized.

After the abortive coup of 29 June, the military offensive in Osorno began. On 9 July, the regional leader of MAPU (one of the Popular Unity parties) was arrested, and, at the time of the interview, was still being held incommunicado.

At the same time, the military patrols began. The way in which these patrols behave, inspecting pedestrians for arms, is humiliating and causes active resentment. Then there are other things; for instance, owing to the state of need brought about by the strike of the lorry owners, we have to organize the distribution of paraffin, petrol and bottled liquid gas. So we

*established workers' guards on the stores selling petrol, where the right had infiltrated.
This is where the Black Market in petrol begins, with these same people who are given a
quota (by DIRINCO, the government distribution agency) and then sell supplies privately.
The CUT (Central Unica de Trabajadores) had called for the formation of workers' guards,
but these guards were opposed by the military, who said: 'Either we are in control, or the
CUT is in control.' And this was when the case of the comrades in the People's Supply
Committee came up.*

*These women were in charge of controlling paraffin and liquid gas being sold in Aliro
Concha's shop. They were under orders from the CUT. And then the officers came, and
these comrades were put out at the point of machine guns, by an enormous detachment of
troops: all this to deal with women who were completely unarmed. Meanwhile, the reactionaries stood by applauding, as they did in the Square on 21 August.*

The confrontation in the square on the 21st was also over the issue of workers'
guards, then being organized by the local DIRINCO in response to a government
order that the trucks held by the strikers should be forcefully 'requisitioned'. In
Osorno, the *Intendant* had agreed to give the CUT police support to carry out these
requisitions – support they would need, as the strikers had sworn not to give over
their vehicles, and were armed. The police were supposed to join the CUT detachment in the square. Instead, soldiers arrived.

*The Square was surrounded by a company of soldiers, who got down from their truck and
marched up the north side. The officer at the head of the column gave orders to the infantry,
who advanced with bayonets. The column stopped about 20 yards away, formed up in a line
in front of the workers, who stood firm. The CUT's chairman talked with the officer,
while those of us who were leading went back along the detachment of workers, informing
them of the details of what was happening. Then we were told that we had five minutes to
disperse.*

*Meanwhile, in front of the Intendancy, they set up three sub-machine guns pointing
directly at the workers. Soldiers were running around with boxes of ammunition and
walkie-talkies, making connection with another detachment of infantry that was marching
into the Square from the South . . . A group of soldiers stepped out and started advancing
towards the crowd.*

*There, we in the first ranks opposed this assault with our arms tensed with rage and
frustration. The call broke out from the ranks of the workers: 'Soldiers, listen! You too
will be one of the exploited! Will you shoot against your fathers, against your class brothers?'
This chant helped determine the nucleus in front, to stand firm by the Intendancy staircase.
The soldiers hit out with the wooden butts of their guns at the iron-hardened bones of the
workers. The soldiers' nerve began to go (they were little more than children) and they
began to pass round ammunition. Suddenly a soldier stepped in, hurled himself against his
comrades, and shouted BACK! and stopped a massacre.*

*Later, we heard the Intendant's voice complaining of the way he had been treated when
his car was searched for arms. But his voice was lost in the shouts of workers who wanted to
do something. 'These lice were going to shoot us' many of them were shouting.*

The Intendant, two carpenters who had been carrying sticks, and the local chief
of DIRINCO were also arrested. The Intendant was later released, but not the
others.

Chile Hoy asked this militant, 'What has happened to the movement of the masses
in the face of this escalation of repression?' This was his reply:

*As in many parts of the country, in Osorno today, the level of consciousness and organ-
ization of the people is something which most people could not have imagined. These repressive actions have only succeeded in speeding up the formation of other industrial cordons,
strengthening the workers' committees for defence and vigilance, and pressing forward the
task of organizing distribution. In summary, this escalation has served to unify and strengthen
the workers of this province.*

As the armed forces began their cautious offensive, right-wing civilians launched their assault too. This time it was the scarcity of spare parts that provided Vilarín and the lorry owners with the pretext for renewed strike action, beginning on 26 July. Once again the right-wing parties joined forces with the lorry owners, as they had in October, while the extreme Right, and Fatherland and Freedom in particular, embarked on a new series of acts of terrorism and sabotage, including the assassination of President Allende's aide, Captain Araya, on 27 July. There were various instances of straightforward industrial sabotage by the capitalists for example; in at least one case a foreign company, the American owned Petrow-Dow company, appealed publicly to its technicians to bring production to a halt; and the leader of a lorry owners' organization which had supported the government was assassinated. These provocations were to continue and intensify during the remainder of the Popular Unity period, as the strike of the lorry-owners spread once again to shop-owners, doctors, and other middle class professionals into a final bosses' strike to provide the excuse for military intervention.

The workers responded, as they had done in the previous bosses' strike, by extending the activities of the cordons and the communal commands to the organization of production and distribution, as well as of self-defence. The demands that came from these organizations were unequivocal – a firm hand against the Right and a continuation of progress towards socialism, which alone could solve their problems in any real sense; the Right too was unequivocal – the process must not only be halted, but turned back upon itself. And the first step in this reversal had to be the crushing of the movement for people's power which had emerged *de facto* in response to the bosses' strike which now involved increasing numbers of *gremialistas* (members of the gremios), who had come out in sympathy with the lorry owners.

Once again, Allende's response was to reopen the dialogue with the Christian Democrats. The PDC was adamant, however, in its insistence that the military should re-enter the cabinet to guarantee 'observance of the Constitution'. On 10 August, Allende complied, and as the tempo of clashes between the armed forces and the people increased and even began to make itself felt in Santiago, where the working class was strongest and the military most cautious, the heads of the armed forces assumed important cabinet posts. The PDC, however, wanted to go still further, putting the officer corps in charge of key areas of the administration – in effect, a 'legal' military takeover. This Popular Unity, under pressure from the workers, refused to accept.

The scenario at this point was different from October 1972. Although the military were supposed to use the threat of martial law against the truck owners, it was clear that they regarded the suppression of the workers as their main priority, as the post-29 June events had shown. Thus while Vilarín and his supporters removed essential components from the lorries, and surrounded them with an armed guard, the armed forces concentrated their efforts against the workers. At the same time, the campaign of provocations by the right-wing continued apace, and the sabotage and terrorism organized by Fatherland and Freedom was intensified. A virulent ideological campaign was launched: *El Mercurio* expounded the benefits of an 'Indonesian solution', while Frei called for the crushing of people's power before it was too late. One writer in *El Mercurio's* columns remarked 'travelling through anti-Communist countries like Brazil is a source of profound satisfaction . . . To start with, there you find the Communists in their proper place – in hiding'.

In this atmosphere there semed to emerge on the Right two separate plans for toppling Popular Unity and suppressing the workers; these became known as the *golpe blanco* and the *golpe negro* – the white coup and the black coup. The first, associated with Christian Democracy, referred to a military coup that would destroy the government, suppress the workers and then return to some form of 'guided' bourgeois democracy. The second, associated with the National Party and Fatherland and Freedom, required a Fascist solution, eradicating all working-class organizations and imposing a corporate State.[4]

Vilarín and his supporters, meanwhile, had the backing of the National Party and the 'unreserved support' of the Christian Democrats. Although Allende had accepted thirteen out of the fourteen points on the lorry owners' programme (relating to new pricing policies, new tariffs, and guaranteed supplies of spare parts etc.) he refused to accede to their main political demand, which was that no more lorries should be transferred to the public sector. On this point alone the lorry owners maintained the strike, though much later they were to add a new political demand – that the government accept the Hamilton-Fuentalba constitutional reform.

In this stalemate, the under-secretary of transport, Jaime Faivovich of the Socialist Party, publicly advocated firmness, a refusal to surrender, the requisitioning of the trucks and the organization of alternative systems of transport. The trade unions, too, offered their support to Allende on this basis, and even agreed to work with the army if necessary; yet Allende preferred to place all his reliance on the armed forces. The military, however, were manifestly unwilling to move against the truck owners. The new Minister of Transport, air force General César Ruiz Danyau, suggested that the government give in to Vilarín, and refused to act further against the lorry owners. Allende then forced him to resign both from the cabinet and from the air force, although the resulting discontent among air force officers theatened for a time to lead to a mutiny. It took all of Allende's considerable political skill to placate them; and even then he felt obliged eventually to sack Faivovich as a concession to the Right.

Time was running out as the coup-minded officers in the armed forces began to close ranks. But General Prats, who remained Chief of Staff of the armed forces, was still a thorn in their side; he alone could have split the armed forces, and he had to be removed. Constant pressure was put on him to resign, and the wives of high-ranking officers demonstrated outside his home, in an effort to bring pressure to bear on his wife. Finally, Prats resigned – 'to preserve the unity of the army' – and Admiral Montero with him. This was probably the last chance Allende had to split the armed forces; but he accepted hierarchical decisions and acceded to the wishes of the generals, appointing General Pinochet as Prats' successor. Thus it was that those who were by now actively planning the coup retained control over the armed forces. Several parts of Chile, particularly in the south, were under military control well before 11 September. The armed forces became increasingly more open in their support of the striking lorry owners and shopkeepers; aeroplanes flew over and buzzed most towns in a show of force designed to frighten any potential opposition; terrorism and sabotage continued. There was no public response from the government, though workers' denunciations of military activities were published in the left-wing press. The president seemed unwilling to admit that his 'loyal' armed forces were in revolt.

What finally goaded the parties of Popular Unity into concerted action were a series of revelations showing that the military were using torture. On 5 August about 100 sailors and workers were arrested in Valparaíso for 'dereliction of military duty' – a blanket charge used in the absence of any concrete offence. It appeared that these men had noticed preparations being made for a coup, and had agreed among themselves that in the event of any military action against the government, they would oppose it. When knowledge of the incident became public, it rapidly became a *cause célèbre*. At first Allende tried to uphold the officers' story, suggesting that the men were MIR sympathizers who had been planning a mutiny. The assessment given by the lawyer representing the arrested men, however, was very different:

'In my opinion the relationship of forces among the officers in the armed forces, and in particular in the navy, is at the present time unfavourable to the Left. Clearly the great majority of officers are hostile to the Left and opposed to the government. I think that government policy towards the armed forces bears some responsibility for this situation. The regime has tried to quarantine the officers from the class struggle in conditions in which such an attitude could not but favour the advance of reactionary sectors, who have thus been able to carry out their plans undisturbed and almost without opposition.

'It has become virtually taboo among the traditional parties of the Left to do any work with a correct orientation aimed at the armed forces. One example: while the workers in the naval yards and the sailors suffered and continue to suffer the most bestial repression within living memory, simply because they are identified with the Left, Dr. Allende, when swearing in his so called "National Security Cabinet" disavowed these workers by saying that they were ultraleftists who were linking up with the far Right. To make statements like that about sailors and workers who are prepared to oppose a coup against the government seems, to say the least, to be a grave mistake.'

Evidence of torture accumulated; at the same time the motives behind it became increasingly clear. The navy laid charges of 'sedition' against Altamirano, Garretón and Enríquez on the grounds that they had organized a conspiracy to infiltrate the armed forces. Whatever the splits within Popular Unity, or its quarrels with Enríquez and the MIR, Popular Unity could not allow this declaration of war against the secretary-general of Allende's own party, and the others, to pass unnoticed. In effect – though Allende refused to recognize it – the navy's charges were a clear warning of an intended coup.

The right-wing offensive had ensured that most of the major factories were working well below capacity. The extreme Right now stepped up its campaign of terrorism and sabotage. By mid-August around twenty people had died in clashes; there were increasing numbers of sabotage attempts on railway lines and oil pipe-lines and numerous attacks on buses, service stations and lorry owners who had not joined the strike. A significant proportion of doctors, nurses, pilots, retailers and professional employees were on strike. By early September over half the country was at a virtual economic standstill.

The Left responded on 4 September with a massive demonstration. On the following day the executive committee of Popular Unity representing *all* the parties, but not Allende, issued a statement of 'solidarity with the sailors and NCOs who have been charged, yet whose intention was only to defend the Constitution and the laws and reject the orders of those who were trying to involve the navy in a military coup'. The statement went on to denounce the use of torture and expressed support for Altamirano, Garretón and Enríquez. The Left, it seemed, was at last becoming united.

Allende himself dithered. His continuing silence could only be interpreted as a tacit acceptance of the right of naval officers to use their military discipline against men who might try to defend Allende and the Left against the treason of their officers. In the last weeks, Allende made no move to condemn the officers who were implicated in the preparations for a coup nor to rally those in the armed forces who remained loyal to the government; his silence allowed the military to continue their preparations with impunity. Workers who had taken over one of the television channels seven months earlier, and made of it the voice of the Left, were expelled. Arms searches among the workers were intensified, while the extreme Right which, according to *Le Monde* had been responsible for more than 500 attacks in the course of two weeks, was left undisturbed to continue its campaign of sabotage.

Conclusions

The six month period between the March elections of 1973 and the military coup of 11 September was the crucial testing time for Popular Unity. From March onwards the Christian Democrats, under the leadership of Frei, tacitly and then more and more explicitly gave support to those forces that were advocating a coup against Popular Unity. Until March, Christian Democrat supporters had tended to take to the streets and go on strike for short periods only. After April, Christian Democrat supporters among students, white collar workers at El Teniente, professionals and lorry owners began to engage in

longer and more determined strikes and in frequent street clashes with government supporters. They may not actually have engaged in sabotage and
bombings, but their support for the escalation of the struggle was an important
contributory factor in encouraging and preparing the ground for a coup.
The party which had once proclaimed itself the advocate of a 'Revolution in
Liberty' in the end abandoned all pretence to either.

In July, the working class responded in a vigorous and determined way to
this new threat. The cordons and the CUT overcame a long standing quarrel
to present a united front in the face of this new and dangerous offensive from
the Right, and made clear demands on the government for a counter offensive –
'a firm hand, a firm hand'. For a time, there was open tension between the
president and his cabinet and the trade unions: in early July, both the Socialist
and the Communist leaders of the CUT served notice on the government that
they would make their own plans for its defence in the event of a coup. The
unwillingness of the working class itself to accept Allende's policy of conciliation provoked a crisis within the Communist Party, previously the most ardent
supporter of negotiations with the Christian Democrats. By the beginning of
September, the signs of a regrouping of the parties in Popular Unity and the
MIR to confront the forces of reaction and even the armed forces themselves
were there. But the regrouping came a little late – too late to provide the working class with any protection against the coup.

The worst record in the last month belongs, sadly, to Allende himself. With
all the weight of responsibility for the 'constitution' and the 'loyal armed forces'
resting on his shoulders, he was unable to confront the reality of the crisis
publicly, and totally unable to offer the working class any indication of what it
should do. Allende genuinely wanted to avoid bloodshed, and held to the
belief that dialogue and compromise could avoid a social conflict even when the
Right had long since abandoned such illusions. He may have felt constrained by
his office; he may have felt that any open commitment on his own part to the
confrontation with seditious elements in the armed forces would itself be
enough to provoke a coup. Nonetheless, he was the acknowledged leader of
Popular Unity itself. There was no ready substitute to hand for the 'people's
president', and the actions of the president himself in that last month were
disastrous, and contributed very largely to the demoralization of the working
class as a whole.

The illusions of the right wing of Popular Unity through three years of
government contributed to Allende's role in this final crisis. If the judgement
of history were moral, then perhaps there would be some concession for the
ability of the Communist Party to respond to the threat of an impending coup
at the final moment, for the ability of its rank and file members to disown their
party leadership when its vacillations obviously became a sign of weakness, and
for the courage with which party members prepared for a battle. If the judgement of history were moral, then Allende's own final battle in the presidential
palace on the day of the coup would count decisively in his favour. But the

judgements of history are above all practical. The illusions in the loyalty of the armed forces, in a bourgeois 'constitution' and the good faith of the opposition, had been sown three years ago and assiduously cultivated by the right wing of Popular Unity until weeks before the coup. There had been no systematic preparation of the people for the inevitability of a confrontation with the armed forces. There were no private armies of the Left. The policy of conceding all possible rights to the military, their right to old traditions and their right to provide the 'ultimate guarantee' of bourgeois constitution, led inevitably in August and September 1973 to the complete passivity of the government, the president, and even of the political parties themselves in the face of every manoeuvre within the armed forces to create the conditions for a coup.

It is true that sectors of the Left believed confrontation to be inevitable, and had made preparations for it. The MIR, for example, had gone underground after the attempted coup of 29 June, and from July onwards had directed a vigorous campaign of propaganda at the rank and file of the armed forces. Indeed, the Left generally stepped up its efforts during the last months to win support among the military. Some arms came in from Cuba and elsewhere and were distributed, particularly among the Socialist Party. Yet there was no overall leadership co-ordinating these various activities, nor any widespread or effective preparation for the coming confrontation. The majority on the Left still believed that massive demonstrations by workers and left wing supporters would deter the plotters from carrying out the coup. Furthermore, many of the policies of the revolutionary Left were based on an assumption that, in the event of a coup, the armed forces would divide and a significant proportion join the workers. The result was a desultory and weak preparation for an armed confrontation; there were no clandestine radio stations, no emergency plans, no clear instructions for Popular Unity and very little evidence of a structure of clandestine organization.

On 11 September, the Left was to fight heroically. Those who had guns used them, but the absence of any plans to deal with a massive and brutal onslaught by the military condemned their resistance to failure in the short term. The future, of course, will be another story.

10 The Coup and its Aftermath

The following account is based primarily on reports in the European press (especially *Le Monde*), supplemented by information which has come out of Chile since the coup through refugees or the underground press. The only newspapers now allowed in Chile are those which give support to the junta. Even the right-wing daily *La Tribuna* was closed in December 1973, for publishing a report on the armed forces themselves with which the junta disagreed. Official Chilean news is useful only as an indication of military thinking and propaganda.

Clearly, not all reports on the situation in Chile since the coup have been reliable. The junta immediately made every effort to control communications with the outside world in the hope of limiting international (and Chilean) awareness of the bloody massacre being perpetrated. A Swedish journalist was arrested and imprisoned in the National Stadium for his role in reporting the massacre, and a warrant was also taken out for the arrest of the *Le Monde* correspondent, though this was not done until he had left for Buenos Aires. In all, the list of foreign journalists beaten up, detained and/or expelled from Chile during the coup numbers eighteen.

But not all the inaccuracies have been due to the instinctive self-protection of the Right. In the first few days after the coup, many rumours were circulating in Chile about the deaths of specific figures (Carlos Altamirano, for example) or about splits within the armed forces, which many left-wing Chileans believed and which were reported in the international press. The most optimistic of these rumours was the one which had General Carlos Prats, former chief of staff of the Chilean armed forces, and a loyal supporter of Allende, marching on Santiago in defence of the government from a base in Concepción, picking up reinforcements in the Central Valley as he went. This rumour appeared during the first week of the coup, when the Left was hoping desperately that such splits would appear in the army, because the whole of their strategy for confronting the forces of reaction had been based on the theory that come a confrontation, the armed forces would split. The rumour was completely untrue. On 14 September, Prats made a television broadcast announcing that he had asked permission to leave Chile. 'I have not the least intention of taking political action,' he said, 'or of trying to split the armed forces. I have always fought for unity within the armed forces.'

Rumours based, now not so much on false hopes as on simple fears, continue to appear. There is a rumour, for instance, that Prats never reached his chosen place of exile in Argentina but was shot on the Chilean side of the border. But such rumours aside, in the months following the coup it has been possible to sift the information on what happened in Chile during and after 11 September, and remove the more obvious distortions. Enough information is now available from eye-witness accounts to confirm that the new military government has carried out a programme of systematic brutality, torture and murder on a massive scale since its seizure of power. Even the bourgeois press outside Chile which originally supported the coup (for instance *The Times* of London) has been forced to disassociate itself from this scale of bloodshed. Meanwhile, the bloodshed continues.

'Plan Z' and other justifications for the Coup.

The references to 'Djakarta' – the systematic massacre of Indonesian Communists in a country-wide pogrom in 1965 – in the right-wing press and on the walls of Santiago suburbs prior to the coup, had not been accidental. For the bourgeoisie, it was the only visible solution. In September 1973, the officer corps and their middle class supporters were faced with the disintegration of the social order on which their lives and careers were based, and they too were prepared to accept a 'Night of the Long Knives', if only it would preserve the existing order. Their privileged social status was now threatening to become a matter of history. Many sectors of the middle class were suffering economic shortages for the first time in their lives, while on television they could see refrigerators going to workers at discount prices, through the good offices of the People's Supply Committees. Unknown forces from the lowest sections of society were taking the control of politics and economics out of their hands. There were rumours that the working class was transforming itself into a professional army, challenging the military monopoly of violence. The level of hysteria prevailing among the middle classes can be judged from the fact that after the coup, ex-President Frei felt able to claim to the Spanish press that the Marxist forces had had more and more powerful weapons at their disposal than those of the armed forces: enough weapons for 30,000 guerrillas, where the armed forces could only equip 20,000 men.

So when the coup came, it was the *golpe negro*, inspired more by the ideas of Fatherland and Freedom than by the professional political manoeuvres which many right-wing Christian Democrats would have favoured. The armed forces not only published an official declaration of internal war: they succeeded in convincing themselves and their middle class supporters that the declaration was no less than the truth. The systematic use of air power against workers, the mass imprisonments and executions, were justified according to the junta because Chile had been invaded by an army of foreign extremists, under Cuban direction, who were planning to kill many thousands of loyal Chileans. The existing government had been implicated in this plot.

This plot was the infamous 'Plan Z', widely reported in the junta press following the coup, the story that the junta did its best to put over to the international press, though without much initial success. In some sectors, however, it met with sympathy: within the British Conservative Party, for instance, where Sir Robert Turton said in a House of Commons debate, 'I have spoken to people who were in Chile then who are convinced that there was a plot to exterminate people. It was to have been carried out on the 17th of September, by an army of 13,000 Cuban, North Korean and Chilean extremists.' The same story also met with acceptance among the Chilean middle classes, who were equally disinclined to consider where President Allende could have hidden several thousand North Koreans, or why Marxists would want to use a code name like 'Plan Z'. Even Frei, who perhaps qualifies as the junta's best straight man, was willing to repeat it in the first few days, when he called his son in London with a message which he suggested could be passed on to the news-papers: 'the only resistance comes from foreigners in the factories, who have been surrounded by troops'.

This was the story 'believed' after one fashion or another by the thousands of respectable people who now set about denouncing to the authorities their neighbours, foreigners, and any suspicious strangers; they must themselves have been responsible for thousands of deaths. However flimsy the basis for such stories, they were still disastrously real in their consequences. The treat-ment of refugees from other Latin American countries was dreadful. There were in fact about 13,000 of them in Chile at the time of the coup, for Chile had been a traditional place of asylum for political refugees. In another sense, the myths were based on reality. They provided powerful symbols of the way in which power had nearly passed out of the hands of the bourgeoisie and its allies. They also mirrored with an amazing accuracy the kind of political action which the generals and their supporters were prepared to take to preserve that power.

More cynical supporters of the regime simply put their heads in the sand. As a Santiago lawyer would later say to a *Newsweek* reporter who had been able to collect firm evidence of massacres: 'I don't believe the stories you tell me, but after all the things which the supporters of Salvador Allende have done to Chile, they deserve whatever happens to them.'[1]

The Seizure of Power

The coup began quietly on 10 September. Troop movements were reported around San Felipe, not far from Santiago. The Minister of Defence telephoned General Brady (commander of the Santiago garrison) and was told that all was calm. In fact, the armed forces were engaged in eliminating dissidents within their own ranks. There were purges and internal 'coups' in the Buin Regiment in Santiago and two of the city's military schools. A similar coup took place in the Caracero Regiment of Viña del Mar.

On the morning of the 11th, at 7.00 a.m., the president was informed that the navy had rebelled in Valparaíso. He now called General Brady, who told him that steps were being taken to deal with the mutiny – a lie. Not reassured, the president left immediately from his home in Tomás Moro for the Presidential palace, with the Director-General of the Police Force, General José Maria Sepúlveda, about 50 police, and the group of personal friends who had served as his bodyguard since his election in 1970. They had difficulty reaching the palace, which was already surrounded by police who supported the coup. Once at the palace, the president learned that the whole of the armed forces was in revolt.

Immediately, he broadcast an appeal for the mobilization of the working class. Some busloads of workers apparently did attempt to reach the palace, but they were turned back: the generals had cordoned off the central area surrounding the palace at a distance of eight blocks. Mobilization around the person of the president was not going to be possible. The armed forces had also learned something from the attempted coup of 29 June.

The CUT broadcast telling all workers to go to their factories and await instructions.

Meanwhile, the three commanders of the armed forces had presented the president with an ultimatum:

> In view of the grave economic, social and moral crisis which is destroying the country, the inability of the government to take steps to put an end to the developing chaos, the constant growth of paramilitary groups organized and trained by Popular Unity, who are leading the country towards an inevitable civil war;
>
> The armed forces and police declare that:
>
> 1) The President of the Republic must resign from his high post immediately, in favour of the armed forces and the police;
>
> 2) The armed forces and the police are united in their determination to assume their historic role of fighting to free their country from the Marxist yoke and to re-establish order and the rule of law;
>
> 3) The workers of Chile may be assured that the social and economic gains which they have obtained up to now, will not be subjected to fundamental changes;
>
> 4) Popular Unity press, radio stations and television networks must suspend their activities immediately. If not, they will be taken by assault by the army and the air force;
>
> 5) The population of Santiago must remain at home to avoid the massacre of innocent people.
>
> Signed: General Augusto Pinochet Ugarta,
>   Commander of the Army.
>   Admiral José Toribio Merino,
>   Commander of the Navy.
>   General Gustavo Leigh Guzmán,
>   Commander of the Air Force.
>   General César Mendoza Durán,
>   Commander of the Police.

General Mendoza was only 'interim commander of the police' at the time of the coup. In order to find someone sympathetic to their plans, the heads of the armed forces had had to remove the others from their positions. But when the ultimatum was published, according to Beatriz Allende, Sepúlveda and some of the police who had accompanied Allende to the palace refused to remain with him and fight.

The president however was adamant. He had already taken the decision to fight to the end, perhaps in the hope that loyal sectors of the armed forces would come to his defence. In any case, he was determined not to cede his legal mandate. One name on the communique came as a bitter surprise: General Pinochet had always been considered the army's leading constitutionalist, and had even sat on Popular Unity's own Security Council, the government's favoured source of information on other officers' seditious plans. By the same token, he had been allowed to listen to all the coalition's own plans for defence.

The *Prensa Latina* correspondent in Santiago was telephoning the presidential palace at regular intervals (*Prensa Latina* is the Cuban news agency). At 1.15, he was told by one of Allende's advisors, Jaime Barrios, 'You can say that we will die here and that we will resist to the last.' Asked who would do the resisting, Barrios replied, 'the palace police guard, 50 other policemen, the president's personal bodyguard and his personal advisors and staff'.

By 8.45, the Socialist Party's radio station had been forced off the air by the simple device of bombing its transmission equipment. By 9.30 a.m., all connections with foreign countries by telephone had been cut, at the same time as the last commercial flight to enter or leave Chile for a week was leaving Pudahuel airport. The border with Peru was closed at 1.00 p.m. The border with Argentina had been closed during the night. Popular Unity was quickly losing access to all means of communication inside and outside the country.

At 9.30 a.m., President Allende delivered his last message to the nation, just before the remaining government radio station went off the air.

The President's last message

Compatriots:

This is certainly the last time I shall speak to you. The air force has bombed all our radio stations. My words flow more from disappointment than from bitterness – let them serve as a moral condemnation of those who betrayed their oath, these Chilean soldiers – so-called Commanders in Chief like the self-appointed Admiral Merino, or that jackal Mr. Mendoza, a general who only yesterday protested his loyalty to the government and has now appointed himself Director General of the Carabineros.

Faced with all these events, there is only one thing I can say to the workers: I shall not surrender.

History has given me a choice. I shall sacrifice my life in loyalty to my people, in the knowledge that the seeds that we have planted in the noble consciousness of thousand of Chileans can never be prevented from bearing fruit.

Our enemies are strong; they can enslave the people. But neither criminal acts nor force of arms can hold back this social process. History belongs to us; it is the people that make history.

Workers of my country:

I want to thank you for the loyalty you have always shown, for the trust you have always placed in a man who has been no more than the interpreter of your great desire for justice, a man who undertook publicly to respect the constitution and the law and who did not betray that undertaking. This is the last chance I shall have to speak to you, to explain to you what has happened. Foreign capital and imperialism have allied with the forces of reaction to produce a climate in which the armed forces have broken with tradition. General Schneider and Commander Araya, who upheld and reasserted that tradition, have fallen victim to those people, to that class which now hopes, through its intermediaries – the armed forces – to regain the interests and privileges it had lost.

Let me speak first to the ordinary women of our country, to the peasant woman who had faith in us, to the working woman who worked even harder, to the mother who knew that her children were our concern.

Let me speak to those members of the professions who acted in patriotic fashion, who a few days ago were still resisting the mutiny led by the professional associations, the unions of the upper class, a mutiny which they hoped would allow them to retain the privileges a few of them had enjoyed under a capitalist system.

Let me speak to the young, to those who sang and who added their joy and their enthusiasm to our struggle.

Let me speak to the workers, peasants and intellectuals of Chile who will now suffer persecution, for Fascism has existed in our country for some time, and has already revealed itself in terrorism, in the sabotage of bridges, railway lines and oil pipelines.

No doubt Radio Magellanes will be silenced very soon too, and my words will no longer reach you. Yet you will continue to hear them; I shall always be with you. And at the very least I shall leave behind the memory of an honourable man, who kept faith with the working class.

The people must defend themselves; but they must avoid needless sacrifice. The people must never be crushed, humiliated or destroyed.

Workers of my country:

I have faith in Chile and its destiny. Other Chileans will come forward. In these dark and bitter days, when treachery seeks to impose its own order, you may be sure that soon, very soon, the broad road towards a new society will open again, and the march along that road will continue.

> *Long live Chile!*
> *Long live the people!*
> *Long live the workers!*

These are my last words. I know that my sacrifice is not in vain. May it be a lesson for all those who hate disloyalty, cowardice and treachery.

The commanders had set a time limit of mid-day for the president to surrender. There was already heavy fighting around the palace. At mid-day, the army moved in with tanks, and the air force with bombs. Allende had ordered all civilians to leave, including his daughter Beatriz. At ten minutes to two, the *Prensa Latina* correspondent telephoned again. Augusto Olivares, Allende's close friend and press advisor, had already been killed. The palace was like a furnace. Barrios told the correspondent that two of Allende's ministers had gone to talk to the generals, presenting the president's demand for guarantees for the working class. 'He will decide what to do, once the guarantees have been obtained.'

But the generals coolly shot at the two envoys as they were returning to the palace, and then took them prisoner.

Some time in the next 25 minutes, Allende also died: according to his daughter Beatriz, with battle helmet on his head and machine-gun in hand, in open battle with the mutinous armed forces entering the palace, just as he had planned. The junta immediately gave it out that he had committed suicide, together with Augusto Olivares. But whether Allende committed suicide or was shot by troops is finally irrelevant: in either case, he died fighting rather than hand over his mandate.

His body was flown the following day to Valparaíso, with his wife and other members of the family in attendance, and buried all but anonymously in the family plot there. Señora Allende was not allowed to see her husband's body.

The epoch of Popular Unity was over. But in Santiago, and to a lesser degree in other cities throughout the country, open resistance to the new regime continued for more than a week.

The Battle for Santiago

The Parties

Faced with the reality of the coup, the original political coalition of the Left dissolved very quickly. Each of the parties gave its own orders to its own militants. There was no united battle command.

It was less than a week since even the Left of Popular Unity had become aware of a real possibility that the armed forces might not split in the face of an attempt at a coup from within their ranks. The existing preparations of all the parties for a confrontation had been based on the expectation that at least a section of the army would remain loyal to the president. With this kind of military strength behind them, the parties were hoping that the government would be able to hold a liberated zone or zones of resistance, where their own militants who were prepared for battle and any other supporters could join the loyal troops fighting against those involved in the coup. Existing contingency plans were for everyone to go to his place of work and wait for splits to appear in the armed forces, and for further instructions. The parties were relying on their own radios to maintain communications: these were broadcasting from the upper floors of central buildings in Santiago, and the Left calculated that they could withstand a siege for several days. It never occurred to the politicians that the attacking force might use bombs.

So the existing plans were for everyone to report to his normal place of work, and wait. If there were any revisions in the plans designed to take into account the possibility of a united move against the president by the three forces, they had not yet filtered down to the base.

At the time of the coup, the Communist Party was still struggling with its own internal divisions. The old party leadership had put all its faith in the possibilities of a compromise with the Christian Democrats, and the success of its campaign to persuade all progressive forces to do everything possible to prevent civil war. It was not prepared for a military battle. The youth section, and some of the party's trade unionists, were aware of the real dangers in the existing situation and had made some preparations for fighting a coup, in line with the prevailing belief that the armed forces would split. In Santiago, they seem to have been virtually in control of the party apparatus. But time was against them: their challenge to the established leadership of the party had only taken form after 29 June – too short a period to allow them to have any real impact on the party as a whole. Their ideas were in contradiction with long-standing party habits, the habit of looking for a solution from Christian Democracy, and the habit of trusting in the constitutionalism of the armed forces. The result was that the party's initial response to the military threat was completely uneven, with some militants and even some of the party's leaders still holding desperately to the security of their old beliefs while others were trying to prepare the membership for the real problems of civil war.

In Temuco, a week before the coup, a member of the party's Central Committee went down from Santiago to advise local Communists on the current political situation. The city was already under military control, but he had no comments to make on how to confront the intervention of the armed forces: he could only advise local militants to wait for the outcome of the negotiations with Christian Democracy. In Santiago, on the other hand, the party's left-wing did a great deal to prepare the masses for what was coming. An official party television broadcast on the night on the 10th warned the Left that a Fascist coup was imminent, and on the morning of the 11th, *El Siglo* (the party's daily paper) came out with a huge headline demanding EVERYONE ON THE ALERT! The instructions were for everyone to go to his place of work. Even here, however, there was confusion at the base. In one of the nationalized textile factories, Ex-Sumar, on the morning of the coup, Communist trade unionists bewildered their Socialist manager by their refusal to believe that the coup was real, or that it would be difficult to put the naval mutiny down. Their own primary concern was that any active plans for resistance in the factory might provoke a final split with the workers and technicians who supported the opposition. In Valparaíso, too, individual Communists had made preparations for confronting a coup. Yet on the morning of the 11th, the party's newspaper only learned that a real coup was happening through a phone call from Santiago: its own sensitivity to what was happening in the armed forces was so limited that it had to be told of a naval mutiny in its own town!

When the armed forces did not split, the divisions within the party healed over very quickly, and by 11.00 a.m. the whole of the party's forces were devoted to organizing an orderly retreat.

The left-wing of Popular Unity, and the MIR, had always predicted that some kind of confrontation was inevitable, and should have been prepared for it. Nonetheless, they too were caught off balance by the timing of the coup and, worse still, by the failure of the armed forces to split. Popular Unity's intelligence sources had predicted that the armed forces would take some kind of action between the 8th and the 10th of September, but this had been universally interpreted as a new, larger-scale version of the old search operations under the 'Law for Arms Control'. The Left was expecting a coup on the 17th or 18th, to coincide with celebrations of Chile's independence. The usual military parades on the 18th would have given the armed forces ample cover for troop movements. Once again, Marxists were caught off balance by their own lack of military experience: they did not expect the armed forces to try to take them by surprise. The first real conviction that a coup was imminent dawned on the night of the 10th.

When it became obvious that there were going to be no significant splits in the armed forces, the MAPU and the MIR organized a strategic retreat, some hours after the Communist Party. For the MAPU, there was very little alternative. Its forces in Santiago factories were very small, and in the South, and the countryside, where it was stronger, the position of the Left already looked very bleak. In any case, party members seem to have believed that all other revolutionary forces were taking the same decision. They were wrong. The Socialists were continuing to fight.

Most of the 'foreigners in the factories, surrounded by loyal troops' to whom ex-President Frei referred in his phone call to London, were in fact Socialists. On the whole, the party seems to have followed its original plan of defending the factories. In some of the nationalized factories (such as Indumet) there were party caches of arms. More arms had been stored in Tomás Moro, the president's private residence, the only place in the country which could be guaranteed against searches for arms in the months before the coup. On the morning of the 11th, these arms were distributed to different factories by trucks, until bombing by the air force made it impossible for party members to remove anything more from the house. Some members of the party's Central Committee and of the executive of the Socialist Youth went to various factories to join the workers in their struggle. (This would seem to have been the basis in fact for the rumour that Altamirano himself was killed fighting in Ex-Sumar, which circulated in the first days of the coup.) Rolando Calderón, not only a member of the Central Committee but also Secretary-General of the CUT, went to join workers fighting in Indumet and stayed there until the factory was taken by the armed forces, when he escaped and joined other comrades still fighting in Ex-Sumar.

When it became obviously impossible to hold the factories in the face of the collapse of any united resistance by other parties in Popular Unity, and the sheer invincibility of a combined attack on individual buildings by troops and bombs, the fighters in the factories organized their retreat. In many cases, the cost in lives was heavy. Twenty-four workers seem to have died in the escape from Ex-Sumar. Those who succeeded in escaping were encouraged by the party itself to hide for a few hours, and then take up the struggle again as snipers: 'urban guerrilla war'.

MIRistas who happened to be factory workers joined the Socialist Party's struggle. Elsewhere, the MIR's conception on how to fight was very different. Its militants were well-drilled and on the whole well-trained, but they were not prepared to lead an armed mass struggle, and the evidence suggests that they did not consider such a struggle appropriate for a battle which, from their point of view, was already lost. *MIRista* interventions in the battle for Santiago and elsewhere in the country were well-planned, self-contained affairs designed to raise the morale of the population without too great a cost. In Santiago, they attacked patrolling soldiers, retreating in good order as soon as they had drawn blood. In Valparaíso a full month after the coup they were able to organize two successive attacks on military barracks, each of them lasting half an hour, and ending in a successful retreat with few casualties and no prisoners. In Santiago, at the same time, there was a brief attack on the National Stadium.

It was a less costly form of military action, useful for keeping the military aware that they had by no means completely won the battle, but in the end it could not amount to a strategy for winning the war.

The People

For those who took part in the battle, the position must have been dreadfully unclear. The last orders which could in any way be said to apply to the Left as a whole had come from the CUT early on Tuesday morning: orders to go to one's place of work and wait for instructions that might or might not come. The last plan formulated publicly by any of the political parties was a plan for turning the factories into fortresses and defending the government there. Thereafter, each party communicated with its own militants by means of whatever direct contacts it was possible to organize. There was no clandestine radio system to which those outside the lines of party communication could turn, because none of the parties had thought to prepare a clandestine broadcasting apparatus. Once the government's radio stations were put out of action, the people as a whole were on their own. Thus militants found themselves in such impossible places to defend as the Central Bank, cheek by jowl with the presidential palace, or the almost equally central Post Office, Ministry of Labour, and Ministry of Social Security. From such positions revolutionary bureaucrats spent the next day and in some cases the next two or three days taking shots at passing soldiers, before they finally evacuated the buildings under cover of night.

Those in the factories were initially in a slightly more favourable position, for in the early hours of the coup it was possible to move about in the industrial suburbs and to transport arms and food. The first concern of the military was to eliminate party headquarters, not industries. But in the long run, the workers in the factories were as exposed as those in the Central Bank. Some of the factories had automatic pistols, machine guns and anti-tank grenades – not all of them – but these weapons were scarcely very useful against the united might of the armed forces. There had been no preparation for attacks from the air. When the armed forces began to attack in earnest it quickly became obvious that the original strategy of defending the factories was absurd.

Perhaps typical of the uncertainty was FENSA, the factory manufacturing electrical appliances which served as the nerve-centre for Cordon Cerrillos. (The report comes from its new capitalist manager, interviewed later by *Le Monde*.) During the morning of the 11th, a government official arrived with fifteen trucks full of workers and arms, presumably from other factories in the Cordon. They waited throughout the day for instructions and information, debating whether they should stay in the factory and defend it, as the Communists there were arguing, or sally out and confront the armed forces, as the Socialists wanted. In the end the defenders left. A 'guard' of older workers was left behind to take care of the plant. When the army arrived the next day, five of these men were killed.

Different again was the story of Ex-Sumar.

The Battle at Ex-Sumar

David Iturra, Socialist Party militant and former government interventor in the nylon plant of Ex-Sumar, now a refugee, gives his account of the resistance. The interview has been summarized from *Chile Nachrichten*, bulletin of the German solidarity committee.

I arrived at the factory for work as usual on September 11th, without any idea of what would happen to Chilean workers during the day. Everything was normal, until I got a telephone call from the executive secretary of CORFO's textile committee. He told me that the navy had taken Valparaíso and were calling for the overthrow of Allende, but that the army had still not committed itself and that the police were on their way to the Presidential Palace to defend the government.

Immediately, I called an emergency meeting of Popular Unity trade union representatives in the factory, to analyse the situation and discuss how we should present it to the workers. This meeting ended in a dispute. Trade union representatives from the Communist Party (who were in the majority) thought that it was not necessary to warn the workers that a Fascist coup might now be beginning. They believed that this attempt at a coup would be a failure [like the one on June 29th *ed.*] and that it was wrong to cause a panic or to provoke unnecessary divisions among the masses. [There were opposition supporters among the workers in the factory, and the Communists' concern seems to have been that no step should be taken which might alienate them *ed.*] I lost my temper. The comrades did not seem to realize the seriousness of the situation. What they wanted to do above all was to ask the Central Committee of their Party for instructions – it was as if they did not want to understand.

So I called an emergency mass meeting of all the workers for 9.00 a.m. to explain the situation. This decision was yet another point of friction between me as the organizer of the meeting, and the Communist comrades . . . [Once again, the friction was caused by different interpretations of what the Christian Democrats would do when confronted with the news: the PC arguing that there was unity in the factory, but unwilling to take steps to organize a resistance which might 'disrupt' this unity, Iturra arguing that there had never been unity and that steps should be taken regardless of the fact that some workers would not support the resistance *ed.*]. The activity of the Communist comrades at this point in time caused a lot of problems, because they prevented an immediate and decisive response to the situation.

The mass meeting decided to stop production, to wait on events and to call further meetings whenever fresh information arrived, in order to prepare for resistance and for taking over the factory. I asked the works manager to stop production, for the first time in the history of Ex-Sumar. But the only fresh information we got was a short speech from Allende, and the broadcasts of the CUT. [The CUT was calling upon workers to go to their factories and wait for further instructions *ed.*]

The situation in the country got worse and worse. We heard about the formation of the junta. But there were no instructions from the political parties, which caused a lot of fruitless discussion within the factory. Time went by without us deciding on any plan for organizing the mobilization of the masses. The Communist comrades were still arguing that there was no need to alarm the workers and that if soldiers attempted to enter the factory, we should not offer them any resistance. They stressed that the class should not be split. The situation was desperate, and the result was that we squabbled among ourselves. While we were disagreeing, opposition supporters within the factory were trying to persuade the workers to leave.

We held another meeting, but the disagreement continued. Finally a resolution was passed, and those who wanted to leave the factory could do so and that those who remained would stay and fight to the bitter end. Only when the opposition supporters began to show their true face as Fascists did the Communist comrades decide to join with the Socialists in occupying and defending Ex-Sumar. By now it was 3 p.m. We started to organize brigades, which was difficult, as we had no weapons and our local political headquarters had already been destroyed. At this moment, fortunately, a contingent of lorries arrived with food, and later some comrades came from Tomás Moro [the president's personal residence *ed.*] with an appreciable number of machine guns, anti-tank grenades and some hundred automatic pistols. These arms would enable us to maintain a resistance for the next few days. We got in touch with two neighbouring factories, PAL and POLAK, in order to organize a united resistance. Our aim was to take over the local police station.

But when we came back to Ex-Sumar from the neighbouring factories we found that the Communist comrades were no longer interested in resistance, having received orders from the Central Committee that the factory was not to resist. Only 200 Socialist Party militants and 3 comrades from the Front of Revolutionary Workers [a MIR organization *ed.*] stayed to defend the factory, among them some comrades from the Central Committee of the Socialist Party Youth who had come to join the struggle.

We organized two fighting groups of 40 people each to leave the factory and confront the enemy outside. The others were to stay and prepare for a prolonged resistance. The women who had remained were put in charge of organizing first aid.

Then we were attacked by planes and helicopters, which caused confusion within the ranks. Simultaneously the factory was surrounded by police and soldiers, who opened fire at once from every side. The comrades who were in charge of military operations distributed our forces in groups of 10, ordering them to leave the factory and fight their way through the surrounding forces, and so retreat out into the surrounding *poblaciones*, La Legua, El Pinar, Esmeralda and Aníbal Pinto. We had reached the conclusion that it would be useless to stay in the factory and organize a resistance there, since there was no longer any organized resistance within the country on the part of the Left as a whole, and only a few factories were still fighting.

The battle against the police and the military was hellish. We heard bursts of machine gun fire and the explosion of bullets ricocheting against the walls. Our people fought tenaciously and with surprising courage. Darting from one side to another, shouts, battle yells which one could not quite make out. It was horrible and staggering to see the first of our comrades fall. But without losing their presence of mind, other comrades picked up the weapons and ammunition of those who had fallen and continued the attack. We could also see the effect of fighting on the enemy. Our comrades brought down many soldiers, and we could see fear and nervousness in the military ranks. They had reason to be nervous, because many of them were fighting against their will, on orders from the Fascist generals, against friends, brothers and neighbours.

At 7 p.m. a prominent leader of the Socialist Party, Rolando Calderón, arrived [Calderón was Secretary-General of the CUT and had been Minister of Agriculture *ed.*]. He said he came from Indumet where the workers had resisted bravely and courageously, and there had been big losses on both sides. The workers had destroyed two military jeeps and their occupants and weapons, and had shot down a helicopter which crashed in the factory grounds. The Party had had a big cache of weapons in this factory, which had been distributed throughout the industrial cordon, where members of our Central Committee had fought shoulder to shoulder with the workers. The factory was taken, but comrades G——, S——, and Calderón himself had got out alive.

Together with Calderón and the six comrades still remaining in Ex-Sumar I left for the *poblaciones*. We went to a house where a female comrade was expecting us. Part of the house's walls had been destroyed and it occurred to us that the house and the surrounding district had been bombed. Our comrade let us in quickly, as one knew that there were informers everywhere waiting to denounce our fighting comrades who were risking their lives to give us refuge. Here we met a member of the Party's Political Committee and another comrade from the CUT, who gave us further news of events and told us that the best thing we could do would be to hide for a few hours, and then go out in small groups of snipers to attack the soldiers. For the first time, we learned that Allende had died fighting.

When the battle in the factories was lost, many turned to a more elementary kind of struggle, taking up positions as snipers during the night in order to make impossible the task of the military patrols. This battle of the rooftops continued for the better part of a week in Santiago, and firing, whether of soldiers or snipers, could be heard in the outlying areas for months after the coup. But if the snipers had some successes, the military had more, for they were prepared to be completely ruthless. In La Legua, the *población* where Ex-Sumar was located, workers who had retreated from the factory succeeded in stopping a bus-load of police reinforcements, and killing most of those inside. The response of the junta was to order an attack on the *población* itself. Many of its inhabitants were killed outright: many more were dragged to the two prison stadiums being used by the junta and killed there, after being savagely tortured.

In any case, where people were not in direct contact with the parties, demoralization set in quickly.

Repression

The military were brutal on a scale which no one on the Chilean Left had imagined was possible. How many people died in the first months of the coup will perhaps never be known. The junta itself has no particular interest in keeping statistics. But the indications are that the figure was very high – perhaps 15,000, the figure estimated in December by the Swedish ambassador to Chile (who played a heroic role himself in helping refugees to find asylum in embassies which had quickly been put under heavy military guard). Perhaps it was twice as high, or more – the kind of figure now suggested by those representing Popular Unity abroad.

In any case, it was the most brutal coup yet in Latin America, in a country known as the heartland of stable democracy.

Concrete evidence on the scale of the massacre is inevitably fragmentary. How many workers were killed during the fighting in the factories, one can only guess: the only figure available is the estimate that 24 died in the battle at Ex-Sumar, made by local residents of the area. *Newsweek* reported that a priest who had gained access to the Technical University to bless the dead, saw the bodies of 200 students piled inside.[2] Reports of the numbers killed at the University of Santiago vary between 200 and 585. After the first two weeks of the coup, according to the same reporter, the official body count at the Santiago morgue was 2,796. His own surreptitious visit to the morgue suggested that most of the dead there had been executed. A *Le Monde* reporter, making a similar visit under official auspices to identify the body of a Bolivian friend, came to a similar conclusion. But the same reporters say that many bodies were found by friends or strangers floating in the river, and others suggest that the police ordered some to be left 'as a warning to others' where they were killed, in the *poblaciones*. There is no reason to think that all the city's dead passed through the hands of its central morgue.

Some of the early killings can be explained as the result of systematic propaganda within the armed forces before the coup, designed to persuade a conscript army that the Chilean working class was trained, armed, and prepared for civil war. The soldiers were afraid of what they would find in the factories and universities, and fear may account for some of their actions – for instance in the Technical University, where students were killed while trying to surrender, according to the testimony of some who survived. The Technical University was known to be a Communist stronghold, and it may be that rank and file soldiers simply could not cope with the possibility that real Communists were not prepared to strike. Ironically, on the day of the coup, students in the Technical University had prepared a concert on the theme 'No to Civil War.'

Soldiers were also under heavy pressure from their officers: some at least of those who refused to obey orders were shot on the spot.

But from the beginning of the coup, the brutality of the armed forces was clearly something which had been carefully planned. On the day of the coup, leaflets were dropped all over Santiago with the message,

No compassion will be shown to foreign extremists who have come here to kill Chileans. CITIZEN, be on the alert to discover who they are, and report them to the nearest military authority.

Many Latin American refugees picked up in this way were shot outright or beaten to death. At least one American student was also shot (and another has since 'disappeared'), even though North Americans and Europeans were generally regarded as 'untouchable' by the military, and after some physical maltreatment were generally released. Refugees from the Latin American dictatorships who survived their initial treatment at the hands of the Chilean armed forces were in great danger of being turned over to their 'own' police. The junta invited the Brazilian secret police into Chile to pick out those on its own wanted list, while simultaneously offering the Chilean armed forces lessons in the more sophisticated techniques of torture. One Brazilian (picked up and subsequently released) has reported that he served as the subject of a well-ordered demonstration in torture, with Chilean officers standing around to watch and learn from his Brazilian interrogators.[3]

The Chileans were scarcely better off. In Santiago, the junta opened the city's two football stadiums, the National Stadium and the Chile Stadium, as concentration camps and centres for interrogation. Nothing smaller was any use, for at any one point in time 7,000 people were being held and processed by the city's military authorities. Workers captured in their factories were brought here, and so were many people from the *poblaciones*. Stadiums were also opened up in provincial cities like Osorno for the same purpose. In Valparaíso, where the navy was busy turning its ships into floating prisons, Admiral Troncoso claimed that he had succeeded in arresting 1,500 people out of a total list of 4,000 in the first two weeks of the coup.

Any evidence of a will to fight on the part of those arrested was met with even heavier repression. In the National Stadium of Santiago, the well-known folk singer Victor Jara tried to raise the spirits of those who had been arrested with him by playing his guitar and singing to them. Guards moved in to take his guitar and break his fingers, and when he still refused to stop singing, to break his back and kill him. In the Chile Stadium, the commander in charge came to lecture the assembled prisoners on the dishonour which Marxists had brought upon the Chilean flag. 'Chile's mountains will be levelled, something which can never happen, before the Chilean armed forces are divided by the Marxists,' he chanted, and forced the prisoners to repeat it after him. Everywhere, prisoners who were in the end to be let go were subjected to mock executions, sometimes one after another, in order to increase the effectiveness of the terror. For those who escaped the tortures and the real executions, beatings, humiliation and fear were the order of the day.

At first the stadiums were the only detention centres, apart from local police stations: they served at once as prison, torture chamber and place of execution. Later, as international outcry about the massacre in Chile grew, other places such as regimental headquarters were used for the initial and bloodiest screening. A clandestine information bulletin published after the coup reported that seven execution camps were functioning in Santiago on the first days of the coup: the regimental headquarters of the Buin and Tacna regiments, the military barracks at Peldahue, the city's three cemeteries, and a place just outside the city airport, Pudahuel. The aim of the military was two-fold: to increase its knowledge of the Chilean Left, through 'interrogation', and to eliminate anyone who might later be capable of leading the resistance. It was a military operation. The cost in lives did not matter. The country was, after all, in a state of internal war.

Perhaps worse than the attempt to identify and kill known militants was the deliberate military policy of creating a reign of terror in the *poblaciones*. Once the initial battle of Santiago was over, the armed forces began a series of systematic raids and exemplary executions. Men, women and children from the city's poorer parts were herded into the stadiums. There was no attempt to check the political record of those who were picked up or simply shot. The victims were a means of terrorizing the working class and its allies into complete passivity: their own personal history mattered very little.

Most of the international reports agree on this facet of the repression. *Newsweek* reported that in the Pincoya *población*, police arrested 50 men and killed all those who belonged to one of the neighbourhood's blocks. *Le Monde* reported a similar incident in the *población* Nueva Matacuna, on the Mapocho river: there the number arrested was 60 and six of them were found dead in the river the next day. In some *poblaciones*, where there was no river to serve as a natural disposal system, police forbade families of the dead to take the bodies away for burial, until they had lain a certain time as a warning. There are even reports of purely gratuitous torture, torture of people with no likely connection with any political party: an exercise for satisfying the sadistic instincts of some of the soldiers and proving to the whole world their complete power over Chile's people.

The following account was published by a Swedish journalist, who was himself arrested and taken to the National Stadium:

> The Swedish journalist Bobi Sourander was one of the foreign journalists most roughly treated by the Chilean junta. He was arrested and held in the National Stadium for more than a week before being expelled from the country. Since returning to Sweden, he has been writing a series of articles on the repression he witnessed. The following article is from the October 28 issue of the Stockholm daily *Dagens Nyheter*. The translation is by Intercontinental Press.
>
> Almost every morning dead bodies turn up lying along the *Avenida Departamental* on the outskirts of Santiago. They appear near bus stops, where they can best frighten people. Their faces are smashed in with rifle butts so that they are unrecognizable. They wear the cheap, worn clothing of Chilean workers.
>   The political persecution in Chile is far from over. It has only changed its form, shifted so as not to be so visible to the world. And it has reached a new level among the poor and the ordinary people.
>   The junta isn't looking for officials in the Allende government any more. They are

dead or deported. Now the Popular Unity politicians are missing or in prison. So the political persecution has another target. It is the Chilean workers who are being persecuted.

The *Departamental* is a long industrial road through Santiago's factory belt, and it passes through campamento after campamento in the working-class slums.

The first dead bodies didn't show up along the road until one morning a few weeks after the military coup. They had been dumped there at night during the curfew period. They were picked up by a passing garbage truck.

Since then, the appearance of such bodies has been a continual occurrence. One morning there were five men lying there in overalls with safety glasses around their necks. Two days later there were two men with their feet tied together. They had obviously been dragged behind a car. I myself saw a man who had been placed in a sitting position on an embankment. He had been shot in the neck with the gun pointed upward so that his face was blown away.

Who killed them? Why? And where did they come from?

The first question can be answered with an ironic 'don't know.' Only the military and the police know. Only they can move around at night when the curfew is on.

As for the second question, Raúl, a friend, can answer it.

He lives in a *campamento* along the *Departamental*, with his wife and ten children. In Allende's time, he was a member of the campamento governing board and head of the health committee. He has never made a secret of the fact that he has been a Socialist Party member for decades.

In front of his house, he hung a picture of Salvador Allende with Fidel Castro. He thought it was funny. In the era of the spiffy Allende, it was the only picture he had seen of Fidel wearing a tie.

The police arrested Raúl on a Saturday night. They came into his *campamento* in a truck and dragged him out of bed. He staggered out carrying his trousers and his shoes and was knocked down and beaten in the street while his children screamed. Finally he was hauled onto the back of the truck with several others. When he asked for a shoe he dropped, the policemen hit him in the eyes and in the testicles with the barrels of their guns.

Raúl was held in the police station for four days. He was tortured for an afternoon, and given the electric shock treatment. When I talked with him, he still had the burn marks on his lips and heels. The police wanted to know where he had hidden Carlos Altamirano, one of those with a half-million escudos price on his head.

'I don't know what you want from me,' Raúl answered. 'I have only seen Altamirano in newspaper pictures.'

He was thrown into a cell with three others. One of them was wearing the same kind of trousers and the other had the same last name. In the middle of the night, his two cellmates were taken out.

In the morning his wife, Carmen, learned that three bodies were lying along the *Departamental*. One had the same kind of trousers on that her husband was wearing. Another had a payslip with the name Gómez, the same last name as Raúl's.

Carmen ran the whole way to the bus stop. She was relieved to see that none of the bodies was Raúl's. But she was also convinced that she would never see him again.

When Raúl came back to the *campamento*, he found out that his job was gone. When Carmen and one of their girls were arrested a little later and held in an army barracks for two days, he gave up.

He fled from the *campamento* and thus lost both the hovel he lived in and the right to one of the new houses that are being built for families in the neighbourhood.

Raúl Gómez, a man who considered himself rich when he was getting about $100 a month in wages, no longer has any hope. He has no job, no home, no future, not even guarantees of his life.

He is a typical case.

Tens of thousands like him, laborers, slum dwellers, and wage workers in the nationalized factories go in fear of their lives. They know that sooner or later, depending on how long the repression lasts, they are going to lose their jobs and their homes.

It is against them that the repression and the pogroms are aimed. A worker in Chile who openly supported Allende and socialism in the past three months knows what can happen to him.

He is a marked man, like a Jew in Nazi Germany.

In Escotilla Tres, Entrance Ramp No. 3 in the National Stadium, the military junta demonstrated this on a massive scale.

This ramp was the 'cell' where all the newcomers landed. A month and two days after the coup, I met eleven workers from Chena in the small suburb of San Bernardo.

They were almost bubbling over and happy to have come to the National Stadium. They thought their lives were saved.

'We don't know how many workers the military shot in Chena. We only heard shooting and found in the roll call that people had disappeared.'

'You didn't see anyone shot, then?' I asked.

'See? We had blindfolds on all the time.' Rómulo, a truck driver, said that he sat in Chena sixteen days blindfolded!

Chena was the military's shooting gallery in San Bernardo. It sits on a hill and is surrounded by barbed wire. There are no buildings, just sheds open on all sides. There is no water and no toilets. And people were held prisoner for weeks there!

A month after the coup, the new methods of repression could be noted in the National Stadium. The first question fellow prisoners asked a newcomer was where he was the day he was arrested – at home, on the job, in the street.

The second question was equally certain. Where were you taken?

If the answer was the National Stadium, they shrugged their shoulders.

He hadn't had anything to complain of yet.

But if the answer was 'the Fifth Precinct,' the 'airbase in Colina,' the 'Tacna barracks,' then a third question was automatically asked. 'How much did they beat you?'

Some didn't have to be asked. The three boys from the René Schneider *campamento* came in with bandaged eyes, swollen lips, and cauliflower ears.

And in the morning inspection, when people could finally take off their clothes and unwind a little, they pointed out the ones who had gone through the barracks and the precinct. Their arms were beaten raw and they had ugly bruises on their backs.

And they were glad to be in the National Stadium, with the International Red Cross and the UN Refugee Committee. Now they only faced questioning, in the bicycle-racing track building.

A month after the coup, almost all of the people coming into Escotilla Tres were workers and poor. They were the new victims of the new methods of repression. And the roundups were so indiscriminate that the results seemed almost ridiculous.

For example, there was the line of newcomers that appeared suddenly in one morning inspection, dominated by five boys in shiny green uniforms with the name of the Savory glass factory on the back.

They had been taken off the job four days before and softened up at a military post.

There were also examples of the monumental stupidity and ignorance underlying the repression. Many of those who came in had been arrested because they had 100-centavo notes in their wallets – worth about a tenth of a cent after the inflation of the Allende period.

'The police told me that this bill was the secret sign of the MIR,' one of them told me. 'Like a lot of other people, I saved one as a curiosity. Never in my life had I had anything to do with the ultra-leftists like the MIR.'

There was a Japanese who had been mistaken for a Brazilian. There was a retired air force noncom who had been going around in civilian clothes but wearing his old service revolver.

And there was a grumbling, ill-tempered old Spaniard. He was the economics secretary to the cardinal in Chile and a personal friend of Pope Paul VI.

The military junta has issued an order that all unregistered guns in the country should be turned in at the churches. So now he was accused of having 'stolen the said weapons from the churches and turned them over to extremists'.

He came in, in shirtsleeves. He had left his coat at his worktable when he came in to the police station to answer the false charge. The prisoners stole a blanket for him and gave him the warmest place to sleep, in the ladies' restroom.

So, Escotilla Tres was a 'safe harbour'. The only thing that could happen to you after you got there was two or three interrogations, which might be rough.

Then came the decision – trial before a military tribunal or release.

For a Chilean worker in the National Stadium there is no difference between trial or release. He can never expect anything more than 'conditional freedom.' That means that every night he must be in his house and if anyone comes looking for him he has to turn himself in immediately to the authorities.

And staying 'home' in a *campamento*, where informers keep a constant eye on people who have been in the National Stadium, can mean ending up face down along the *Avenida Departamental*.

The military 'search' these *campamentos* in raids for weapons and political leaders. They are appointing informers as the new leaders and re-naming the settlements. 'New Havana' is now called 'New Dawn', and 'Ho Chi Minh' is called 'Happy Valley'. The settlement of 'Three Bullets' got the name 'Virgin María'.

And if you get through the military's 'house-by-house searches,' there are still the night raids, when the police come. The police know their districts well. They do not come looking for weapons. They know that there aren't any. They go directly after the people they want.

But even if everything goes all right at 'home', there is still the problem of making a living. Workers are sent out of the National Stadium with the notation 'Marxists' on their work permits. They have no chance of finding work in today's Chile.

National Reconstruction.

The work of reorganizing Chile began immediately. The day after the coup, the junta announced that congress was dissolved and all its seats now fell vacant. The existing Constitution was indefinitely suspended. All parties which had formed part of Popular Unity were declared illegal, together with the MIR. As for the Christian Democrats and the National Party, their activities were temporarily suspended. All political activity was effectively banned.

In October, a commission was set up to study the legal possibilities of a new Constitution possibly on corporativist lines, one which would ensure that a Marxist government never came to power again. The constitutional suggestions of the junta made no provision for giving the working class any kind of representation in parliament. Privately, military officers indicated that the right of the working class to vote would not be returned until they had been purged of their Marxist superstitions. In December came the news that the old electoral register had been withdrawn.

Meanwhile, the junta ruled by decree. A state of siege was declared, which the generals predicted could last for seven or eight months. The nation was put under curfew from ten o'clock in the evening to the following morning, a curfew which has still not been withdrawn. For the time being, late-night parties were forbidden.

The first sector of society to be reorganized by the junta was the press. On the day of the coup, the junta had ordered all news media, newspapers, radio or television to cease publication. On 12 September, two newspapers were allowed to resume publication: *El Mercurio* and *La Tercera*, a paper closely connected with the family of ex-President Alessandri. The same decree announced that any unauthorized newspapers would be taken over and destroyed, and the junta simultaneously set out its principles for the future:

> The Military Government is determined to clean up press publications in accordance with what is considered to be the immediate solution for the re-establishment of national harmony and ethical norms. It will not, therefore, accept insults to individuals or institutions, nor impertinent language in the press.

Four other daily newspapers were later authorized. (Two of them however have since closed down: *La Prensa*, the Christian Democrats' paper, and *Tribuna*, which represented the National Party.) Censorship remained: an office was established in the Military Polytechnic to which editors were told to submit their first editions. All communications media were compelled to provide free advertising for the junta's campaign of National Reconstruction, with the result that the television stations were flooded for the first weeks with soldiers making speeches on the traditional virtues and singing the National Anthem.

As for the newspapers and journals which had supported Popular Unity, their premises were raided during the coup, their journalists arrested or killed and the papers themselves closed down. The junta had no illusions about the dangers of freedom of the press.

Much the same fate befell the universities. On 3 October, the junta appointed new military rectors or chancellors throughout the country, to carry out a complete reorganization. Some university departments, particularly those in the faculties of arts and social science, were closed down temporarily to allow for the pruning of Marxists from their staff. In Valparaíso's Technical University, all Marxist books in the library were weeded out and burned. At the University of Chile in Santiago, the departments of sociology, philosophy, journalism and psychology were closed down pending an even more thorough reorganization. The university year was declared at an end, two months before its natural term, and all students were forced to re-register if they wanted to finish their courses. Many thousands of those who re-applied were refused entry. In this fashion, 6,600 students were effectively expelled from the University of Concepción (out of a total student body of 18,600), from the University of Chile in Santiago, and from the Catholic University.

Within a month, the military had let it be known that all factories and farms taken over illegally by workers would be restored to their former owners. Where foreign businessmen were concerned, the return of private property was accomplished very quickly. The junta announced that it would keep the copper mines, but would pay their owners 'adequate compensation'. Other foreign businesses nationalized under Allende, such as Petrodow, were simply returned. Where it was a question of local business, the generals could not afford to be so generous. Businesses which had been taken over illegally by Popular Unity were returned to their former owners, but at the cost of the owners' assuming responsibility for all debts incurred during the previous government. The monopolies and banks which had been nationalized legally were sold back to their former owners. The desire to restore Chile to a complete free enterprise economy was there, reiterated almost daily, but in the existing economic circumstances the junta could not afford to be too generous.

A fund for National Reconstruction was started, financed out of private donations from wealthier citizens and a levy on soldiers' wages. For a time, the press made much of this fund. Instructions were published in *El Mercurio* for Chileans living abroad who wished to contribute, and the Banco Central (now under the management of a general) announced ceremoniously that the vast majority of donations had come in the form of wedding rings.

Meanwhile, the rate of exploitation of the working class was increased. Salaried workers were forced to work for an extra four hours a week without pay, as their contribution to National Reconstruction. The right to strike and the right to be represented by a trade union in wage negotiations, were withdrawn. The CUT was declared an illegal organization. The junta's original promise, that Chilean workers would be allowed to keep all the gains they had made under Allende, was of course completely forgotten. Gains made by the working class in the fifty years since the Constitution of 1924 were wiped out.

In the mines, workers were forced back to work at gunpoint. Everywhere, known sympathizers of Popular Unity were dismissed. The junta declared that Popular Unity had packed the factories with its own supporters, to the detriment of production. Now, unemployment surged, until the junta itself felt so threatened by the prospect of a large mass of starving militants with nothing to lose, that it introduced a tribunal to examine the appeals of those who felt they had been unfairly dismissed, and provided unemployment relief for the others for a six month period.

The only sector of the poorer classes which did not lose everything it had gained under Popular Unity was the peasantry. Initially farm workers and peasants in the newly reformed sector were as maltreated by the military and their own old landlords as workers in the towns. But in the countryside, the generals themselves intervened to replace Jaime Silva, vice-president of CORA

(Agrarian Reform Corporation) and himself a landlord, with a military representative prepared to listen to the demands of the peasantry. They were obviously worried by the twin threats of loss of agricultural production (which would have made any successful programme of economic reconstruction impossible) and the possibility that the countryside might provide cover for a successful rural guerrilla war. Peasants who had gained a legal title to their land under Allende, were allowed to keep it. The generals insisted only that the previous landlord's right to eighty hectares of reserve land for his own use was respected.

The New Order

The initial intervention of the Chilean armed forces was a classic political success. When the coup came, the task of persuading Chile's middle class that a violent overthrow of Popular Unity was necessary and even in some sense 'constitutional' had already very largely been accomplished. Virtually every institution with some claim to constitutional respectability had committed itself publicly to the campaign against the president – parliament, the judiciary, even the secondary schools and universities. The non-Marxist political parties of the centre and right were united in claiming that democracy could only be preserved if Allende went. By August 1973, there was very little credibility left in the president's legal title. Only the Church remained ambiguous, or showed any interest in continuing the dialogue between opposition and Popular Unity, or any evidence of unwillingness to face the prospect of a bloody civil war.

More important still, the politicians of the Centre and Right had succeeded in organizing a very large section of the population prepared to take action in its own right to force the president to go. Chile has a disproportionately large middle class element in its working population. (One need only remember that in the 1970 Census, 700,000 of those at work were self-employed, and another 350,000 were employed by the State.) This petty bourgeois layer of shopkeepers, independent producers, professionals and white-collar employees had suffered from the economic disruption of the last three years and was in any case worried about the prospect of losing its social position under a real Marxist government. It was the ideal material for a mass movement of reaction, and its organization had proceeded with great efficiency. In 1973, a whole sector of pseudo-trade unions or *gremios* set their face against the president's continuing in office, organizations based on the petty bourgeoisie at work and thus able to convince at least their own kind that they represented the working population of Chile. Doctors, lawyers, self-employed shopkeepers, white-collar workers, truck owners and small industrialists, all had their *gremio*. So did the genuine large-scale capitalists. The grand and petty bourgeoisie were almost completely united in their opposition to Allende, although Popular Unity's fundamental strategy had been based on the theory that their interests were in direct conflict with one another and politically it was logical for them to be diametrically opposed.

The political power of the *gremios* had already been demonstrated in two national strikes. Their bitterness against the incumbent government can be measured by the statement made by the Secretary General of the Colegio Médico in August 1973, asking doctors to go on strike for a second time: 'Either people will die, or this country itself will die. It's the same as war. No one takes to the streets prepared to kill voluntarily, but in war one must be prepared to kill.' Not surprisingly, then, members of the *gremios* cooperated actively with the military even in the most gruesome aspects of the junta's work. The Colegio Médico itself drew up a list of those of its membership who had opposed the August strike, recommending that some of them should be disqualified and others should be turned over to the military authorities. Fourteen doctors were shot. As for the other *gremios*, privately, their membership must have provided the backbone of the middle class campaign of denouncing local Marxists and suspicious activities to the military. Publicly, the *gremios* put all their force behind the new regime. Leon Vilarín, president of the truck-owners union, undertook an international tour to defend the junta against the supposed international Marxist campaign of defamation, as soon as it became obvious that the generals' willingness to indulge in wholesale bloodshed was not acceptable even to the capitalist Free World.

The campaign to bring down Allende had thus provided the junta with a large, ready-made popular base, and ironically, with an opportunity to replace the professional politicians once and for all. The *gremios* were not tied to the traditional political parties, however much Christian Democrats and Nationalists had contributed to their rapid growth. The junta itself was obviously inclined to distrust the professional politicians, as people who had contributed a great deal to the existing social crisis through their own mismanagement of the country from 1958 to 1970. For anyone seriously interested in creating a different political structure in Chile which would by-pass traditional politics completely, the *gremios* should have been a heaven-sent opportunity. Many foreign observers were quick to point out the parallels with European Fascism in its heyday: it, too, was based on the petty bourgeoisie, favouring corporativist forms of organization which gave capitalists and wage-labour a spurious equality, both being represented through their work; it, too, claimed to want to abolish class conflicts in the interests of national harmony and was prepared to support any kind of authoritarian measures to achieve this end. It seemed that with the existing power of the *gremios*, all the military needed to do was to establish a corporativist parliament, in which the nation would be represented by the *gremios* themselves rather than by traditional political constituencies: in other words, to give the existing mass movement some permanent constitutional form.

But those who saw the new Chile as a perfect example of a Fascist regime were wrong. The junta toyed briefly with the idea of introducing a new

Constitution on corporativist lines, which would have given direct parliamentary representation not only to the *gremios* but also to women, youth, and the armed forces and police. Comments about the generals' admiration for the Spanish and Portuguese political systems were allowed to filter through to the press. But although a commission of right-wing jurists was set up to investigate the possibility of a new Constitution, it was a commission of civilians. The generals themselves quickly lost interest. Rather than share their power with the middle class, under any circumstances, they preferred to govern alone.

Five months after the coup, General Pinochet announced that he expected the military to be in power for another five years. In the interim, signs of the armed forces' preference for their own kind had become very plain. The junta made no attempt to bring prominent activists from the *gremios* into positions of power or influence within the new regime. Vilarín was allowed to make propaganda for the junta abroad, but even he was given very little public recognition from the government at home for his role in bringing down Allende. Even positions of status rather than power were kept in the military camp. In the universities, the junta appointed retired or serving officers to replace the chancellors who had been dismissed in the first days of the coup. Doctors were also slighted: in the hospital of San Bernardo, one of Santiago's largest, the vacant post of chief administrator was entrusted to an army surgeon, not to a prominent activist of the Colegio Médico.

When a national conference of the *gremios* suggested reorganization of the provinces in order to give the *gremios* control of local administration, their suggestions were quietly ignored by the military authorities. The task of determining government policy was entrusted to the traditional representatives of big business. It was Fernando Leniz, president of *El Mercurio*, (a key link in one of Chile's biggest conglomerates) who was invited to become Minister of the Economy and he was not prepared to make any immediate concession to the economic interests of the middle class, as the results of his policies very quickly showed.

Immediately after the coup, the economic pressure on the middle classes eased dramatically as long-hoarded goods were put back in shop windows. The stocks which had been accumulated by shopkeepers during Allende's presidency were enough to satisfy short-term demand. The junta imposed tough penalties on shopkeepers who were discovered still to be hoarding goods, and for the first two weeks, no price increases were allowed. Shopkeepers accepted the emergency regulations. For the rest of the middle class, consumption became possible once again. But this period of economic relief was quickly over. Economically, all sectors of the Chilean middle class – salaried employees, shopkeepers and even small capitalists – were badly hit by the traditional economic policies favoured by the Minister of the Economy in the months following the coup.

The junta maintained a list of 30 goods with official, i.e. government-established prices. However, prices were raised to approximate to what their own economic advisors considered a realistic level. Thus the price of a kilo of sugar jumped from 24 escudos in September to 120 escudos in October and 280 escudos at the end of the following January. Unlisted goods were allowed to find their 'free market' price level, with similar results. The price of a pair of shoes rose from 1,000 escudos to 8,000 or 9,000 in the first months following the coup, dropping back to 5,000 and 6,000 escudos in December because nobody could be found to buy them at such a price. Rents in Santiago rose to ten times their pre-coup levels. The escudo was devalued several times over, to bring it into line with international prices, with the usual result of raising the cost of imports. Inflation, already out of control under Popular Unity, ran wild under the generals. Where the rise in the cost of living had been 192% in the first eight months of 1973, by the end of the year it was 508%. The junta themselves considered this figure an achievement: General Pinochet had predicted in October that the total figure for the year would be closer to 1,600%.

In December, the Jesuit monthly *Mensaje* estimated that essential foods had risen in cost 400–500% since the coup, while officially announced wage increases amounted to 67%. For those still at work, the bulk of the wage packet was obviously going on food. There were many reports that the Chilean working class was facing starvation. Even the lower middle class found itself in a grim situation. In December, the Confederation of White Collar Workers in Private Industry published its own report on the cost of living. It estimated that the absolute subsistence minimum for a family of four was 48,660 escudos a month – providing the family ate no macaroni, jam, biscuits, fish or cheese, or any other luxury, drank neither coffee nor wine, and read no papers. The average legal wage of one of its own members with 10 years' service, it reported, was 23,420, leaving more than 25,000 escudos to be met by the new government 'bonuses' or by private loans.

The junta had called for all citizens to accept the need for sacrifices in the interest of National Reconstruction. But in the existing circumstances of hyper-inflation, it could not impose a freeze on wages for very long. In spite of the continuing toll of repression, the massive dismissals, and the imprisonment and murder of accepted leaders, the Chilean working class quickly recovered enough to mount a fight against starvation. In October, workers constructing Santiago's underground railway briefly went on strike. In December, the bakery workers, traditionally one of the most difficult sectors of Santiago's working class to organize, spontaneously boycotted their bakeries in a protest against the low level of wages. Once again there were bread-queues in the city, and the government had to explain that the cause was worker 'absenteeism', and not a national shortage of flour.

Thus it was obvious even to the generals that an attempt to freeze wages at pre-coup levels would be counter-productive. In mid-October, the new policy of 'bonuses' was declared, which in effect doubled existing salaries. The wages for October were to be paid at mid-month rather than at the month's end, the wages for November were to be paid at the beginning of the month, and a 'bonus' equal to a month's wages was to be paid at the end of November. The same pattern was to be repeated for December. In November, the official minimum monthly wage was raised from the pre-coup level of 4,000 escudos to 12,000 escudos, and the junta announced that in 1974, the minimum wage in the public sector would be 16,500 escudos, and in the private sector 18,000 escudos.

In practice, even for white-collar workers who could be sure of getting their 'bonus', the new wage increases were not very generous. The 'bonus' would have brought the salary of an office worker earning 23,420 escudos and with a family of three, to just under what his *gremio* declared was the minimum subsistence level. The bonus ensured survival, and not much more. The situation was, of course, far worse for the working class. With the price of a kilo of beef at 1,000 escudos and the price of a pair of shoes 6,000, a minimum wage of 12,000 or 18,000 escudos meant very little – particularly since the take-home pay of a man nominally earning 18,000 was now about 14,000. Even this absolute minimum had to be fought for. Small capitalists had their own troubles; many of them were unable to pay the 'bonuses', while others were willing to take whatever further advantage could be had from the smashing of working-class organization following the coup. Strikes broke out with the declared aim of forcing employers to live up to their commitments under the new regime's laws.

One of the traditional patterns in Chile's class structure was beginning to reassert itself: the pattern of a large, poor lower middle class of salaried employees who have to fight in order to preserve their existing level of wages against inflation, privileged only if one chooses to compare them with a working class which is even worse off. In the past, that pattern had served to make Chilean white-collar workers into a well-unionized and even a militant sector of the population, willing to strike, willing to join the CUT, willing to support the struggles of the working class, and open to the influence of any philosophy calling for radical social change. Under Popular Unity, the pattern had changed: a bare majority of white-collar workers had joined the fight to bring down Allende. Whether the generals realized it or not, the prospect of the pattern changing once again into its old direction posed a considerable political danger for them.

It was not only the working class and the salaried middle class which suffered from the junta's pricing policy after the coup. Hyper-inflation also very quickly embittered the junta's relations with another *gremio* which had actively participated in the campaign against Allende, the National Confederation of Retailers. The generals' intention to keep a strict control over shopkeepers' economic behaviour was not, retailers learned, a matter of a few weeks' emergency regulations. On the contrary, official prices were rigidly enforced. General Pinochet and other leading officers made a point of regular public tours of local markets, to see if the proper price was being charged for goods on the official list, and to make sure that the quality of food was maintained and customers were sold the proper weight. Hoarding, or any other attempt to circumvent the junta's decrees, was met with arrests and fines. In October and November alone, 1,381 shops were prosecuted for infringing regulations, and 11 million escudos levied in fines (though only 2 million were collected without appeal), 45 shops were closed by the authorities. When fines had obviously failed to work, the authorities turned to more drastic measures. In January, several shopkeepers were imprisoned for five days and had their shops closed for another fifteen days. The president of the National Confederation of Retailers protested that the junta was mounting a campaign against his members, but the protests did very little good. The following week a new Law on Economic Crimes was published, with the shopkeeper who overcharged or hoarded goods or otherwise fell foul of the junta's decrees on consumer standards, as its chief target.

It seems likely that the junta's campaign against shopkeepers was partly a remnant of old-style populism: once again, though with less justification, it was government policy in Chile to focus wage-earners' resentment against inflation on the figure of the overcharging shopkeeper. In other areas the same kind of heavy-handed authoritarianism was used to impose the norms of the free market where they had never operated before. When in mid-November the College of Engineers proposed to raise the scale of fees charged by its members, *El Mercurio* denounced it as a purveyor of monopoly practices; in January, the junta announced the creation of a new Anti-Monopoly Commission which would have the power to dissolve societies guilty of such practices, remove the incumbent officers of professional associations or *gremios* if they were guilty of them, and apply a fine of up to 150 times the prevailing legal annual minimum salary.

Small capitalists too had problems with the junta. Because of the failure of wages to keep pace with prices, Chile was suddenly hit by a crisis of under-consumption. In November, sales had slumped 25% on August levels.[4] The owner of a small textile factory commented to a foreign reporter:

> People have no money, so they cannot buy anything. Nothing is sold – there is no demand, and so no production. In my factory, we haven't had one important order in the last three months. By the end of last month, I hadn't any money to pay Friday's wages, so I asked for credit from a bank. I was told that credit was suspended, but that I could ask for advice at the Ministry of Economic Affairs. So I did, and received a visit from a Colonel. I explained that I had no money to pay wages, to which he replied, 'Well, tell them to sell the TV's their precious Allende gave them, and if that doesn't satisfy them, let me know – we'll shoot a few, and you'll see how they obey.'[5]

Credit for small businessmen was out of the question. The junta had very little money to spare, and what it had was now committed to necessary works of infrastructure, many of them designed to lessen the likelihood of a successful urban guerrilla movement. There was no compensation for industrialists even for damage caused by soldiers during the coup; the military had taken refuge in the doctrine of internal war to disclaim any legal responsibility. Even the bad debts of industries now being returned to their owners, debts taken on by Popular Unity, were set at the door of the businessmen who had legal title to the factory concerned.

In all, the junta did very little to ensure that it kept the support which it had originally enjoyed among Chile's middle class. In part, this failure was the result of simple economic constraints. Only an immediate and massive influx of foreign aid could have returned the Chilean middle classes to the standard of living they had enjoyed under President Frei. At that time, aid from the US government alone amounted to more than $100 million a year, and the various US-dominated international agencies contributed half as much again. Chile's short-term economic problems were now much worse. For three years, there had been virtually no investment in industry. Because of the American blockade, even spare parts for existing machinery had become difficult to obtain. There was the damage caused during the coup itself. Furthermore, Chile still had to renegotiate a foreign debt of some $3,500 million, almost four times its annual income in foreign exchange, much of it incurred by the Frei regime. For the junta, anxious to re-establish its credit with international capital, the comfort of the middle classes was not an economic priority.

International capital could have done a great deal to ease the internal political situation in Chile. But there was no massive influx of foreign aid. The US government only managed a credit of $24 million to finance the import of American wheat and another $28 million through a semi-public agency to finance the import of corn: hardly a generous contribution. Among the international agencies dominated by the Americans, the reaction was equally cautious. The IMF finally awarded the junta Special Drawing Rights of $95 million after a several-month long investigation, half what the junta had asked for as a contribution to its attempts to solve balance of payments difficulties. The Inter-American Development Bank lent $65 million for a hydro-electric plant. Credits came piecemeal, tied to specific imports from the country of origin: £36 million from the City of London to finance the construction of a new copper smelter by British construction firms, $33.5 million from Spain to finance the import of its own Pegasos lorries, tools and spare parts, a credit of $10 million from Argentina for the import of Argentinian capital goods and a 73 million cruziero credit from Brazil to purchase Brazilian sugar. There was enough confidence in the new regime to ensure the resumption of normal commercial relations. But international capital was not prepared to give the junta a massive political boost.

However, economic constraints cannot explain why, time and again, the military should have resorted to simple compulsion as a way of handling relations with their own political base. There was no need to pass a decree against monopolies in order to hold the fees charged by the College of Engineers to a reasonable level. Nor was there any need to mount a political campaign against shopkeepers for charging prices marginally higher than the official prices which the junta itself had raised to astronomical levels. A similar mistake was made with the bus owners' *gremio* in Valparaíso, when its leaders protested publicly against the junta's refusal to keep transport prices in line with the rising cost of fuel, they were jailed for distributing 'subversive pamphlets'.

Once in power, the generals were clumsy in their handling of the civilian population. It was as if the military arrangements for the coup itself and for the subsequent brutal 'internal war' against Marxist militants had exhausted all their existing capacity for inventing a consistent political strategy. After the first weeks, a number of distinct and mutually incompatible political themes began to emerge: corporativism was a possibility, and so was an attempt to recreate Chilean society on the model of a pure free market system, as favoured by the president of *El Mercurio*. Perhaps the most consistent political line was a kind of crude and classically inappropriate populism, favoured by Generals Pinochet and Bonilla and their followers within the junta. The generals made a great deal of their interest in talking to the people at large, of visits to *poblaciones* where they heard the complaints of workers who had not been paid their legal 'bonus', of visits to local markets to make sure that local shopkeepers were not exploiting the population. There were even public announcements that television sets had been donated to the poorer *poblaciones*, and a tax was imposed on workers to provide a fund for the poor.

But this populist tack lacked any firm support even within the junta itself, and with good reason. Rather than a consistent political strategy, it represented a reflex action: a remnant of the days when populism had been the most constant element in the Chilean political system, perhaps the result of latent sympathies with the old Christian Democracy on the part of the generals. For the junta, a populist solution was simply not feasible. Reduced to the simplest, its own economic policy was to force the working class to sacrifice its existing standard of living for 'National Reconstruction'. To make such a policy possible, all signs of independent action on the part of the working class had to be crushed – even the economic protests raised by former Christian Democrat trade unionists. Nor could any real support be gained now from the classes who used to be the marginals of Chilean society, the lumpenproletariat existing on casual labour or on what it could sell at street corners. For one thing, this class now included many Marxists, dismissed from their own work. For another, the money to buy them out and turn them against their working class brothers was simply not available. In any case, too many people had lost relatives who may or may not have been political militants in that first indiscriminate wave of the internal war, when the military turned their apparatus loose on the *poblaciones*. Any new sign of resurgence among the *pobladores* would pose a political threat to the regime, the more so if it took the form of a solid political organization of the lumpenproletariat on the old Christian Democrat lines.

The generals were partially trapped by their own military training. Even Pinochet, trying hard to improve relations with the people at large, managed in the course of his efforts to deal a blow at the shopkeepers and retailers from whom he should have been looking for support. The only consistent strategy adopted by the generals was a strategy of continuing military control and military repression, which had all the advantages of inertia. If shopkeepers do not obey, fine them: if they still do not obey, lock them up. If workers become restive, threaten to shoot them. It was the kind of authoritarianism on which the internal life of the armed forces had always been based, and the easiest form of government for them to fall into now.

For the hard-liners within the junta, repression was itself a strategy. On the whole, their line seems to have prevailed. The police apparatus was expanded, drawing upon the pool of unemployed which the coup itself had created. When this investment was announced, it was characterized as an example of 'social promotion' (*promoción social*), drawing on an old Christian Democrat expression for public works designed to improve the position of the marginals in a way which should have had the ghosts of old politicians turning in their graves. Other improvements of the kind designed to make a policeman's life easier were provided for the *poblaciones*. Consistent street lighting was introduced in the suburbs surrounding Santiago. Lengthy discussions were reported in *El Mercurio* about the need to improve the living conditions of the poorer people by building them new houses – thus incidentally breaking up the old functioning neighbourhoods, and reducing the opportunities for a resurgence of mass organization among the poor, or for a successful urban guerrilla war.

The new Chile is not Fascist then, and by the same token, it lacks the kind of political stability which a true Fascist regime would have provided. The junta has imposed a government solidly based upon the repression of the majority of the population, even the repression of some of those sectors who originally gave it support. This apparent failure of the generals to understand their own need to consolidate a political base has been one of the most surprising aspects of the new order, and if one is looking for its overthrow, the most promising.

One of the results of the junta's failure to make use of the *gremios* has been the revival of the old bourgeois democratic parties, particularly the Christian Democrats. At the time of the coup, it looked as though Christian Democracy might well disappear forever. Throughout the period of Popular Unity, its own traditions of a 'Revolution in Liberty' had looked rather shopworn. In 1973, following first one and then another national strike, its parliamentarianism and formal commitment to the constitution had been outflanked by the emergence of the *gremios*, committed to more direct action, and it was in real danger of losing its own petty-bourgeois base (with the natural result that in order to recapture it, the party moved sharply to the right). Any serious attempt to construct a Fascist regime would have left the party without any political role to play at all. But the gradual alienation of the petty bourgeoisie from the junta has given it a new place in the existing order of things: as the potential and powerful voice of their opposition to military rule.

Originally, both the Christian Democrats and the National Party fell over themselves in an effort to give the new regime their encouragement. On 12 September, both parties sent official missions of congratulation. The president of the Christian Democrats, Senator Patricio Aylwin, made a public statement saying 'the manifest intention of the junta is to re-establish our political institutions, according to the constitution, and bring peace and unity to Chileans. It reflects public opinion, and deserves the full cooperation of all Chileans'. The evidence suggests that Aylwin and the majority of the party (with the exception of a tiny left wing) were hoping that the junta would place Frei in power as a more acceptable 'civilian' strong man. Frei himself mentioned a six month interregnum of military rule before a democratic regime was re-established, in his phone call to London, and the interview he gave in October to a Madrid paper (the *ABC*) was an obvious and deliberate demonstration of total support for the coup. At the time, supporters of the National Party and the Christian Democrats were already rumoured to be competing openly for places vacated by Popular Unity supporters.

But it soon became very clear that the junta had no intention of restoring Frei to power. If anything, the junta favoured National Party men in the scramble for places; but on the whole, it was much more inclined to favour its own. Retired and serving officers were appointed to replace the outgoing university chancellors, with the bizarre result that two Christian Democrat chancellors were forced to look for employment abroad like any Marxist refugee. One of them, Edgardo Boeninger, had played a prominent part in the campaign to bring Allende down. As time went on, the junta's distrust of all politicians became increasingly obvious. In October all political activity was banned, even political activity by the National Party or the Christian Democrats. Later in the month both parties were declared temporarily 'suspended'. In December, both were asked to furnish the junta with lists of their party members. At roughly the same time, the parties' chief source of patronage, the government apparatus, was closed to them forever by a government decree forbidding civil servants to have any kind of party connections.

In January came General Pinochet's statement that the military could be in power for five years. The job of national reconstruction was to remain in the hands of soldiers, not to be entrusted to politicians (and particularly, perhaps, not to a man like Frei, whose relations with the armed forces had been strained during his term in office, and whose demagogery had played an active part in creating the conditions for Allende's later success). The Christian Democrats had already protested publicly against the banning of party activity and the creation of a commission to draw up a new Constitution. But previously their protests had been muted, because of their general support for the coup. Now, still more grievously wounded, and with the growing support of the middle classes behind them, they began to move into a position of declared opposition to the junta.

On 18 January, a 'private but official letter' from Senator Aylwin was handed to General Pinochet; it said:

> A lasting order cannot be created on the basis of repression. Many Chileans have lost their jobs, been denied civil service promotions, been arrested, harassed, threatened or pressured in different forms without any evidence or concrete charge being brought against them ... In view of the level of prices and the fact that the earnings of workers are insufficient to cover the cost of food and other vital items, we feel it is no exaggeration to say that many of these people are going hungry ...
>
> We are convinced that the absolute inactivity of the democratic sectors facilitates the underground efforts of the Marxist groups. Without guidelines from their leaders, our rank and file members and sympathizers are at the mercy of rumour, trickery and infiltration.

A cynic might have noted that the scale of murder, torture and imprisonment under Chile's new rulers seemed to have passed the Christian Democrats by almost unnoticed, and commented perhaps that its view of the junta reflected very well the level of inconvenience suffered by a right-wing petty bureaucrat. In any case, the key to the letter is provided by its last sentence. Once before Christian Democracy had felt that its base among the petty bourgeoisie was threatened: then it had moved to the Right, to pre-empt any successful competition from the National Party. Now it felt that its bases could slip away towards the Left. In the face of such a threat, the Christian Democrats were forced to move.

As the letter was handed over, Christian Democrat women began a simultaneous campaign of writing to the wives of junta members, as once they had written to the wife of General Carlos Prats, calling for the junta to resign. On February 8, Aylwin's 'private but official' letter was made public in Buenos Aires. Before the end of the month, the Christian Democrats' semi-official daily newspaper, *La Prensa*, was closed. *El Mercurio* explained that it had been forced to shut down for financial reasons.

The Left in Retreat

11 September 1973 was a massive defeat for both the parties of the Left and the Chilean working class. Whatever the junta's original promises, the working class lost not only what it had gained under Popular Unity, but the elementary rights which had been won through hard struggle fifty years before: the right to be represented by trade unions, the right to belong to a confederation of unions, the right to strike, even the right to vote. Its traditional leadership was an easy target for the tidal wave of denunciations. Within every factory and every *población*, local activists were known by name. Only one right-wing

white-collar worker, one local shopkeeper, one person with a personal grudge was needed to make sure that they were picked up.

In some *poblaciones*, people who denounced their neighbours were found hanged with a note on the body explaining their crime, the only effective possible deterrent against denunciations. But where this practice was most successful, it led to immediate retaliation by the military forces. In Temuco, after a wave of such executions immediately following the coup, the military announced that for 'every innocent' who died they would kill ten prisoners. The executions stopped.

So the immediate possibilities for action open to the working class or its parties were drastically limited by the brutality of the new regime – which was, after all, its function. The massacres of September and October could not wipe out the Chilean Left (still less of course the working class) but they could and did make it very dangerous for anyone to take a position of political leadership. After a fashion, repression worked. Traditional working class leaders were too vulnerable to be relied on, even supposing that they survived arrest and execution or the massive dismissals of those known to be Marxists. Party militants were forced to be circumspect, as were the parties to which they belonged. There are still more than 20,000 political prisoners in Chilean jails, and at both the national and the local level they serve as hostages for the good behaviour of the rest. One of the first united actions of the Left was to ban all guerrilla activity, since it was likely to give the junta an even better excuse for further repression against those inside the prisons as well as those still at liberty.

The coup did not destroy party organizations – in spite of the massacre and the denunciations – but it did considerable damage. Worst hit was the Socialist Party, many of its local and even regional units disappearing completely because of the scale of the repression. In Rancagua, a city of 90,000, it seems that the Socialist Party was destroyed. The Communist Party fared better, both because it was less hated by the Right and because it had a much larger political base. The MIR and the MAPU, smaller organizations, also succeeded to some extent in preserving their cadre: the MIR in particular because it had gone underground some months before the coup. Even these suffered important losses: the Communist Party saw its Secretary-General, Luís Corvalán, taken prisoner even while arrangements were being made to smuggle him out of the country. The MIR lost Bautista Von Schauwen, their second in command. Both remain prisoners of the junta. Carlos Altamirano, however, managed to escape.

Where local party organizations survived, what they could do was severely limited. Recruitment or public discussion of policy was impossible, and even the passing on of party decisions to those in need of leadership was suddenly fraught with dangers. Some sections had been infiltrated by spies in the days of open mobilization, and in any case, in the prevailing situation, no strangers could be trusted. Even small meetings in private houses were difficult (though they were held) while neighbours might denounce 'suspicious activity' to the police. Thus mass organizations were suddenly reduced to a much smaller network of trusted comrades – the oldest members of the party, in some cases, and in others those who had fought together for a particular political line. The Socialist Party immediately split into different political fractions.

Everywhere, there was a sudden loss of contact between the parties and their bases: a contact which could only slowly and painfully be rebuilt.

The most surprising and most hopeful development in Chile since the coup has been the ability of the working class itself to fight back in some fashion, in spite of the weakness and fragmentation of its leadership. There have been a number of strikes – very localized, often lasting no more than a day, often motivated solely by economic reasons but still strikes, in a situation where one would have expected a terrified passivity. In Santiago, metro workers and bakery workers have been on strike, together with some factory workers (most of these, apparently, trying to force employers to pay out what the junta had already declared to be the legal minimum wage). In Lota there was a brief strike of coal miners against the low level of wages and the murder of trade union officials, coupled with a massive demonstration which ended when the town was surrounded by tanks. There have been a series of one day general strikes in small towns in the south. There have also been strikes by traditional right-wing unions angered by the junta's policy of giving orders first and consulting afterwards. During the first weeks of the coup there was a strike of dockworkers in Valparaíso (the dockworkers have traditionally had one of the most corrupt unions in Chile, a union modelled on Hoffa's Teamsters in the United States, and well-endowed with American aid). Six dockworkers were shot. In Puerto Montt, the similarly right-wing seamen's union went on strike in early 1974, only to have its leader Juan Elpido González Gómez, thrown in jail.

In fact, Chilean workers have proved that they are willing to fight against the starvation wages being imposed on them by junta, and indirectly against the repressive regime as a whole. This remarkable resilience has already produced some results. Junta supporters have begun to discuss the 'problems' posed by the government's 'relationship' with the working class, where two months before they had assumed that no problems would exist, and the 'relationship' would be dictated by the gun. The government's economic policy was based on the assumption that it could force the working class to make huge sacrifices: now it has some doubts. Some concessions have been made in particular struggles, and one notable pseudo-concession: the military have agreed to recognize a right-wing, CIA-financed trade union confederation (the *Confederación Nacional de Trabajadores*), which previously only existed on the docks. Even this attempt to build a 'tame' union system to replace the old one is fraught with dangers, for the junta's own economic policies have succeeded in bringing an impossible pressure even on right-wing trade unions: as one can see in its history of problems with the *gremios*, the seamen's union, and the docks.

The work of rebuilding the Chilean Left has gone forward much more slowly. Chilean Marxists have had to solve the twofold problem of managing to organize at all in a clandestine fashion, and trying to work out how the existing military dictatorship can be overthrown. There have been no easy solutions.

After the coup there was a certain amount of guerrilla activity, spontaneous or planned – planned in Santiago and Valparaíso, where the MIR had a hand in it, spontaneous in the south where in many places peasants and UP officials took to the hills. The short and severely limited initiatives taken by the MIR were on the whole successful: the retreat to the hills in the countryside was not, for Chilean country is relatively open, and the would-be guerrillas were quickly picked off. Within the first few weeks, the parties of the Left all decided that guerrilla warfare was not going to provide them with the means of overthrowing the junta, and would only increase the repression. A tactical retreat was called.

Meanwhile the different parties began to make an attempt to patch up their own divisions, on the theory that any continuing sectarianism would be virtually suicidal in the present circumstances. *Le Monde* reported that a meeting of all left-wing organizations (including the MIR) was held in Santiago on 29 September, to co-ordinate the struggle against the junta. Its most concrete result was a directive that militants should end all individual initiatives and wait for the parties to elaborate a new strategy. Party differences over the kind of organization which was wanted in order to co-ordinate the resistance still remained. The Communist Party wanted a 'Democratic Front', which would include at least some sections of Christian Democracy. The MIR wanted a 'Revolutionary Front' which would only contain the parties of the Left. The Socialists, at least the left-wing of the Party, were supporting the MIR.

By the end of 1973 the question of how the united front should be composed had been solved, at least for the moment. The growing isolation of the junta within Chile freed new sectors of the middle class which it was imperative for the resistance to capture, whether the fight was one to restore democracy or to create a new socialist order. On this basis, a broad Anti-Fascist Front was formed. Whether it would include sectors of the progressive, anti-Fascist bourgeoisie (who would certainly be unwilling to struggle for socialism) or parties committed to the maintenance of bourgeois democracy, such as the Christian Democrats, was left deliberately vague. In the end, the Front was formulated so as to allow each party to put forward its own policy. A declaration issued in Rome in December, signed by all the parties of Popular Unity and the MIR, put it this way:

> The Chilean people are reorganizing their ranks. They are regrouping for the struggle in the midst of a difficult clandestine environment. A far-reaching and united movement is being set up for mobilizing the great majority of our compatriots. *The anti-Fascist resistance is headed and shaped by the Chilean people inside the country. They must decide on its character, form,*

scope, and the factors making it up. They will surely set it up as strong as possible, with absolute determination to win, with a spirit of unity that seeks to increase the vast well-spring of anti-Fascist feeling that is developing throughout the country.

The more difficult problem still of how one overthrows an armed Fascist regime in practice, still remained to be solved.

Paradoxically, the situation in Chile in 1974 once again opened up possibilities for the reformists on the Left – the parties and the politics which had led the working class into a whirlwind not five months before. Once again, it was possible for those of the Left to believe that Christian Democracy was a progressive force, at least to the extent of opposing the existing dictatorship (though their opposition was still very cautious, and its very publication set it out as a substitute for a Marxist-led resistance, not part of an anti-Fascist front). Still, an anti-Fascist movement aiming to restore the old order with a few suitable modifications must seem very attractive to those who are suffering under a savage authoritarian regime. By the beginning of 1974, the Left in Chile was in a dangerous political vacuum, without a clear concrete policy as to how it could move forward on its own: it was a breeding ground for false hopes.

In February, the MIR felt it necessary to publish a statement abroad emphasizing that only an armed struggle would overthrow the dictatorship: it would not collapse as a result of its own contradictions. In a sense, the point was obvious. The junta's repressive policies had been a success, from the point of view of international and even national capitalism. The armed forces had stopped one incipient revolution in its tracks, and were making it exceedingly difficult to prepare another one in its place.

By 1974, whatever the fate of the Anti-Fascist Front, one could predict that it would take the Left some time to recover the initiative it had lost with the coup. Perhaps that should have been expected. The Chilean working class has suffered massive defeats before – in 1926, with the imposition of a military dictatorship by Ibáñez, and in 1948 with the passing of the *Ley Maldita* which outlawed the Communist Party and established concentration camps for Communists and trade union activists alike. In each case, the working class and its parties have survived to take up the struggle again. But in each case it has taken the parties of the Left several years to recover, and has involved sections of the Left in a profound rethinking of their own political position.

The coup of 1973 was a much bigger disaster. The working class lost more than its traditional economic and political liberties – it lost a chance for a socialist revolution, which had never seemed so close. Many more people were killed, tortured, imprisoned or dismissed from their work than ever before, in spite of the black record of nineteenth century labour relations in the nitrate mines. From being a stable liberal democracy, Chile was suddenly plunged into a military dictatorship as vicious as any other in the world.

Some of the responsibility of the disaster rests with the Chilean Left: they might well be expected to need a few years' grace, both to work out their own conclusions about the period of Popular Unity and to find a new strategy capable of putting Socialism back on the agenda.

Conclusions

One should always be suspicious of people who draw cut and dried 'lessons', according to their own political formula, from the experiences of other countries and other times. 'Men make history, but they do not make it just as they please; they do not make it under circumstances chosen by themselves, but under circumstances directly encountered, given and transmitted from the past. The tradition of all the dead generations weighs like a nightmare on the brain of the living . . .'[1] Even the working class suffers from the weight of the traditions of its dead generations. Successful revolutions are made partly in spite of those dead generations, and partly by drawing on their accumulated strength. The task is never cut and dried: certainly it was not so in Chile.

Nonetheless, there is a basic similarity of historical situation between Chile's experience in 1970-1973 and the possible future experiences of the Left in Europe. Chile was a democratic country, with a social structure and a culture not all that unlike western European countries such as Italy and France, or even Britain: a large middle class, a strong proletariat, perhaps fewer peasants than France, a large Communist Party and Socialist Party. Even members of the British Labour Party were sufficiently struck by the reasonableness of Allende's road to socialism, judged in their own terms, to think momentarily in September 1973, *it could happen here*. Interpretations of the Chilean experience are therefore not just academic exercises: Chile is too close for comfort to the world we live in ourselves.

A revolution in Europe would scarcely break out in more favourable conditions, at least in this present century. It, too, would have to cope with the problem of a strong Social Democrat or Communist Party deeply rooted in the working class, advocating the parliamentary road to socialism. In Europe, too, the revolutionary Left would be in a minority – probably in a much smaller minority than it was in Chile, where there was a strong revolutionary current in the Socialist Party, the MAPU and the Christian Left within Popular Unity, as well as the MIR. One should not forget that in Chile there genuinely was a revolutionary upsurge of the urban proletariat, gathering other classes around it to demand the overthrow of the bourgeois congress and the bourgeois law courts and their replacement by popular justice and workers' control. The tragic history of Chile is not simply a reflection of the fact that reformists never make revolutions: primarily, it is the tragedy of a revolution that failed, inspiring a violent mass movement of reaction with Fascist inclinations and a military massacre of the working class.

The readiness of the European and American Right to justify the coup and overlook the massacre should chill their fellow-citizens, even those who are not socialists. The day after the coup, *The Times* of London editorialized the general view of the British bourgeois press: '. . . whether or not the armed forces were right to do what they have done, the circumstances were such that a reasonable military man could in good faith have thought it his constitutional duty to intervene'.[2] Predictably, the magazine *Encounter* offered an academic gloss on the myths of reaction,[3] also reiterated in a book by Robert Moss, in which the perpetually quarrelling parties of Popular Unity are seen as having been on the point of turning Chile into a 'monolithic State ruled by a narrow ideological elite'.[4] After that, it only remained to tut-tut about the brutality of the military and the 'temporary death of democracy in Chile',[5] circulate the junta's rumour of any army of 13,000 left-wing foreign extremists – war is a nasty business – and leave it to the Chilean military to get on with the business of 'eradicating Marxism' and introducing 'economic discipline' once again.

What is more disturbing is that the Right has been, on the whole, quicker to recognize the real significance of the coup in Chile than the Left.

On the British Left, there have been two important currents of interpretation. The Communist Party and the left-wing of the Labour Party have described what happened in Chile as a brutal and unjustifiable assault on democracy by a small group of capitalists and military officers, aided and abetted by the USA. In this view, the fact that Popular Unity remained within the confines of bourgeois legality was one of its virtues: the essence of the Chilean process was that it was a peaceful, that is parliamentary, transition to socialism.

The answer to all such arguments is offered by *The Times* editorial quoted above. It could also be found in Lenin: the State consists of bodies of armed men, whose role it is to maintain the capitalist order. Or in Marx: the working class cannot simply lay hold of the ready-made State machinery and wield it for its own purposes. In practice, Allende's faith in bourgeois legality was suicidal: it was responsible for his death and for the death of some tens of thousands of other men, some of them supporters of Popular Unity, some of them not. The prospect of a coalition of Communists and Social Democrats taking the same road in Europe is not encouraging.

On the whole, Social Democrats have dodged any such conclusions, taking refuge in a series of explanations which have in common a tendency to locate the causes of the coup anywhere but in the internal dynamics of the class struggle in Chile – in the intervention of US imperialism, in the comforting thought that after all Chile was only a relatively democratic country (democratic for Latin America, but not to be compared to the 'mature' western democracies), in the equally comforting belief that it was an underdeveloped country with a totally dissimilar class structure, and occasionally in theories that the Chilean revolutionary Left itself was partly responsible for provoking the coup. Characteristic of this school of thought is the belief that if Allende had won 51% of the vote, rather than 44%, the outcome of Popular Unity would have been different.

Some of these theories have been discussed elsewhere in the book. It may be that if the Chilean road to socialism had been successful, the US would have intervened, but as it happened any open intervention was unnecessary – and we have argued that even the informal blockade was less important in bringing down the government than has often been claimed. Chile does have a unique class structure, but its large middle class is not substantially different from Europe and, on the whole, if anything the Chilean middle class has had a history of much longer contact with working class trade unionism and a much firmer bias to the Left.

As for the theory of provocation, there is a danger of falling into the right-wing habit of looking for 'agitators' behind every popular demand. The MIR in Chile were just too weak to be held responsible for mass actions, even among the peasantry. If the theory of provocation is seriously held then it was the bulk of the working class and peasantry who were provocative. For it was they who took over factories and farms in response to the right-wing threats of October 1972 and June 1973, and it was they who demanded that Allende and his government take 'a firm hand' against the Right. The UP could have suppressed this movement to conciliate the Right, but it would have meant abandoning its base and its programme. Preparations for the coup, and the events leading up to the coup, were not 'spontaneous' reactions to extreme-left provocations, but a well-organized campaign to bring down the government and defeat the working class. If there was provocation, Carlos Altamirano's comment was perhaps the closest to the mark: 'The best way to precipitate a confrontation, and to make it even more bloody is to turn one's back upon it.'[6]

There is a second misconceived analysis of the Chilean experience, often found on the revolutionary Left. It suffers less from faulty theoretical premises than from a simple mis-reading of the Chilean situation. The analysis usually begins by criticizing the theory of a peaceful transition to socialism and arguing that what was needed in Chile was a revolutionary party with mass support, having a coherent strategy for dealing with the army and taking power. So far so good; this is precisely what this book has tried to argue. The tragedy of Chile is that this did not happen. The proponents of this argument then go on to analyse the reformist nature of Allende's policies and say, either that Allende was 'administering capitalism'; or that the Popular Unity was a bourgeois, popular front government; or that it was a united front dominated by the politics of reformism, or more simply still, that it was another Stalinist betrayal of the working class.

Now it is true that Allende's policies were reformist and that the Popular Unity government's policies in power were largely controlled by the Communist Party. But what this argument misses, or more usually underemphasizes, is the size and importance of the revolutionary wing both inside and outside the UP coalition, and more generally inside the working class.

By not fully appreciating the importance of the revolutionary Left in Chile, revolutionaries in Europe and the USA reduce the possibility of a Chilean revolution to an abstract, purely formal proposition. Revolution is always possible.   But the argument then proceeds that with no revolutionary party capable of successfully challenging a reformist leadership, 'the workers were left to confusion and demoralization',[7] and there was no real alternative to the military coup, no other possibility than another bloodbath occasioned by another Stalinist betrayal.   Willy-nilly one is led to the conclusion that the Allende regime was doomed to failure from the start, or perhaps that the real cause of its failure was that it was not sufficiently efficient in administering capitalism and restraining the workers' movement.   The wheel has very nearly come full circle, and the Communist Party analysis is reproduced.

Any analysis of the 'failure' of the Chilean road to Socialism must begin with the disunity within the Left and the failure to provide an alternative leadership. The revolutionaries in Chile were dispersed among a number of different parties.   The MIR was the most consistently revolutionary of these, but its organizational structure, lack of base among the organized proletariat, and guerrilla tendencies meant that on its own it could not provide a revolutionary vanguard.   The Socialist Party contained within it large numbers of revolutionary militants, but was encumbered with bureaucratic careerists and a powerful group of reformists.   Furthermore the Party remained essentially a loose amalgam of competing fiefdoms, each stalemating the other.   Its weak internal organization was an important factor in preventing the Party from developing into a revolutionary vanguard.

The other two potentially revolutionary parties, the Christian Left and MAPU, both contained important nuclei of revolutionaries but, for historic reasons, had developed as separate parties and, like the MIR, were too small to provide on their own the necessary mass base for a vanguard party.

That was the situation facing Chilean revolutionaries: three small parties (MIR, MAPU, Christian Left) with predominantly petty-bourgeois leaderships and only small working class bases, and a massive working class party (the Socialist Party) which had the necessary base but lacked a consistently revolutionary line.   In addition, the hold of the Communist Party over large sectors of the Chilean working class must be remembered.   The thoroughly reformist nature of the leadership of the PC, together with the tight organizational discipline within the Party, meant that many working class cadres remained trapped within the theoretical and practical framework of reformism until shortly before the coup.   Until July and August 1973 – virtually the final moments – the Communist Party's sectarianism kept its militants isolated from the cordons and at the margin of any plan for the defence of the working class.

The crux of the problem for the revolutionary Left then, was somehow to combine the mass working class base of the Socialist Party with a consistently revolutionary line so as to produce a genuine vanguard party.

Shortly after Allende's election as president, the left wing within the Socialist Party gained nominal control of the Party in the 1970 conference, and Carlos Altamirano, their spokesman, was elected secretary-general of the Party.   It seems likely that the continued control of the leadership of the Party by

Altamirano was an important factor in persuading many revolutionaries who might otherwise have broken with the UP to stay in the Socialist Party and in the UP. We believe this was a serious mistake. In our opinion, the Socialist Party (or at least a large fraction of it) should openly have broken with the UP and provided the mass base for the building of a vanguard party.

The revolutionary Left would still of course have continued to vote with the government, and support it against the opposition. But by 1972 it was clear that President Allende and the Communist Party were not capable of providing the sort of leadership needed to combat right-wing violence. It was the Right which turned the class struggle into class war, and it was a matter of life and death for the working class to prepare its defences. If the government was unwilling to do it, then alternative leadership had to be provided. This leadership could only have been given by the revolutionary Left distancing itself from President Allende. For by remaining within the structures of the UP the revolutionary Left and the working class movement as a whole were forced to adapt themselves to Allende's policy of restraint and of relying on the bourgeois armed forces rather than their own strength to prevent a coup.

There were good arguments against such a break. There was a fear that a split with Popular Unity would disorientate much of the working class and play into the hands of the opposition. There was also the fear that to do so would be to condemn the Socialist Party to a sectarian isolation should the mass of the working class not see clearly the reason for a break with the UP. It was feared that the net result would be a weakening of the revolutionary position within the Chilean Left and a strengthening of reformism in the Allende administration. These were compelling arguments. They were compelling in 1970, when Allende had just been elected and the working class and peasantry were waiting expectantly, but at the same time passively, to see what the new government would do for them. But by 1972, when the working class and peasantry had begun to take massive actions on their own, and were continually going beyond Popular Unity's programme in attempts to solve for themselves the problems they faced, particularly the problem of right-wing attacks against them, these arguments had begun to lose much of their persuasiveness.

It was essential for the successful development of the revolutionary process that there should be a party with a solid working class base that was capable of leading the working class in a consistently revolutionary manner. But the vanguard party does not appear out of thin air; it is not a *deus ex machina*. We think that if the Socialist Party had split from the UP sometime in mid-1972 the process of building a vanguard party would have been aided considerably. A split would have helped expose the reformist nature of the Allende leadership and would have helped sharpen the difference between the revolutionary position and that of the reformists, particularly on the crucial question of self-defence. It would also have provided the mass base and organizational impetus for the construction of a vanguard party. Doubtless such a move would have accelerated the split within the MAPU and would have produced a regroupment of the revolutionary Left as a whole. Unless Socialist Party militants took such a step, the final confrontation with the bourgeoisie in Chile in 1973 was bound to find the mass of the working class unprepared and confused.

Some part of the failure to split openly with the reformists must be attributed to Altamirano who, although revolutionary in words, tended to vacillate at crucial moments. The clearest example of this came in June 1973. During the congressional election campaign of March, and in the weeks after the election, Altamirano had adopted a tough militant line. Yet, when the going began to get rough after May 1973, Altamirano began to make overtures to bring the military back into the cabinet, thereby disorientating and confusing the working class. This was crucial, for the question of the nature of the military and the attitude of the working class towards it becomes of fundamental importance in a prerevolutionary period.

However, it would be unfair to put the blame entirely on Altamirano's shoulders. A break with the UP and a decision to prepare seriously for a revolutionary seizure of power in the immediate future required an act of will, an act of courage. Whether it resulted from organizational weakness, fears of becoming isolated from the working class, or the continuing dead weight of reformist practice, we cannot say; the point is, that act of will was not forth-coming.

This coexistence of revolutionary theory and reformist practice in the Socialist Party was not unique to that party alone; it was shared by much of the Chilean Left. Revolutionaries in Chile were clear on two central theoretical points: that in moments of crisis, the military will intervene to safeguard bourgeois rule; and that when threatened by a mass working class movement, the bourgeoisie will generate a mass Fascist movement to oppose it. Both happened in Chile.

As soon as the results of the 1970 election were known, the bourgeoisie began to organize to meet the threat. Not disdaining to employ Leninist methods of organization, the bourgeoisie began to orchestrate a mass movement with Fascist tendencies which would be capable of toppling the government. *El Mercurio*, the most highly respected of Chilean bourgeois newspapers, put it like this:

'However the opposition organizes itself, its methods of action must have an immediate root in the bases of society: it cannot confine itself to the general propaganda and traditional use of assemblies by the old political parties. Neighbourhood councils, mothers' unions, cooperatives, trade unions and other professional bodies require the permanent involvement of those representing the best political thinking of the citizens: not the reduced contacts characteristic of an electoral campaign. The explicit or implicit unity of the opposition should give rise to concrete actions at work, in the suburb, in the supermarket, which will be capable of counteracting the dictatorship which the Marxists are preparing to put into practice at the base.

It is not enough for the democratic forces to try to reach the public through the mass media. They must link themselves with the masses. Such a programme implies great sacrifice, often a substantial change of people's habits and style of life . . .'[7]

What *El Mercurio* meant by democracy has been obvious since the coup of 11 September.

If it was not clear in 1970, it must have been obvious at least from October 1972 onwards that a mass movement of the petty bourgeoisie, with marked Fascist tendencies, was growing rapidly, and would have to be confronted on its own terms; with the mass mobilization of the working class. And it became clear after several attempted coups that the military, if left to their own, would remain true to their class position in the final showdown.

But while this was known at the level of theory, lamentably little was done in practice to prepare for the armed confrontation, even though Altamirano had himself said that an armed confrontation was inevitable.

This inability to move from theory to concrete practice was not unconnected with the failure to develop a unified revolutionary party. Without an organized revolutionary intervention, reformist conceptions tended to set limits to what the parties did in practice. And although the most conscious elements of the working class, often in advance of the parties and the leadership, were 'spontaneously' throwing up revolutionary forms of organization at the base (the *cordones*, for example), spontaneous interventions of this kind were not sufficient to tackle the problem of the winning and transference of State power.

A central element in the question of the seizure of State power was the military aspect of the insurrection. The 'military question' was not a 'technical' question that the Left somehow overlooked, or failed to deal with adequately. Of course there were many technical aspects to it, such as the accumulation of arms, the drawing up of plans of action, and so on, but fundamentally it was a *political* question.

By and large, Popular Unity attempted to deal with the military, by means of manoeuvres among the generals. In addition, there were attempts by all parties to infiltrate the ranks (without a great deal of success), while each small group hoarded its own small supply of arms. What was needed was, firstly, a campaign in the armed forces around issues which related to the felt needs of the soldiers and linked them to the ongoing process of working class mobilization. Demands for free speech, soldiers' trade unions, and increased democracy within the armed forces (for example) could have helped politicize the military and make it harder for the officers to use their troops against workers and peasants. Secondly, the core of the insurrectionary forces had to be organized, equipped and trained. These would be relatively small groups of revolutionary cadres from the political parties of the Left, but they should at least have been co-ordinated and had an overall strategic plan for neutralizing fascists in the armed forces and coping with the technical problems of seizing power. Thirdly, the working class as a whole (or at least large sections of it) had to be prepared as adequately as possible for the military confrontation.

To some extent these tasks were carried out. But as the events of 11 September demonstrated, the preparations had been grossly inadequate. The battle of Santiago was essentially a defensive battle, fought by small, isolated groups of workers. There was not even an adequate clandestine radio system. By and large, the bourgeois armed forces remained intact, and within a relatively short space of time overcame the inadequately armed workers.

In large part, these shortcomings and mistakes can be attributed to the absence of a vanguard party capable of taking on the responsibility for an armed insurrection. The result of the failure to forge such a party from the material available was the success of the military coup of 11 September, 1973. Since that date Chileans have lived under a reign of terror. The organizations of the working class, the parties, the unions, the *cordones*, the JAPs have been smashed. They have been proscribed, banned, decapitated, or taken over by the military. And tens of thousands of men, women, and children have been hunted down, imprisoned, tortured and killed. One can expect no mercy at the hands of one's enemies: he who half makes a revolution digs his own grave. Such is the price exacted by imperialism and the bourgeoisie as the ruling class attempts to ensure that its power and privileges will not again be challenged. The working class and the people of Chile are to be beaten into a bloody silence for the next decade.

Under such conditions any resistance is in itself an act of heroism. Yet resistance in Chile continues. Furthermore, the savagery of the military junta daily forces more and more people to join it. Large sectors of the Christian Democratic Party are now working with the MIR and the parties of the UP in a united resistance against the junta.

As part of this continuing struggle against the repression in Chile we in Britain have our part to play. It may not require the same heroism, but it does require persistence, and it is not the less important. Chile remains a dependent country, highly sensitive to international economic and political pressure. The campaign to black Chilean goods has been effective; the international protests have had effects in Chile. These activities must be continued, stepped up, and made more widespread.

Ustedes que ya escucharon	You who have heard this story
la historia que se contó	don't sit in your easy chair
no sigan allí sentados	and think that the matter's over,
pensando que ya pasó.	and it all finishes here.
No basta solo el recuerdo,	It's not enough to remember,
el canto no bastará.	it's not enough to sigh.
No basta solo el lamento,	It's not enough to make up songs
miremos la realidad.	for more men still will die.
Quizás mañana o pasado	If not today, tomorrow,

o bien, en un tiempo más,
la historia que han escuchado
de nuevo sucederá.
Es Chile un país tan largo
mil cosas pueden pasar
si es queno nos preparamos
resueltos para luchar . . .
Unámosnos como hermanos
que nadie nos vencerá.
Si quieren esclavizarnos
jamás lo podrán lograr.
La tierra será de todos,
también será nuestro el mar.
Justicia habrá por todos
y habrá también libertad.
Luchemos por los derechos
que todos deben tener.
Luchemos por lo que es nuestro
de nadie más ha de ser.

or before the year's old,
the story you've been listening to
will once again unfold.
For Chile is a very big country,
a thousand things could come to light,
if we aren't prepared to meet them,
if we aren't prepared to fight.
No one'll be able to put us down,
United we're strong enough,
If they intend to make us slaves
They'll never pull it off.
The land will belong to everyone
and so in turn will the sea.
Everyone will have justice
and everyone will be free.
Let us be ready to battle
for what all should have by right.
Let us be ready to fight for our own,
For no one else will fight.

From the folk opera *Santa Maria de Iquique*, written by Luis Advis and sung by the Quilapayun in 1971.

Postscript: Illusions and Prospects

In the space of a year and a half since the last chapter was written, very little of significance has changed. Repression continues, although as it has become more systematic the absolute number of political prisoners has declined. The international campaign of condemnation of the Chilean regime continues, but it has been too ineffectual to bring about any major change within the country. It has, however, been successful in securing the release of some of those imprisoned and in finding homes in Europe for the first wave of Chileans to flee the country after the coup. The number of exiled Chileans outside Latin America now numbers in tens of thousands, and refugees continue to drift into Argentina or apply directly to foreign embassies in Chile. There is now a Chilean community abroad, making an effort to grapple with the new Chilean reality from a distance of many thousands of miles and subject to the wishful thinkings which are characteristic of exiles everywhere, as a recent attempt to re-form Popular Unity shows.[1]

Meanwhile, in Chile itself, the junta continues to lose popular support among the classes who were Allende's erstwhile opponents, those who formed the *gremios* and now, it seems, also the industrial bourgeoisie. However, as yet there is no sign of any force within the country capable of toppling it. Within the armed forces, General Pinochet has consolidated his position, and internal repression combined with the judicious retirement of potential rivals seems to have ensured so far that no effective opposition can emerge. General Prats, commander-in-chief of the armed forces under Allende, and the likeliest rallying point for those within the military who wanted to repudiate the extremes of the coup, was removed from the political scene by his assassination on 30 September 1974. General Bonilla, a possible 'populist' rivel to Pinochet within the ruling junta and an old Christian Democrat, died in a helicopter accident in March 1975.

Economically, the junta has been a disaster. The original economic model introduced by Leniz was based on the belief that Chile's structural problems could be solved by dismantling State interference in the economy, allowing free play to market forces, and gearing the entire economy to the export sector: the so-called 'social market economy'. This model closely followed the ideas of Milton Friedman and his associates in the University of Chicago. Two years later, it still continues to dominate the junta's thinking. Leniz, however, was unable to contain Chile's spiralling rate of inflation (between September 1973 and October 1975 the Consumer Price Index rose a total of 3,367.4%, surpassing even Allende's dismal record). In April 1975, Leniz was replaced by two professional economists, Jorge Cauas, the Chicago-trained professor of economics at the Catholic University, and Raul Saez, the man who negotiated the 'Chileanization' of copper during the administration of President Frei. Following the personal advice of Friedman and Arnold Harberger, a new 'shock treatment' of the economy was announced, applying the original principles of the social market economy with even greater stringency and further reducing State expenditure. A third of the workforce in the National Electricity Company was dismissed, and plans were announced to dismiss 5,000 workers in the State Railway Company as well as to cut off all State support for the National Health Service by the beginning of 1976.[2]

As a result, the rate of inflation began to fall in the latter months of 1975. So, however, did industrial production. After only two months of Cauas's 'shock treatment', the general index of industrial production registered a drop of 18.9% for the first six months of 1975 as compared with 1974. After three months, a survey by a government department of 250 industrial enterprises in metropolitan Santiago estimated that manufacturing production had fallen by approximately 60% since the second quarter of 1974.[3] Industries in the monopoly sector of the economy were now being affected: for example, INSA (the National Tyre Industry) and SUMAR, one of the largest textile firms, were closed 'temporarily' in June, and the BATA Shoe Corporation, a Canadian multi-national which controlled a third of Chile's internal market, asked the government for permission to close. Suppliers of primary and intermediate goods such as the Pacific Steel Company and the coal industry sent their workers on an indefinite, unpaid winter holiday. Unemployment rose even higher – from 10.3% in June 1974 to 16.1% in June 1975, according to University of Chile statistics for greater Santiago – and such prominent representatives of the bourgeoisie as Orlando Saenz, past President of SOFOFA, and ex-President Frei himself, were moved to protest. Frei drew attention to the essential role which State investment had played in the past in creating such industries as steel, electricity, petroleum and telecommunications. Cauas, himself a former protege of Frei's, replied:

> . . . Chile's sickness is serious and requires drastic treatment. It serves little purpose to say, like children, that the medicine is bitter or the operation painful . . . Only demagogy, or an inadequate understanding of modern social science, could lead one to claim that inflation is due to anything other than the deficit in the public sector.[4]

Under the military, Chile has been made the subject of an even more radical economic experiment than that envisaged by Allende. Allende stood for the extension of a State apparatus which had been the pivot of the Chilean economy for almost a century, and the end or at least the curtailment of a system whereby the State invested but the profits went to private capital. The military have undertaken to dismantle the State intervention in the economy entirely, thus depriving private capital of what has been, historically, its most important source of support. They have also undertaken to prune drastically the distributive role of the State as a source of social services and indeed of employment, thus contracting the internal market for Chilean goods and reversing the logic of Chile's original process of industrialization. One reporter has compared this process to vivisection: certainly it can be of little consolation to those now being laid off or dismissed in their thousands that the junta's experiments are carried out in the name of Milton Friedman and the principles of modern American social science.

Perhaps not surprisingly, the junta has felt the need to re-assert that the country faces an immediate threat from a 'clever and pitiless'[5] Marxist enemy, from which only the military can save it. To emphasize this point it conveniently discovered new guerilla bases in Talca in the height of winter, and a clandestine military organization headed by that martial figure, Allende's widow, Hortensia Bussy Allende.[6] Simultaneously, Chilean exiles abroad have discovered the hope that such widespread economic suffering would cause some officers to have a change of heart, leading to the emergence of differences of opinion within the military and some form of political opening or democratization. The most obvious force capable of leading such a 'bourgeois change of face' seemed to be Christian Democracy: President Frei was still an international figure of some standing, in spite of his support for the military in the immediate aftermath of the coup, and the party was popularly supposed to have retained a number of sympathizers within the officer corps. Accordingly, in late 1974, the Communist Party sent an open letter to army officers pleading with them to think how they would look in the light of history, and once again began to make approaches to the Christian Democrats (as it had done so often during the heyday of Popular Unity), for an alliance of all forces, whatever their class composition, as the best hope of removing the incumbent regime.

Once again this alliance with the Christian Democrats has proved to be an illusion: while certain left-wing elements in the party in exile, such as Renan Fuentealba and Bernardo Leighton, came out publicly in favour of it, the right wing of the party within the country rejected it out of hand. Patricio Aylwin, President of the party, made a public statement in reply claiming that:

> our task as a party is to reach an agreement with the groups that formed the opposition to the Allende regime, and with the armed forces, in order to restore democracy in Chile . . .[7]

He received a public rebuke for his pains from the Ministry of the Interior, which put out its own statement re-emphasizing that the armed forces had taken power to build a new type of democracy without political parties, and insinuating that Aylwin's suggestions were an infringement of the conditions of political recess imposed on all the old parties in the wake of the coup.[8] In fact, with the mysterious death of General Bonilla in March 1975, Christian Democrat influence within the armed forces seems to have waned considerably. Certainly the military were no longer willing to give the party the virtual status of a 'loyal opposition' which it enjoyed in the immediate aftermath of the coup. In the last few months of 1975, an increasing number of Christian Democrats have been arrested and forced into exile. One of the party's founding fathers, Bernardo Leighton, a former vice-President of Chile and Minister of the Interior, was the victim of an attempted assassination in Rome in October 1975, while two others, Gabriel Valdes and past Presidential candidate Radomiro Tomic in the USA were forced to seek the protection of the FBI against assassination threats.[9] Thus the initial political advantages which Christian Democracy seemed to retain after the coup, as a force with some cohesion and room for manoeuvre under the new regime representing sectors of the bourgeoisie and the political movement of the *gremios*, have fast disappeared. At the end of 1975 the party was divided and increasingly itself the victim of repression.

More and more, the role of 'loyal opposition' and even occasionally of disloyal opposition has devolved upon the Church, the only institution which retains sufficient autonomy to provide a permanent focus for criticism under the military regime. Prominent religious figures such as the Lutheran Bishop Frenz and the Catholic Bishop Enrique Alvear were involved in setting up a 'Committee for Peace' less than a month after the coup to look after the interests of thousands of Chileans in prison or missing, and their families. The hierarchy of the Catholic Church has used increasingly bitter language in its criticisms of the junta: in September, 1975, the Bishop's Conference brought out a document which said among other things,

> ... We cannot refrain from insisting on the extreme gravity, in the light of the gospel, of the fact that there are homes where there is no food to be cooked, children begging for bread, schoolchildren who cannot study because they have not eaten sufficient to be able to concentrate ...

while simultaneously recognizing the 'service' of the armed forces in freeing the country from the prospect of an inevitable Marxist dictatorship.[10] Recently, two American nuns were forced to take asylum following their apparent involvement in hiding a wounded leader of the MIR, Nelson Gutierrez, while an English doctor, Sheila Cassidy, with close ties to the Church, was arrested and imprisoned for treating his wounds. In the subsequent scandal, as Nelson Gutierrez and the Secretary-General of the MIR, Andres Pascal Allende, took asylum and escaped the junta's security forces, Cardinal Silva Henriquez himself publicly defended the right of the Church to come to the aid even of those fleeing from the junta's secret police.

With the decision of Andres Pascal Allende to seek asylum in November 1975, the old leadership of the MIR and indeed the old leadership of all the left-wing parties, ceased to play an active part in the struggle within the country.[11] After the coup, the MIR, under the leadership of Miguel Enriquez, took a firm stand against its militants taking asylum and bitterly critized those leaders of other political parties who sought safety abroad. Miguel Enriquez himself set the example, an example which cost him his life in a gun-battle in Santiago in September 1974. The policy was probably romantic: Enriquez, Pascal Allende, Altamirano and other such figures were too well-known easily to play a role in the new circumstances, and outside the ranks of the MIR itself, few politicians had any experience of clandestine organization. Andres Pascal's decision not to provide the Chilean resistance with another martyr and another myth was sensible. But the destruction of the MIR central committee and the apparent inability of the Popular Unity parties to function effectively does underline the ineffectual nature of left-wing response to the coup to date. Chile in 1975 is very far from the prospect of a successful guerrilla war or even a Christian Democrat inspired coup within the armed forces, and a massive return of exiles, the myths of Right and Left notwithstanding. More than two years after the coup, the task of rebuilding a political organization to undertake the struggle against the military remains; and as time passes, it seems if anything more likely that the re-emergence of the Chilean Left as an effective political force within the country will take some years.

For its part, the USA continues to prop up the regime it helped to create in spite of some doubts among liberals in Congress. Contact between the American and the Chilean armed forces continues to be strong: on a recent visit to Chile, Denis McAuliffe, head of the US Southern Command, is reported to have told General Pinochet that he found Chile 'serene and tranquil' and promised that the armed forces 'would continue to do everything possible to help the Chilean armed forces'.[12] American aid and assistance also continues: 85% of the US Food for Peace programme in Latin America went to Chile during 1975. But aid has not been able to halt the catastrophic decline of the economy. Ironically, the promise US Ambassador Korry made to Frei before Allende's inauguration has been fulfilled under the junta: 'Once Allende comes to power we shall do all within our power to condemn Chile and the Chileans to utmost deprivation and poverty.'[13]

November 1975

Chronology of Main Events

1969

October
Coordinating committee of Popular Unity formed.
December
Basic programme of Popular Unity approved.

1970

January
Salvador Allende nominated as Popular Unity presidential candidate.
September
Presidential Elections: Salvador Allende (UP) 36.2%; Radomiro Tomic (Christian Democrat) 27.8%; Jorge Alessandri (Independent) 34.9%. Although Allende has won, he does not receive a majority of the total vote, and so a special vote will be necessary in the legislature in October to confirm him as president.
Christian Democrat Party demands that Allende sign 'guarantees'.
US expresses 'dismay' at Allende's election.
Run on banks and loan institutions follows Allende's victory.
October
Allende accepts the statute of guarantees, and Christian Democrat party officially supports him. Allende is proclaimed president.
Commander in Chief of the Army, René Schneider, shot during a kidnap attempt.
US stops aid to Chile.
In London, executives of the big copper corporations meet to deplore the 'protectionist' policies of copper-producing countries in the Third World.
November
Allende is inaugurated and chooses his first cabinet.
December
Gun battles at Concepción University. One student killed.
Land occupations by the Mapuche indians begin.

1971

January
Bill for the nationalization of copper presented to congress.
Two retired generals implicated in Schneider assassination plot.

Government announces plans to take over private banks and coal mining industry.

February

Allende announces plans to nationalize the nitrate industry.

March

President Nixon's foreign policy statement, full of ominous references to governments who behave in an unfriendly way. US begins to adopt an attitude of open hostility towards Chile.

Government takes over complete control of Chuquicamata and El Salvador copper mines, previously jointly owned by Anaconda and Chilean government.

April

CODELCO, the State copper corporation, takes over sales of copper abroad, which had previously been in the hands of subsidiaries of the great copper corporations.

4 April: municipal elections: UP wins 50.9% of the votes, Christian Democracy 26.2% and the National Party 18.5%.

A meeting of eighty priests from working class areas of Chile declares its support for UP.

Nathaniel Davis is to replace Edward Korry as US Ambassador to Chile. Davis was formerly in Guatemala, and is known as an 'anti-Marxist' expert.

May

Allende's first 'State of the Nation' message promises to forge ahead with the UP programme and 'the second model for the transition to a socialist society'.

MIR warns UP that it must desist from sending the police in to throw landless peasants off the land which they have occupied, or it will defend the actions of the peasantry itself.

El Teniente copper mine, previously owned by Kennecott, taken over by the State.

June

As the takeovers of land organized in conjunction with the MIR come nearer to Santiago, Allende moves to stop them altogether. The result is a number of violent clashes between police and peasantry.

Christian Democrat ex-Interior Minister Perez Zujovic (who as Minister of Interior had ordered police to open fire on demonstrators at Puerto Montt in 1969) assassinated by the shadowy VOP (*Vanguardia del Pueblo*) group. Allende responds by declaring a state of emergency, and by sending to congress a bill to reintroduce capital punishment for political assassination.

Christian Democrat demand that Allende disband his personal guard rejected by the government, but all ministers are now given bodyguards.

July

11 July: ratification of the copper nationalization bill by unanimous vote of congress. Celebrated by big demonstration of copper workers.

Panamanian vessel discovered in the attempt to smuggle arms into Chile.

August

Movement of the Christian Left (IC) splits from Christian Democrats. It represents the left of the party, opposed to the policy of obstructionism from the Christian Democrats towards UP. It takes with it some 13% of the Christian democrat party members, and joins UP.

Other splits follow, e.g. in the Radical Party.

Miners on strike over wage dispute; but later settle.

ExImBank refuses Chile a $21m. loan to buy Boeing 707s from the US.

Allende departs for a Latin American tour.

September

Cabinet reshuffle.

October

Announcement of compensation to copper companies provokes violent reaction among some foreign sectors. Their compensation, minus 'excess profit' over the years, amounts to almost nothing.

Government presents new bill to congress, defining the three areas of the economy – the 'social' (public), mixed, and private sectors. Firms in key areas of the economy, with over 14m. escudos capital, are to be nationalized. This would imply 150 companies in all.

November

Allende sends a bill to Congress to replace two houses with a single chamber assembly.

MIR attacks Allende openly, and Allende responds by condemning the extremism of groups like MIR.

The Chamber of Deputies rejects Allende's proposal for restructuring the economy.

Fidel Castro arrives in Chile for a one-month visit.

December

The march of the empty pots, led by the opposition, takes place to coincide with Castro's visit. A state of emergency and curfew are declared in Santiago after clashes arising from the demonstration.

General Prats declares that the Army holds to its constitutional role, and will continue to do so.

1972

January

José Tohá, Interior Minister, suspended after censure vote in congress; transferred to Defence Ministry.

Statement by Nixon advocates a hard line against countries which fail to pay adequate compensation to expropriated companies.

February

Chilean representatives meet international creditors in Paris; US demands that International Monetary Fund be given right to 'oversee' repayment. Chile refuses.

State takeover of cigarette industry: announcement of plan to take over 120 further companies.

Congress (dominated by Christian Democracy and the Right) passes measures designed to hold back process of nationalization. Allende says he will appeal to Constitutional Court.

Constituent parties of Popular Unity meet at El Arrayán to discuss next phase. Allende reaffirms the constitutional path.

New cabinet reshuffle.

March

The CUT, in a statement, promises immediate action from the workers if there is any attempt to hold back nationalization.

Banco Continental de Chile taken over by government.

UP and the Christian Democrats reach an agreement over the elections of March 1973. Agreed that parties will be able to offer their individual candidates, and also participate in federations of parties whose vote will be taken as a whole. A Christian Democrat spokesman (Fuentealba) describes the March elections as 'a popular referendum on UP government'.

The National Party (PN) will be taken to court for infringements of state security. The PN expresses anger at its exclusion from talks with UP over the March elections.

Revelations of ITT's (International Telephone and Telegraphy Corporation) involvement in a plot to overthrow Allende immediately after the election of 1970.

Two more plants – Ceresita (paint) and Comandari (woollens) – taken over by the State.

General John Ryan of the US Air Force visits Santiago.

April

The organization of the Mapuche indians (FNI) joins UP, after the Christian Democrats had opposed a Congressional bill to organize and develop cooperatives in the Mapuche areas.

Formal talks begin between the UP and the Revolutionary Movement of the Left (MIR).

The Left Radical Party (PIR), withdraws from UP after Allende has used his veto to stop the Christian Democrat sponsored bill to deprive executive of the right to carry out nationalizations. Talks between UP and the Christian Democrats on the question break down.

UNCTAD meeting in Santiago.

May

UP leadership confers at Lo Curro.

US announces military grants to Latin America; Bolivia gets $5m., Chile $3m.

Jorge Tapia, Justice Minister, announces plans for future talks with Christian Democracy on question of Chile's future economic structure. He points out, however, that the right of the executive to order nationalizations will not be negotiable.

12 May: in Concepción, a ban on demonstrations defied both by the extreme Right and the MIR. Street fighting occurs leaving one *MIRista* dead and 42 people injured. The Communist Under-secretary of State, Daniel Vergara, issues a statement deploring extremist violence whether of the Right or of the Left. His statement angrily condemned by other elements of the UP.

Rodrigo Ambrosio, secretary general of MAPU, killed in a car crash.

June

Crisis talks within the UP begin, to discuss the question of relations between UP and the MIR. Communist Party insists that MIR be condemned for its illegal seizures of land, and that UP break off relations with the MIR. They present this as a prelude to a general offensive on the Right, in the context of 'the struggle against extremism'.

UP unable to reach agreement; final statement simply acknowledges the status quo.

12 June: cabinet resigns *en bloc*.

Despite growing criticism from the left, particularly the Socialists, talks between UP and the Christian Democrats continue.

23 June: new cabinet announced. Shows significant changes: Pedro Vuskovic, Economy Minister since 1970 and a constant target for right-wing attacks, is dismissed from his post (though not from the cabinet).

Elections for officers of the CUT take place.

July

'Amicable breakdown' of talks on the economy between UP and Christian Democrats.

Two federations are officially registered for the March elections: the Federation of the Right (CODE) and the Left Federation (UP).

UP candidates successful in various elections: UP wins presidency of the National Student Association and the Technical University, as well as the Coquimbo bye-election. In the CUT elections, results announced show a total vote for UP of 70%, and of 26% for Christian Democracy.

Government arrests 14 members of the *Comando de Liberación Nacional 16 de julio*, an extreme left urban guerrilla group, for armed robbery.

26 July: call for a Popular Assembly in Concepción.

August

4 August: the Popular Assembly meets in Concepción, though it fails to take legislative powers as the MIR had advocated. Nevertheless, it is condemned by some sections of the UP, particularly the Communist Party, as representing a move outside the framework of legality.

18 August: in Lo Hermida, a Santiago shanty town, 100 policemen attempt to enter the area in order to arrest a leader of the *MLN-16 de julio* said to be hiding there. The population resisted, and a battle ensued in which one man was killed, 11 wounded, and 160 detained. At the funeral of the dead man, the inhabitants distributed leaflets demanding the resignation of those responsible. The head of the Criminal Investigation Department and his deputy are dismissed; at the same time, UP issues a condemnation of the activities of the ultra-left.

A statement from MIR sets aside the armed struggle 'for the moment'.

25 August: a group of Argentine guerrillas escape from prison at Trelew Argentina, and after a gun battle at the airport, 16 of them seek asylum in Chile. After some hesitation, Allende accepts them as political refugees.

September

State of Emergency declared in Bio Bio province after right-wing attacks on radio stations in the area.

Anniversary celebrations bring new clashes between Right and Left in the streets of Santiago and Concepción.

Kennecott Copper Corporation announce that they will stop negotiations with Chilean government over the compensation issue, and pursue instead a blockade on Chilean copper throughout the world.

MIR intelligence reveals the existence of a plan for a military coup – the *Plan Septiembre* – and decides to set aside its differences with the CP and march alongside them in demonstrations.

24-hour shopkeepers' strike.

Cardinal Silva Henríquez warns against the dangers of civil war.

Chilean Army begins negotiations for the purchase of military equipment abroad; financial sources unknown.

Appearance of armed vigilante groups, called PROTECO and SOL, in the middle class suburbs, for self-defence in the event of a left-wing takeover.

A statement from the Christian Democrat party totally rejects the use of unconstitutional methods to overthrow Allende. At the same time, it demands the resignation of the mayor of Concepción for forbidding a right-wing demonstration.

October

In response to the *Plan Septiembre* General Prats makes statement reaffirming the constitutional role of the armed forces.

Government closure of *Radio Agricultura* (owned by the big landowners) for 48 hours for 'false and alarmist reporting' of an encounter between soldiers and peasants in the South.

Discussions begin between the judiciary and the executive aimed at 'curbing the extremist violence of Right and Left'.

Loans to Chile from Dutch and Canadian banks suspended as a result of pressure from Kennecott.

Director of the Central Bank of Chile attacks World Bank for its steadfast refusal to extend loans to Chile.

Lorry owners begin strike in the South: short strike at Chuquicamata copper mine. Allende puts the economy on a war footing. A number of factories taken over by workers to prevent their closure. Curfew imposed in Santiago as tension grows over the lorry owners' strike. Formarion of industrial cordons. Shopkeepers and some professionals join lorry owners' strike.

Sabotage on the Santiago-Valparaiso railway.

Christian Democrats refuse to discuss the crisis with the government.

November

Allende forms a new cabinet which includes 3 military officers. This provokes protest from within the UP; the Christian Left (IC) resigns from the cabinet at continued policy of courting the middle class.

December

Allende speaks at the United Nations, condemning the subversive role of multi-national companies in underdeveloped countries and visits a number of Latin American countries.

Talks between the US and Chile to renegotiate the foreign debt are broken off.

1973

January

Government announces it will establish a monopoly control of the distribution of all agricultural products. This brings violent reactions from the business-men's organization SOFOFA and from the *Comando Nacional de Accion Gremial* (coordinating the activities of trade and professional associations), which organizes to resist handing over of goods to the government.

Allende responds by putting Air Force General Bachelet in charge of a new Secretariat of Distribution and Trade.

Copper miners on strike over a wage dispute.

Allende responds to miners' strike with a public self-criticism on the one hand, and an exhortation to the miners to return to work in a revolutionary spirit, on the other.

Minister of Economy, Orlando Millas, proposes a bill returning 123 factories, seized by workers during October, to their original owners. Much opposition from within UP.

February

The campaign for the March elections intensifies; it is seen by both sides as an election that will determine the fate of UP.

MIR announces its support for Socialist Party (PS) and Christian Left (IC) candidates in the elections.

9 February: UP publishes its political programme; its major points are:
a) a single chamber Popular Assembly to replace congress and senate.
b) Legislation to be initiated by popular demand, either by collection of 5000 signatures or through CUT.
c) reshaping of the economy, especially distribution, in favour of the people.
d) a broadening of the role of the military.

In a speech Allende warns that if the violence of the Right continues, UP will be forced to abandon the constitutional road and respond in kind.

Build up as elections approach: mutual accusations of terrorism; Allende pro-poses new wage increases for 2 million lower-paid workers, but stresses that the burden must be borne by the rich through higher and more progressive taxes. Christian Democracy bitterly opposed.

March

Congressional elections: UP increases its share of the vote from 36%+ (in 1970) to 43.4% of the total. Those who lost votes mainly the smaller parties.

4 days after the election, the right-wing paper *El Mercurio* publishes the full text of a MAPU internal document criticizing many aspects of government policy, particularly the inclusion of the military in the cabinet. This leads to a deep split in MAPU between left and right of the organization, and to an angry response from Allende, saying he would suspend MAPU from UP unless disciplinary measures were taken. 15 members expelled from MAPU. MAPU divides into two parties.

Renewed negotiations with US over foreign debt.

Under-secretary of House Committee on Interamerican Affairs in Washington states categorically that there can be no compromise with Chile over question of compensation to foreign corporations nationalized in Chile.

US vetoes Panamanian resolution at UN Security Council over Panama's right to control the Canal. Britain abstains.

Senate Committee to investigate ITT affair opens in Washington.

30 March: Allende forms a new cabinet, in which the military have been replaced. Allende also suggests that UP should consider forming itself into a single party.

April

In an interview with an Italian paper, Frei, leader of Christian Democrats, stresses that his party will no longer collaborate with UP in any way.

Faced with US insistence on payment of $700m. compensation before talks begin, negotiations between Chile and the US on foreign debt break down almost immediately.

MIR announces plans for further land takeovers.

National committee of Christian Democrat Party asserts that the door is still open to UP.

In congress, the Right combines against a bill to nationalize 42 companies and threatens to impeach the whole cabinet.

Allende attacks the ultra-left on radio and TV.

A number of strikes in industry and in the mines.

Proposed bill calling for unification and development of educational system (ENU) leads to street clashes between Left and Right.

May

In Santiago a worker dies during a demonstration outside the HQ of the Christian Democrat Party.

State of Emergency in Santiago, after death of a militant of Fatherland and Freedom (extreme-right terrorist group).

Strikes in the copper mines continue.

Aylwin elected new president of Christian Democrat party and Frei becomes president of the senate.

June

Socialist Party congress; the right of the party led by Allende and Almeyda wins the day.

The miners' strike continues and grows more serious. Allende confronts the strikers and asks them to return to work.

Lorry owners' strike begins again, ostensibly in protest at lack of spare parts, but also because of project to establish a State transportation system.

29 June: the *tancazo:* an attempted coup carried out by Col. Roberto Souper and his tank regiment, together with armed members of Fatherland and Freedom group. The coup fails.

Miners return to work, and the workers occupy factories and working class districts in response to the coup.

July

The armed forces decide not to join cabinet (as they had done after strike of October 1972). New cabinet, therefore, has no military members, and has a 'moderate' and technocratic character.

Leaders of Fatherland and Freedom take refuge in Ecuadorean embassy.

Conflict arises between government and CUT on question of the return of factories taken over by workers during and immediately after the *tancazo*.

Christian Democrats insist that the Law for the Control of Arms (passed 1972) be put into effect, and the army used to carry out searches for arms. Allende agrees to this.

Allende's naval aide, Captain Araya, assassinated.

Christian Democracy reopens talks with UP.

Lorry owners' strike declared on 26 July.

August

Socialist Party threatens to withdraw from UP if any unacceptable compromise is reached with Christian Democracy.

Christian Democrats break off talks with UP, because Allende will not accept the military into the cabinet.

In Punta Arenas a worker is killed during an arms search in a factory.

The army protects convoys of government lorries loaded and driven by volunteers.

Lorry strike continues, and sabotage on power lines and railway lines mounts. Christian Democrats declare their support for the lorry owners.

The military return to the cabinet – one each from the Army (Prats), the Navy (Montero), the Air Force (Ruiz) and the Carabineros (Sepulveda). But pressure builds, until eventually General Prats and General Ruiz are both forced to resign by pressure from within the armed forces and are replaced by others less sympathetic to UP.

Taxi drivers, bus drivers and owners, some small shopkeepers and professionals (e.g. two-thirds of the medical profession) join the 'bosses' strike'.

In Valparaiso, a group of loyal sailors and workers at the naval base reveal preparations for a coup in the Navy. They are arrested and tortured by the Navy; the cabinet is ambiguous in its response.

In Cautín province, the discovery of a so-called cache of arms provides justification for widespread torture of peasants. The Arms Control Law leads to searches often of a very brutal nature, carried out by the Army, throughout the country.

September

4 September: the Anniversary celebrations bring three quarters of a million workers on to the streets of Santiago in support of Popular Unity.

11 September: the combined armed forces launch a coordinated military coup. Popular Unity is overthrown.

Notes

Chapter 1

1. Stanley J. Stein and Barbara H. Stein, *The Colonial Heritage of Latin America*, Oxford UP, N.Y., 1970.
2. F. Gil, *The Political System of Chile*, Houghton Mifflin, Boston, 1966, p. 36.
3. Hernán Ramírez Necochea, *Balmaceda y la Contrarrevolución de 1891*, Editorial Universitaria, Santiago, 1972.
4. Sergio Ramos, *Chile, una Economía Transición?*, Editorial Prensa Latinoamericana, Santiago, 1972.
5. H. Ramírez, *Historia del Movimiento Obrero*, Santiago, 1956.
6. Cf. B. G. Burnett, *Political Groups in Chile*, Texas UP, Austin, Texas, 1970.

Chapter 2

1. L. Corvalán, *Ricardo Fonseca Combatiente Ejemplar*, Austral, Santiago, 1971, p. 93.
2. Alejandro Chelén Rojas, 'Flujos y Reflujos del Socialismo Chileno', in Julio César Jobet and Alejandro Chelén Rojas (eds.), *Pensamiento Teónico y Politico del Partido Socialista*, Quimantrí, Santiago, 1972, p. 213.
3. Speech by Kennedy, 13 Mar. 1961.
4. Jorge Ahumada, *La Crisis Integral de Chile*, Editorial Universitaria, Santiago, 1966, p. 25.

Chapter 3

1. For an analysis of the PDC see J. Petras, *Politics and Social Forces in Chilean Development*, University of California Press, Berkeley and Los Angeles, 1969.
2. NACLA, *New Chile*, Berkeley, 1972, p. 82.
3. For an analysis of US aid policies before Popular Unity, see P. J. O'Brien, 'La Alianza para el Progreso y los préstamos por programa á Chile', *Estudios Internacionales*, Vol. 2, No. 4, 1969.
4. ODEPLAN, *La Inversión Pública en el período 1961-70*, Santiago, 1971.
5. Garretón and Cisternas, 'Algunas caracteristicas del proceso de toma de decisiones en la gran empresa: la dinámica de concentración', mimeo, Santiago, 1970.
6. NACLA, op. cit., p. 84.
7. For a detailed analysis, see ODEPLAN, *Antecedentes Sobre el Desarrollo Chileno, 1960-70*, Santiago, 1971.
8. R. R. Kaufman, *The Politics of Land Reform in Chile, 1950-1970*, Harvard UP, Cambridge, Mass., 1972.
9. J. Petras, op. cit., p. 199.
10. D. J. Morris, *We Must Make Haste – Slowly*, Vintage Books, N.Y., 1973, p. 41.
11. E. Labarca Goddard, *Chile Al Rojo*, Ediciones de la Universidad Técnica de Estado, Santiago, 1971, p. 149.
12. *Ibid*, p. 160.
13. *Ibid*, p. 187.
14. *Ibid*, p. 197-8.

15. Florencia Varas, *Conversaciones con Viaux*, Santiago, 1972, p. 100.
16. Labarca, op. cit., p. 57.

Chapter 4

1. The full text of the UP programme is reprinted in A. Zammit (ed.), *The Chilean Road to Socialism*, Institute of Development Studies, University of Sussex, Brighton, Sussex, 1973.
2. For an analysis of Tomic's programme see J. E. Garcés, *La Pugna Política por la Presidencia de Chile*, Editorial Universitaria, Santiago, 1971.
3. Sergio Ramos, *Chile: Una Economía de Transición?*, CESO, Santiago, 1972.
4. S. Barraclough, 'The Structure and Problems of the Chilean Agrarian Sector', in Zammit, op. cit.
5. P. Vuskovic, 'The Economic Policy of the Popular Unity Government', in Zammit, op. cit.
6. H. Zemelman and P. León, 'Political Opposition to the Government of Allende', in K. Medhurst (ed.), *Allende's Chile*, Hart-Davis, MacGibbon, London, 1972.
7. R. Debray, *Conversations with Allende*, New Left Review, London, 1971.
8. ODEPLAN, *Informe Económico Anual, 1971*, Editorial Universitoria, Santiago, 1972.

Chapter 5

1. H. Zemelman and P. León, 'El Comportamiento de la bourguesía chilena en el primer año de Gobierno de la Unidad Popular', *Revista de Sociología*, No. 1, Santiago, Aug. 1972.
2. The text of the ENU was published by the Ministry of Education in March 1973; *Informe sobre la Escuela Nacional Unificada*.
3. *El Mercurio*, 26 June 1973.
4. NACLA, *New Chile*, Berkeley, 1972.
5. *El Caso Secreto de la ITT*, Quimantú, Santiago, 1972.
6. D. Eisenhower and D. Johnson, 'The low profile swings a big stick', in D. Johnson (ed.), *The Chilean Road to Socialism*, Anchor, N.Y., 1973.
7. *Punto Final*, No. 169, 24 Oct. 1972.
8. *Chile Hoy*, No. 65, 7 Sep. 1973.

Chapter 6

1. M. Najman (ed.), *Le Chili est Proche*, Francois Maspero, Paris, 1974.
2. A. Zimbalist, 'Workers Control; its Structure under Allende', *Monthly Review*, Vol. 25, No. 10, Mar. 1974.
3. For an analysis of the aims and results of the Christian Democrat agrarian reform see S. Barraclough, 'Reforma Agraria; Historia y Perspectivas', *Cuadernos de la Realidad Nacinal*, No. 7, Mar. 1971.
4. C. Kay, 'Chile: An Appraisal of Popular Unity's Agrarian Reform', *Occasional Paper*, No. 13, Institute of Latin American Studies, University of Glasgow, 1974.
5. I. Roxborough, 'Agrarian Policy in the Popular Unity Government', *Occasional Paper* No. 14, Institute of Latin American Studies, University of Glasgow, 1974.
6. Quoted in *ibid*.
7. *Bank of London and South America Review*, Oct. 1974.
8. R. Moss, *Chile's Marxist Experiment*, David and Charles, Newton Abbot, 1973.

9. W. Baer and I. Kerstenetsky (eds.), *Inflation and Growth in Latin America*, Richard Irwin Press, Homewood, Ill., 1964.
10. For an analysis of the IMF stabilization programme in Chile see E. Sierra, *Tres Ensayos de Estabilización en Chile*, Editorial Universitaria, Santiago, 1970.
11. Quoted in Spokesman Pamphlet No. 31, *Chile: No More Dependence*.
12. *Subversion in Chile: a case study of US corporate intrigue in the Third World*, Bertrand Russell Peace Foundation, Nottingham, 1972.
13. *Le Monde*, 7–8 Oct 1973; *Le Monde Diplomatique*, Nov. 1971.
14. NACLA, *New Chile*, Berkeley, 1972.
15. Ibid.
16. Ibid.
17. A. Zammit, *The Chilean Road to Socialism*, contains the Popular Unity programme.
18. *Bank of London and South America Review*, Feb. 1974.
19. Article by Hugh O'Shaughnessy, *Financial Times*, 11 Apr. 1974.
20. *Ercilla*, June 1974.

Chapter 9

1. MAPU, *La Revolution Chilienne 1970–73; Recueil de Textes*, Politique Hebdo, Paris, 1974.
2. A. Zimbalist and B. Stallings, 'Showdown in Chile', *Monthly Review*, Oct. 1973.
3. Quoted in *Chile Hoy*, 31 July 1973.
4. *Chile Hoy*, 7 Sep. 1973.

Chapter 10

1. *Newsweek*, 8 Oct. 1973.

Conclusions

1. K. Marx, *The Eighteenth Brumaire of Louis Bonaparte*, Moscow, 1967, p. 10.
2. *The Times*, 13 Sep. 1973.
3. *Encounter*, Jan. 1974.
4. R. Moss, op. cit., p. 205.
5. Ibid.
6. *Nouvel Observateur*, 17 Sep. 1973.
7. *International Socialism*, No. 63, p. 16.
8. *El Mercurio*, 9 Nov. 1971.

Postscript

1. La Unidad Popular y las Tareas del Pueblo de Chile, 'Documento de Berlin', *Chile America*, No. 10–11 (1975).
2. These and subsequent figures are taken from Latin America Vol. 9, No. 36, 12 Sep. 1975. Chile Committee for Human Rights, Report No. 3 (1975). 'El Hambre Aprieta', *Chile America*, No. 10–11 (1975).
3. Survey by SERCOTEC (Servicio de Cooperación Técnica) published in Ercilla, 10 Sep. 1975.
4. *Latin America*, Vol. 9, No. 22, 6 June 1975.
5. General Leigh on the occasion of the visit of the commander-in-chief of the Argentine air forces, General Héctor Luis Fantario. Quoted in ibid, Vol. 9, No. 24, 20 June 1975.

6. Ibid., Vol. 9, No. 44, 7 Nov. 1975.

7. Ibid., Vol. 9, No. 39, 3 Oct. 1975.

8. Ibid.

9. The FBI had apparently informed Valdes and Tomic that the brothers Jorge and Jaime Melgoza, responsible for the assassination of General Schneider in 1970 and reported to have been subsequently released by the Chilean junta, had been given the task of assassinating them. Interpress, quoted in *Chile America*, No. 10–11 (1975).

10. Quoted in 'Contradicciones en la Iglesia Chilena', *Chile America*, No. 10–11 (1975).

11. With the sole exception of Jaime Gazmuri, the leader of the relatively insignificant MAPU – Obrero Campesino.

12. Quoted in *Latin America*, Vol. 9, No. 39, 3 Oct. 1975.

13. Quoted in US Senate Report on CIA Assassination Plots (Nov. 1975).

Select Bibliography

Historical Background

Blakemore, H., *British Nitrates and Chilean Politics* 1886–1896; *Balmaceda and North*, Athone Press, London, 1974.

Burnett, B. G., *Political Groups in Chile*, Texas University Press, Austin, 1970.

Corvalán, Luis, 'Communists' Tactics Relative to Agrarian Reform in Chile', in *Agrarian Reform in Latin America*, ed. T. Lynn Smith, Knopf, N.Y. 1965.

Ellsworth, Paul T., *Chile: An Economy in Transition*, Macmillan, New York, 1945.

Felix, David, 'Chile', in *Economic Development*, ed. Adamantios Pepelosis et al. Harper, N.Y., 1961.

Halperin, E., *Nationalism and Communism in Chile*, MIT, Cambridge, Mass., 1965.

Kaufman, R. R., *The Politics of Land Reform in Chile*, Harvard UP, Cambridge, Mass., 1971.

Kinsbrunner, Jay, *Chile: A Historical Interpretation*, Harper Torchbooks, N.Y., 1973.

Mamalakis, Marcos & Reynolds, Clark (eds.), *Essays on the Chilean Economy*, Richard Irwin Press, Homewood, Ill., 1965.

McBride, George, *Chile: Land and Society*, American Geographical Society, N.Y., 1936.

Morris, James O., *Elites, Intellectuals and Consensus: A Study of the Social Question and the Industrial Relations System in Chile*, Cornell University Press, Ithaca, N.Y., 1966.

Petras J. and Zeitlin M. (eds.), *Latin America: Reform or Revolution?* Fawcett, 1966.

Stephenson, John Reese, *The Chilean Popular Front*, University of Pennsylvania Press, Philadelphia, 1942.

Swift, J., *Agrarian Reform in Chile*, D. C. Heath, Lexington, Mass., 1971.

Zañartu, S. and Kennedy, J. J. (eds.), *The Overall Development of Chile*, University of Notre Dame Press, 1969.

Ahumada, Jorge, *En vez de la miseria*, Editorial del pacífico, Santiago, 1958.

Barrera, Manuel, *El sindicato industrial*, INSORA, Universidad de Chile, Santiago, 1965.

Barría, Jorge, *El Movimiento Obrero en Chile*, Santiago 1972.

Barría, Jorge, *Trayectoria y estructura del movimiento sindical Chileno, 1946–1962*, Instituto de Organización y Administración del Departmento de Relaciones Laborales, Santiago, 1963.

Cademártori, Jose, *La Economía Chilena: un enfoque marxista*, Editorial Universitaria, Santiago, 1968.

Casaneuva, Fernando and Fernández, Manuel, *El Partido Socialista y la lucha de clases en Chile*, Quimantú, Santiago, 1973.

Castillo Velasco, Jaime, *Las fuentes de la democracia cristiana*, Editorial del pacífico, Santiago, Chile, 1963.

Centro de Estudios Socio-Económicos, *Chile Hoy*. Siglo XXI, Mexico City, 1970.

Comité Interamericano de Desarrollo Agrícola (CIDA), *Chile: Tenencia de la tierra y desarrollo socio-económica del sector agrícola*, Santiago, 1966.

Edwards, Alberto, *La fronda aristocrática.*, Ediciones del pacífico, Santiago, 1952.

Frei, Eduardo, *Chile desconocida*, Editorial del pacífico, Chile, 1958.

Instituto de Economía. *La economía de Chile en el período* 1940–1956, Santiago, 1963.

Jobet, Julio César, *El socialismo Chileno a través de sus congresos*, Editorial Latinoamericana, Santiago, 1965.

Ensayo critico del desarrollo económico – social de Chile, Editorial universitaria, Santiago, 1965.

El Partido Socialista de Chile, 2 vols., Santiago, 1971.

Joxe, Alain, *Las Fuerzas Armadas en el sistema Político Chileno*, Editorial Universitaria, Santiago, 1970.

Labarca, Eduardo, *Chile al Rojo*, Ediciones de la Universidad Técnica del Estado, Santiago, 1971.

Chile Invadido, Reportaje a la Intromision Extranjera, Editorial Austral, Santiago, 1968.

Corvalán, 27 Horas, Quimantú, Santiago, 1972.

Lagos, E. Ricardo, *La concentración del poder económico*, Editorial del pacífico, Santiago, 1965.

Mattelart, Armand and Garrelón, Manuel (eds.), *Integración nacional y marginalidad*, Editorial del pacífico, Santiago, 1965.

Molina, Sergio, *El Proceso de Cambio en Chile*, Editorial Universitaria, Santiago, 1972.

Muñoz, Oscar, *Proceso a la Industrialización Chilena*, Ediciones Nueva Universidad, Santiago, 1972.

ODEPLAN. *Antecedentes sobre el Desarrollo Chileno* 1960–1970, Santiago, 1971.

Pinto, Anibal, *Chile: una economía dificil*, Fondo de cultura económica, Mexico City, 1964.

Chile, Un caso de desarrollo frustrado, Chile, Edit. Universitaria, 1959.

Ramírez Necochea, Hernan. *Historia del movimiento obrero en Chile, siglo XIX*, Editorial Austral, Santiago, 1956.

Origen y Formación del Partido Communista de Chile, Editorial Austral 1965.

El Imperialismo en Chile, Editorial Austral 1970.

Sierra, Enrique, *Tres Ensayos de Estabilización en Chile*, Editorial Universitaria, Santiago, 1969.

Vera Valenzuela, Mario, *La política económica del cobre en Chile*, Universidad de Chile, Santiago, 1961.

Vitale, Luis, *Esencia y apariencia de la democracia cristiana*, Arancibia, Santiago, 1964.

Historia del movimiento obrero, Editorial POR, Santiago, 1962.

(ed.), *Los discursos de Clotario Blest y la revolución Chilena*, Editorial POR, Santiago, 1961.

(ed.), *Obras escogidas de Luis Emilio Recabarren*, Editorial Recabarren, Santiago, 1965.

Interpretación Marxista de la Historia de Chile, Prensa Latinoamericana, Santiago.

Popular Unity and After

Castro, F., *Fidel in Chile*, International Publishers, N.Y., 1972.

Clarke, Kate, *Reality and Prospects of Popular Unity*, Lawrence and Wishart, 1973.

Feinberg, Richard E., *The Triumph of Allende: Chile's Legal Revolution*, Mentor, 1972.

Horne, Alistair, *Small Earthquake in Chile*, Macmillan, 1972.

IDOC, 'Chile – The Allende Years, The Coup, Under the Junta', 'Chile Under Military Rule'.

Subversion in Chile: a case study of US corporate intrigue in the Third World, Bertrand Russell Peace Foundation, 1972.

Medhurst, Kenneth, *Allende's Chile*, Hart-Davis MacGibbon, 1972.

Chile: A Diary of Recent Events – A selection of articles translated from *Le Monde*.

Morris, David, *We Must Make Haste Slowly: The Process of Revolution in Chile*, Random House (Vintage), N.Y., 1973.

Moss, R., *Chile's Marxist Experiment*, David & Charles, Newton Abbot, 1973.

NACLA's *Latin America and Empire Report*, Oct. 1973, (Chile: The Story Behind the Coup).

Petras, J. and Zemelman, H., *Peasants in Revolt*, Texas University Press, Austin, 1972.

Prieto, Helios, *The Gorillas are Amongst Us*, Pluto Press, 1974.

Sampson, Antony, *The Sovereign State*, Coronet, 1974.

Zammit, J. Ann (ed.), *The Chilean Road to Socialism*, Institute of Development Studies, University of Sussex, Brighton, 1973.

Arriagada, Genaro, *La Oligarquía Patronal Chilena*, Ediciones Nueva Universidad, Santiago, 1970.

20

Bardon, A., y otros, *Itinerario de Una Crisis Política Económica y Transición al Socialismo*, Editorial del Pacífico, Santiago, 1972.

Canihuante, Gustavo, *La Revolución Chilena*, Santiago, 1971.

Corvalán Luis, *Camino de Victoria*, Santiago, 1971.

Foxley, Alejandro y otros, *Chile: Busqueda de un Nuevo Socialismo*, Ediciones Nueva Universidad, Santiago, 1971.

Garcés, Joan, 1970, *La pugna política por la presidencia en Chile*, Editorial Universitaria, Santiago, 1971.

Desarrollo Político y Desarrollo Económico, Editorial Andres Bello, 1972.

Revolutión, Congreso y Constitución. El Caso Tohá, Quimantú, Santiago, 1972.

Giusti, Jorge, *Organización y participación popular en Chile – el mito del 'Hombre marginal'*, Ediciones Flasco, 1973.

Huneeus, Pablo et al., *El Costo Social de la Dependencia Ideológica*, Santiago, 1973.

Jarpa, Sergio Onofre, *Creo en Chile*, Santiago, 1973.

Labreveux, Philippe, *Chile bajo las botas – crónicas del terror*, Editorial Abraxas BA, 1973.

MacHale, Tomas, *El Frente de la Libertad de Expresión*, Santiago, 1972.

Martner, Gonzalo y otros, *El pensamiento económico del Gobierno de Allende*, Editorial Universitaria, Santiago, 1971.

Musalem, José, *Crónica de un Fracaso*, Santiago, 1973.

Orrego, Claudio, *El Paro Nacional*, Santiago, 1972.

Ossa, Juan Luis, *Nacionalismo Hoy*, Santiago, 1972.

Parker, D., *La Nueva Cara del Fascismo*, Quimantú, Santiago, 1972.

Ramos, Sergio, *Chile, una economía de transición?*, Editorial Prensa Latinoamericana, SA, 1972.

Saenz, Orlando, *Chile, un País en Quiebra*, Santiago, 1973.

P. Sweezy, J. Chonchol et al., *Transición al Socialismo y Experiencia Chilena*, PLA, 1972.

Universidad de Chile, 'Taller de Coyuntura', *Comentarios sobre la Situación Económica*, 1971–1973.

Universidad de Chile, Instituto de Economía, *La Economía Chilena en 1971*, Santiago, 1972.

Varas, Florencia, *Conversaciones con Viaux*, Santiago, 1972.

Varas, Florencia and Vergara, José Manuel, *Operación Chile*, Editorial Pomaire Argentina, 1973.

Vidales, Carlos, *Contrarrevolución y dictadura en Chile*, Ediciones Tierra Americana, Bogota, Colombia, 1974.

French-language: recent commentaries

Acquaviva Fournial, Gilhodes Marcelin, *Chili, 3 ans d'unité populaire*, Collection Notre Temps/Monde, Paris, 1974.

Cerda, Carlos, *Génocide au Chili*, Francois Maspero, Paris, 1974.

Chili, l'affrontement de classes (1970–1973) dossier réalisé par le comité de soutien à la lutte révolutionnaire du peuple chilien, supplément au no 29 du *Bulletin de liaison du CEDETIM*, Paris, Oct. 1973.

Delcourt, Francois 'Pouvoir Populaire', in *Politique Aujourd'Hui*, Paris, Jan. 1974.

Debray, Régis, *La Critique des Armes I*, Editions du Seuil, Paris, 1974.

Labrousse, Alain, *L'Expérience Chilienne*, Editions du Seuil, Paris, 1974.

Lamour, Catherine, *Le Pari Chilien*, Stock, Paris, 1972.

MAPU, 1970–1973, *La Révolution Chilienne*, Recueil de Textes, Édité par Politique Hebdo.

Mattelart, Armand, 'La bourgeoisie a l'école de Lenine: le gremialisme et la ligne de masse de la bourgeoisie chilienne', in *Politique Aujourd'Hui*, Jan. 1974, Paris.

Touraine, Alain, *Vie et Mort du Chili Populaire*, Editions du Seuil, Paris, 1973.

Uribe, Armando, *Le Livre noir de l'intervention americaine au Chili*, Editions du Seuil, Paris, 1974.

Articles, essays, etc. in English-language journals

Alexander, R., 'Socialism's Uncertain Future', *New Politics*, Vol. 9, Fall 1971.

Angell, A., 'Counter-revolution in Chile', *Current History*, Jan. 1974.

Ayres, R., 'Economic Stagnation and the Emergence of the Political Ideology of Chilean Underdevelopment', *World Politics*, Vol. 25, Oct. 1972.

'Political History, Institutional Structure and Prospects for Socialism in Chile', *Comparative Politics*, Vol. 5, July 1973.

Chaparro, P. and Prothro, J., 'Public Opinion and the movement of the Chilean government to the left 1952–72', *Journal of Politics*, Vol. 36, Feb. 1974.

Francis, M. and Vera-Godoy, H., 'Chile: Christian Democracy to Marxism', *Review of Politics*, Vol. 33, 1971.

Gedicks, A., 'The Nationalization of Copper in Chile', *Review of Radical Political Economics*, Vol. 5, Fall 1973.

Gil, F. G., 'Socialist Chile and the United States', *Inter American Economic Affairs*, Vol. 27, Autumn 1973.

Hanson, S., 'Kissinger on the Chilean Coup', *Inter American Economic Affairs*, Vol. 27, Winter 1973.

Holden, D., 'Allende and the Myth Makers', *Encounter*, Jan. 1974.

Kay, C., 'Chile: An Appraisal of Popular Unity's Agrarian Reform', *Occasional Paper No. 13*, Institute of Latin American Studies, Glasgow, 1974.

O'Brien, P. and Roddick, J., 'Chile: Too Close for Comfort', in *Latin America Review of Books No. 2*, 1974.

Petras, J., 'Achievements of the Allende Government', *New Politics*, Vol. 9, Fall 1971.

'Chile: The Political Labyrinth', in *Latin America Review of Books No. 1*, 1973.

Recent Developments in Chile, *Hearing before the Subcommittee on Inter-American Affairs of the Committee on Foreign Affairs, US House of Representatives,* 92nd Congress, 15 Oct. 1971, US Government Printing Office.

Roxborough, I., 'Agrarian Policy in the Popular Unity Government', *Occasional Paper No. 14,* Institute of Latin American Studies, University of Glasgow, 1974.

Steenland, K., 'Two years of Popular Unity in Chile', *New Left Review,* No. 78 Mar.–Apr. 1973.

Sinding, S., 'The Evolution of Chilean Voting Patterns', *Journal of Politics,* Vol. 34, 1972.

Valenzuela, A., 'The Scope of the Chilean Party System', *Comparative Politics,* Vol. 4, Jan. 1972.

Veliz, C., 'The Chilean Experiment', *Foreign Affairs,* Vol. 49, 1971.

Whitehead, L., 'The Socialist Experiment in Chile', *Parliamentary Affairs,* Vol. 25, Summer 1972.

'Why Allende Fell', *World Today,* Vol. 29, Nov. 1973.

Win, P. and Kay, C., 'Agrarian Reform and Rural Revolution in Allende's Chile', *Journal of Latin American Studies,* Vol. 6, 1974.

Zeitlin, M., 'Chilean Revolution: the Bullet or the Ballot', *Ramparts,* Apr. 1971.

Chilean newspapers and journals

El Mercúrio (right-wing)
El Siglo (Communist Party)
La Prensa (Christian Democrat)
El Rebelde (MIR)
Aurora de Chile (Socialist Party)
Mensaje (Jesuit monthly)
Ercilla (weekly)
Qué Pasa? (weekly)
Panorama Económico (independent)

Punto Final (leaning to the MIR)
Política y Espíritu (Christian Democrat)
Chile Hoy (excellent independent left weekly)
Principios (Communist Party)
Posición (Socialist Party)
De Frente (MAPU)
Causa Marxista-Leninista (Maoist)

Cuadernos de la Realidad Nacional, Centro de Estudios de la Realidad Nacional (CEREN)
Sociedad y Desarrollo, Centro de Estudios Socio-Económicos (CESO)
Estudios de Planificación, Centro de Estudios de Planificación Nacional (CEPLAN).

Government

ODEPLAN – Informe Económico Anual
            – Nueva Economía
            – Vía Chilena
Banco Central de Chile – Balanza de Pagos
                       – Boletín Mensual
                       – Noticias Económicas

Other newspapers and journals

Le Monde	Latin America
The Times	Latin America Economic Report
New York Times	Intercontinental Press
Financial Times	Encounter
Guardian	Economist Intelligence Unit Quarterly
Morning Star	Review: Chile
Bank of London and South	Monthly Review
American Review	

Various theoretical journals and newspapers of left-wing groups, e.g. *Red Weekly*.
United Nations Economic Commission for Latin America – *Economic Survey of Latin America*.
Economic Bulletin for Latin America.
Organization of American States, Inter-American Committee on the Alliance for Progress (*CIPA*), *Domestic Efforts and the Needs for External Financing for the Development of Chile*.

Current news analyses

Apart from *Le Monde*, the Chilean resistance and the various Chilean Solidarity Campaigns provide thorough analysis and news on Chile.
The British Chile Solidarity Campaign produces two first-class magazines:
  Chile Fights (incorporating Chile Lucha and New Chile).
  Chile Monitor.
These, and other information can be obtained from: Chile Solidarity Campaign, Cooperative Centre, 129 Seven Sisters Road, London, N7. Tel: 01-272-4299.
A detailed bibliography on the coup is Cooperation in Documentation and Communication, *Bibliographical Notes For Understanding The Military Coup in Chile*, Washington, 1974.
Si Companero, c/o ESG Koblenzer Str 8, West Berlin 1, Berlin 31 – Excellent journal produced by Chilean exiles.
Chile – Nachtrichten, c/o ESG Koblenzer Str 8, West Berlin 1, Berlin 31 – Very useful German magazine.
Information on other bulletins, etc. can be obtained from the British Chile Solidarity Campaign.

Short reading list

The following books have been selected to meet the needs of those readers who have little knowledge of Chile and require a list of introductory works.
Allende, Salvador, *Chile's Road to Socialism*, Penguin, 1973. This is a selection of

speeches made by Allende during the first months of his government. They set out, in Allende's own words, the ideas behind the 'Chilean road to socialism', but do not contribute greatly to an understanding of the later difficulties faced by the regime.

Angell, Alan, *Politics and the Labour Movement in Chile*, Oxford UP, 1972. While this book does not deal with the Popular Unity period, it provides essential background information on the history of the Chilean working class movement.

Debray, Régis, *Conversations with Allende*, New Left Books, 1971. Besides containing a fascinating discussion between Debray and Allende, the book also has a lengthy and critical introductory essay by Debray, useful historical notes, and MIR's assessment of the significance of Allende's victory in 1970.

Evans, Les (ed.), *Disaster in Chile: Allende's Strategy and Why it Failed*, Pathfinder Press, 1974. A useful left-wing collection of articles and newspaper reports taken from the Trotskyist Intercontinental Press. Unnecessarily dogmatic and sectarian in places.

Frank, André Gunder, *Capitalism and Underdevelopment in Chile and Brazil*, Penguin, 1972. Stimulating historical sweep within Frank's now famous thesis on underdevelopment. But should be treated with caution.

Garcés, Joan, *El Estado y los problemas tácticos en el gobierno de Allende*, Siglo XXI, 1973. Is an important analysis by President Allende's political advisor.

Gil, Frederico, *The Political System of Chile*, Houghton Mifflin, Boston, 1966. This is a standard work on the subject and contains a useful historical section.

Johnson, Dale (ed.), *The Chilean Road to Socialism*, Anchor, 1973. This is a lengthy collection of numerous articles written by Chileans and North Americans covering a wide variety of points of view and of uneven quality.

Miliband, Ralph, *The Coup in Chile*, in The Socialist Register 1973, ed. Ralph Miliband and John Saville. A succinct and important statement on the main lessons socialists should draw from the Chilean coup.

NACLA, *New Chile*, 1973, North American Congress on Latin America, 1973. Contains a lot of useful information on US economic interests in Chile.

Petras, James, *Politics and Social Forces in Chilean Development*, University of California Press, 1969. Probably the single best systematic analysis of Chilean society by a Marxist sociologist, but marred by inaccuracies.

Najman, Maurice (ed), *Le Chili est Proche: Révolution et Contre-révolution dans le Chili de l' Unité Populaire*, Francois Maspero, 1974. Is an invaluable collection of Chilean left-wing statements and positions together with some reports from the excellent Chilean weekly, *Chile Hoy*.

Pike, Frederick, *Chile and the United States* 1880–1962, University of Notre Dame Press, 1963. While this book concentrates on US–Chilean relations, it also provides an invaluable history of Chilean society.

Index